Takeshi Obata

Hotta Sensei recently gave me a pair of green Go stones. They're so nice and smooth, I wouldn't mind playing a game with them myself. But come to think of it, doesn't that mean Hotta Sensei is short a couple of stones?
—Takeshi Obata

t all began when Yumi Hotta played a pick-up game of Go with her father-in-law. As she was learning how to play, Ms. Hotta thought it might be fun to create a story around the traditional board game. More confident in her storytelling abilities than her drawing skills, she submitted the beginnings of **Hikaru no Go** to **Weekly Shonen Jump**'s Story King Award. The Story King Award is an award that picks the best story, manga, character design and youth (under 15) manga submissions every year in Japan. As fate would have it, Ms. Hotta's story (originally named, "*Kokonotsu no Hoshi*"), was a runner-up in the "Story" category of the Story King Award. Many years earlier, Takeshi Obata was a runner-up for the Tezuka Award, another Japanese manga contest sponsored by **Weekly Shonen Jump** and **Monthly Shonen Jump**. An editor assigned to Mr. Obata's artwork came upon Ms. Hotta's story and paired the two for a full-fledged manga about Go. The rest is modern Go history.

HIKARU NO GO VOL. 8
The SHONEN JUMP Manga Edition

This manga contains material that was originally published in English from
SHONEN JUMP #43 to #46.

STORY BY YUMI HOTTA
ART BY TAKESHI OBATA
Supervised by YUKARI UMEZAWA (5 Dan)

Translation & English Adaptation/Andy Nakatani
English Script Consultant/Janice Kim (3 Dan)
Touch-up Art & Lettering/Inori Fukuda Trant
Design/Courtney Utt
Additional Touch-up/Josh Simpson
Editor/Yuki Takagaki

Editor in Chief, Books/Alvin Lu
Editor in Chief, Magazines/Marc Weidenbaum
VP, Publishing Licensing/Rika Inouye
VP, Sales & Product Marketing/Gonzalo Ferreyra
VP, Creative/Linda Espinosa
Publisher/Hyoe Narita

Printed in the U.S.A.

Published by VIZ Media, LLC
P.O. Box 77010
San Francisco, CA 94107

SHONEN JUMP Manga Edition
10 9 8 7 6 5 4 3 2
First printing, November 2006
Second printing, October 2008

www.viz.com

THE WORLD'S
MOST POPULAR MANGA

www.shonenjump.com

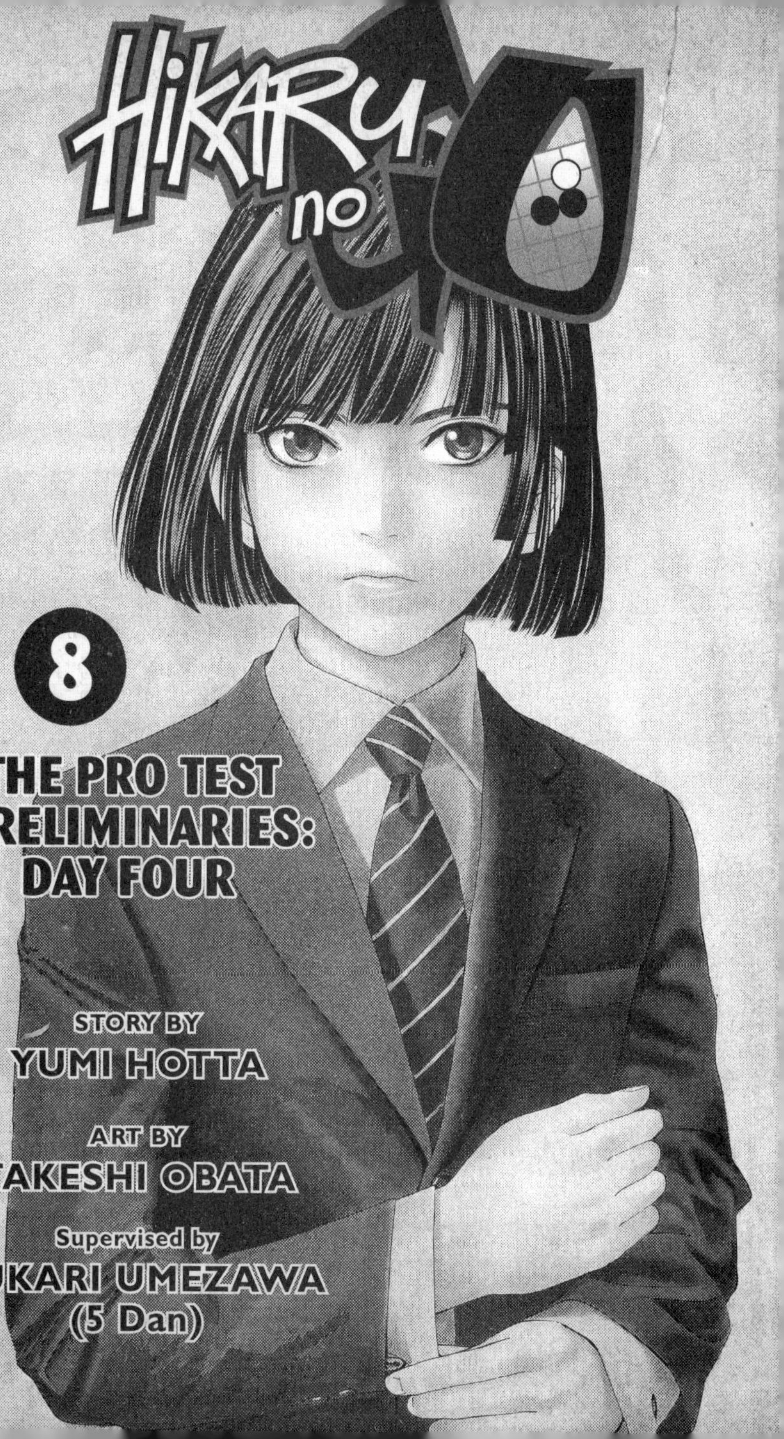

Hikaru no Go

8

THE PRO TEST PRELIMINARIES: DAY FOUR

STORY BY
YUMI HOTTA

ART BY
TAKESHI OBATA

Supervised by
YUKARI UMEZAWA
(5 Dan)

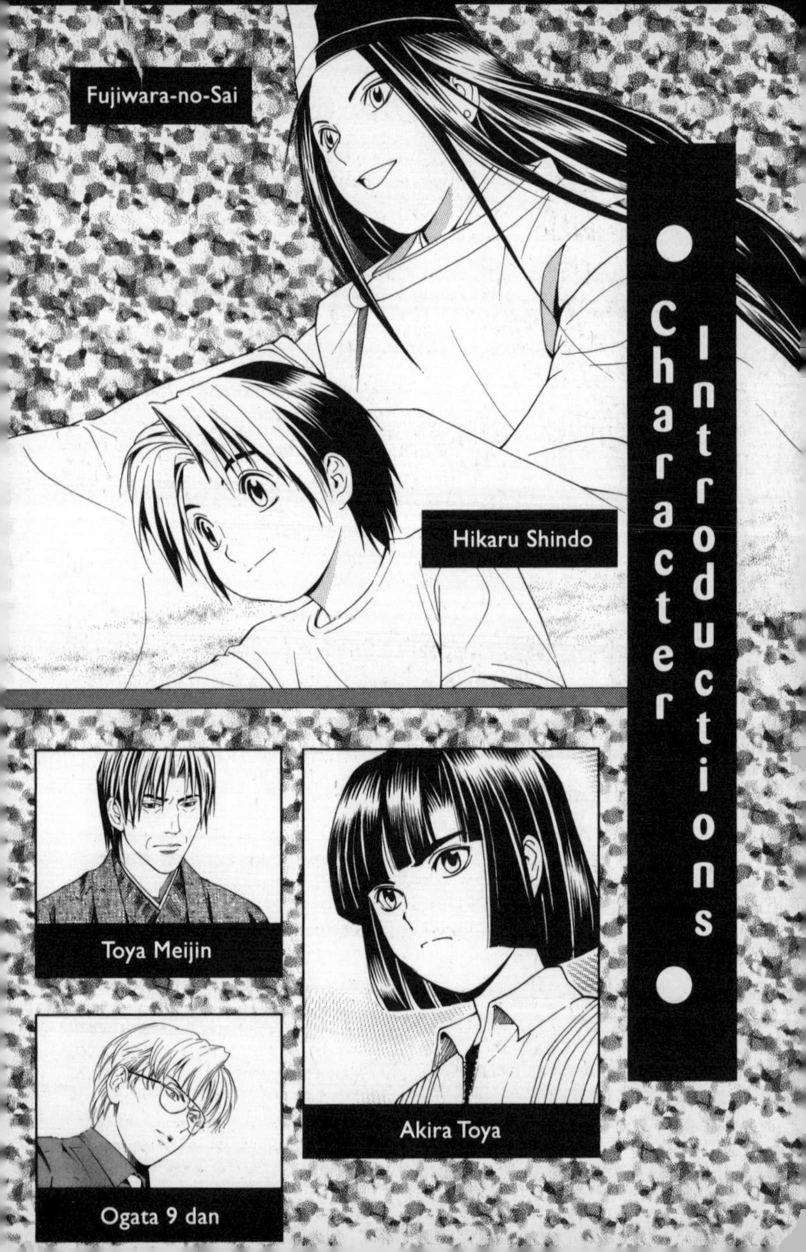
Character Introductions
Fujiwara-no-Sai
Hikaru Shindo
Akira Toya
Toya Meijin
Ogata 9 dan

Shinichiro Isumi

Kuwabara Sensei

Asumi Nase

Hikaru's mother

Yuta "Fuku" Fukui

Kosuke Ochi

Yoshitaka Waya

The Story Thus Far

One day a sixth grader named Hikaru discovers an old Go board in his grandfather's attic. Hikaru touches the board, and in that instant, the spirit of Fujiwara-no-Sai, a genius Go player from Japan's Heian era, enters his consciousness. Hikaru is gradually drawn to the game, inspired by Sai's love of Go and by a meeting with the prodigy Akira Toya, the son of Go master Toya Meijin.

Hikaru sees his chance to play Akira for a fifth time at the Young Lions Tournament, but to enter it he must rank at least 16th in A League. Alas, he loses some games, which leads Sai to believe that Hikaru is afraid to attack his opponents. Once Hikaru knows the source of his weakness, however, he manages to qualify, but he still has to win his first round to play Akira. Hikaru is eliminated after a close game, but he's excited to discover how much his game has improved. When Akira sees the game board, he realizes that Hikaru is no longer the player he once was.

CONTENTS

8

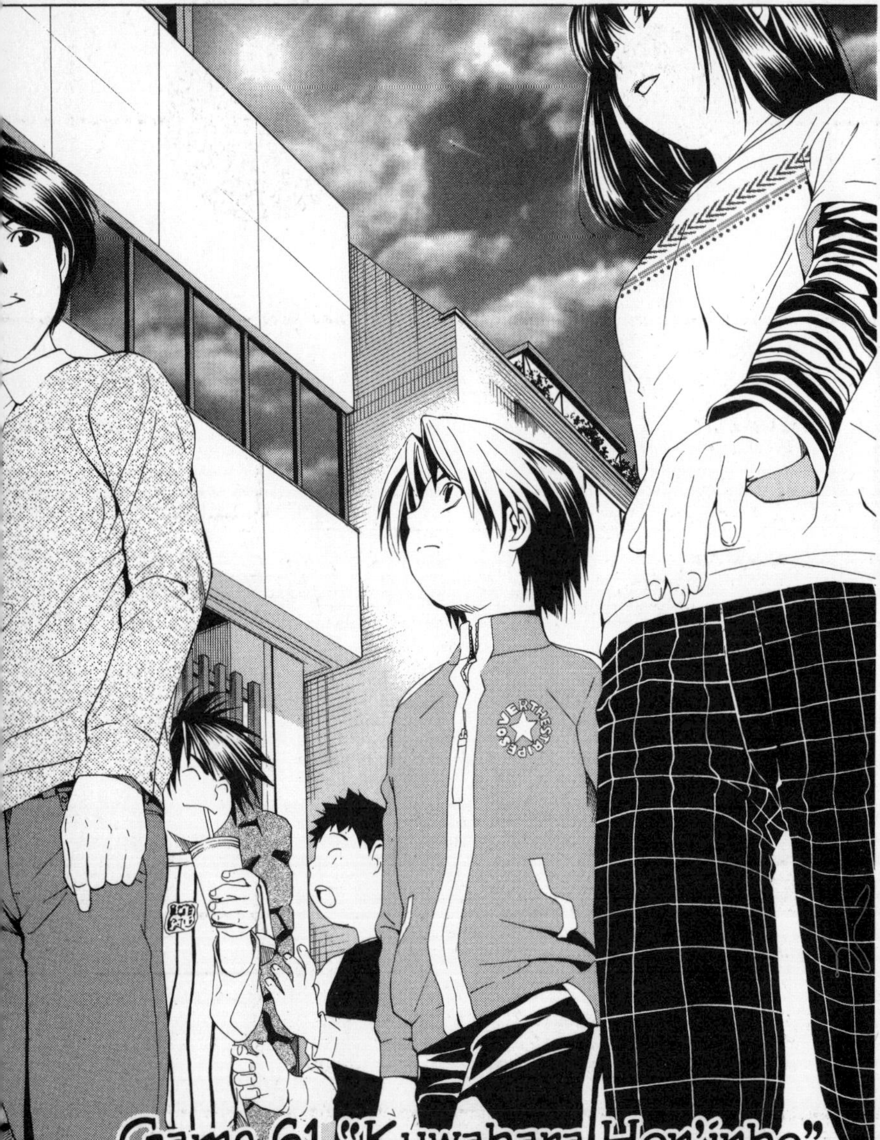
VERTHESTRIPES

Game 61 "Kuwabara Hon'inbo"

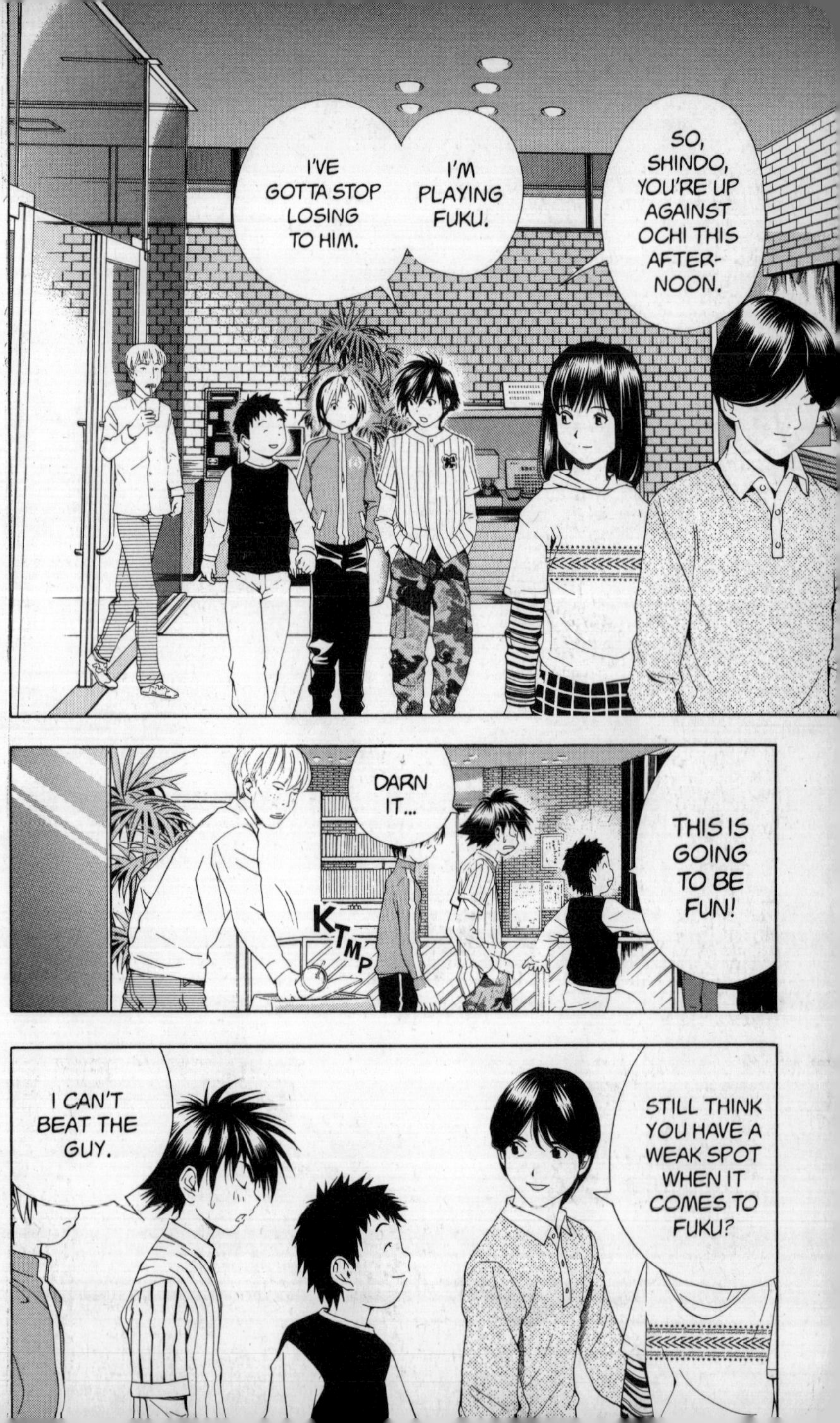
SO, SHINDO, YOU'RE UP AGAINST OCHI THIS AFTER-NOON.
I'M PLAYING FUKU.
I'VE GOTTA STOP LOSING TO HIM.
THIS IS GOING TO BE FUN!
DARN IT...
KTMP
STILL THINK YOU HAVE A WEAK SPOT WHEN IT COMES TO FUKU?
I CAN'T BEAT THE GUY.

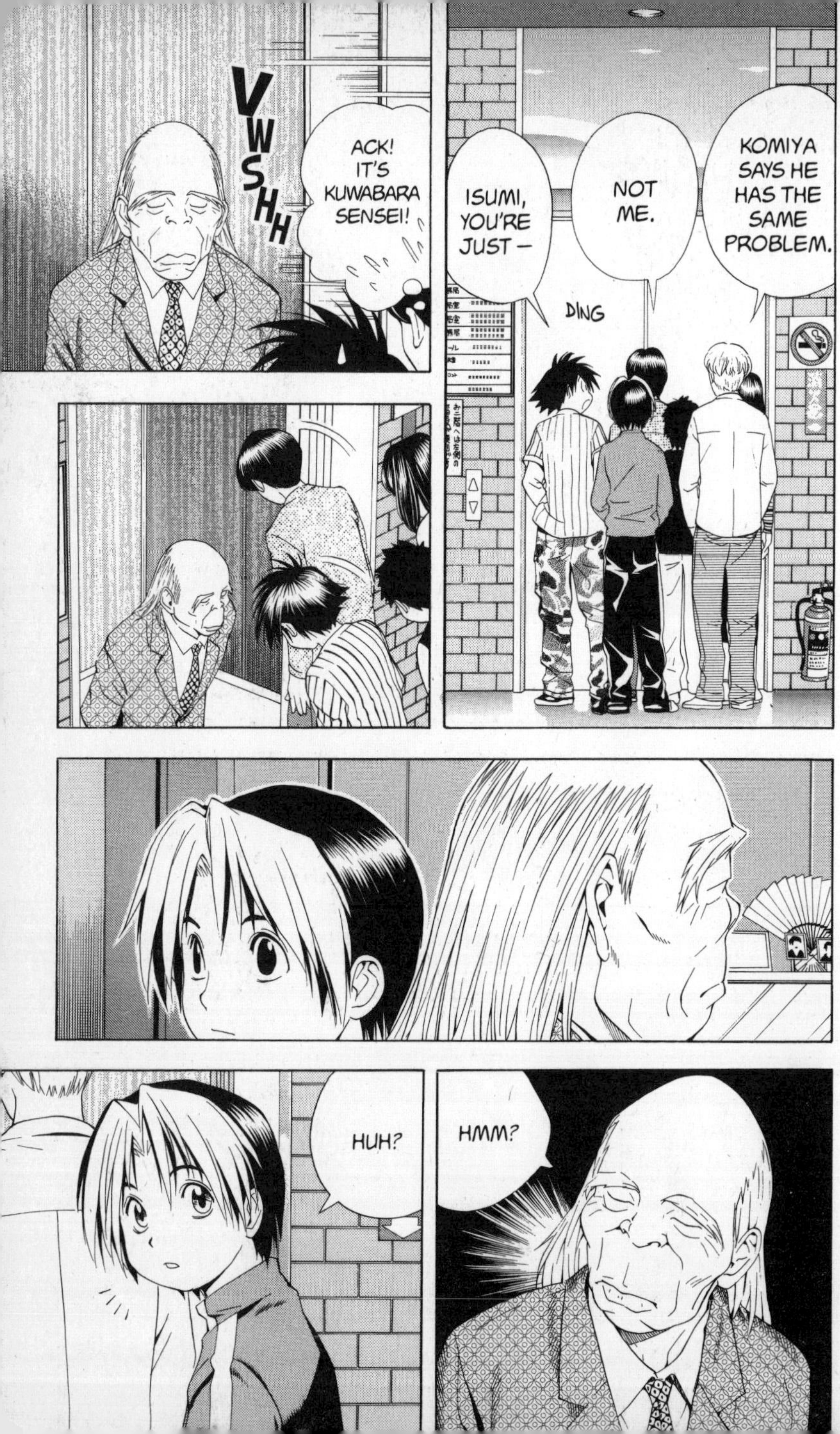
KOMIYA SAYS HE HAS THE SAME PROBLEM.
NOT ME.
ISUMI, YOU'RE JUST —
DING
VWSHH
ACK! IT'S KUWABARA SENSEI!
HMM?
HUH?

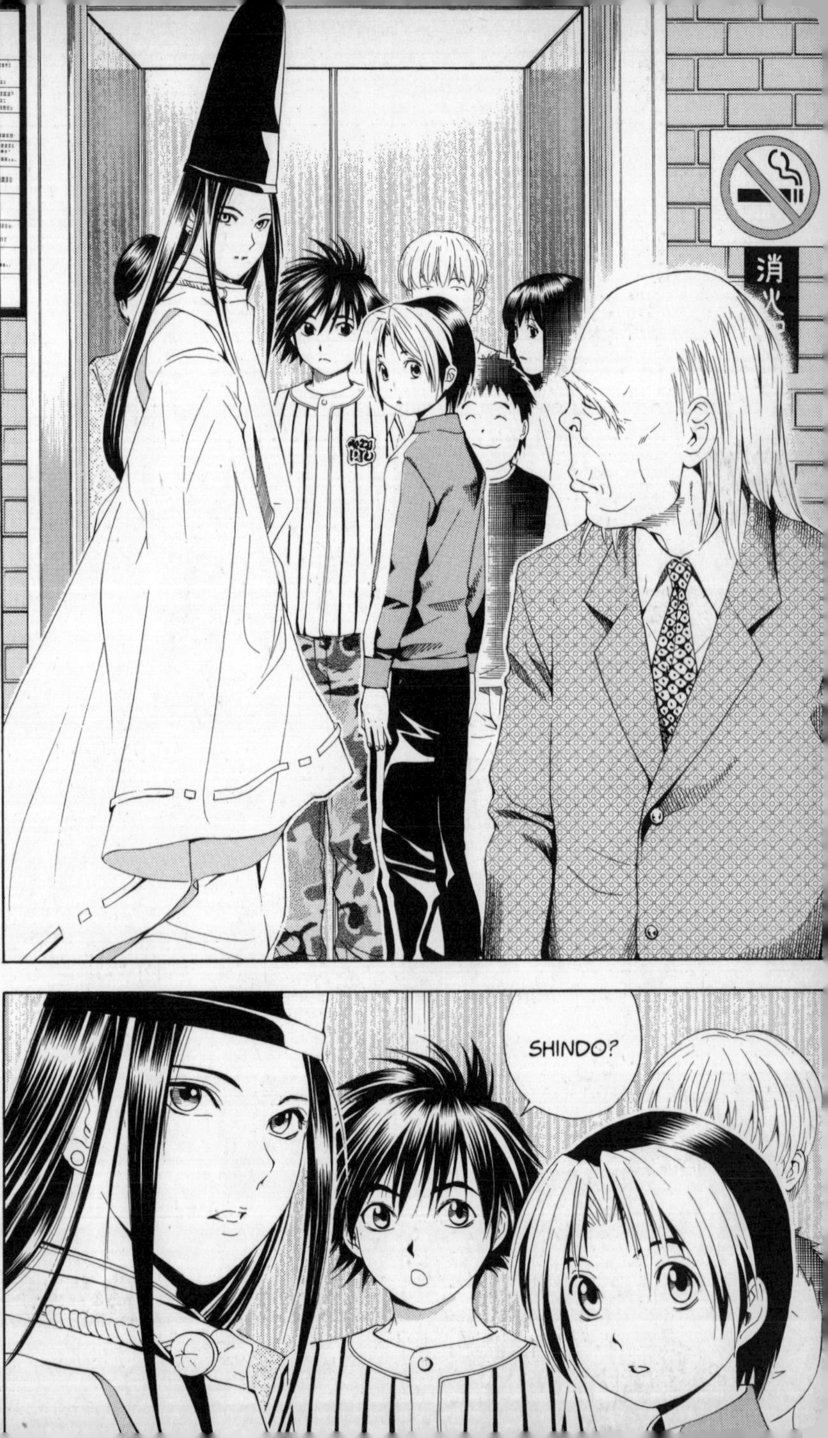
消火
SHINDO?

READ THIS WAY

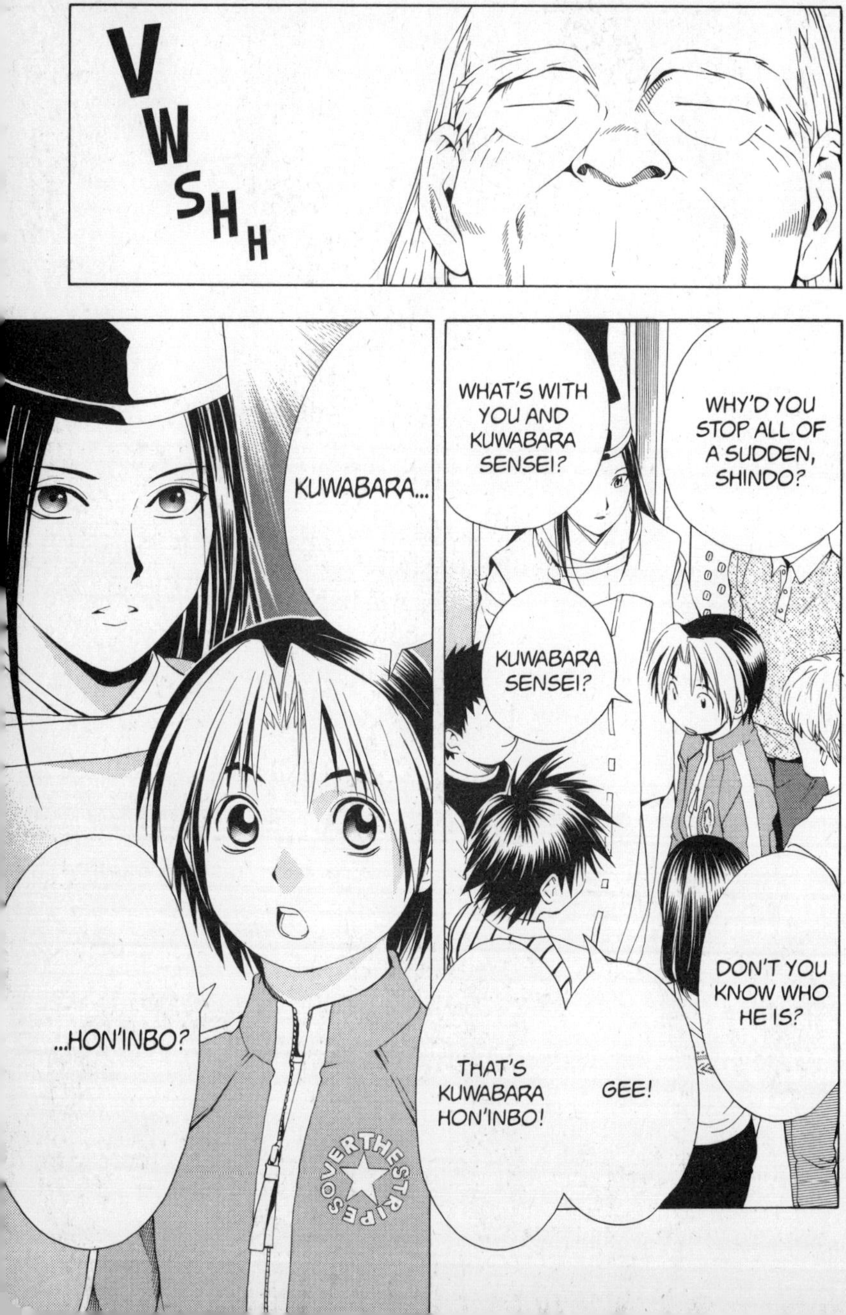
VWSHH
WHY'D YOU STOP ALL OF A SUDDEN, SHINDO?
WHAT'S WITH YOU AND KUWABARA SENSEI?
KUWABARA SENSEI?
DON'T YOU KNOW WHO HE IS?
GEE!
THAT'S KUWABARA HON'INBO!
KUWABARA...
...HON'INBO?
OVER THE STRIPES

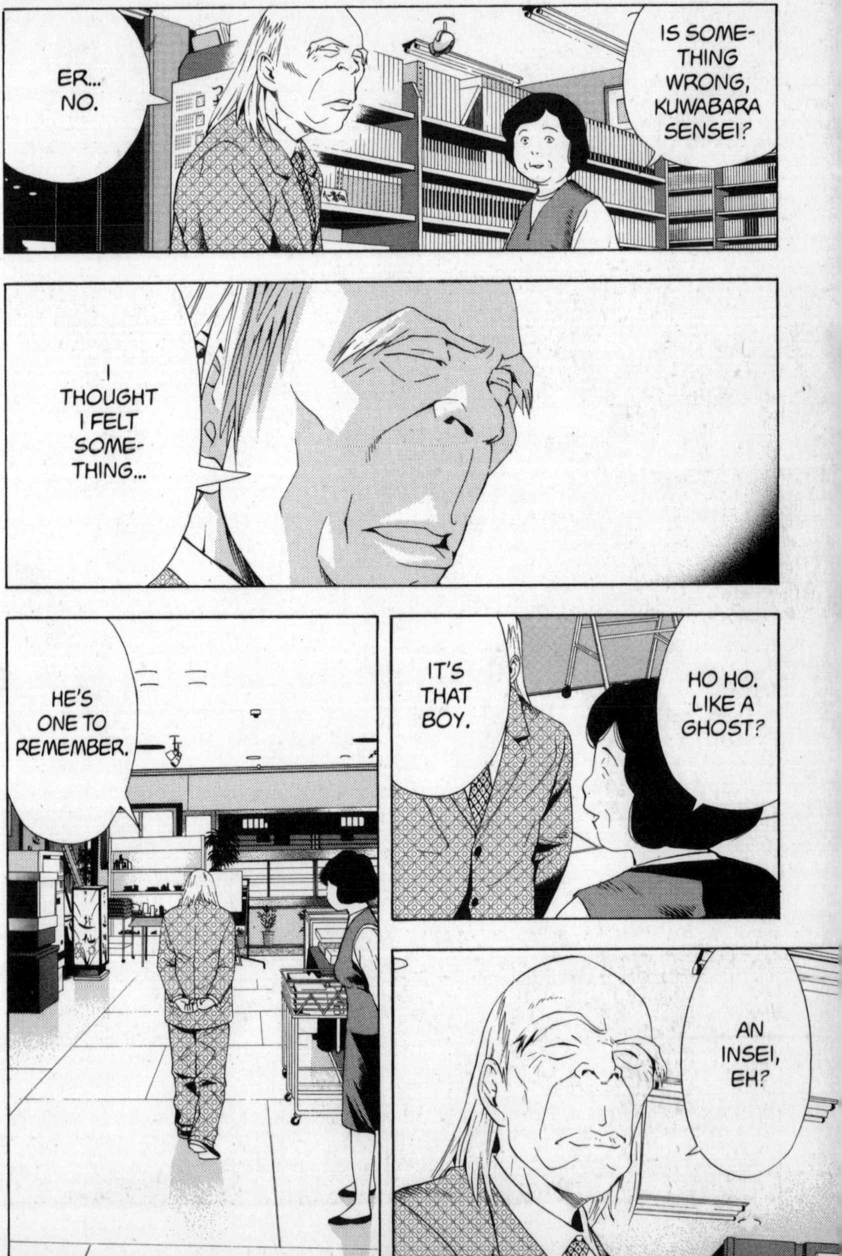
IS SOME-THING WRONG, KUWABARA SENSEI?
ER... NO.
I THOUGHT I FELT SOME-THING...
HO HO. LIKE A GHOST?
IT'S THAT BOY.
AN INSEI, EH?
HE'S ONE TO REMEMBER.

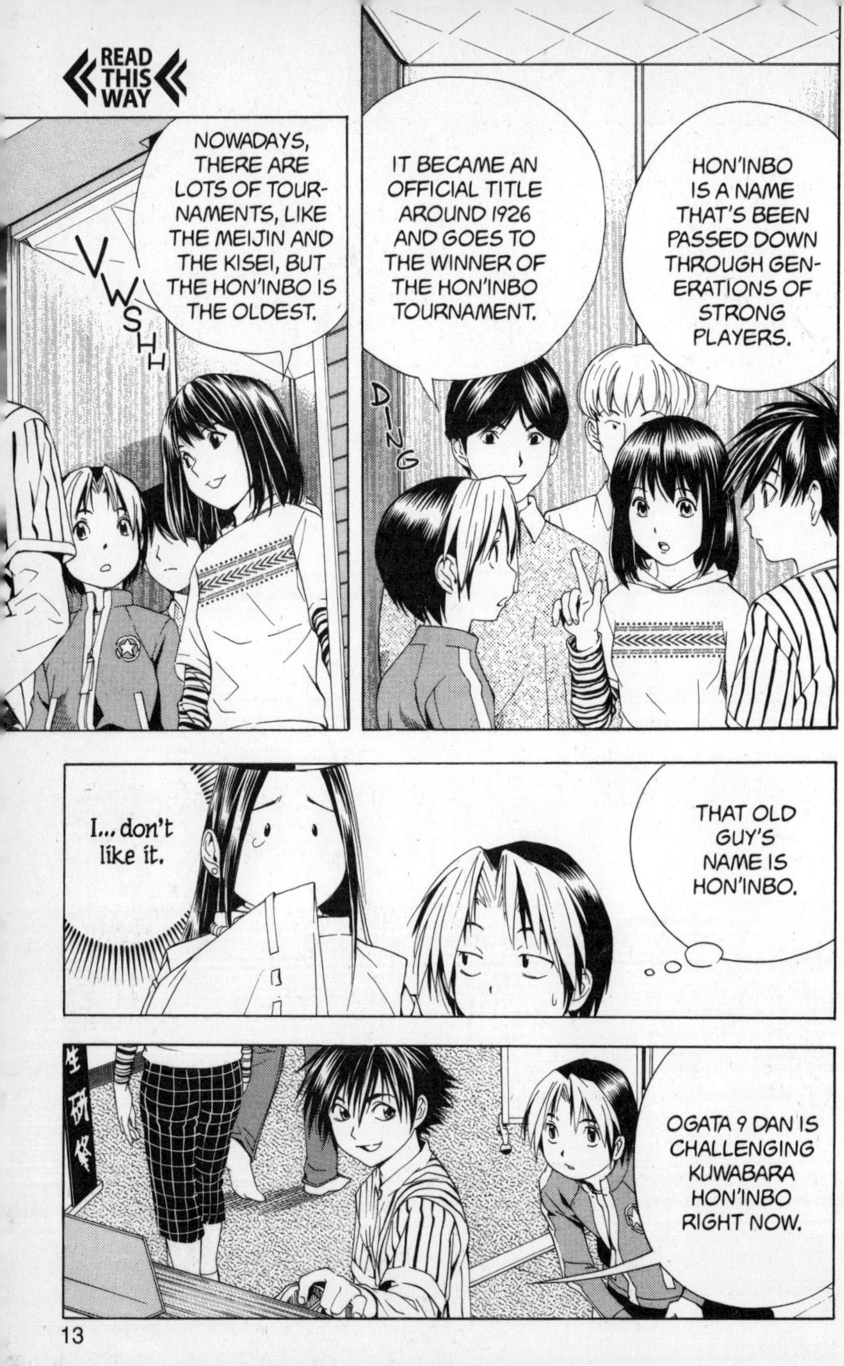
READ THIS WAY
HON'INBO IS A NAME THAT'S BEEN PASSED DOWN THROUGH GENERATIONS OF STRONG PLAYERS.
IT BECAME AN OFFICIAL TITLE AROUND 1926 AND GOES TO THE WINNER OF THE HON'INBO TOURNAMENT.
DING
NOWADAYS, THERE ARE LOTS OF TOURNAMENTS, LIKE THE MEIJIN AND THE KISEI, BUT THE HON'INBO IS THE OLDEST.
VWSHH
THAT OLD GUY'S NAME IS HON'INBO.
I... don't like it.
OGATA 9 DAN IS CHALLENGING KUWABARA HON'INBO RIGHT NOW.

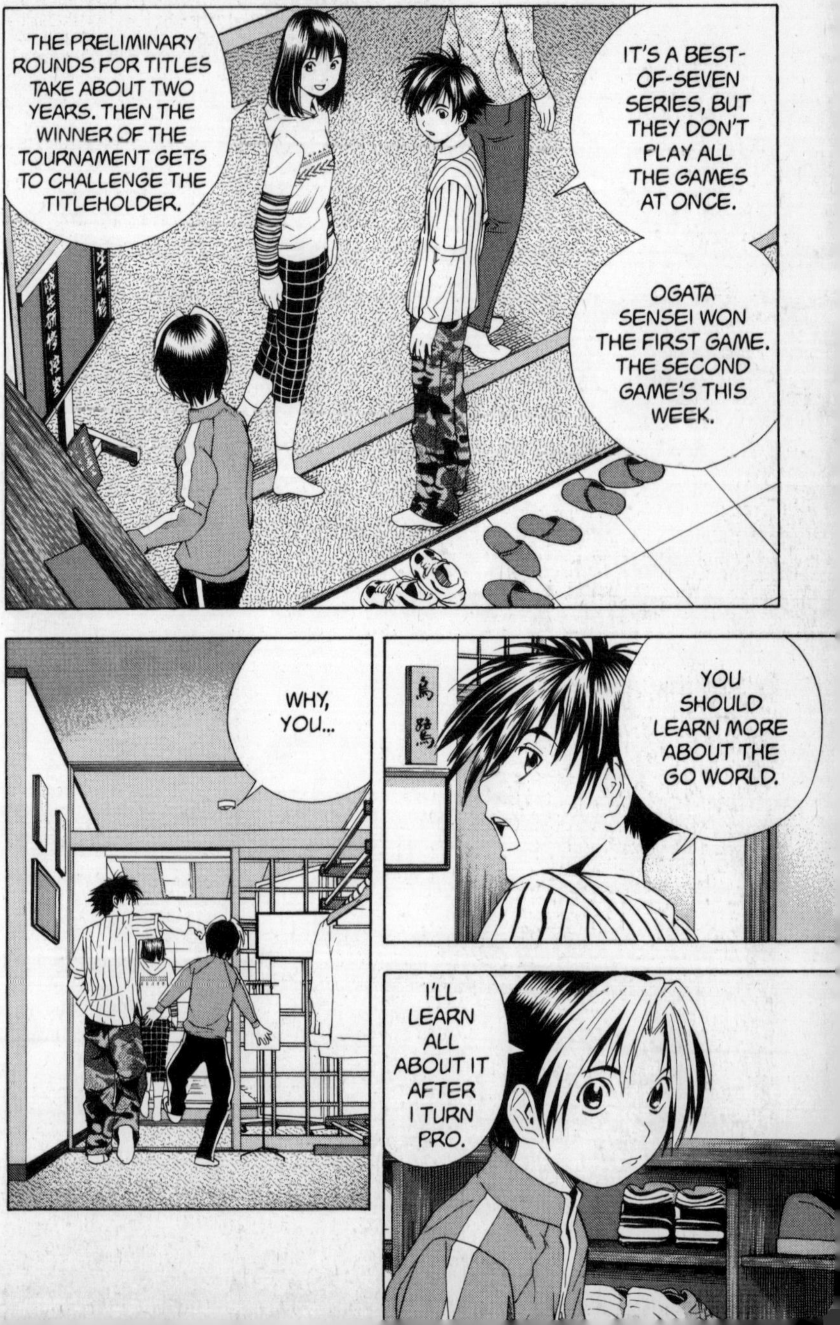
IT'S A BEST-OF-SEVEN SERIES, BUT THEY DON'T PLAY ALL THE GAMES AT ONCE.
OGATA SENSEI WON THE FIRST GAME. THE SECOND GAME'S THIS WEEK.
THE PRELIMINARY ROUNDS FOR TITLES TAKE ABOUT TWO YEARS. THEN THE WINNER OF THE TOURNAMENT GETS TO CHALLENGE THE TITLEHOLDER.
YOU SHOULD LEARN MORE ABOUT THE GO WORLD.
I'LL LEARN ALL ABOUT IT AFTER I TURN PRO.
WHY, YOU...

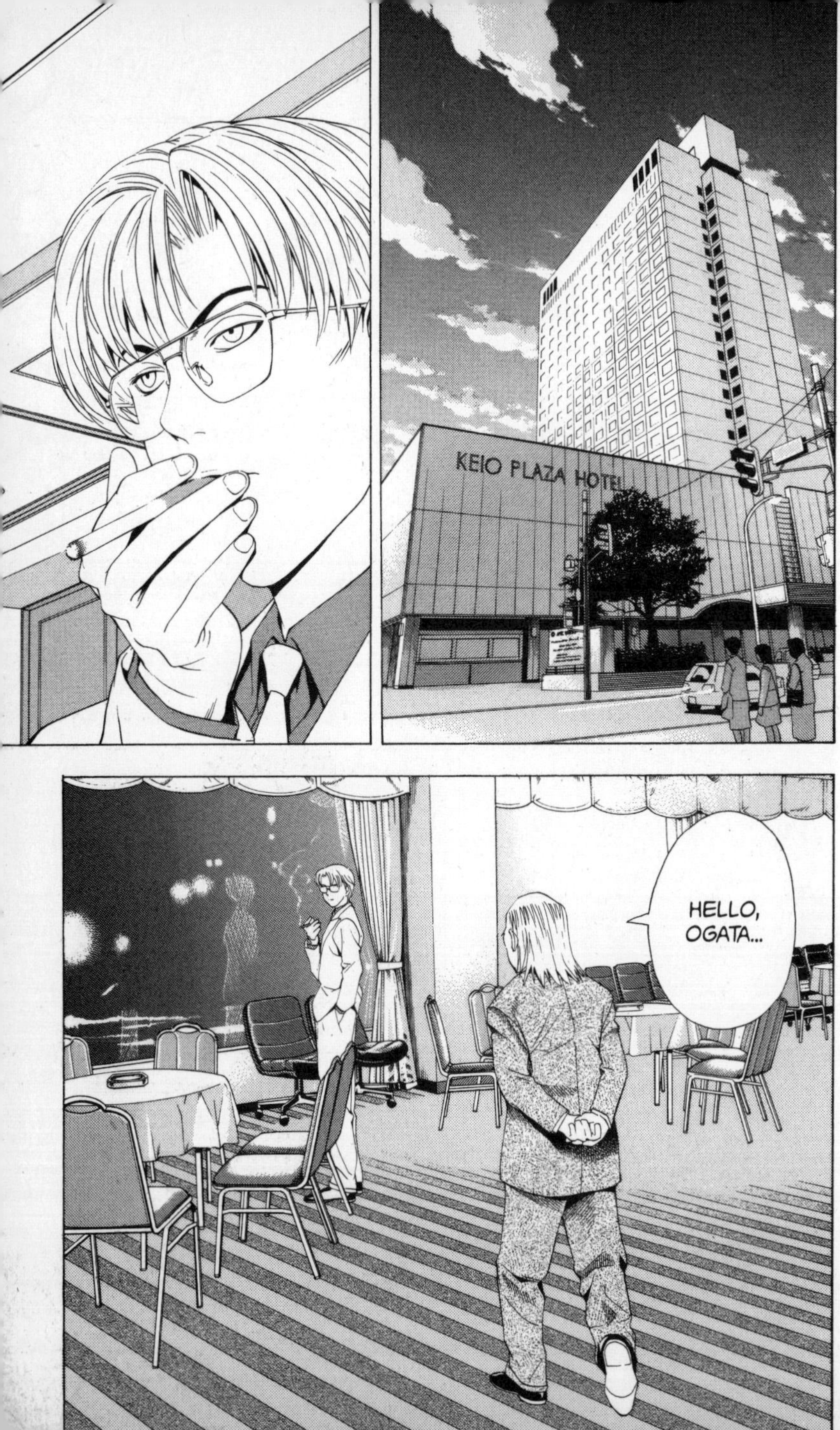
KEIO PLAZA HOTEL
HELLO, OGATA...

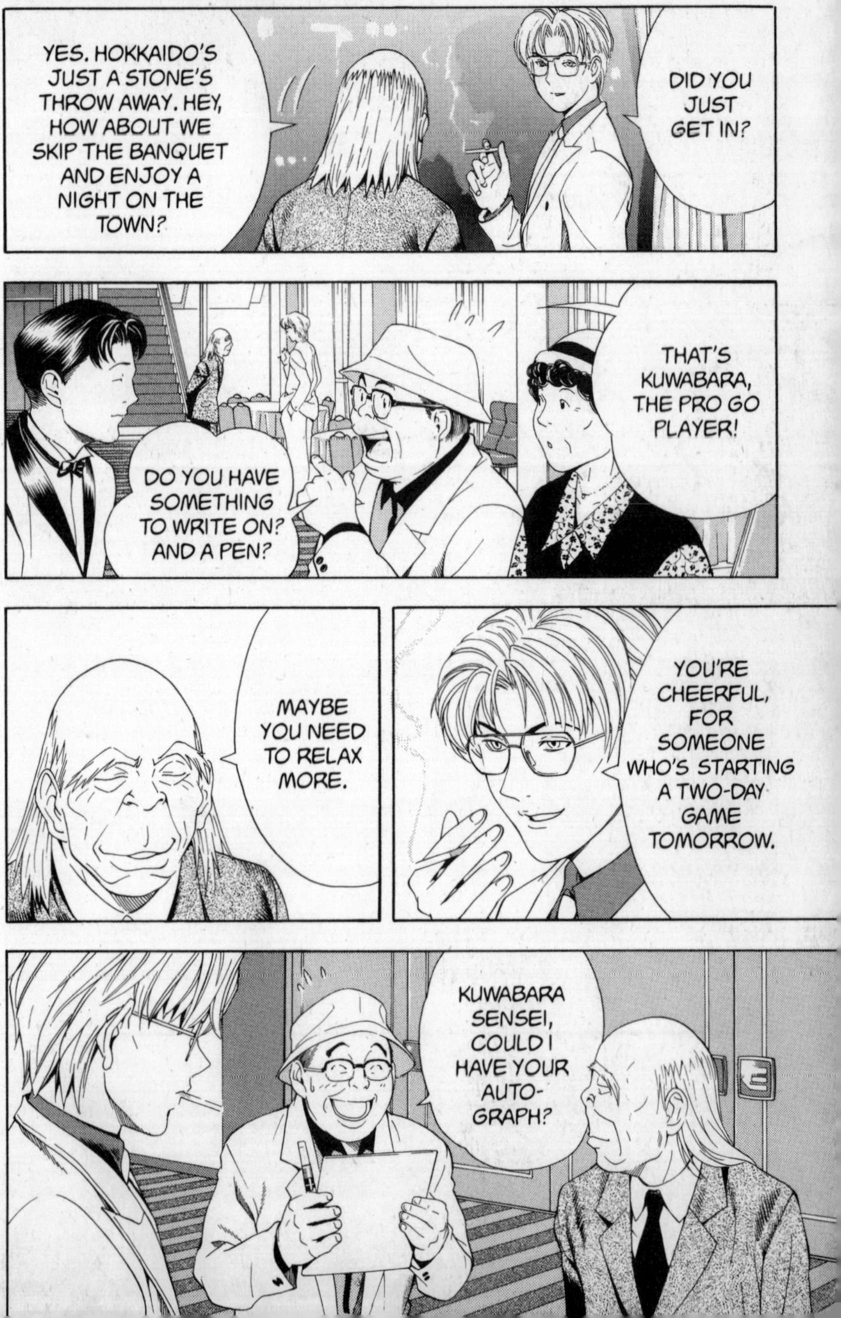
DID YOU JUST GET IN?
YES. HOKKAIDO'S JUST A STONE'S THROW AWAY. HEY, HOW ABOUT WE SKIP THE BANQUET AND ENJOY A NIGHT ON THE TOWN?
THAT'S KUWABARA, THE PRO GO PLAYER!
DO YOU HAVE SOMETHING TO WRITE ON? AND A PEN?
YOU'RE CHEERFUL, FOR SOMEONE WHO'S STARTING A TWO-DAY GAME TOMORROW.
MAYBE YOU NEED TO RELAX MORE.
KUWABARA SENSEI, COULD I HAVE YOUR AUTO-GRAPH?

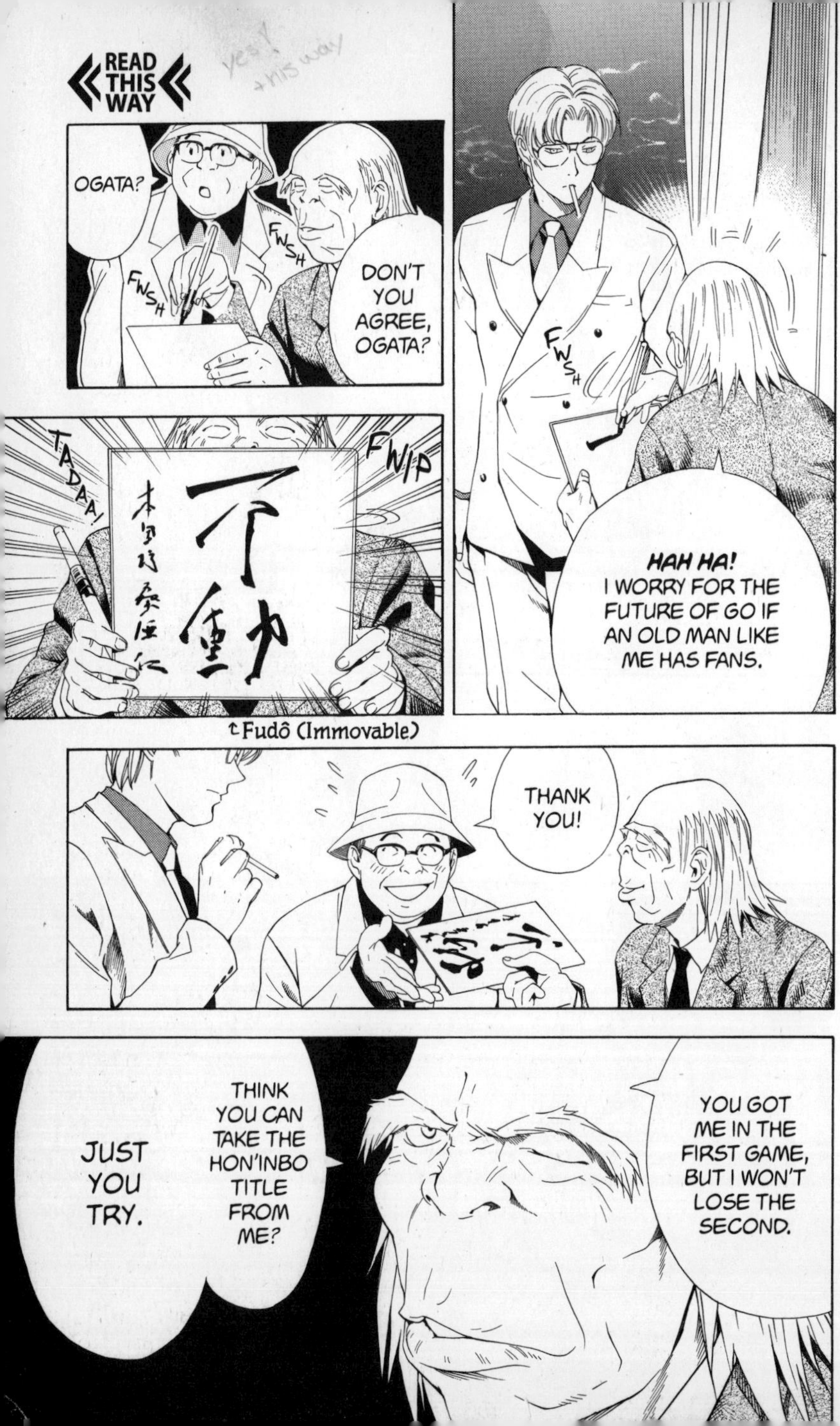
READ THIS WAY
yes! this way
HAH HA! I WORRY FOR THE FUTURE OF GO IF AN OLD MAN LIKE ME HAS FANS.
FWSH
DON'T YOU AGREE, OGATA?
FWSH
OGATA?
FWSH
FWIP
TADAA!
THANK YOU!
YOU GOT ME IN THE FIRST GAME, BUT I WON'T LOSE THE SECOND.
THINK YOU CAN TAKE THE HON'INBO TITLE FROM ME?
JUST YOU TRY.
↑Fudô (Immovable)

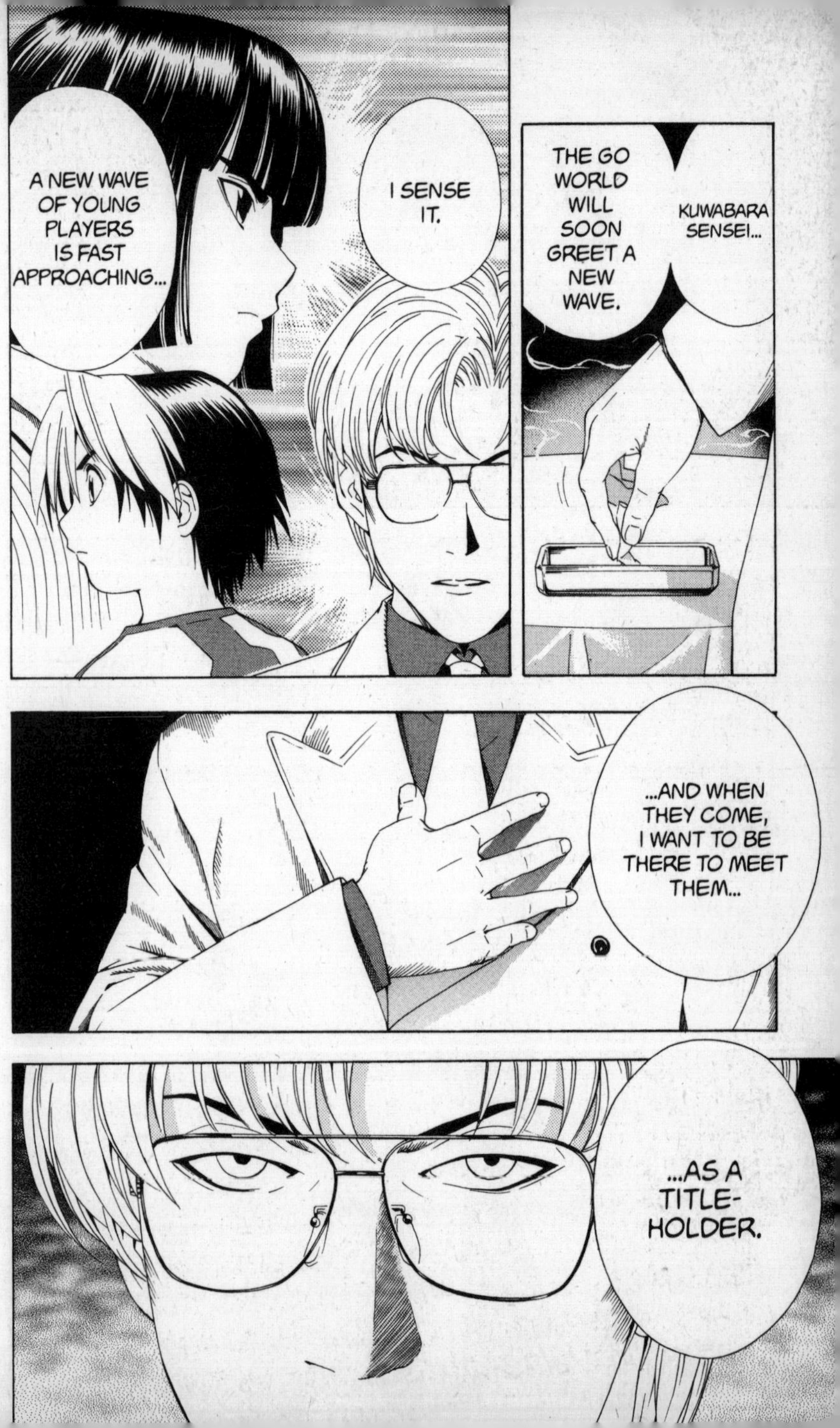
KUWABARA SENSEI...
THE GO WORLD WILL SOON GREET A NEW WAVE.
I SENSE IT.
A NEW WAVE OF YOUNG PLAYERS IS FAST APPROACHING...
...AND WHEN THEY COME, I WANT TO BE THERE TO MEET THEM...
...AS A TITLE-HOLDER.

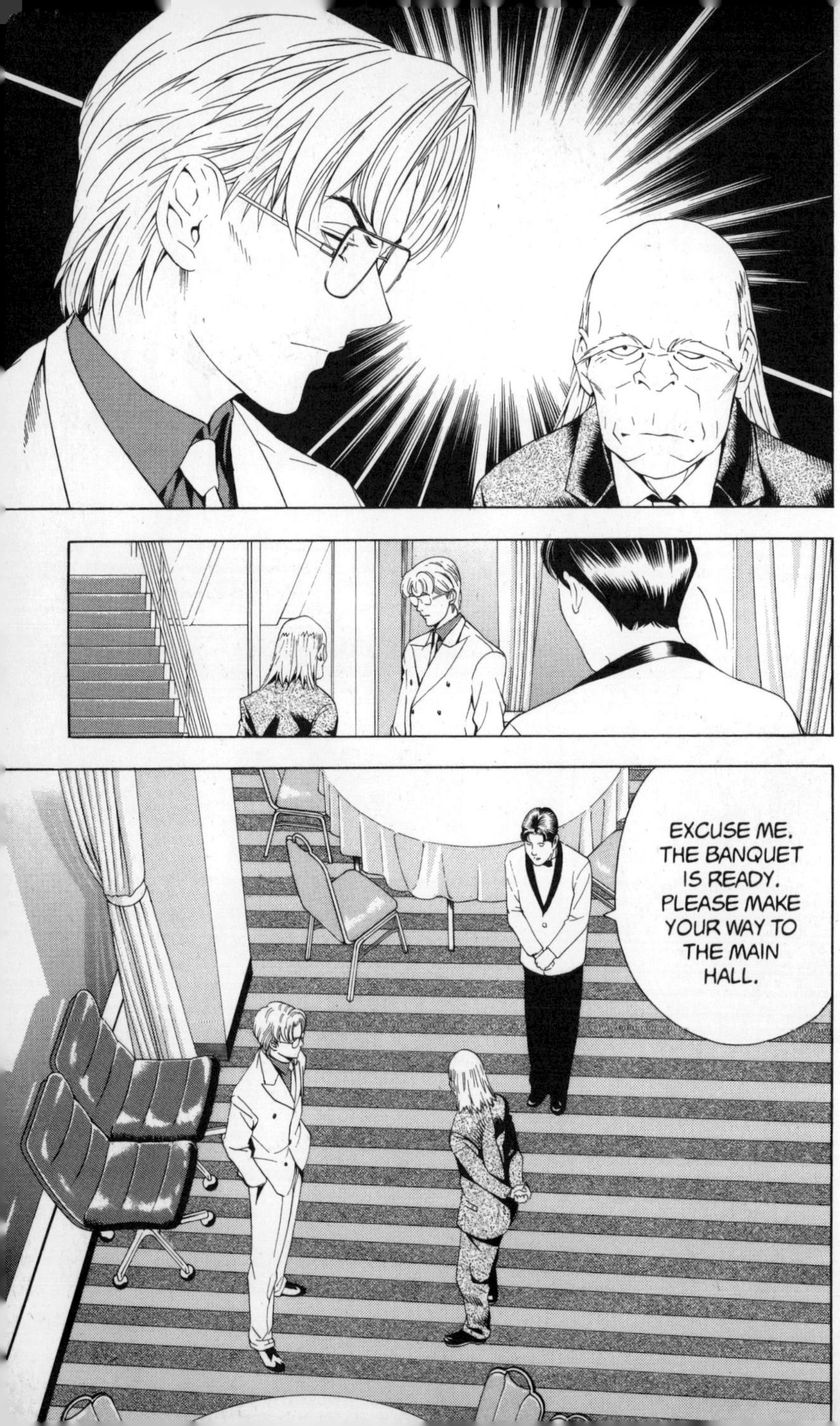
EXCUSE ME. THE BANQUET IS READY. PLEASE MAKE YOUR WAY TO THE MAIN HALL.

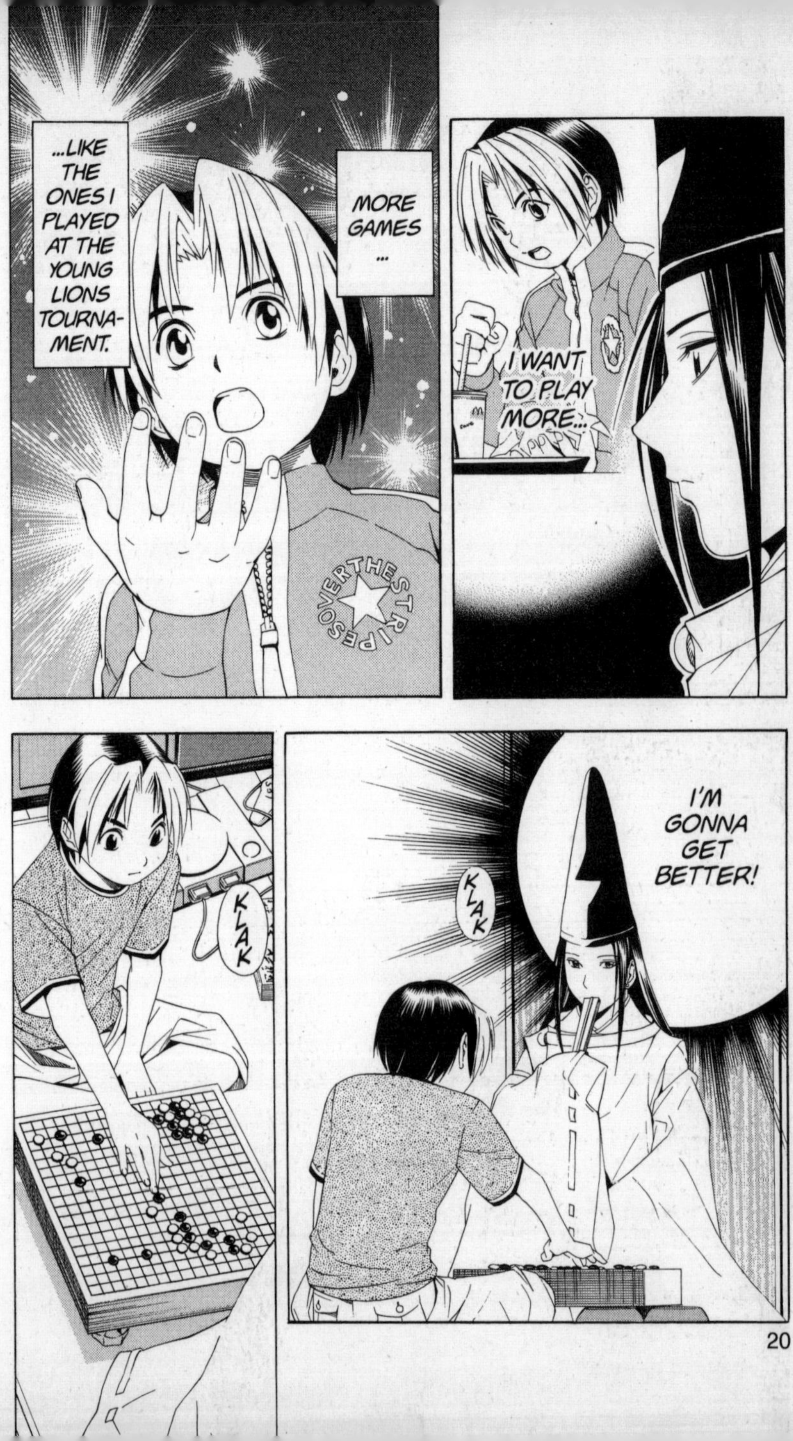
I WANT TO PLAY MORE...
MORE GAMES ...
...LIKE THE ONES I PLAYED AT THE YOUNG LIONS TOURNAMENT.
I'M GONNA GET BETTER!
KLAK
KLAK

Hikaru, you should play a large knight's move there, instead of a small knight's move.*

*The small knight's move is 1 down and 2 across, like in chess. The large knight's move is 1 down and 3 across.

A LARGE KNIGHT'S MOVE?

BUT A SMALL KNIGHT'S MOVE ISN'T BAD...

If we say the large knight's move is worth 100 points, then the small knight's move is worth 99.

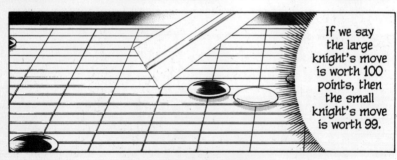

The small knight's move was good enough until now.

The moves after the small knight's move are predictable, and you're not likely to make a mistake.

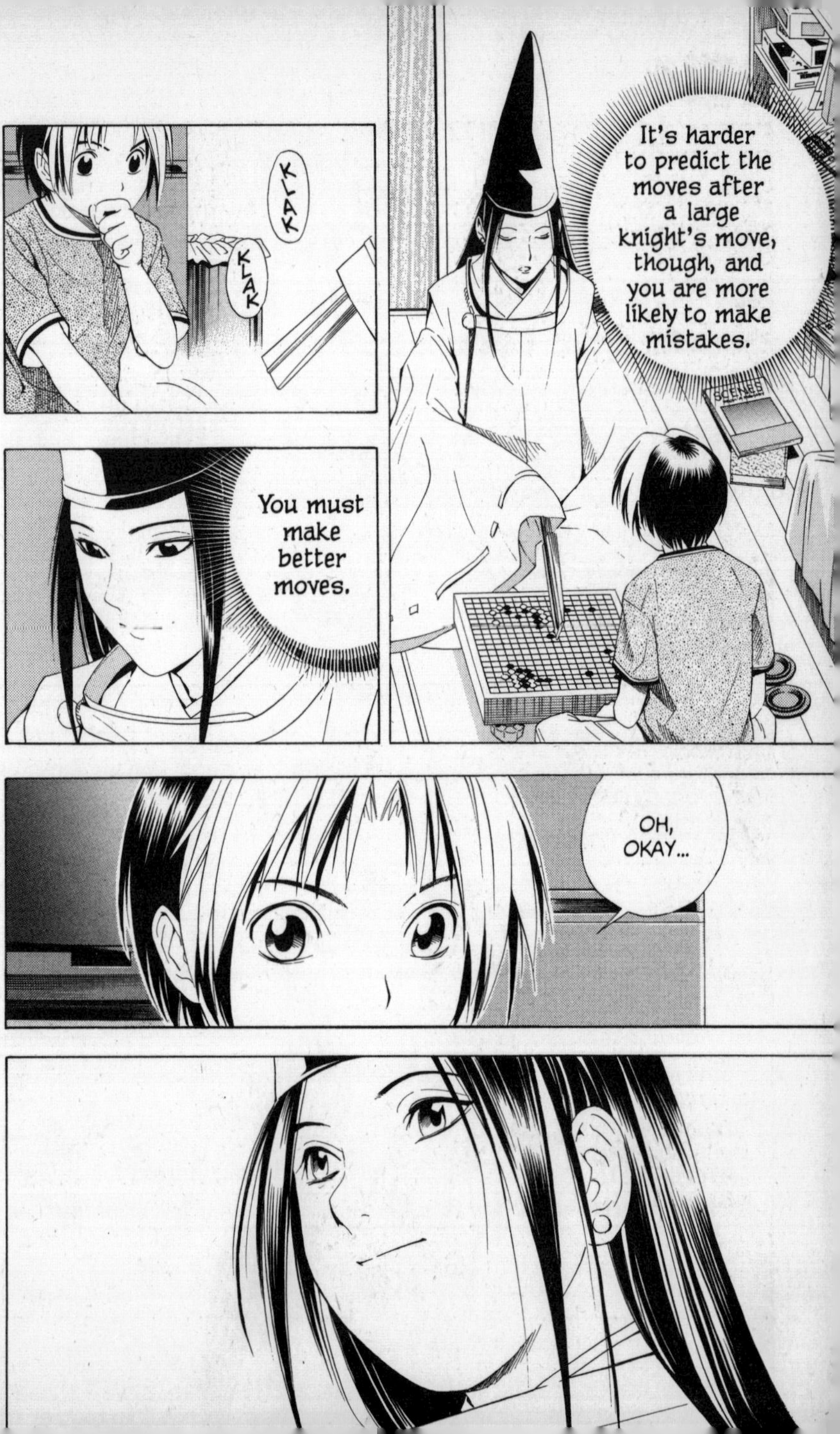
It's harder to predict the moves after a large knight's move, though, and you are more likely to make mistakes.
KLAK
KLAK
You must make better moves.
OH, OKAY...

READ THIS WAY

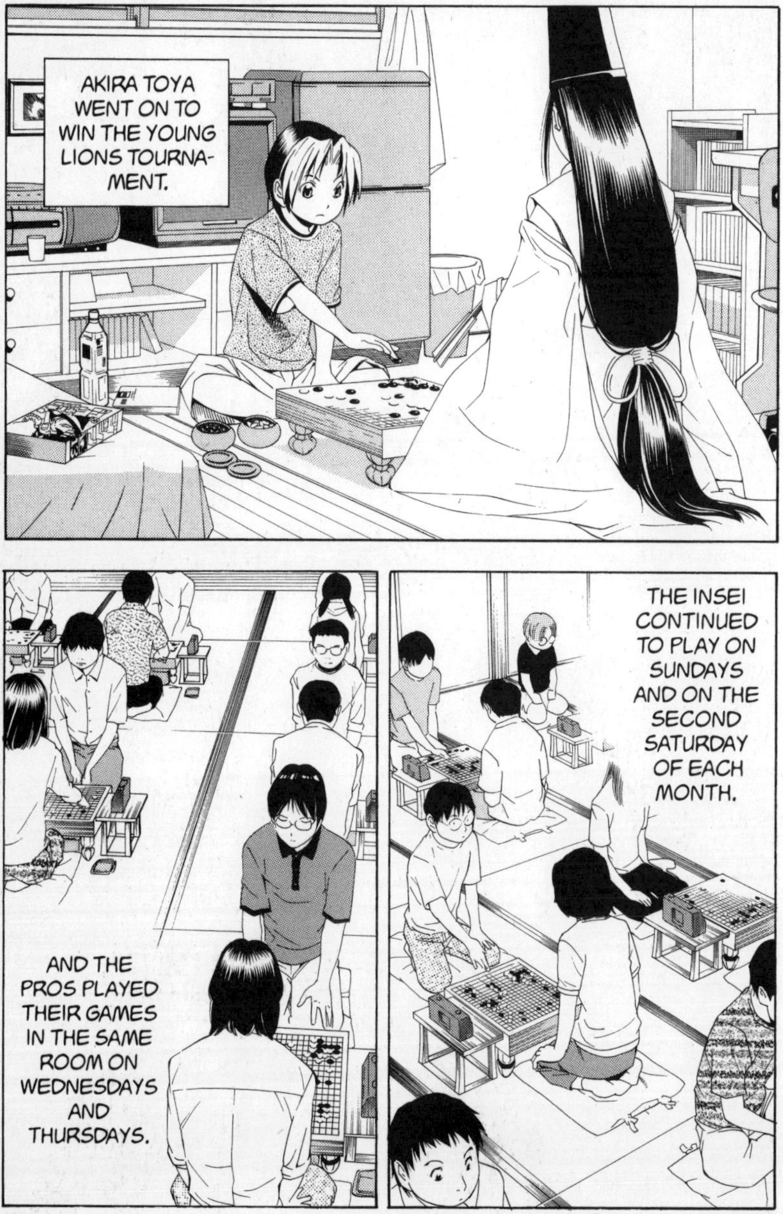
AKIRA TOYA WENT ON TO WIN THE YOUNG LIONS TOURNAMENT.
THE INSEI CONTINUED TO PLAY ON SUNDAYS AND ON THE SECOND SATURDAY OF EACH MONTH.
AND THE PROS PLAYED THEIR GAMES IN THE SAME ROOM ON WEDNESDAYS AND THURSDAYS.

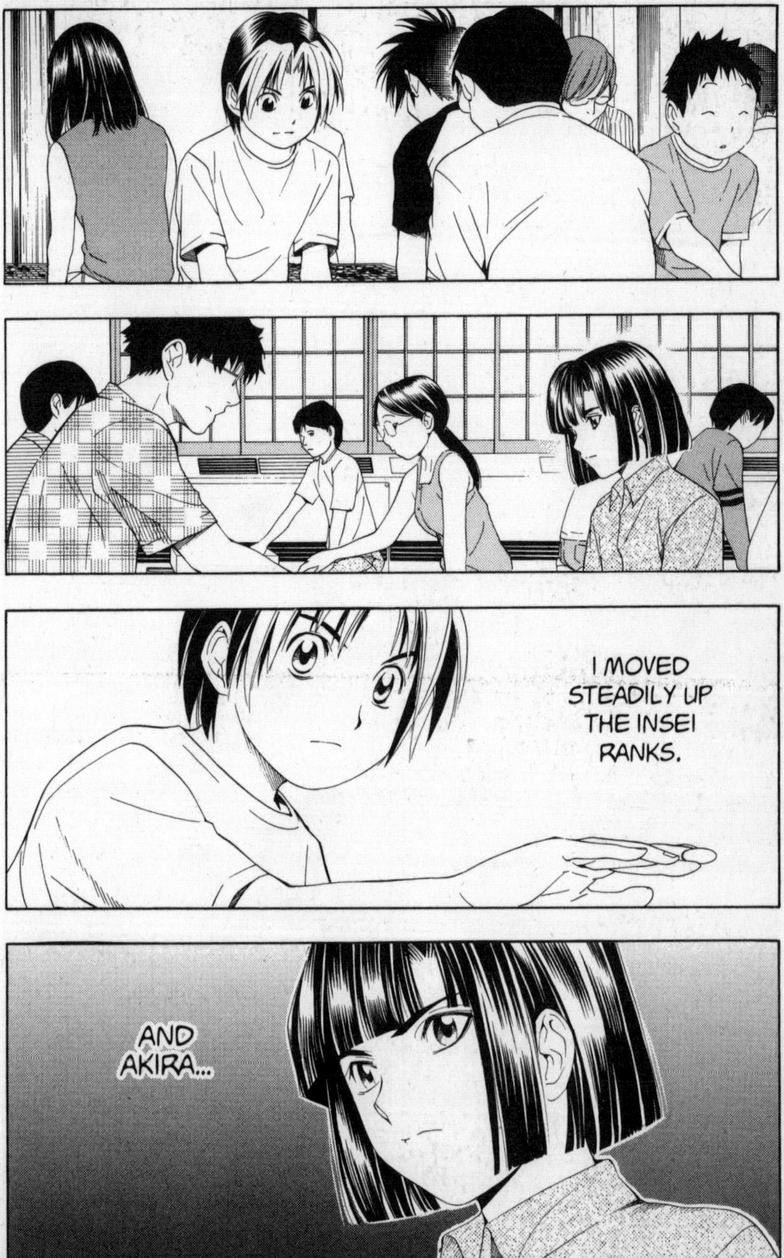
I MOVED STEADILY UP THE INSEI RANKS.
AND AKIRA...

READ THIS WAY

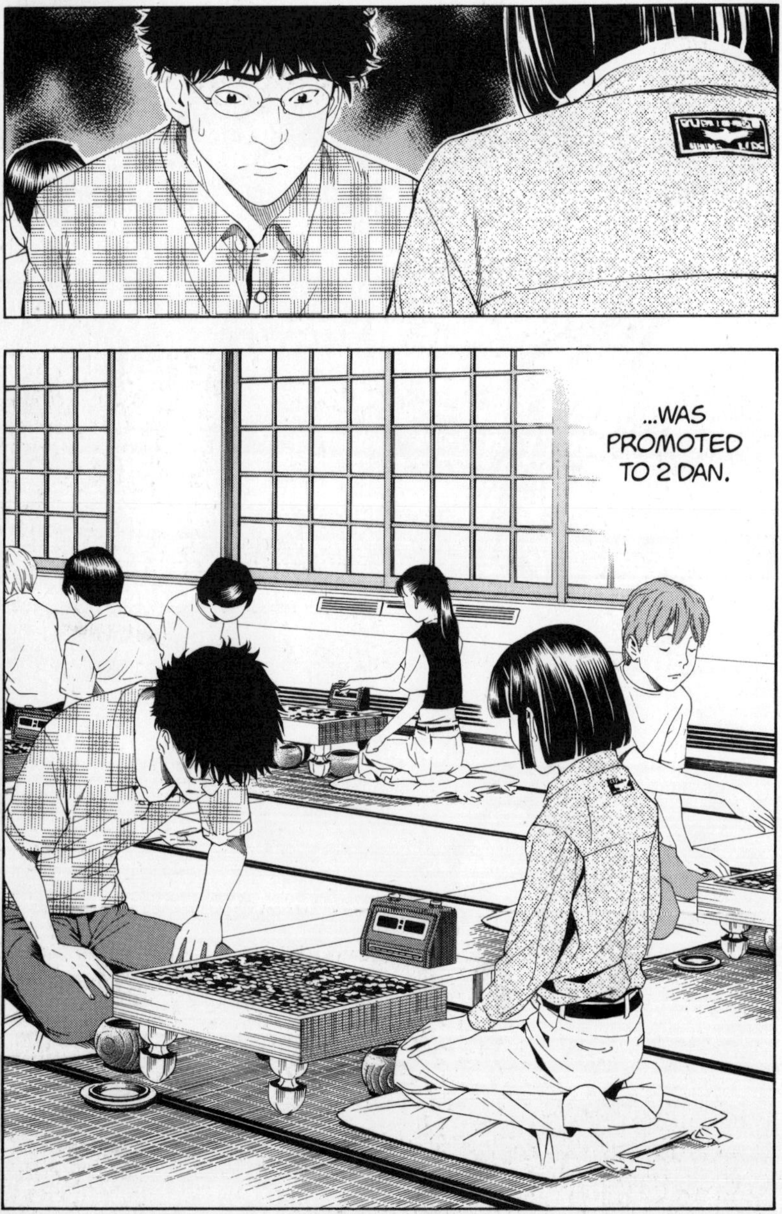
...WAS PROMOTED TO 2 DAN.

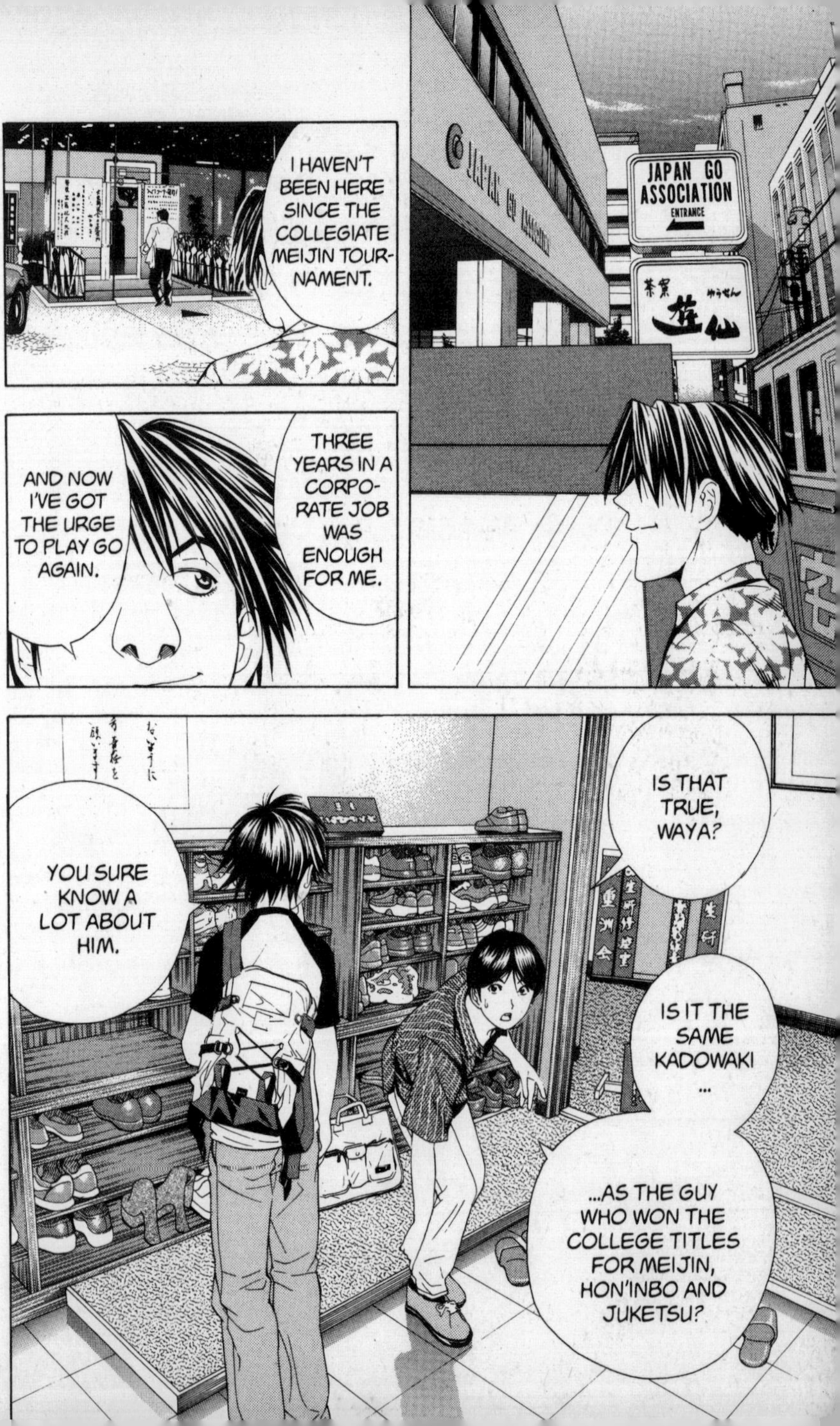
JAPAN GO ASSOCIATION
ENTRANCE
I HAVEN'T BEEN HERE SINCE THE COLLEGIATE MEIJIN TOURNAMENT.
THREE YEARS IN A CORPORATE JOB WAS ENOUGH FOR ME.
AND NOW I'VE GOT THE URGE TO PLAY GO AGAIN.
IS THAT TRUE, WAYA?
IS IT THE SAME KADOWAKI ...
...AS THE GUY WHO WON THE COLLEGE TITLES FOR MEIJIN, HON'INBO AND JUKETSU?
YOU SURE KNOW A LOT ABOUT HIM.

READ THIS WAY

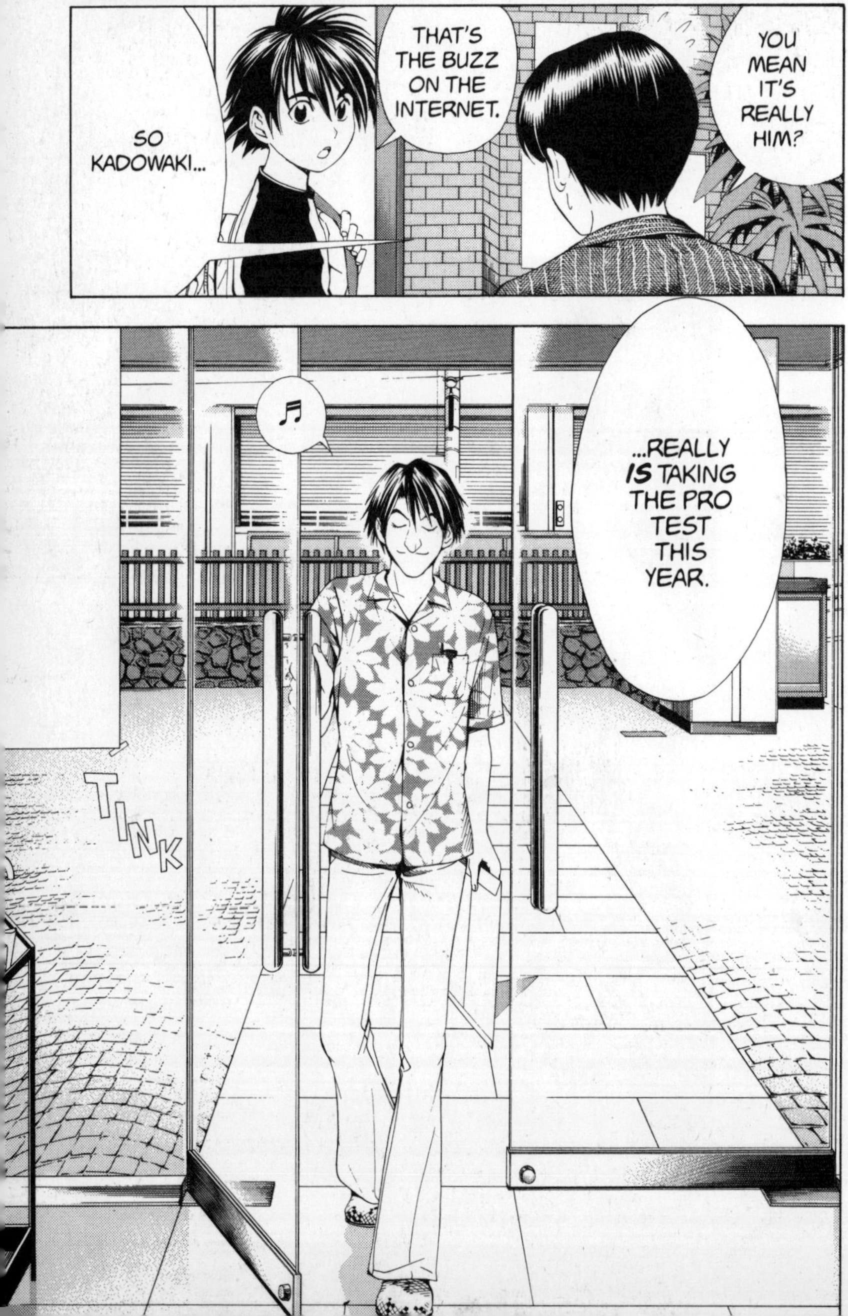
YOU MEAN IT'S REALLY HIM?
THAT'S THE BUZZ ON THE INTERNET.
SO KADOWAKI...
...REALLY *IS* TAKING THE PRO TEST THIS YEAR.
♬
TINK

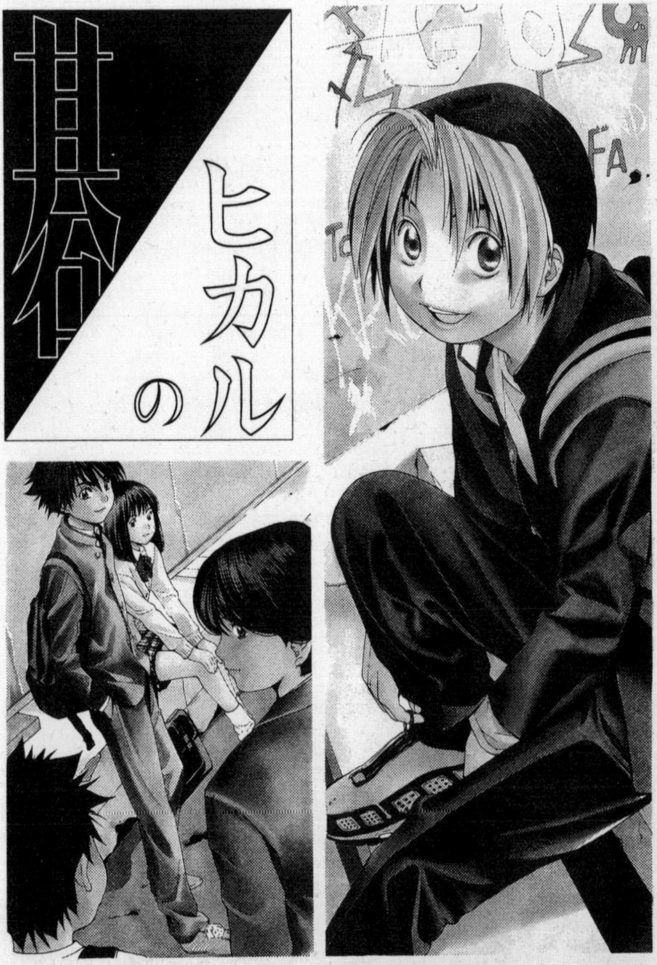
ヒカルの碁

Game 62 "A Chance to Play"

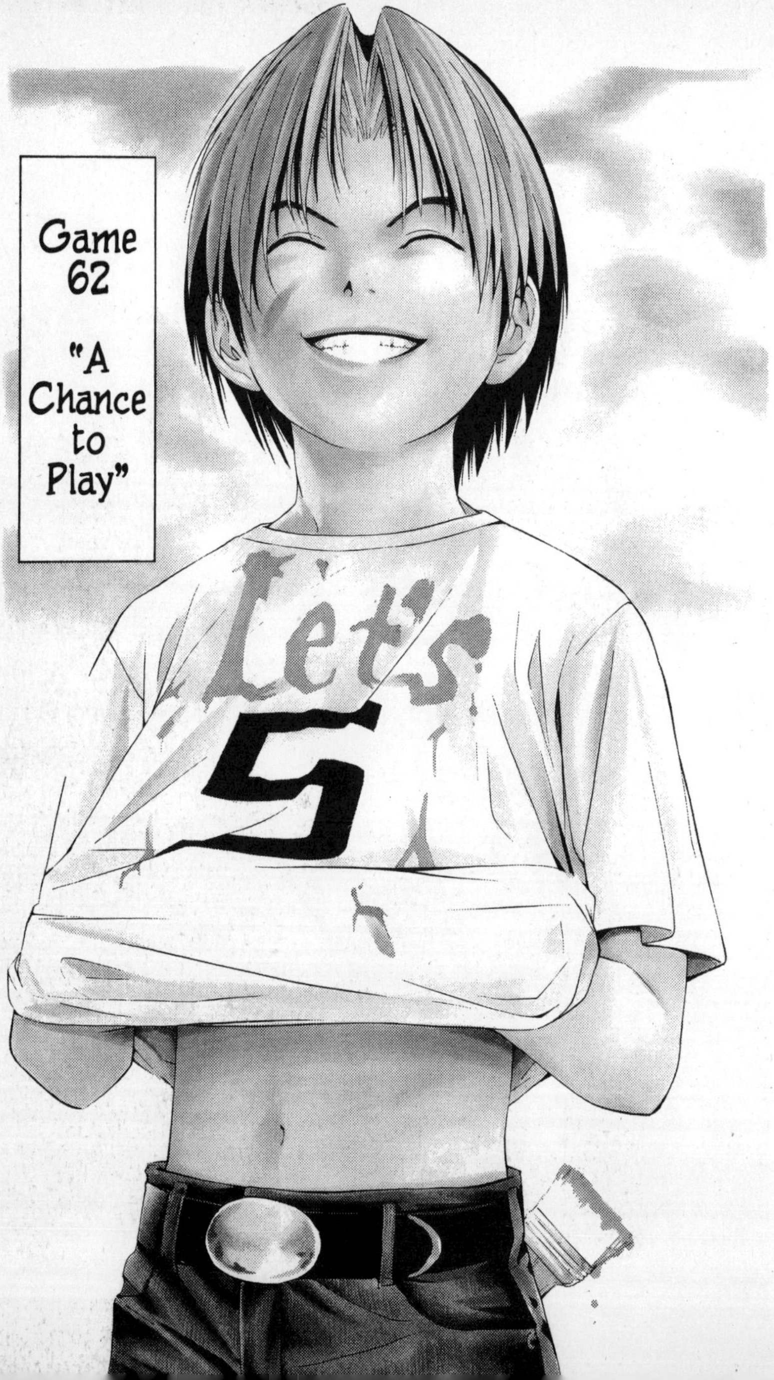
Let's
5

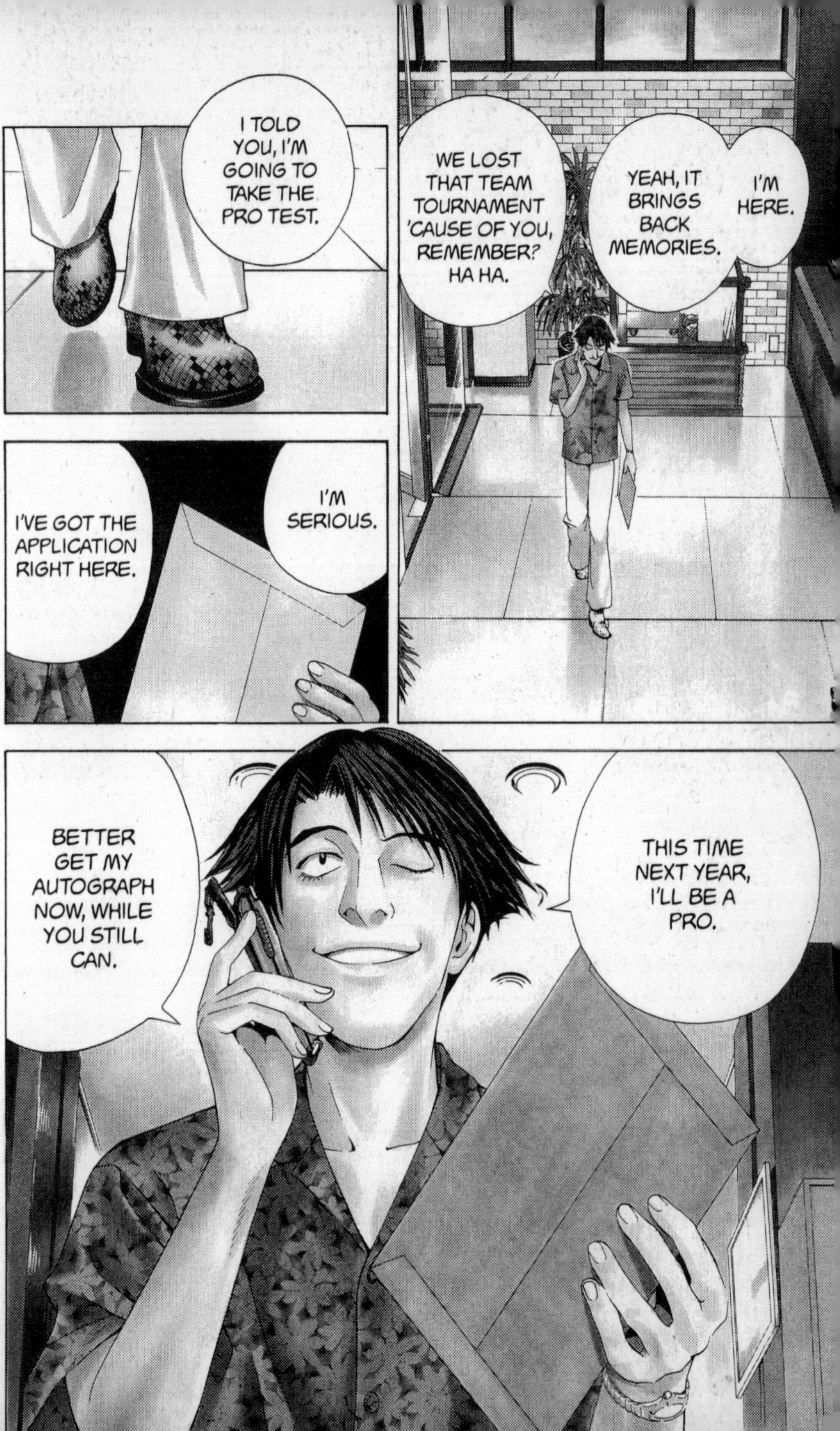
I'M HERE.
YEAH, IT BRINGS BACK MEMORIES.
WE LOST THAT TEAM TOURNAMENT 'CAUSE OF YOU, REMEMBER? HA HA.
I TOLD YOU, I'M GOING TO TAKE THE PRO TEST.
I'M SERIOUS.
I'VE GOT THE APPLICATION RIGHT HERE.
THIS TIME NEXT YEAR, I'LL BE A PRO.
BETTER GET MY AUTOGRAPH NOW, WHILE YOU STILL CAN.

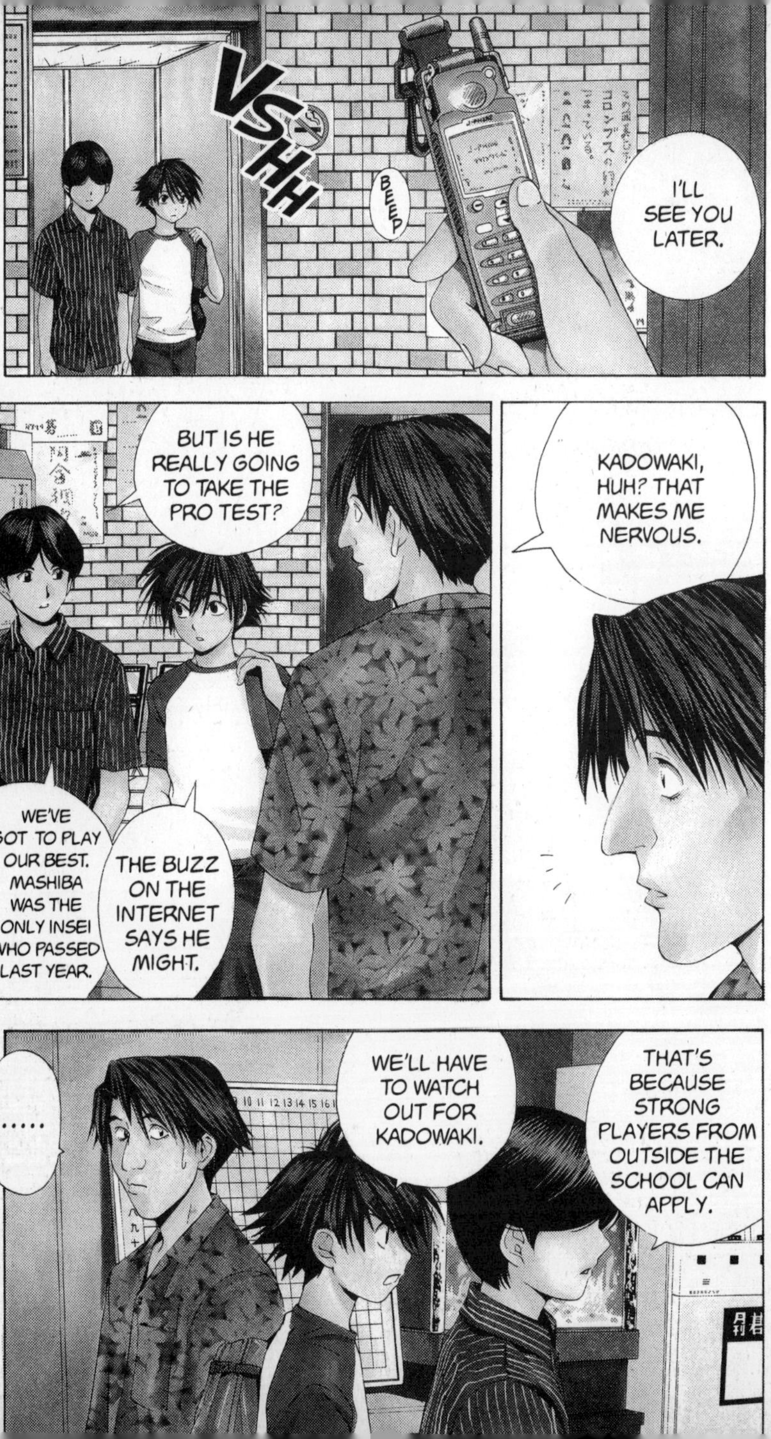
I'LL SEE YOU LATER.
BEEP
VSHH
KADOWAKI, HUH? THAT MAKES ME NERVOUS.
BUT IS HE REALLY GOING TO TAKE THE PRO TEST?
THE BUZZ ON THE INTERNET SAYS HE MIGHT.
WE'VE GOT TO PLAY OUR BEST. MASHIBA WAS THE ONLY INSEI WHO PASSED LAST YEAR.
THAT'S BECAUSE STRONG PLAYERS FROM OUTSIDE THE SCHOOL CAN APPLY.
WE'LL HAVE TO WATCH OUT FOR KADOWAKI.
.....

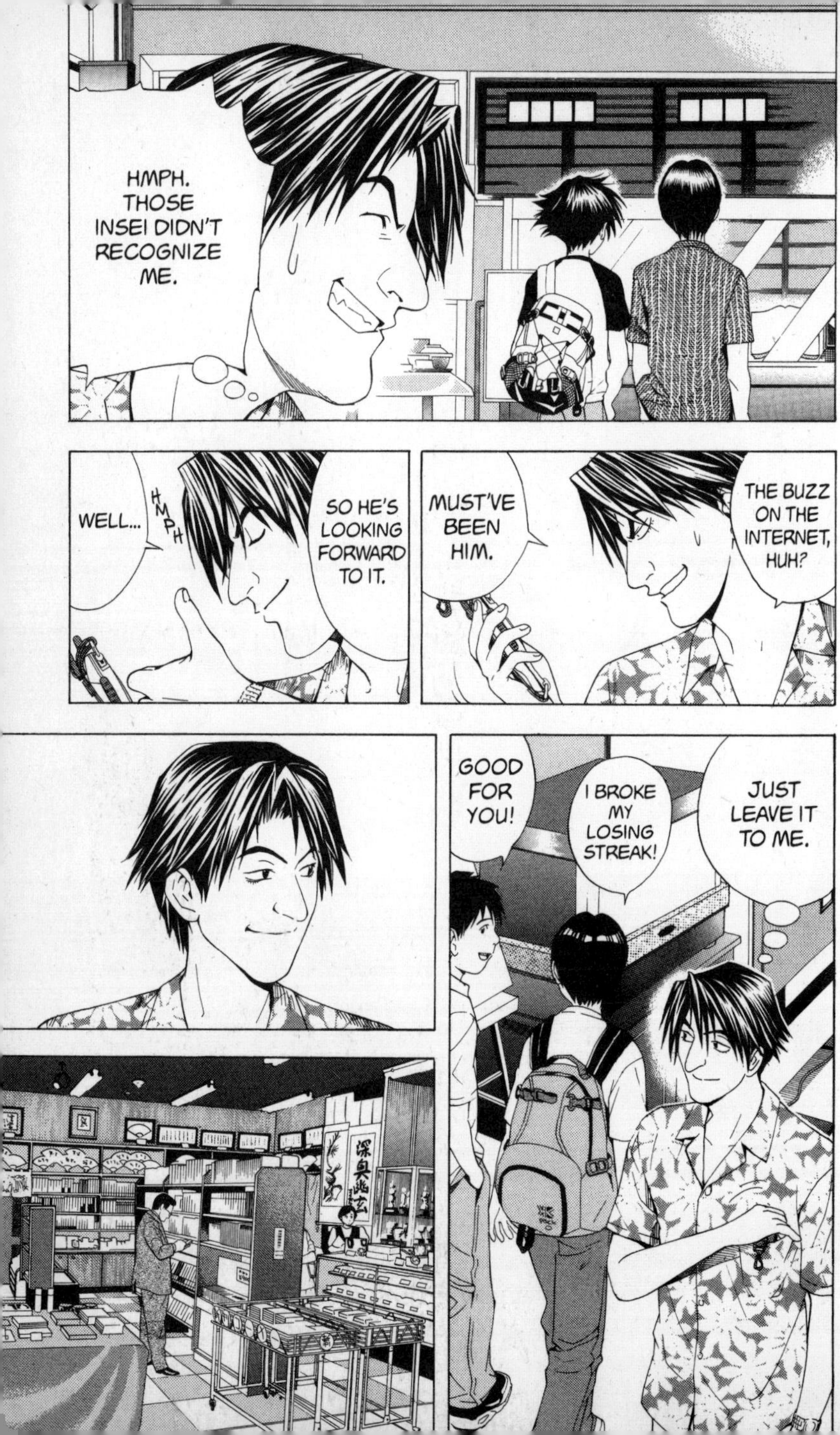

HMPH. THOSE INSEI DIDN'T RECOGNIZE ME.
THE BUZZ ON THE INTERNET, HUH?
MUST'VE BEEN HIM.
SO HE'S LOOKING FORWARD TO IT.
HMPH
WELL...
JUST LEAVE IT TO ME.
I BROKE MY LOSING STREAK!
GOOD FOR YOU!
深奥幽玄

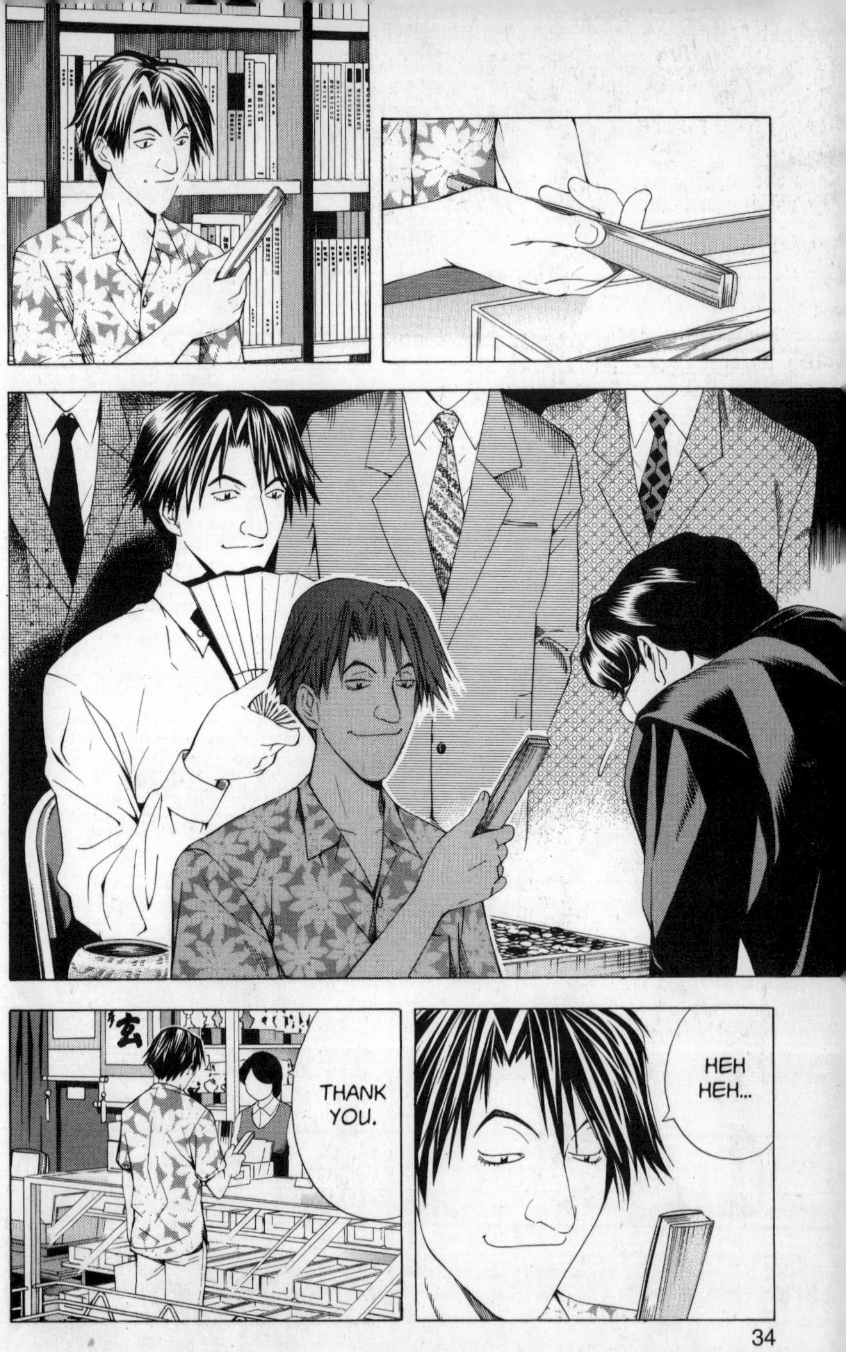
HEH HEH...
THANK YOU.

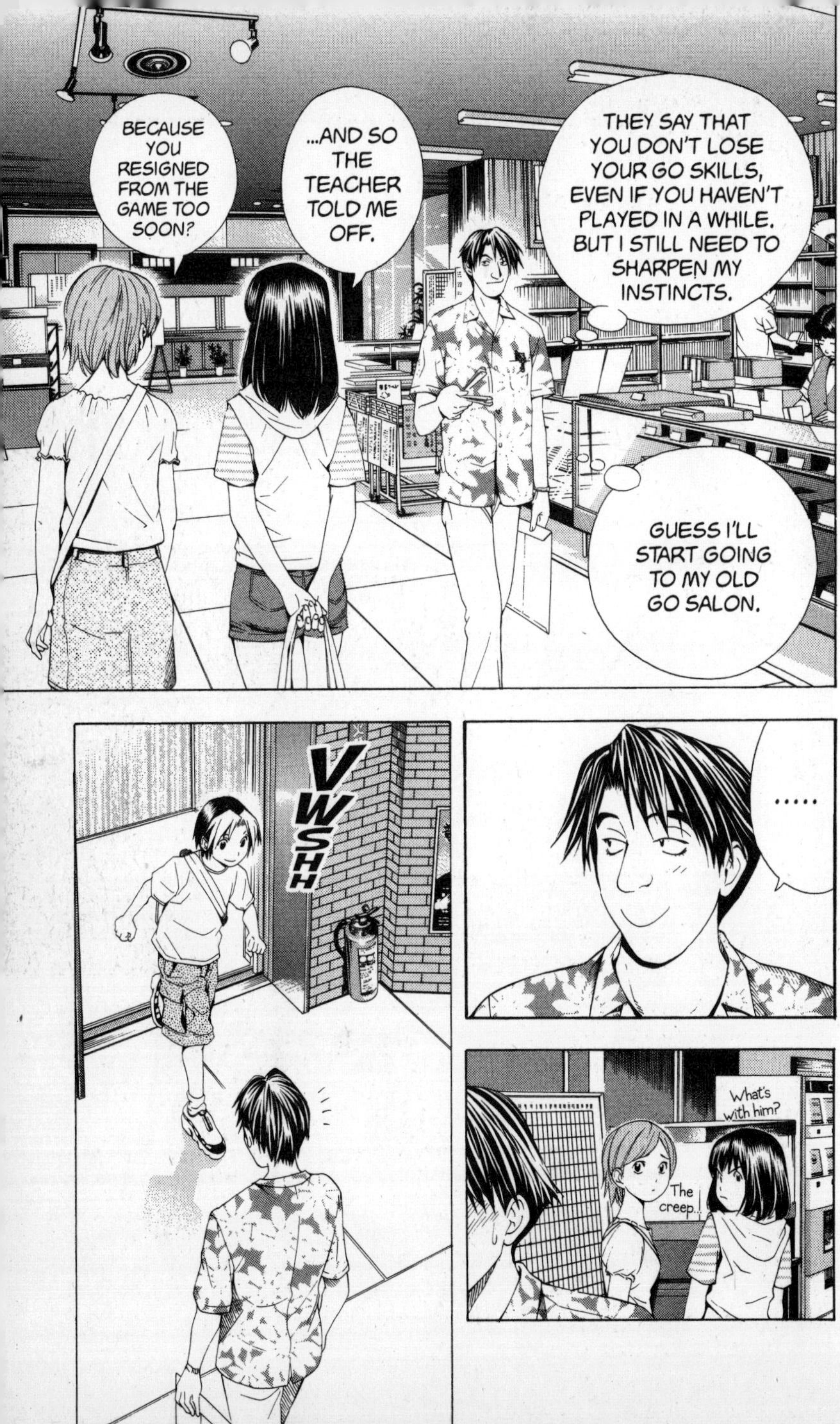
THEY SAY THAT YOU DON'T LOSE YOUR GO SKILLS, EVEN IF YOU HAVEN'T PLAYED IN A WHILE. BUT I STILL NEED TO SHARPEN MY INSTINCTS.
...AND SO THE TEACHER TOLD ME OFF.
BECAUSE YOU RESIGNED FROM THE GAME TOO SOON?
GUESS I'LL START GOING TO MY OLD GO SALON.
.....
What's with him?
The creep...!
VWSHH

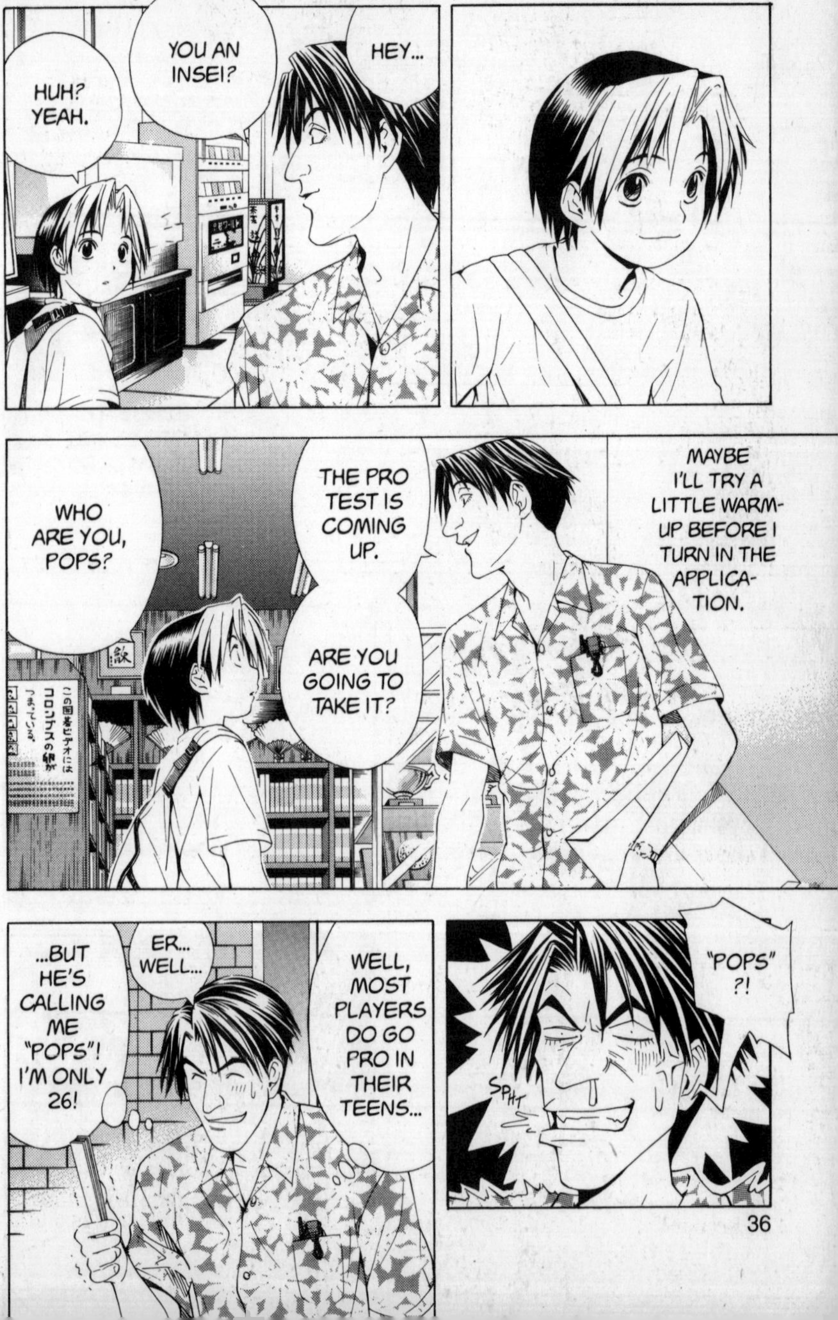
HEY...
YOU AN INSEI?
HUH? YEAH.
MAYBE I'LL TRY A LITTLE WARM-UP BEFORE I TURN IN THE APPLICA-TION.
THE PRO TEST IS COMING UP.
ARE YOU GOING TO TAKE IT?
WHO ARE YOU, POPS?
この囲碁ビデオにはコロンブスの卵がつまっている。
"POPS" ?!
SPHT
WELL, MOST PLAYERS DO GO PRO IN THEIR TEENS...
ER... WELL...
...BUT HE'S CALLING ME "POPS"! I'M ONLY 26!

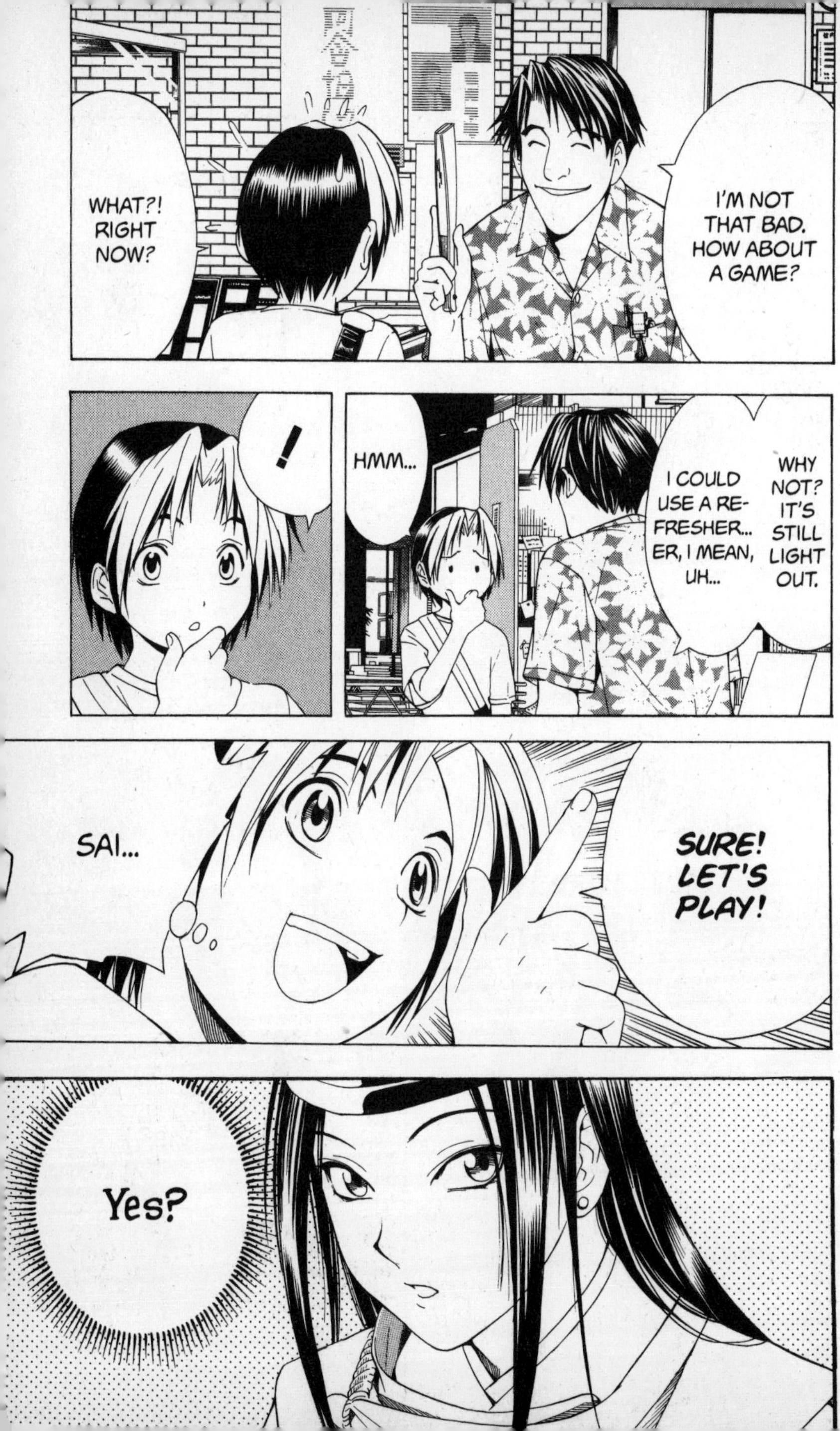
I'M NOT THAT BAD. HOW ABOUT A GAME?
WHAT?! RIGHT NOW?
WHY NOT? IT'S STILL LIGHT OUT.
I COULD USE A RE-FRESHER... ER, I MEAN, UH...
HMM...
!
SURE! LET'S PLAY!
SAI...
Yes?

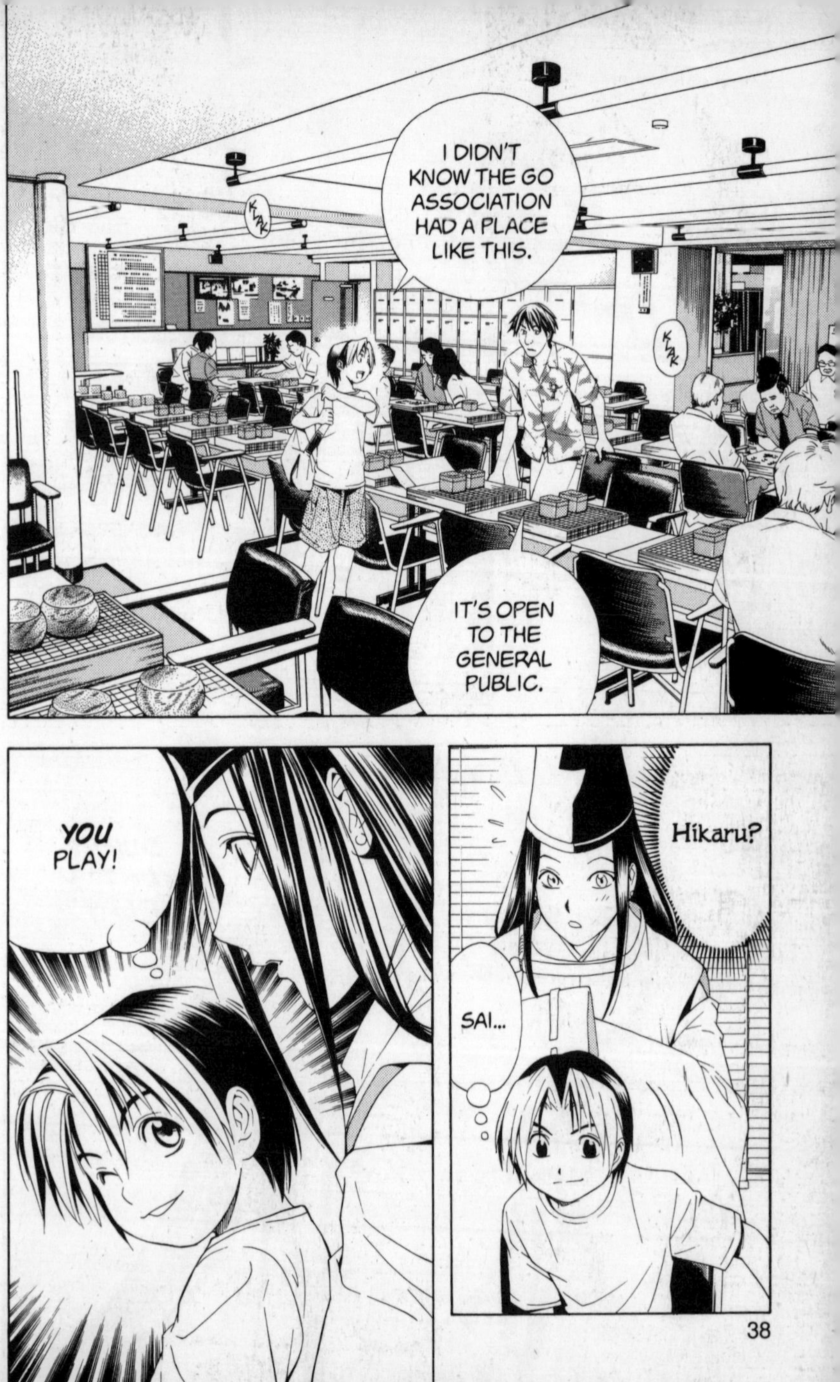
KLAK
KLAK
I DIDN'T KNOW THE GO ASSOCIATION HAD A PLACE LIKE THIS.
IT'S OPEN TO THE GENERAL PUBLIC.
Hikaru?
SAI...
YOU PLAY!

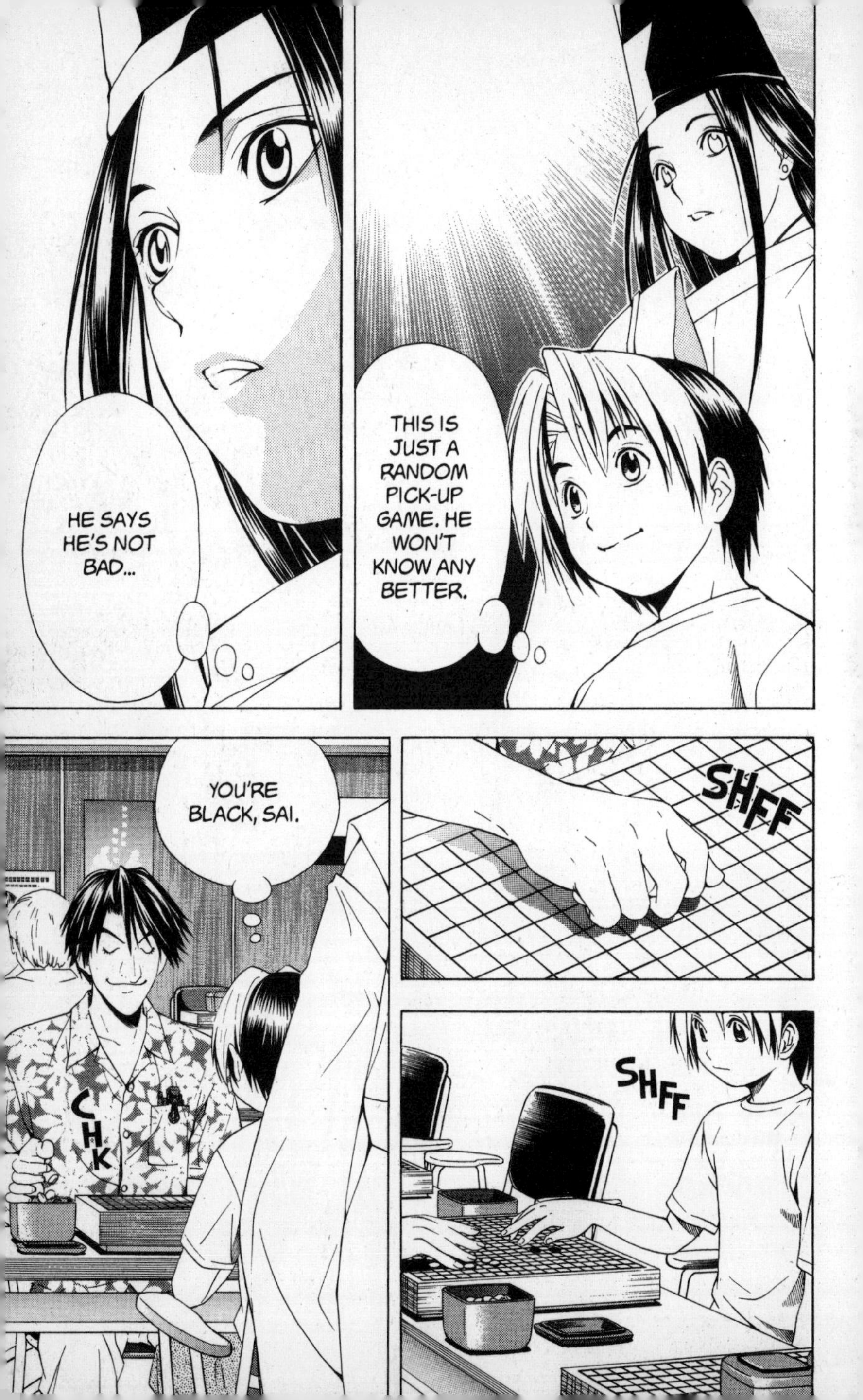
THIS IS JUST A RANDOM PICK-UP GAME. HE WON'T KNOW ANY BETTER.
HE SAYS HE'S NOT BAD...
SHFF
SHFF
YOU'RE BLACK, SAI.
CHK

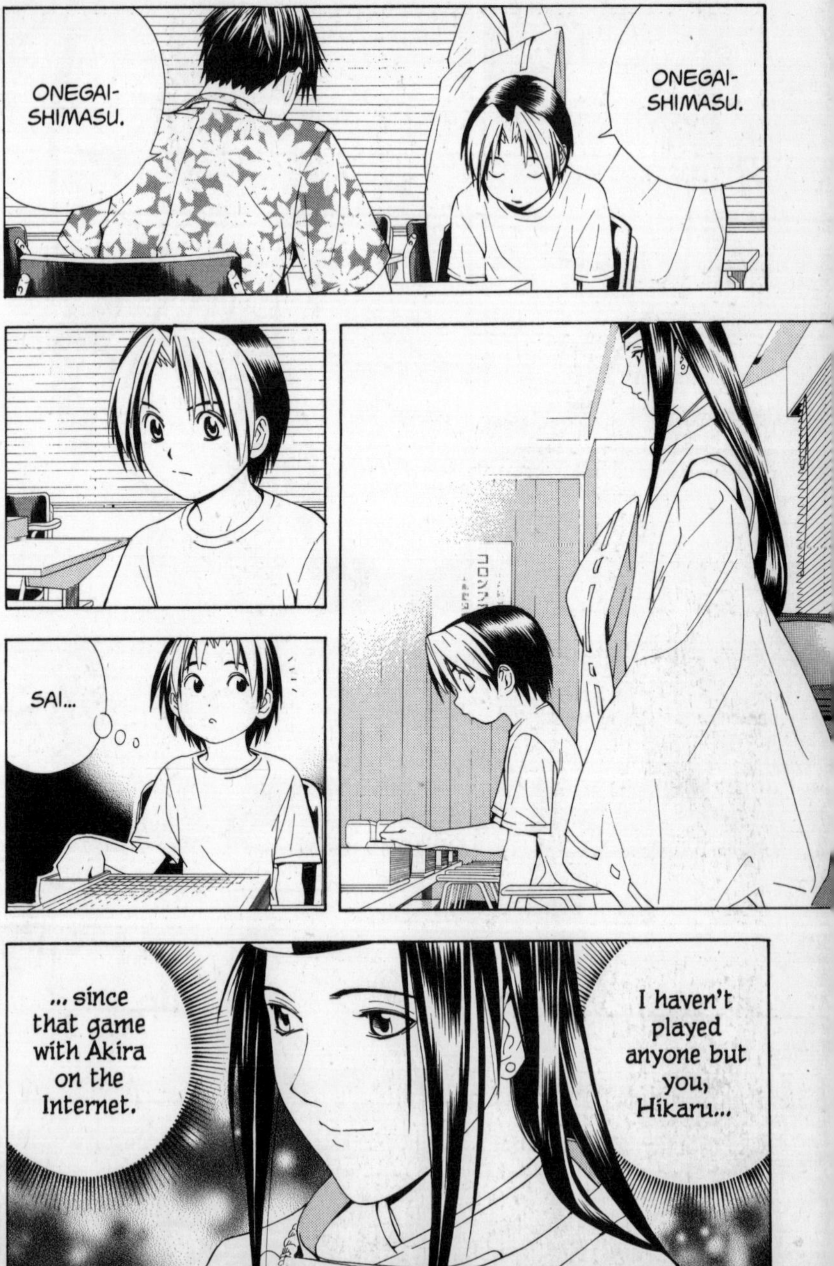
ONEGAI-SHIMASU.
ONEGAI-SHIMASU.
SAI...
I haven't played anyone but you, Hikaru...
... since that game with Akira on the Internet.

DON'T TAKE TOO LONG TO THINK, SAI. I WANT TO GET HOME BEFORE DARK.

.....

Of course.

WELL?

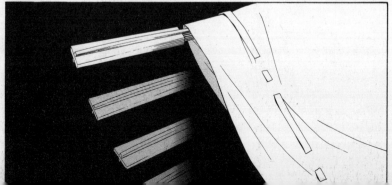

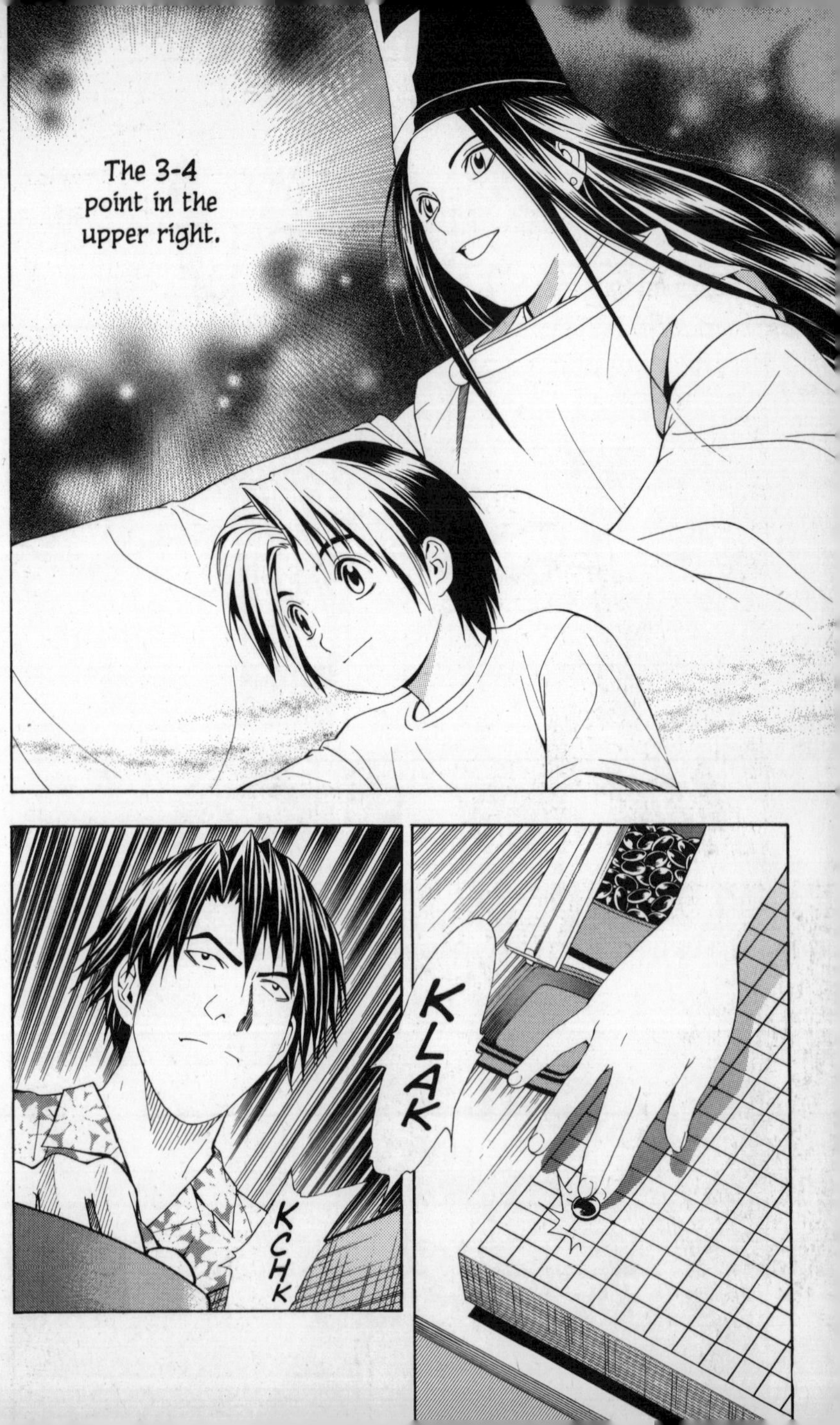
The 3-4 point in the upper right.
KLAK
KCHK

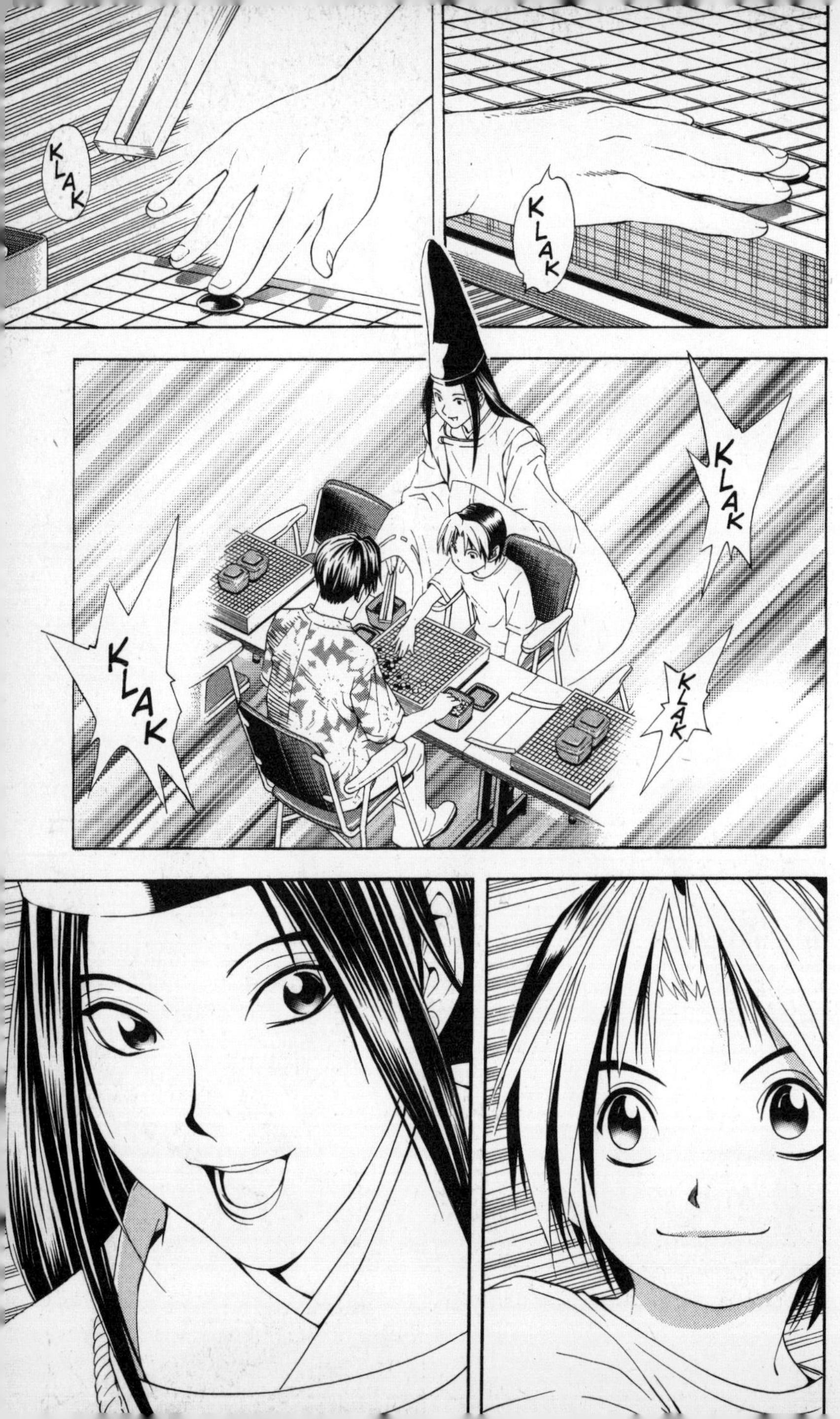
KLAK
KLAK
KLAK
KLAK
KLAK

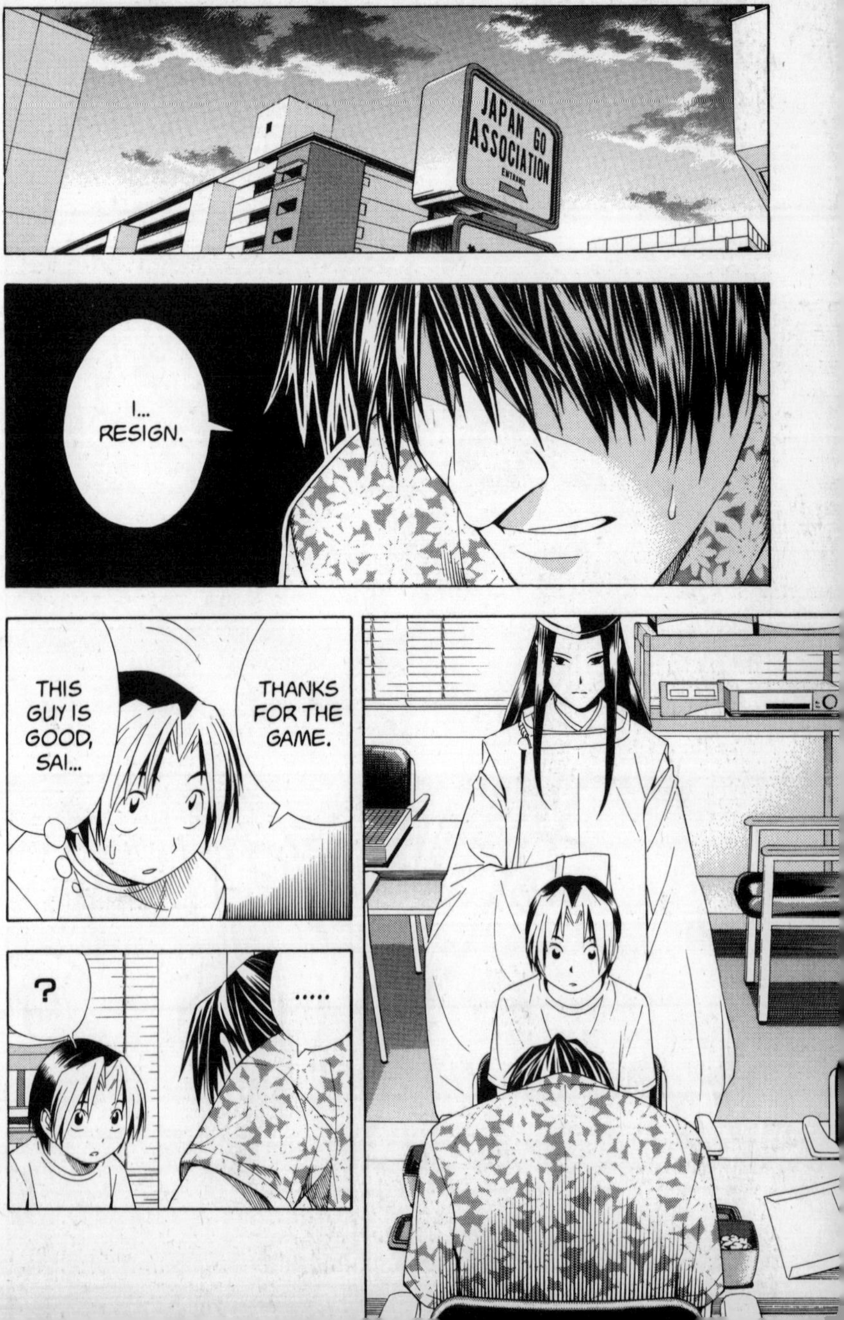
JAPAN GO ASSOCIATION
ENTRANCE
I... RESIGN.
THANKS FOR THE GAME.
THIS GUY IS GOOD, SAI...
.....
?

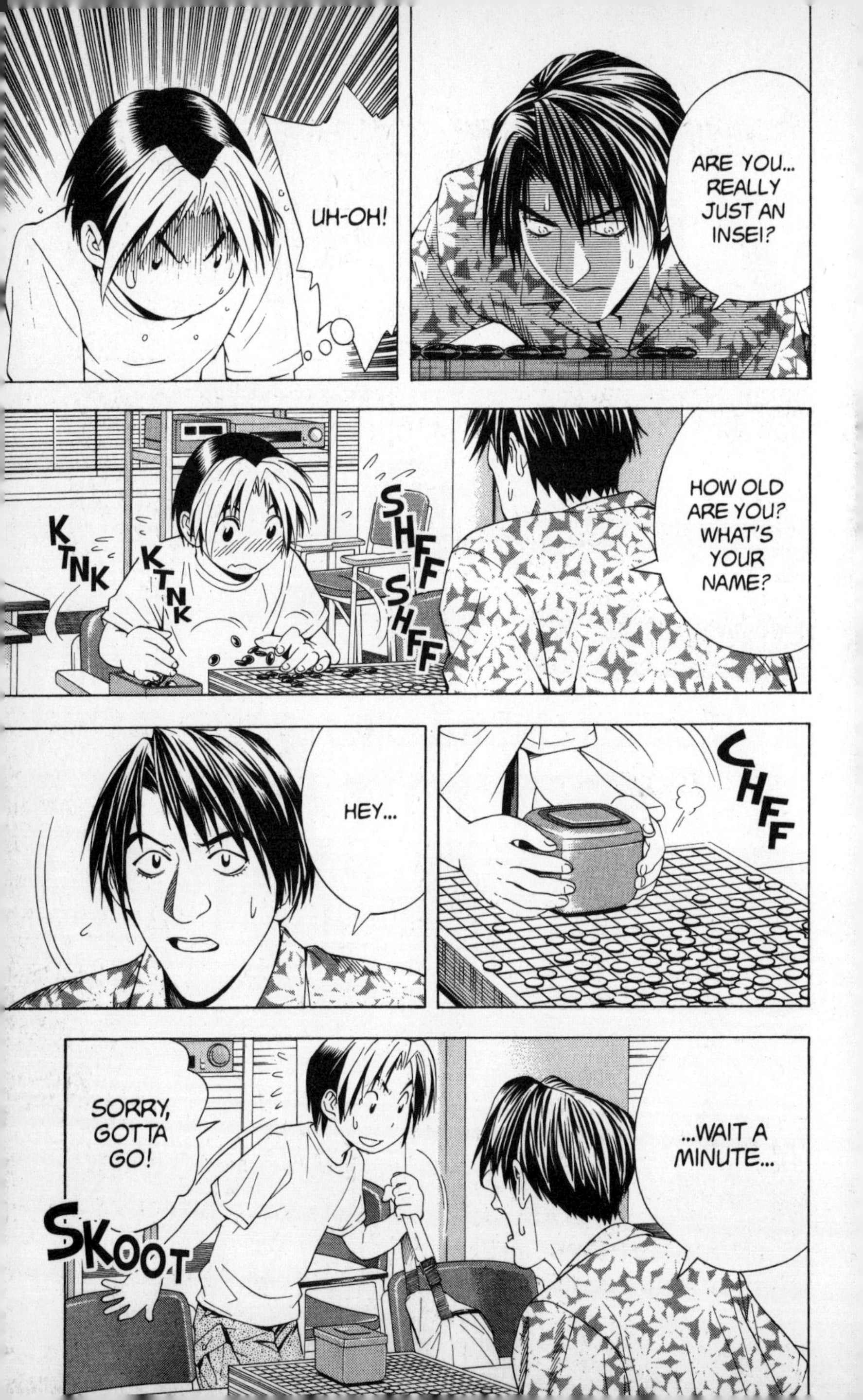
ARE YOU... REALLY JUST AN INSEI?
UH-OH!
HOW OLD ARE YOU? WHAT'S YOUR NAME?
SHFF
SHFF
KTNK
KTNK
CHFF
HEY...
...WAIT A MINUTE...
SORRY, GOTTA GO!
SKOOT

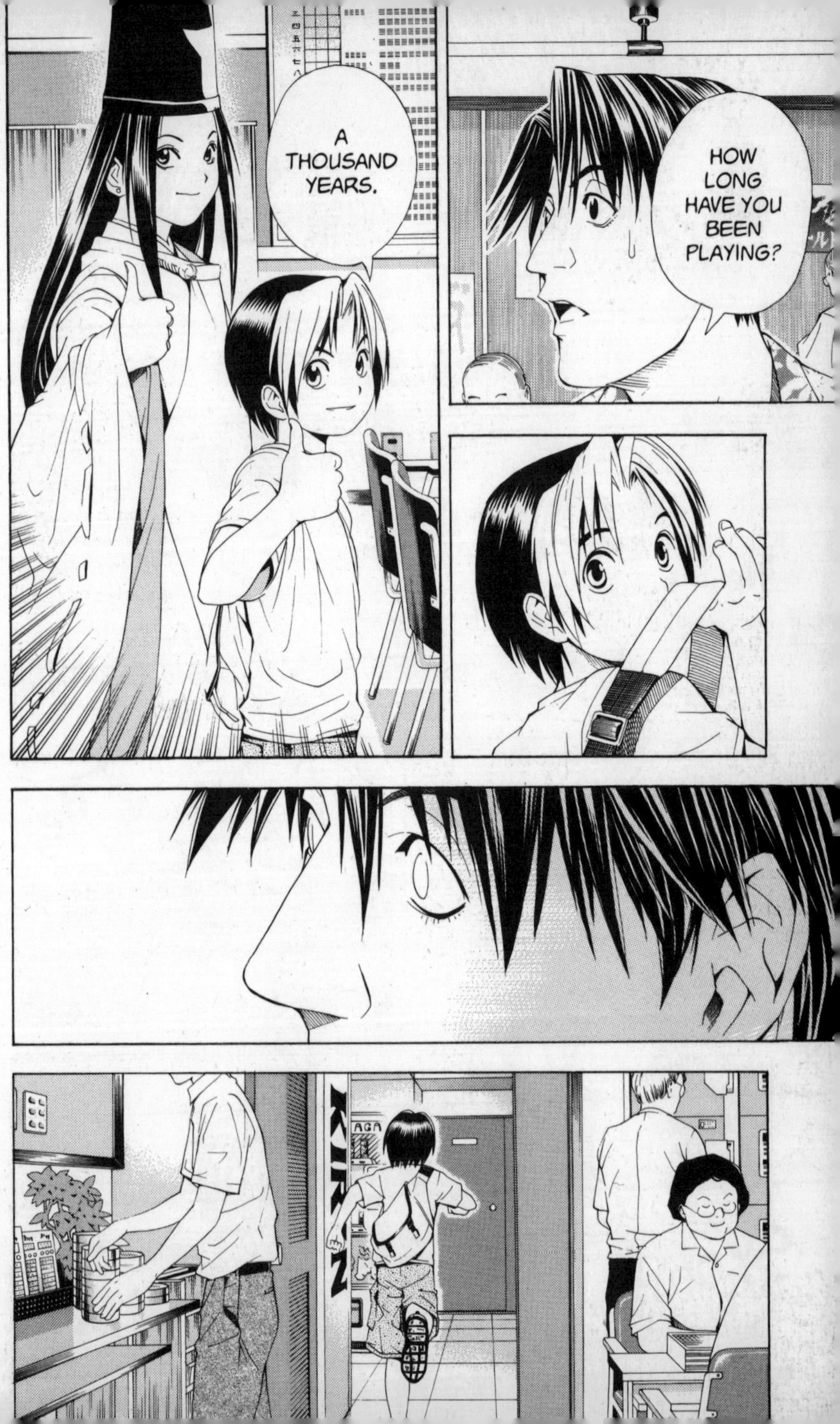
HOW LONG HAVE YOU BEEN PLAYING?
A THOUSAND YEARS.
KIRIN

READ THIS WAY

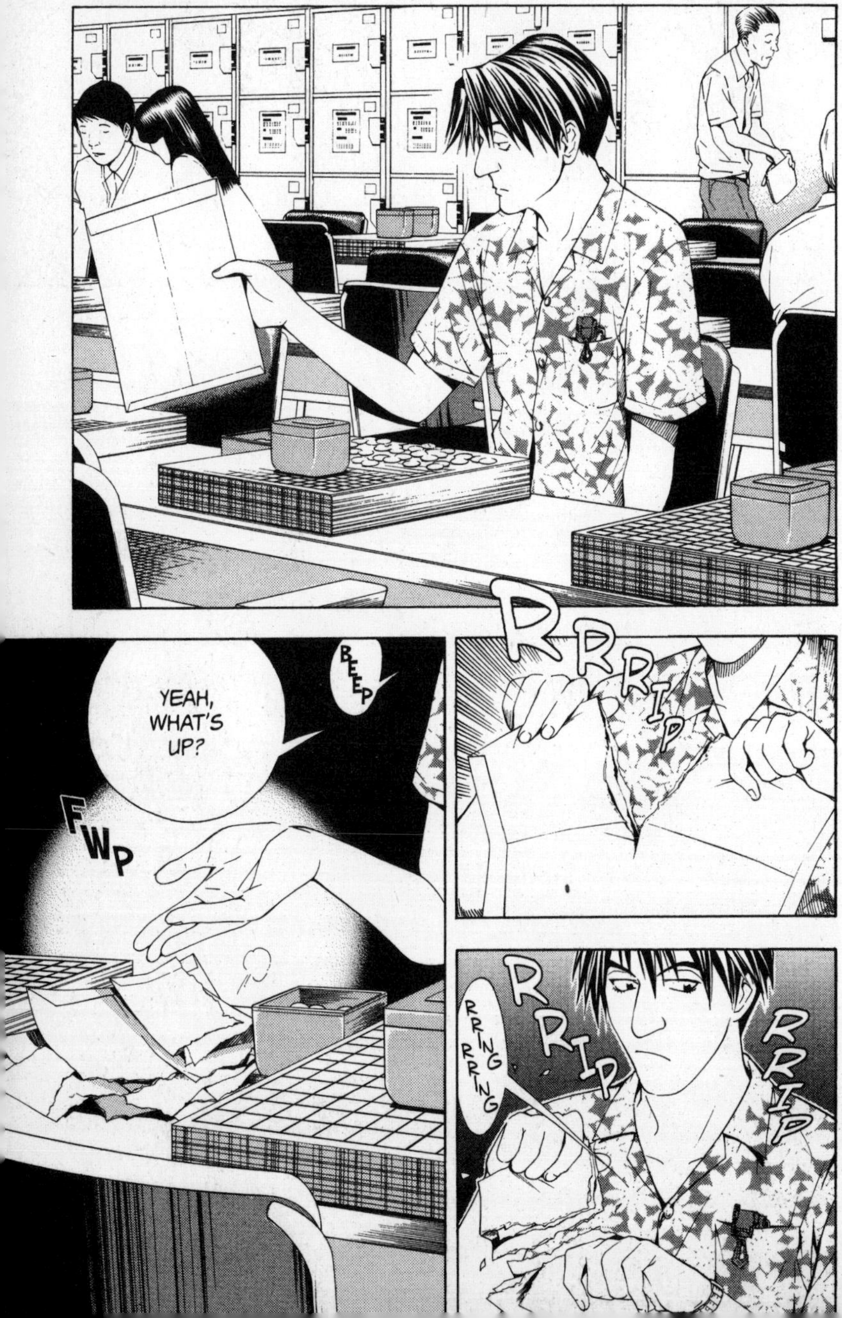
RRRRIP
RRIP
RRING RRING
RRIP
BEEP
YEAH, WHAT'S UP?
FWP

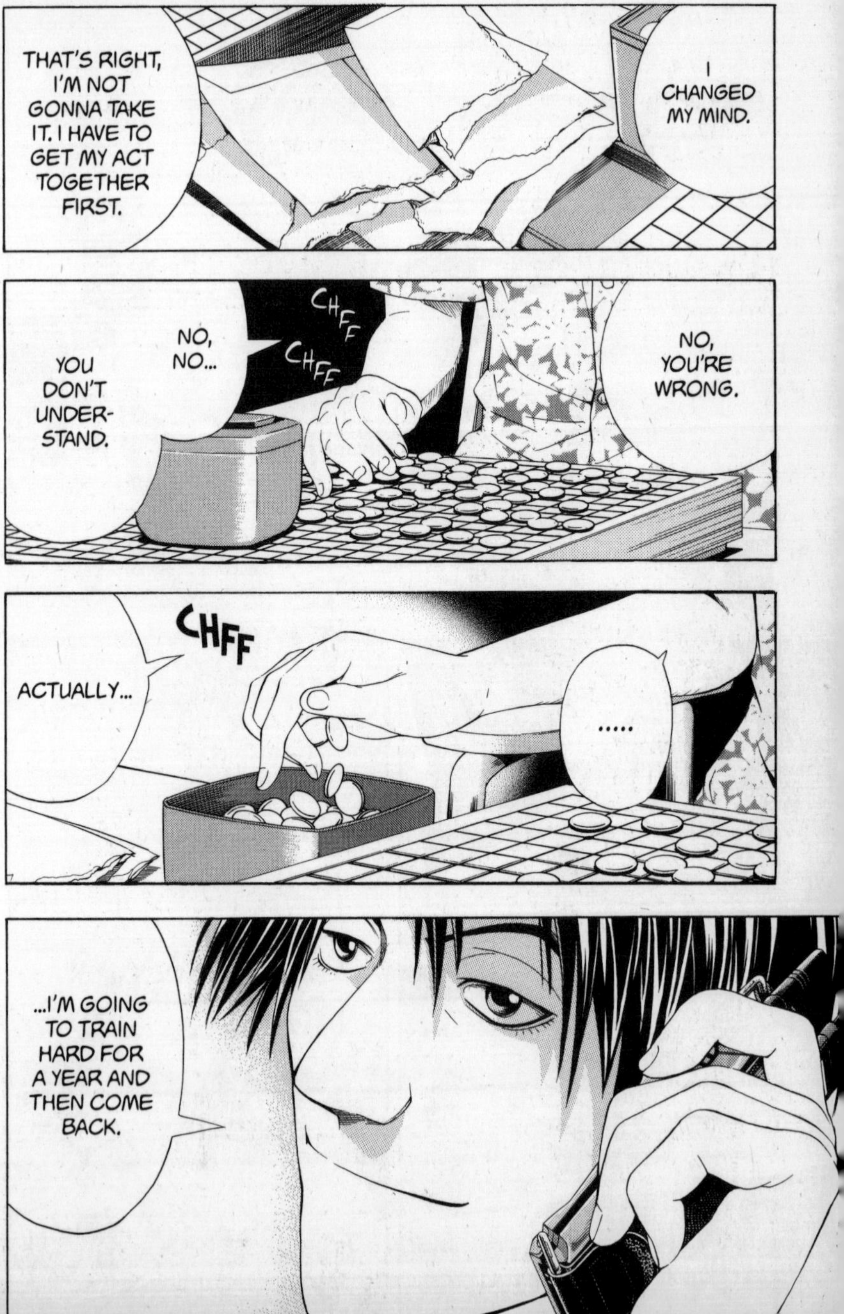
I CHANGED MY MIND.
THAT'S RIGHT, I'M NOT GONNA TAKE IT. I HAVE TO GET MY ACT TOGETHER FIRST.
NO, YOU'RE WRONG.
CHFF
CHFF
NO, NO...
YOU DON'T UNDER-STAND.
.....
CHFF
ACTUALLY...
...I'M GOING TO TRAIN HARD FOR A YEAR AND THEN COME BACK.

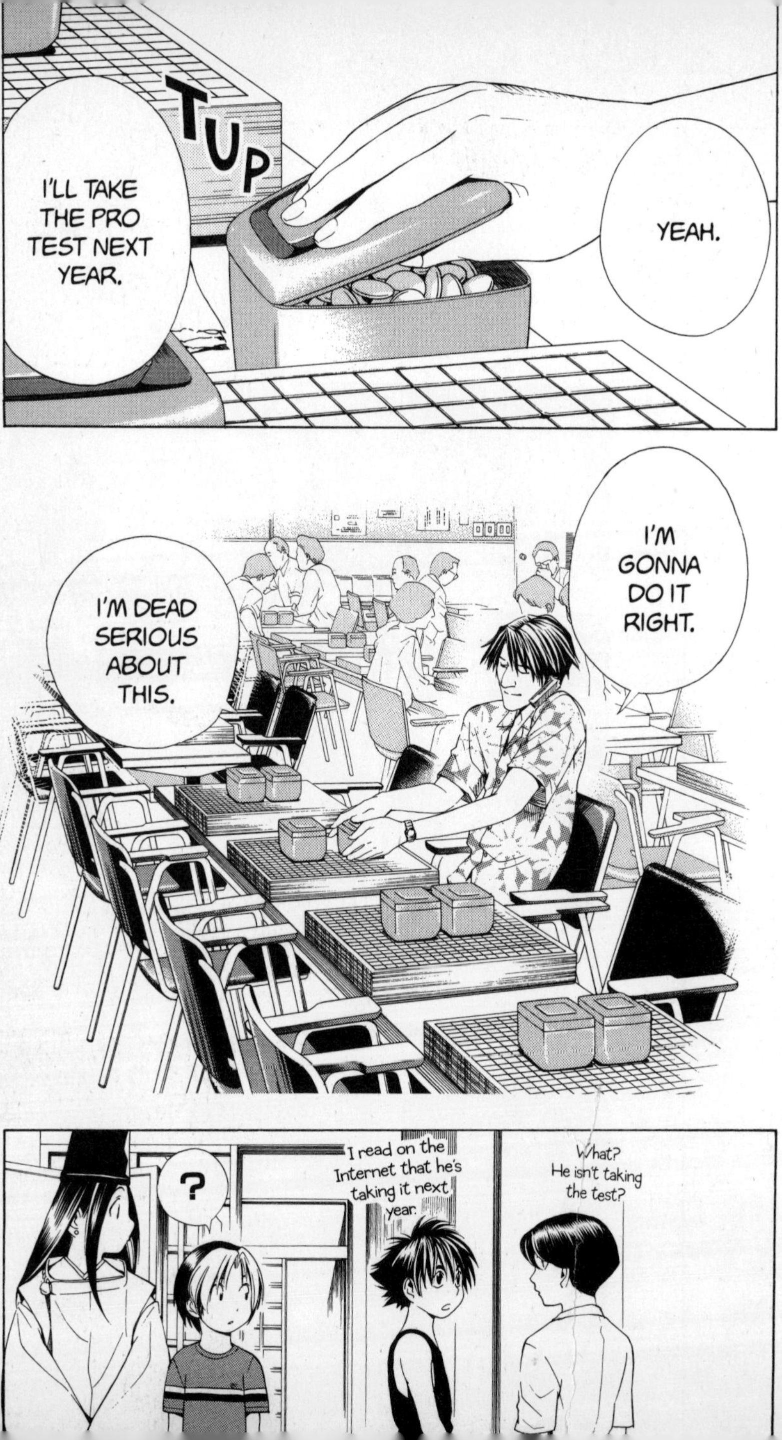
YEAH.
TUP
I'LL TAKE THE PRO TEST NEXT YEAR.
I'M GONNA DO IT RIGHT.
I'M DEAD SERIOUS ABOUT THIS.
What? He isn't taking the test?
I read on the Internet that he's taking it next year.
?

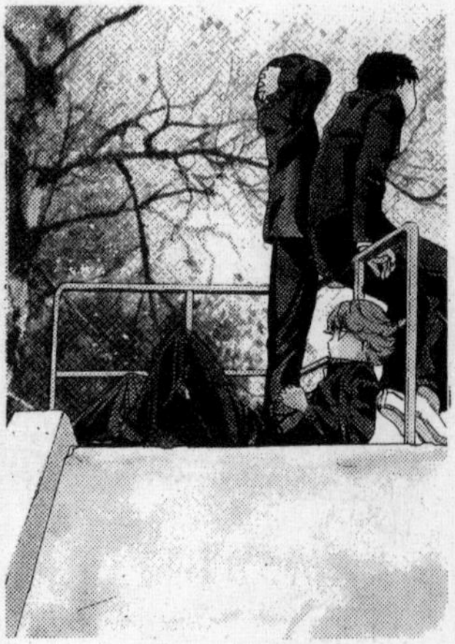
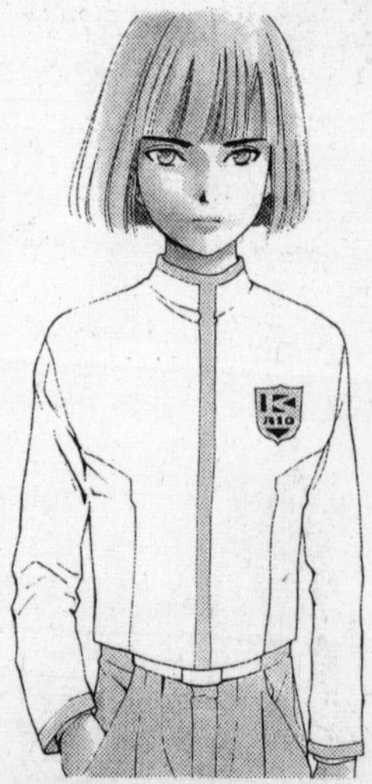
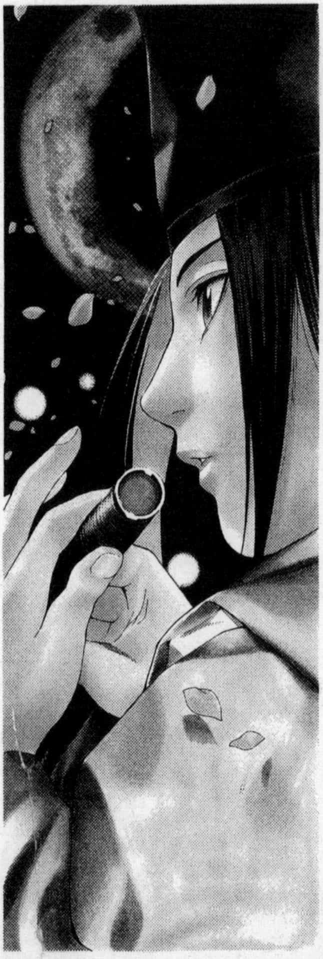

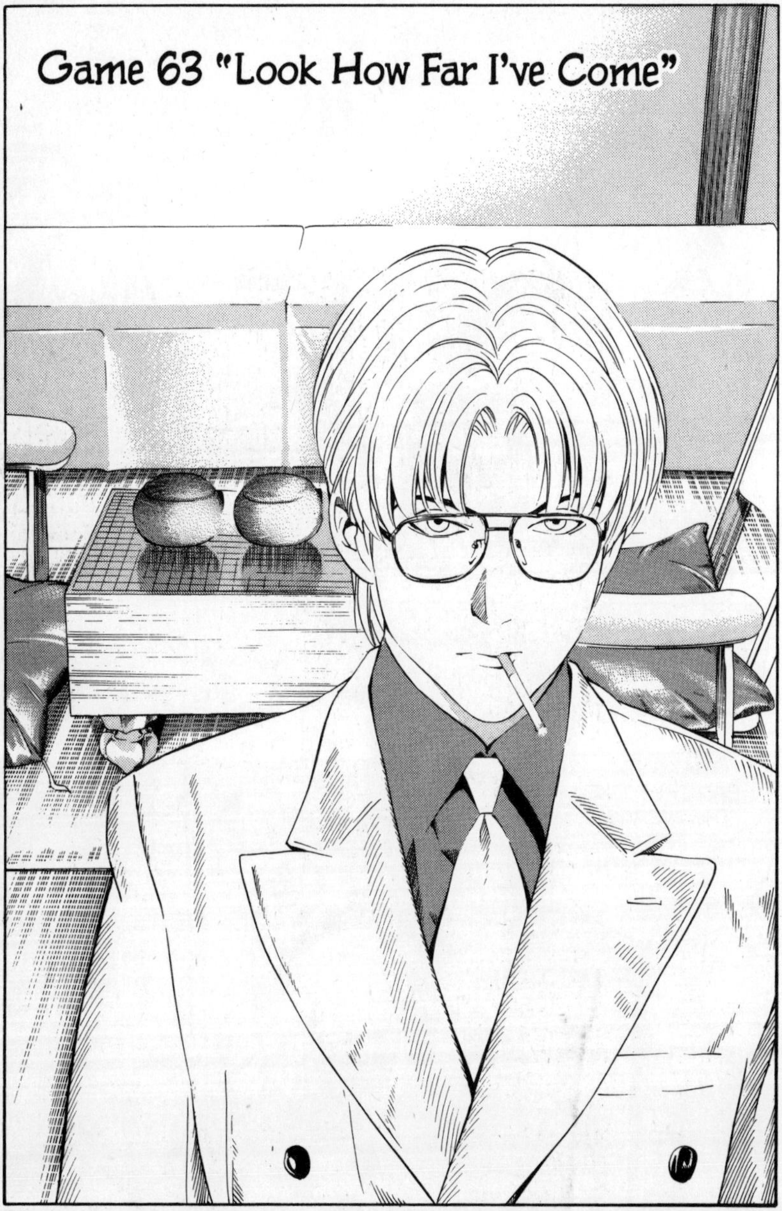
Game 63 "Look How Far I've Come"

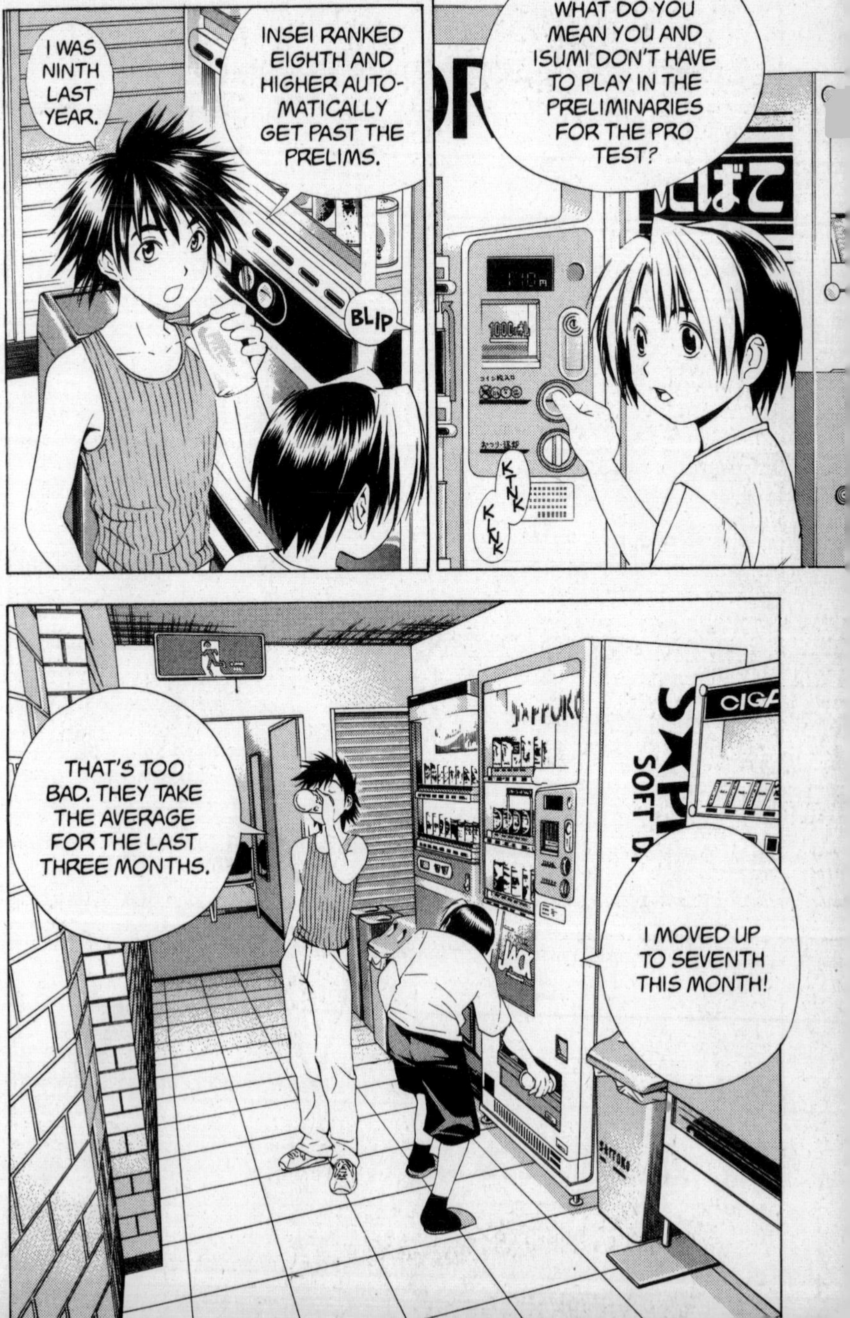
WHAT DO YOU MEAN YOU AND ISUMI DON'T HAVE TO PLAY IN THE PRELIMINARIES FOR THE PRO TEST?
KTNK
KLNK
INSEI RANKED EIGHTH AND HIGHER AUTO-MATICALLY GET PAST THE PRELIMS.
I WAS NINTH LAST YEAR.
BLIP
I MOVED UP TO SEVENTH THIS MONTH!
THAT'S TOO BAD. THEY TAKE THE AVERAGE FOR THE LAST THREE MONTHS.

READ THIS WAY

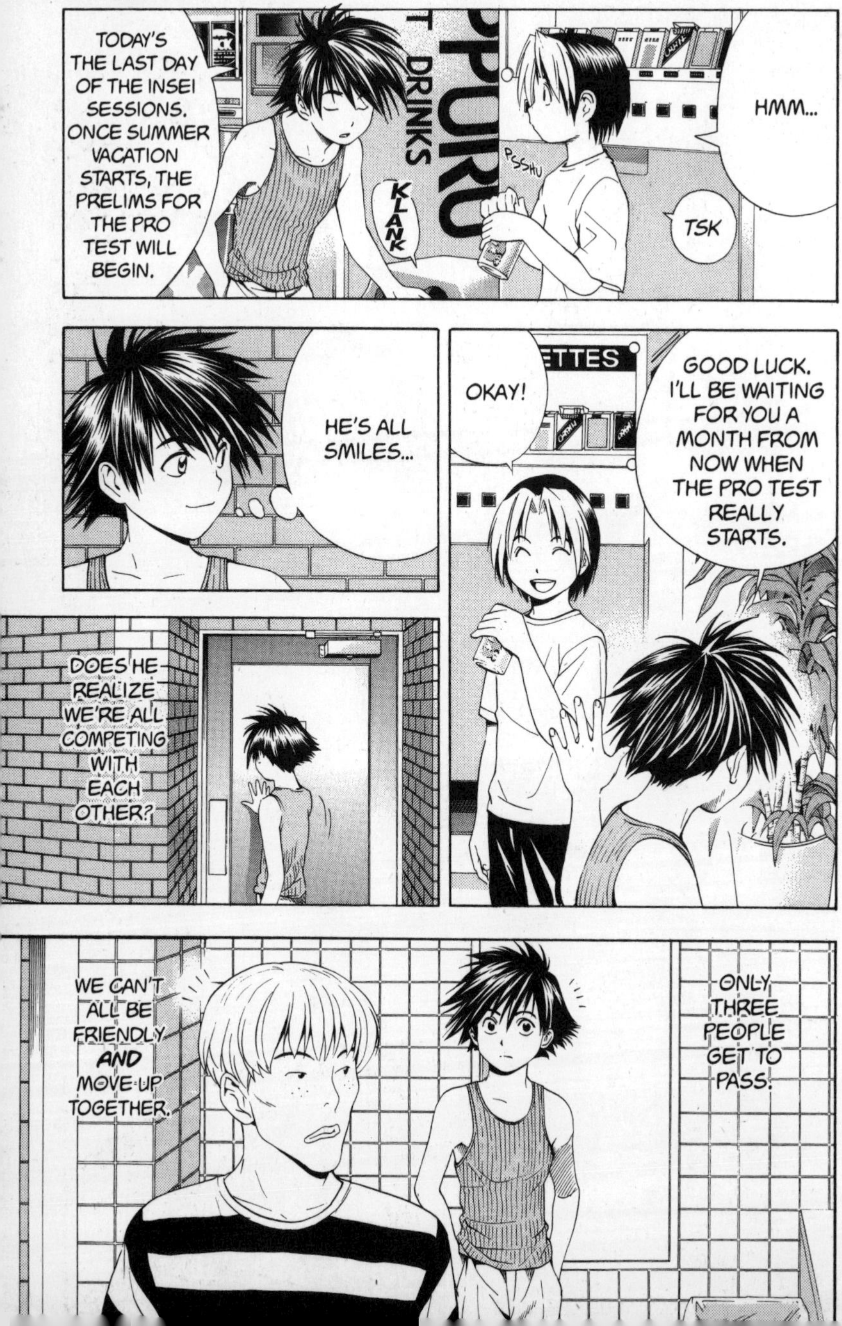
HMM...
PSSHU
TSK
DRINKS
TODAY'S THE LAST DAY OF THE INSEI SESSIONS. ONCE SUMMER VACATION STARTS, THE PRELIMS FOR THE PRO TEST WILL BEGIN.
KLANK
GOOD LUCK. I'LL BE WAITING FOR YOU A MONTH FROM NOW WHEN THE PRO TEST REALLY STARTS.
ETTES
OKAY!
HE'S ALL SMILES...
DOES HE REALIZE WE'RE ALL COMPETING WITH EACH OTHER?
ONLY THREE PEOPLE GET TO PASS.
WE CAN'T ALL BE FRIENDLY *AND* MOVE UP TOGETHER.

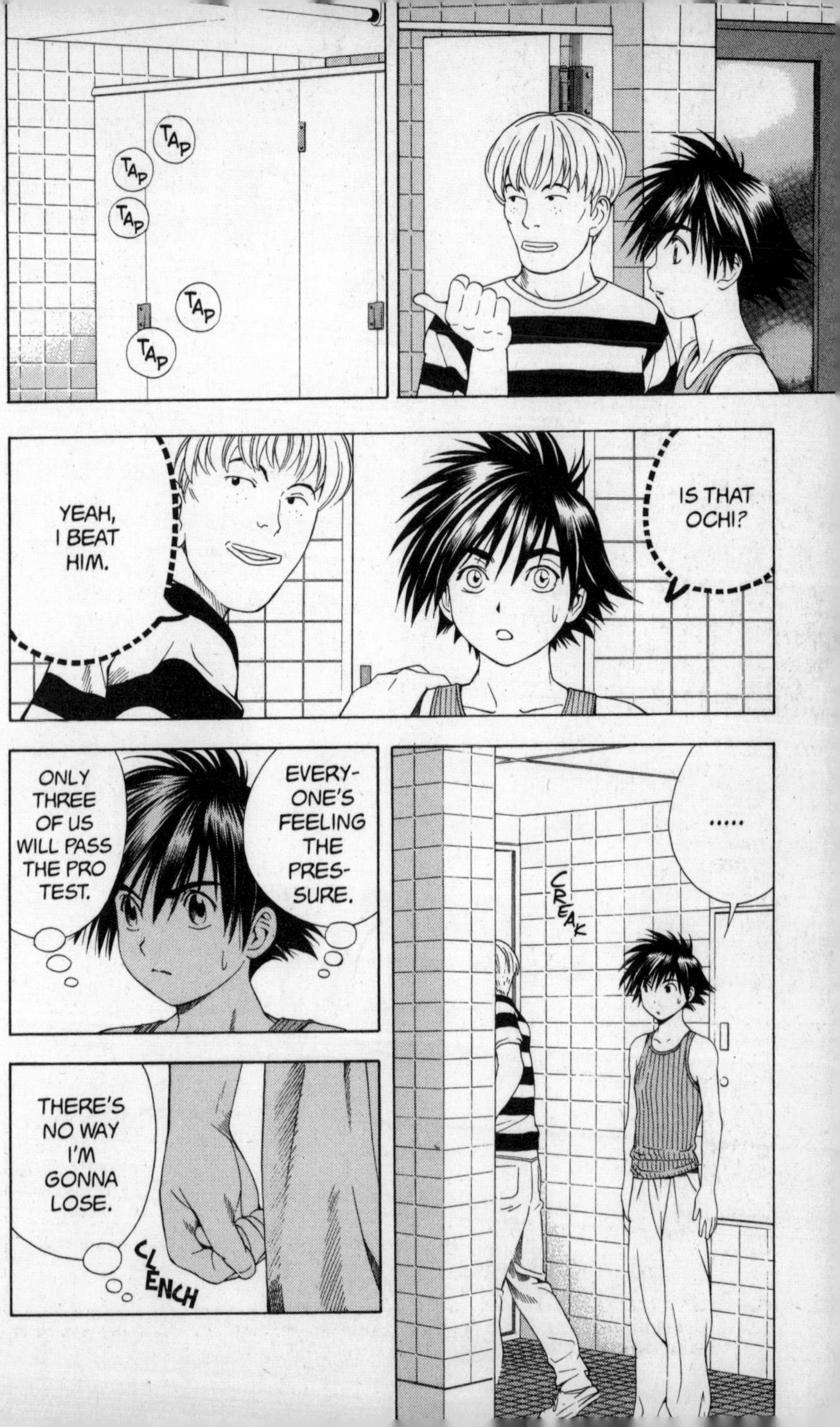
TAP
TAP
TAP
TAP
TAP
IS THAT OCHI?
YEAH, I BEAT HIM.
.....
CREAK
EVERY-ONE'S FEELING THE PRES-SURE.
ONLY THREE OF US WILL PASS THE PRO TEST.
THERE'S NO WAY I'M GONNA LOSE.
CLENCH

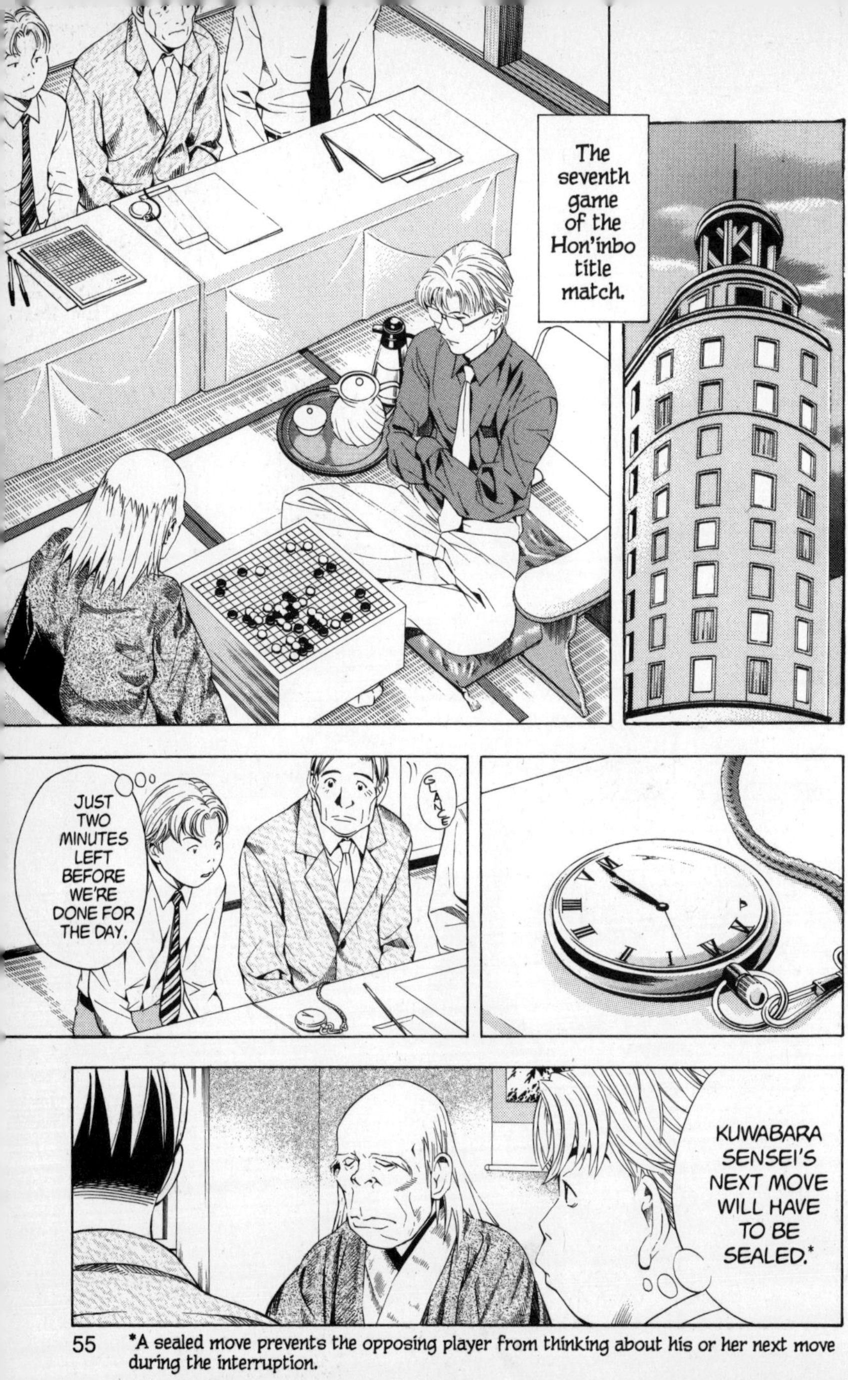
The seventh game of the Hon'inbo title match.
GLANCE
JUST TWO MINUTES LEFT BEFORE WE'RE DONE FOR THE DAY.
KUWABARA SENSEI'S NEXT MOVE WILL HAVE TO BE SEALED.*

*A sealed move prevents the opposing player from thinking about his or her next move during the interruption.

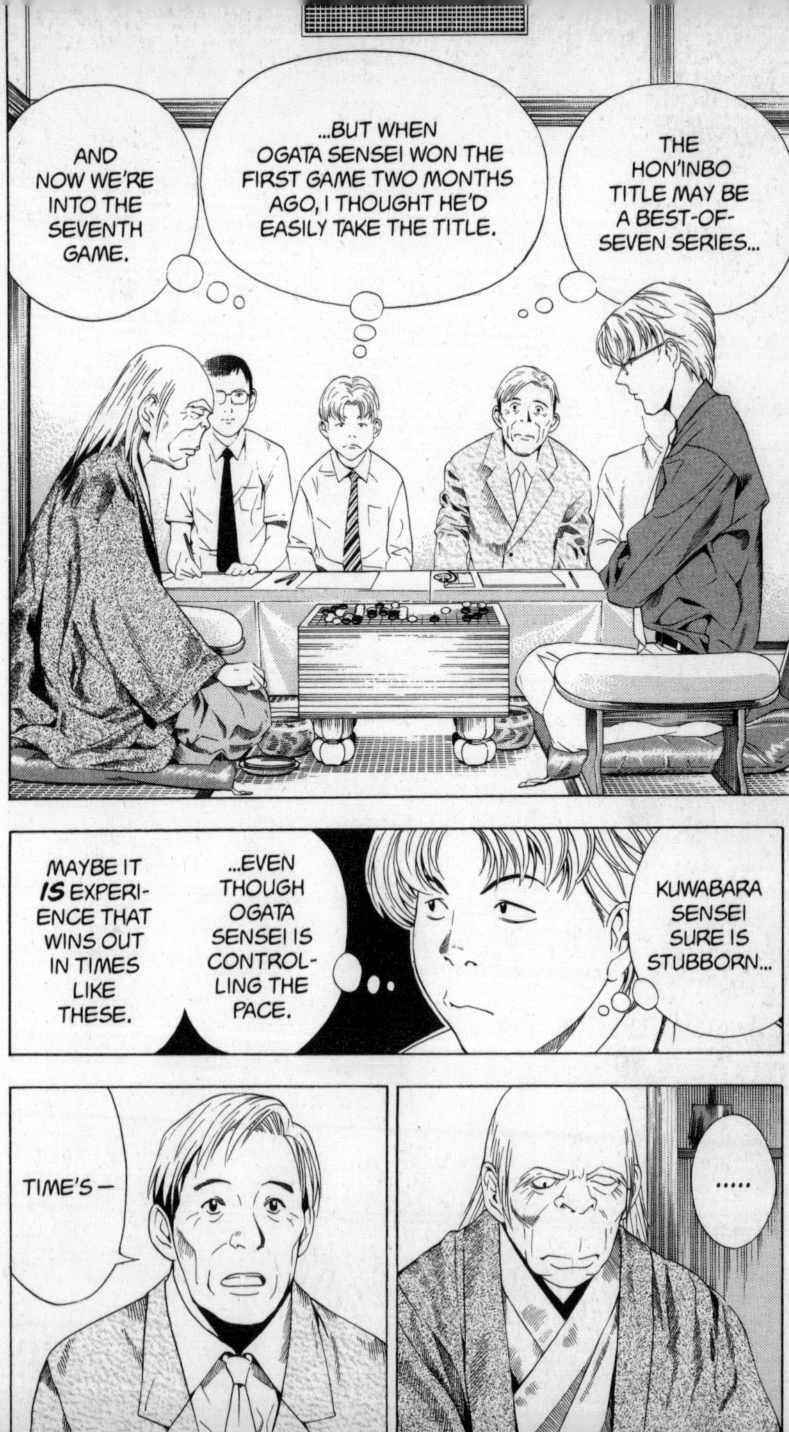
THE HON'INBO TITLE MAY BE A BEST-OF-SEVEN SERIES...
...BUT WHEN OGATA SENSEI WON THE FIRST GAME TWO MONTHS AGO, I THOUGHT HE'D EASILY TAKE THE TITLE.
AND NOW WE'RE INTO THE SEVENTH GAME.
KUWABARA SENSEI SURE IS STUBBORN...
...EVEN THOUGH OGATA SENSEI IS CONTROLLING THE PACE.
MAYBE IT *IS* EXPERIENCE THAT WINS OUT IN TIMES LIKE THESE.
.....
TIME'S—

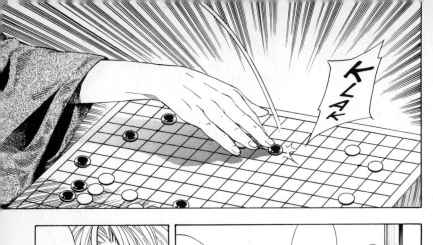

KLAK

. . . . .

. . . . .

AHEM

TIME'S UP FOR TODAY. THE NEXT MOVE WILL BE SEALED.

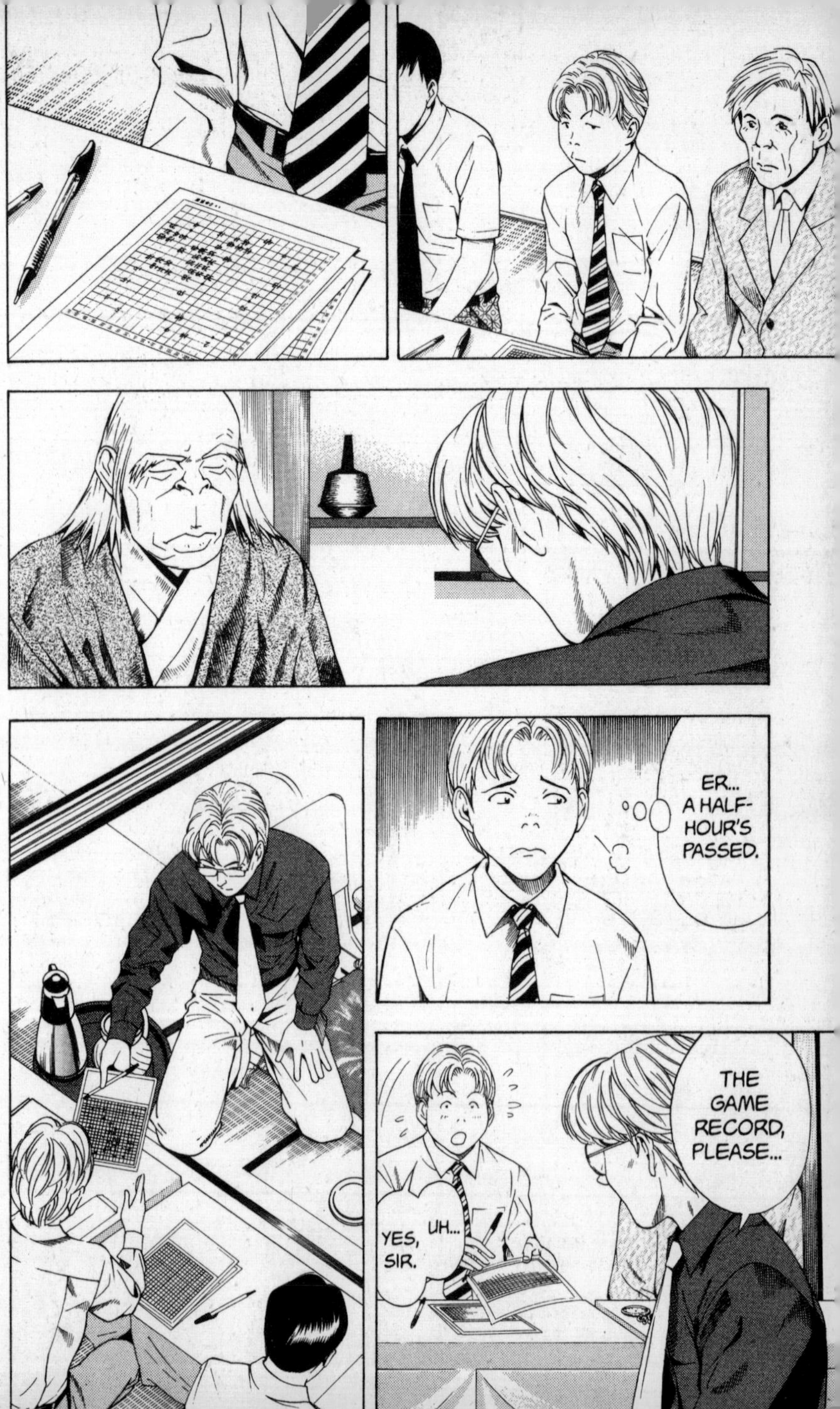
ER... A HALF-HOUR'S PASSED.
THE GAME RECORD, PLEASE...
UH...
YES, SIR.

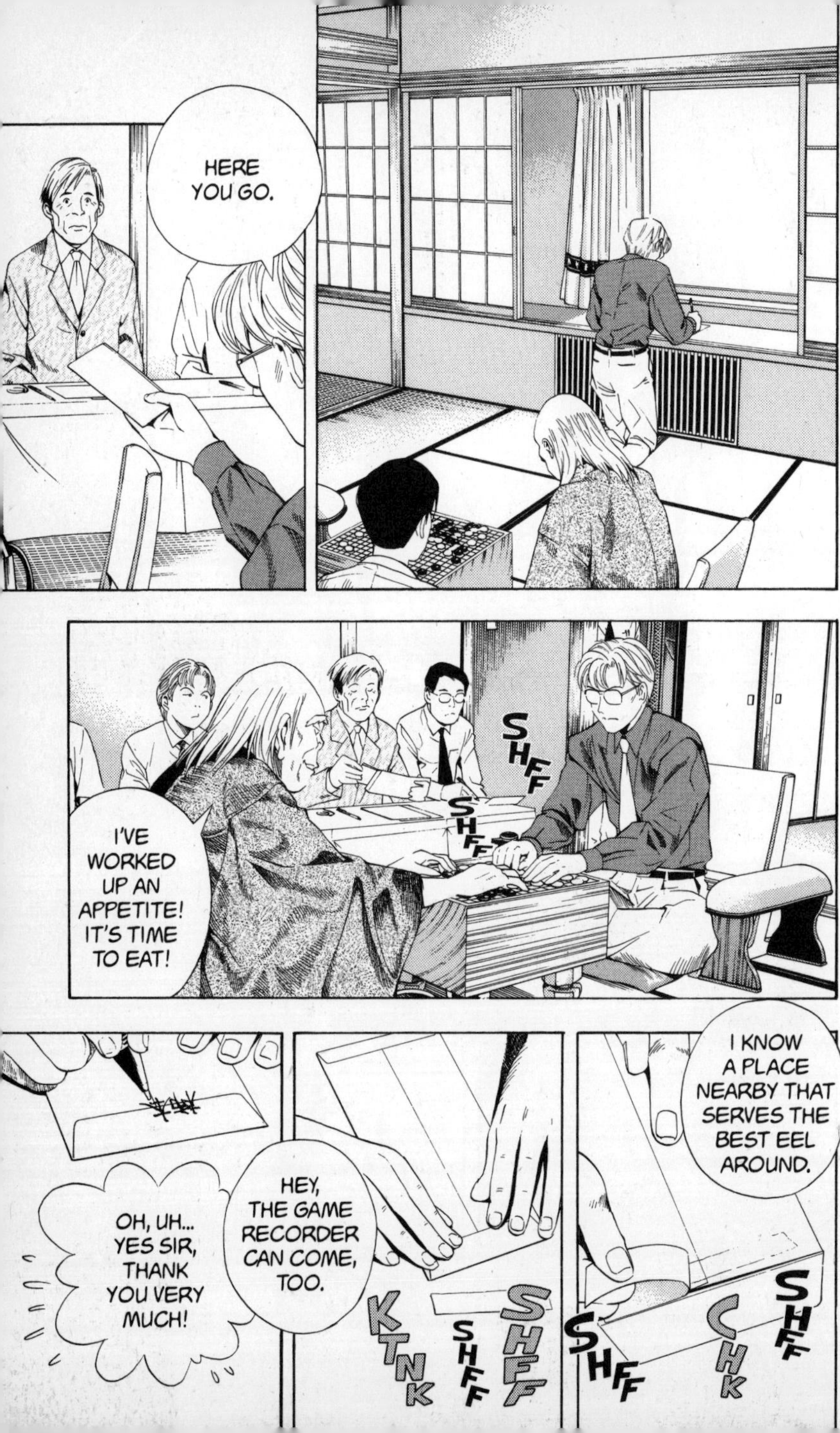
HERE YOU GO.
SHFF
SHFF
I'VE WORKED UP AN APPETITE! IT'S TIME TO EAT!
I KNOW A PLACE NEARBY THAT SERVES THE BEST EEL AROUND.
SHFF
CHK
SHFF
HEY, THE GAME RECORDER CAN COME, TOO.
SHFF
SHFF
KTNK
OH, UH... YES SIR, THANK YOU VERY MUCH!

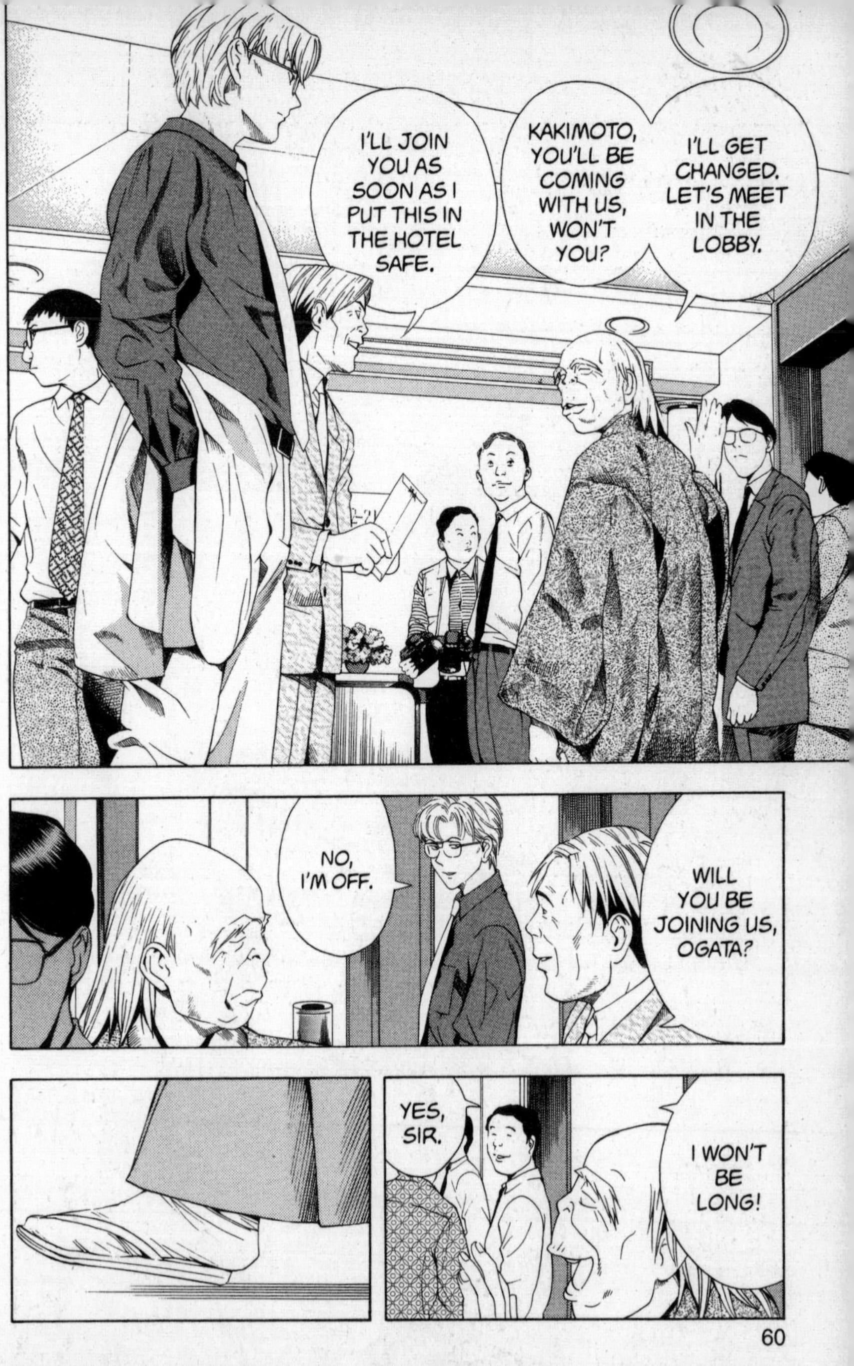
I'LL GET CHANGED. LET'S MEET IN THE LOBBY.
KAKIMOTO, YOU'LL BE COMING WITH US, WON'T YOU?
I'LL JOIN YOU AS SOON AS I PUT THIS IN THE HOTEL SAFE.
WILL YOU BE JOINING US, OGATA?
NO, I'M OFF.
I WON'T BE LONG!
YES, SIR.

READ THIS WAY

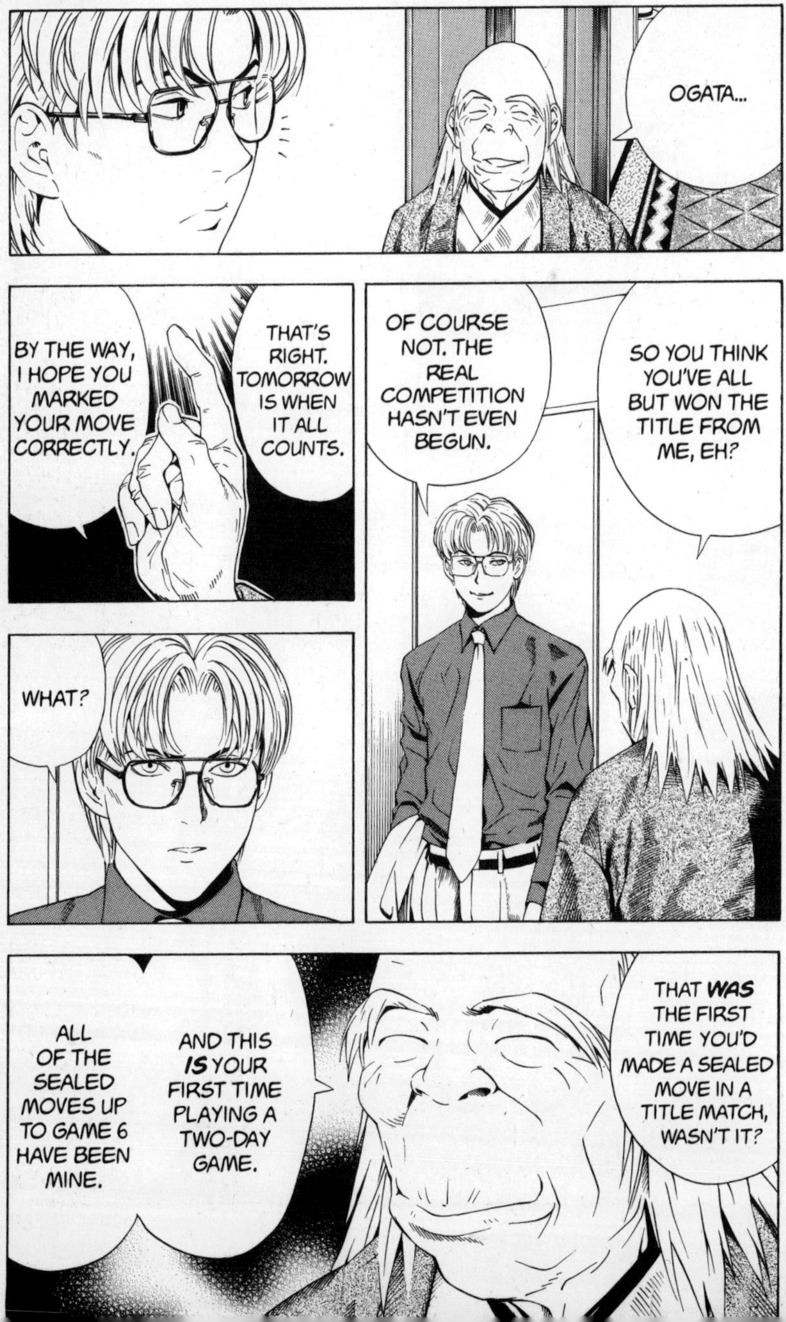
OGATA...
SO YOU THINK YOU'VE ALL BUT WON THE TITLE FROM ME, EH?
OF COURSE NOT. THE REAL COMPETITION HASN'T EVEN BEGUN.
THAT'S RIGHT. TOMORROW IS WHEN IT ALL COUNTS.
BY THE WAY, I HOPE YOU MARKED YOUR MOVE CORRECTLY.
WHAT?
THAT **WAS** THE FIRST TIME YOU'D MADE A SEALED MOVE IN A TITLE MATCH, WASN'T IT?
AND THIS **IS** YOUR FIRST TIME PLAYING A TWO-DAY GAME.
ALL OF THE SEALED MOVES UP TO GAME 6 HAVE BEEN MINE.

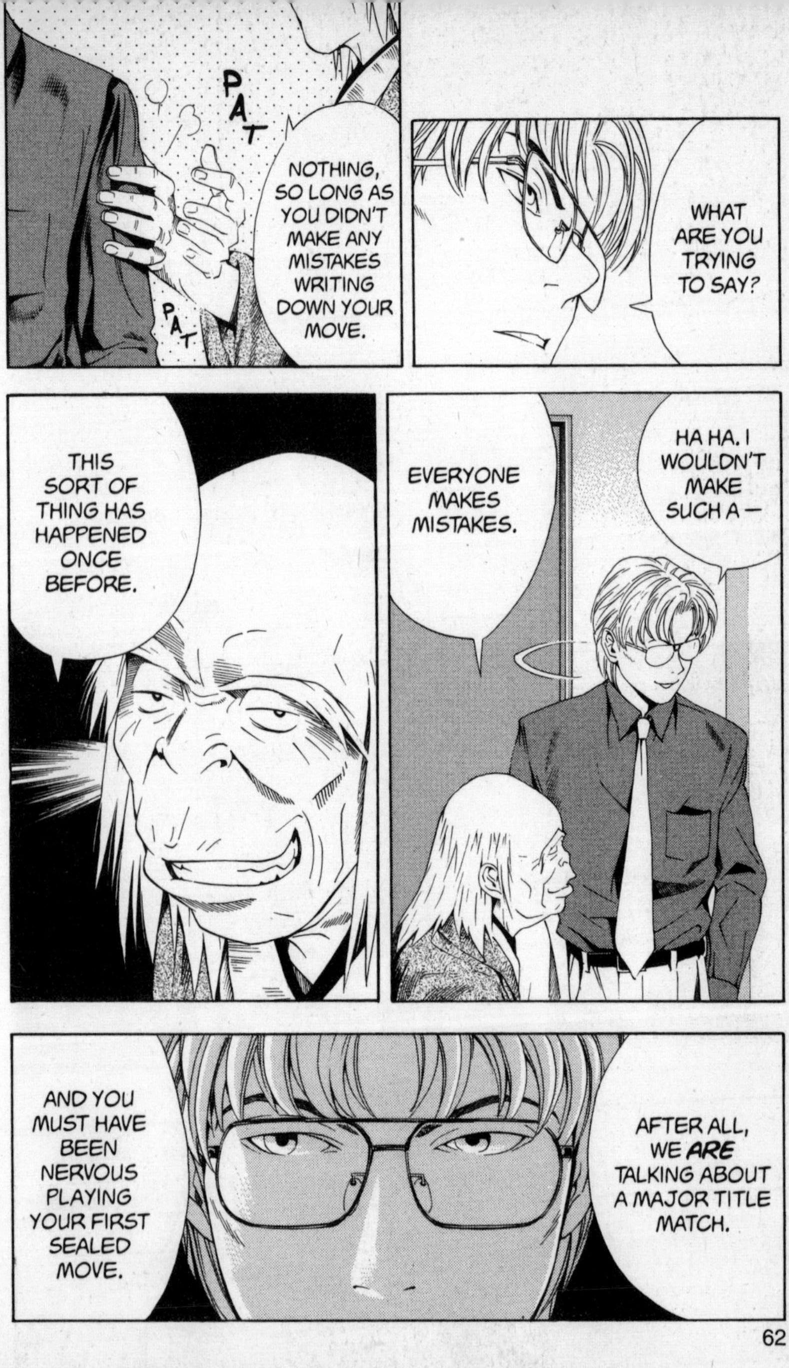
WHAT ARE YOU TRYING TO SAY?
PAT
NOTHING, SO LONG AS YOU DIDN'T MAKE ANY MISTAKES WRITING DOWN YOUR MOVE.
PAT
HA HA. I WOULDN'T MAKE SUCH A—
EVERYONE MAKES MISTAKES.
THIS SORT OF THING HAS HAPPENED ONCE BEFORE.
AFTER ALL, WE *ARE* TALKING ABOUT A MAJOR TITLE MATCH.
AND YOU MUST HAVE BEEN NERVOUS PLAYING YOUR FIRST SEALED MOVE.

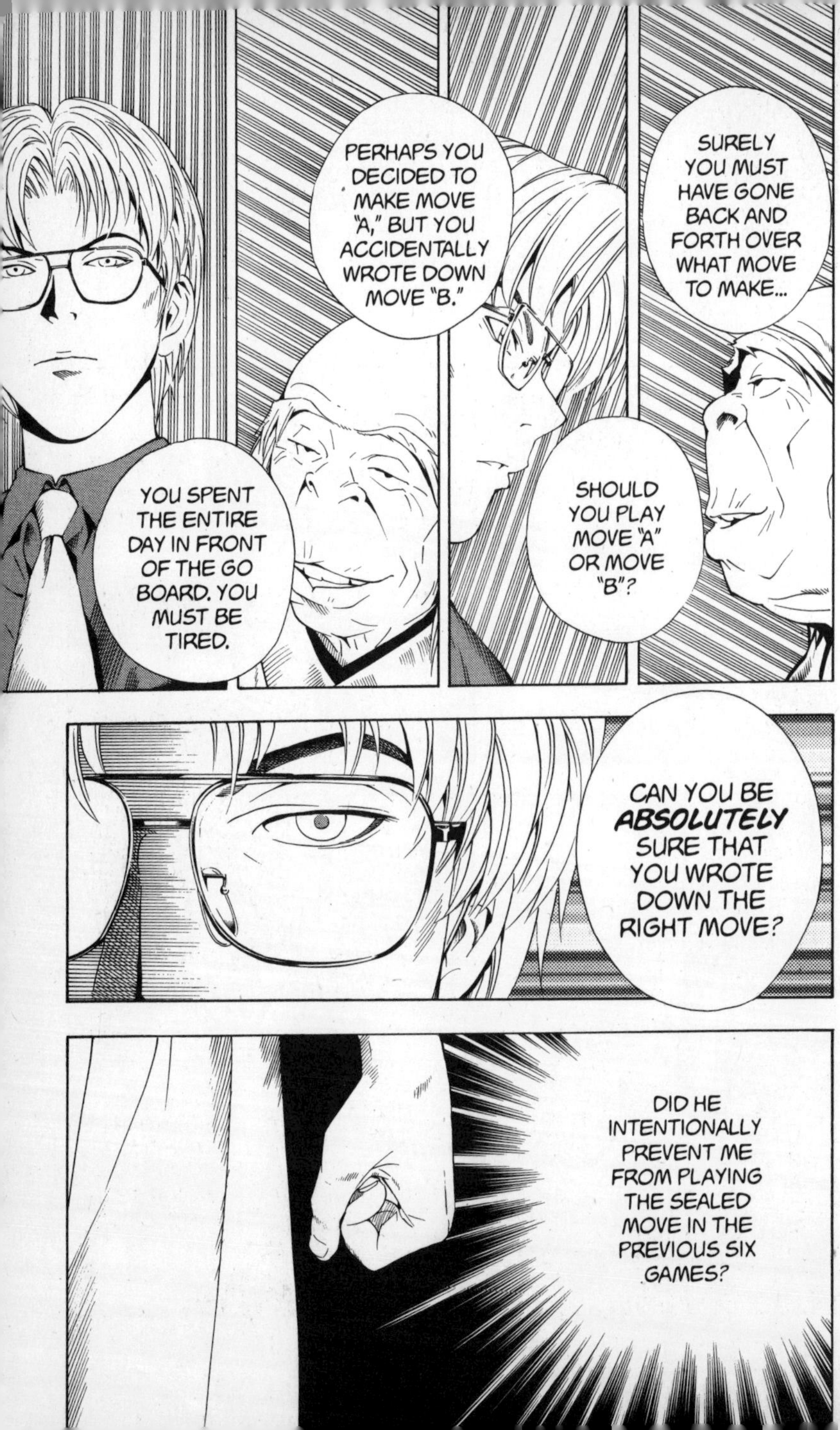
SURELY YOU MUST HAVE GONE BACK AND FORTH OVER WHAT MOVE TO MAKE...
SHOULD YOU PLAY MOVE "A" OR MOVE "B"?
PERHAPS YOU DECIDED TO MAKE MOVE "A," BUT YOU ACCIDENTALLY WROTE DOWN MOVE "B."
YOU SPENT THE ENTIRE DAY IN FRONT OF THE GO BOARD. YOU MUST BE TIRED.
CAN YOU BE ***ABSOLUTELY*** SURE THAT YOU WROTE DOWN THE RIGHT MOVE?
DID HE INTENTIONALLY PREVENT ME FROM PLAYING THE SEALED MOVE IN THE PREVIOUS SIX GAMES?

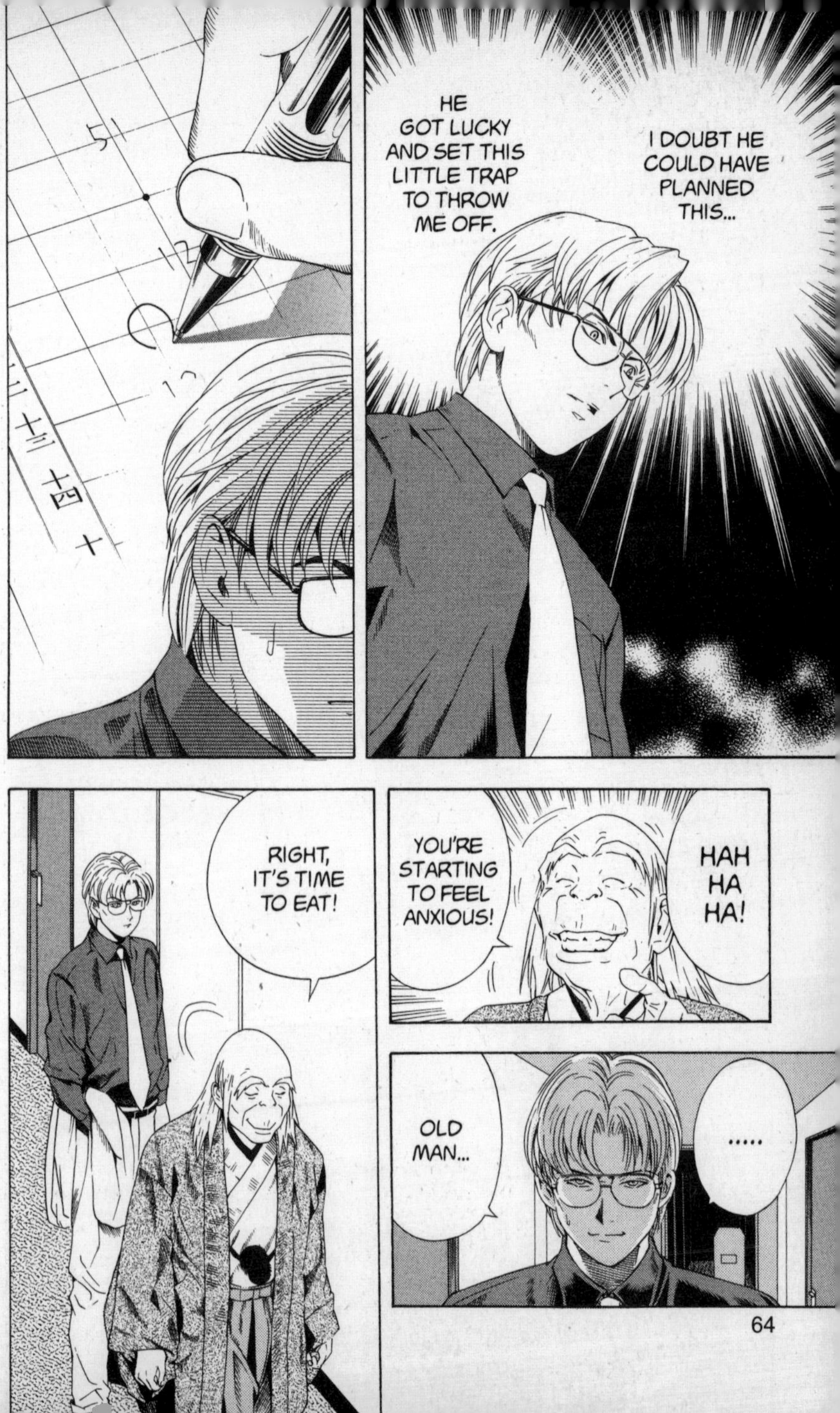
I DOUBT HE COULD HAVE PLANNED THIS...
HE GOT LUCKY AND SET THIS LITTLE TRAP TO THROW ME OFF.
HAH HA HA!
YOU'RE STARTING TO FEEL ANXIOUS!
.....
OLD MAN...
RIGHT, IT'S TIME TO EAT!

READ THIS WAY

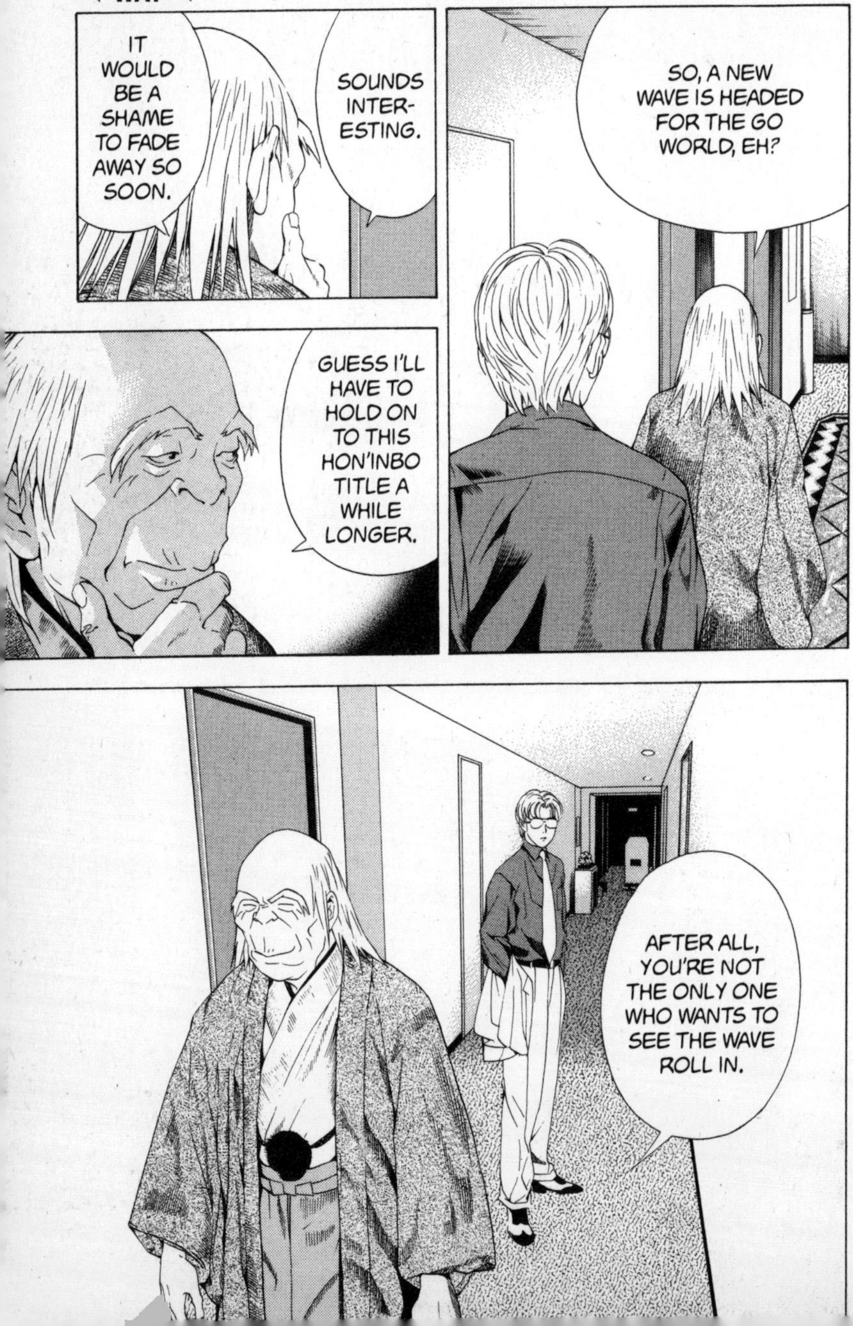
SO, A NEW WAVE IS HEADED FOR THE GO WORLD, EH?
SOUNDS INTER-ESTING.
IT WOULD BE A SHAME TO FADE AWAY SO SOON.
GUESS I'LL HAVE TO HOLD ON TO THIS HON'INBO TITLE A WHILE LONGER.
AFTER ALL, YOU'RE NOT THE ONLY ONE WHO WANTS TO SEE THE WAVE ROLL IN.

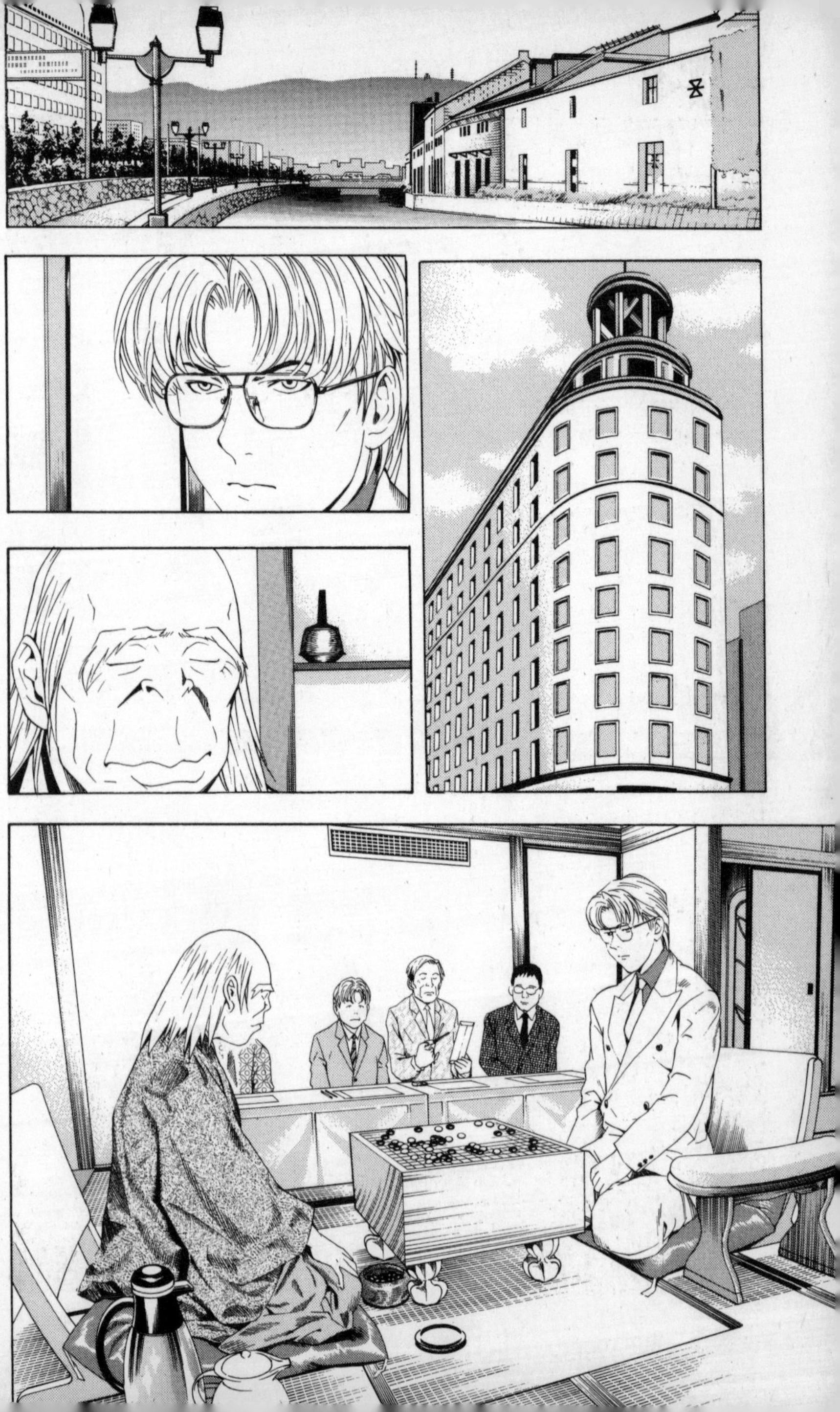

READ THIS WAY

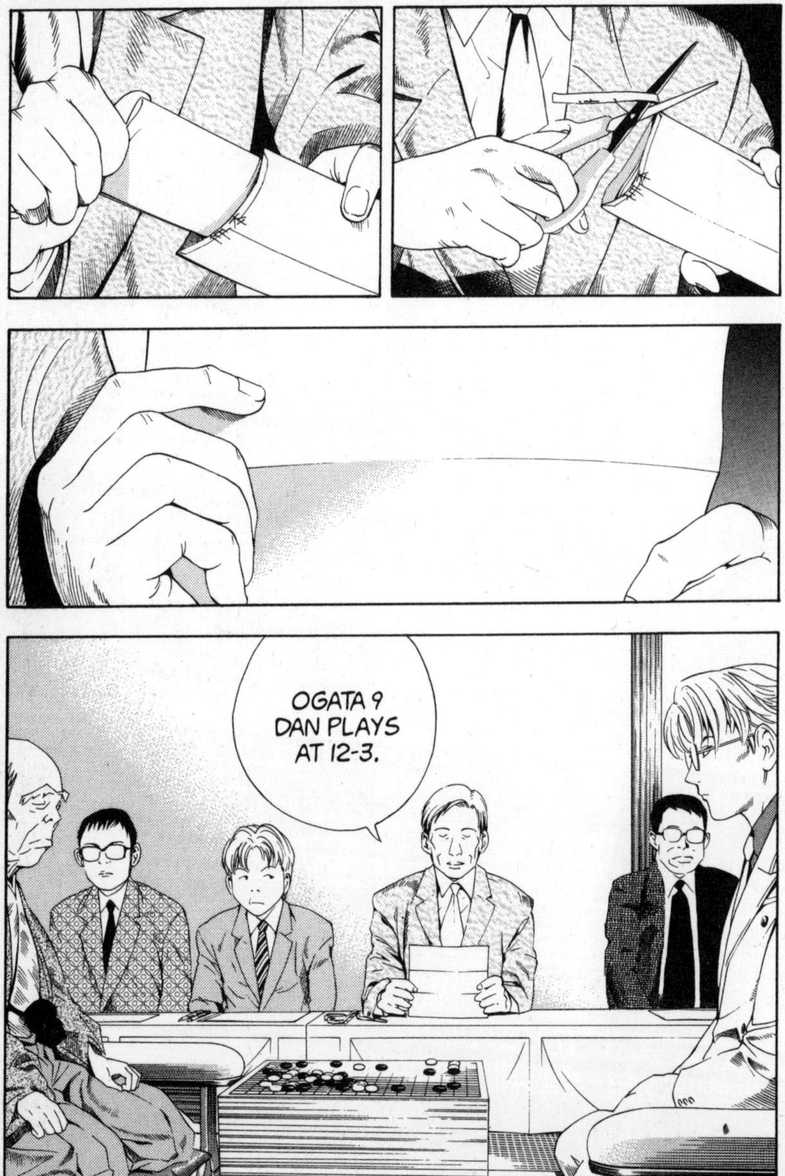
OGATA 9 DAN PLAYS AT 12-3.

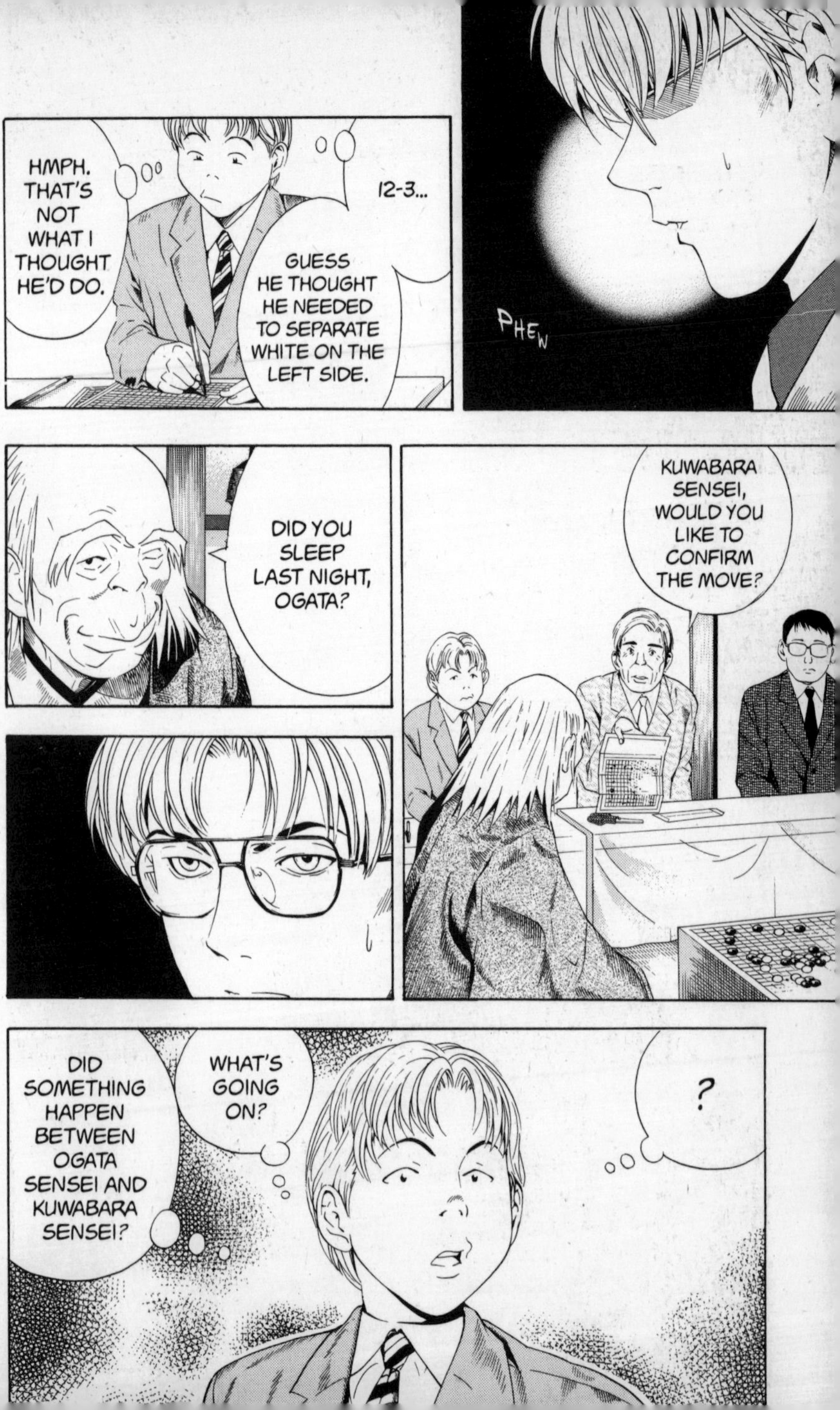
PHEW
12-3...
GUESS HE THOUGHT HE NEEDED TO SEPARATE WHITE ON THE LEFT SIDE.
HMPH. THAT'S NOT WHAT I THOUGHT HE'D DO.
KUWABARA SENSEI, WOULD YOU LIKE TO CONFIRM THE MOVE?
DID YOU SLEEP LAST NIGHT, OGATA?
?
WHAT'S GOING ON?
DID SOMETHING HAPPEN BETWEEN OGATA SENSEI AND KUWABARA SENSEI?

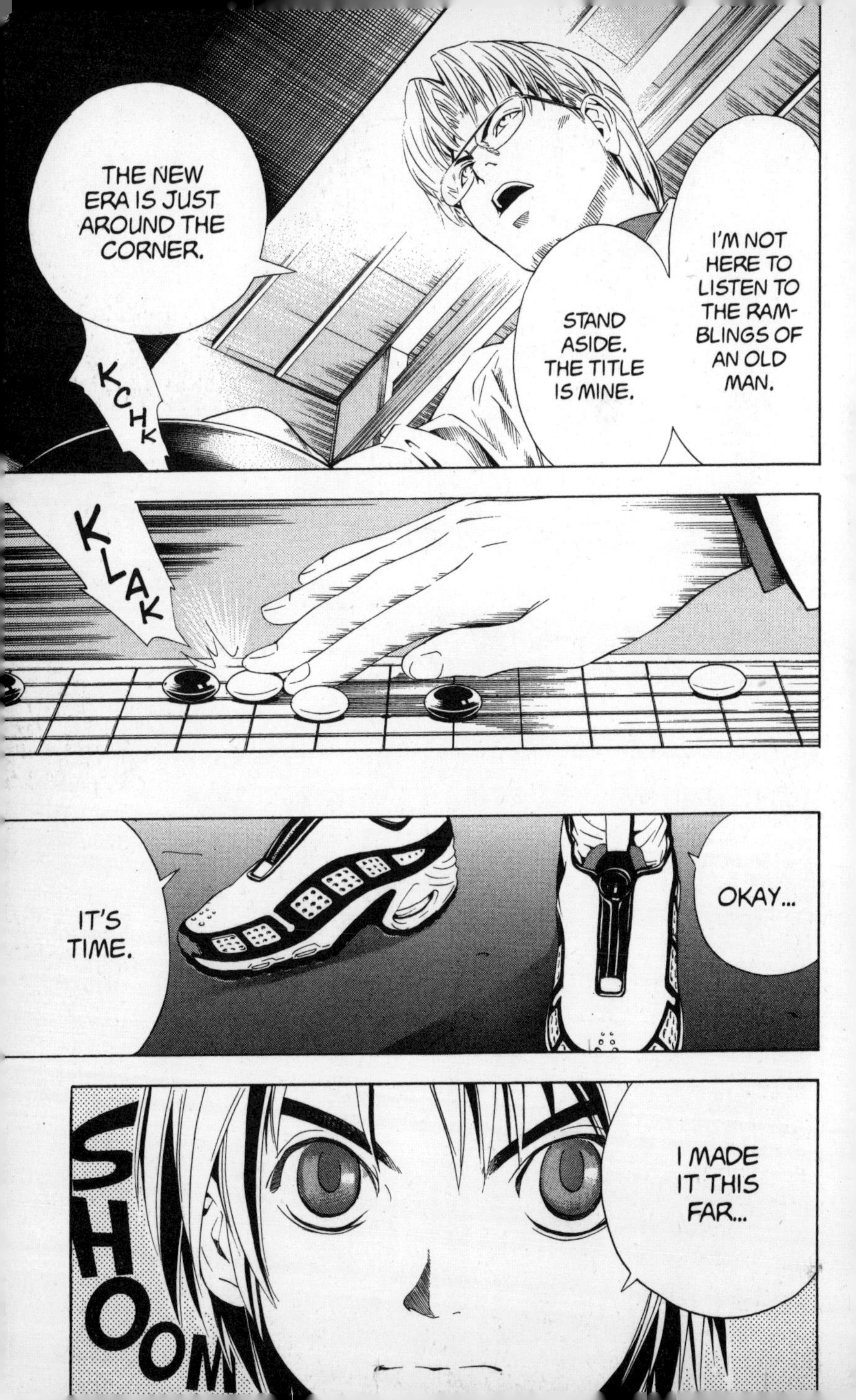
I'M NOT HERE TO LISTEN TO THE RAM-BLINGS OF AN OLD MAN.
STAND ASIDE. THE TITLE IS MINE.
THE NEW ERA IS JUST AROUND THE CORNER.
KCHK
KLAK
OKAY...
IT'S TIME.
I MADE IT THIS FAR...
SHOOM

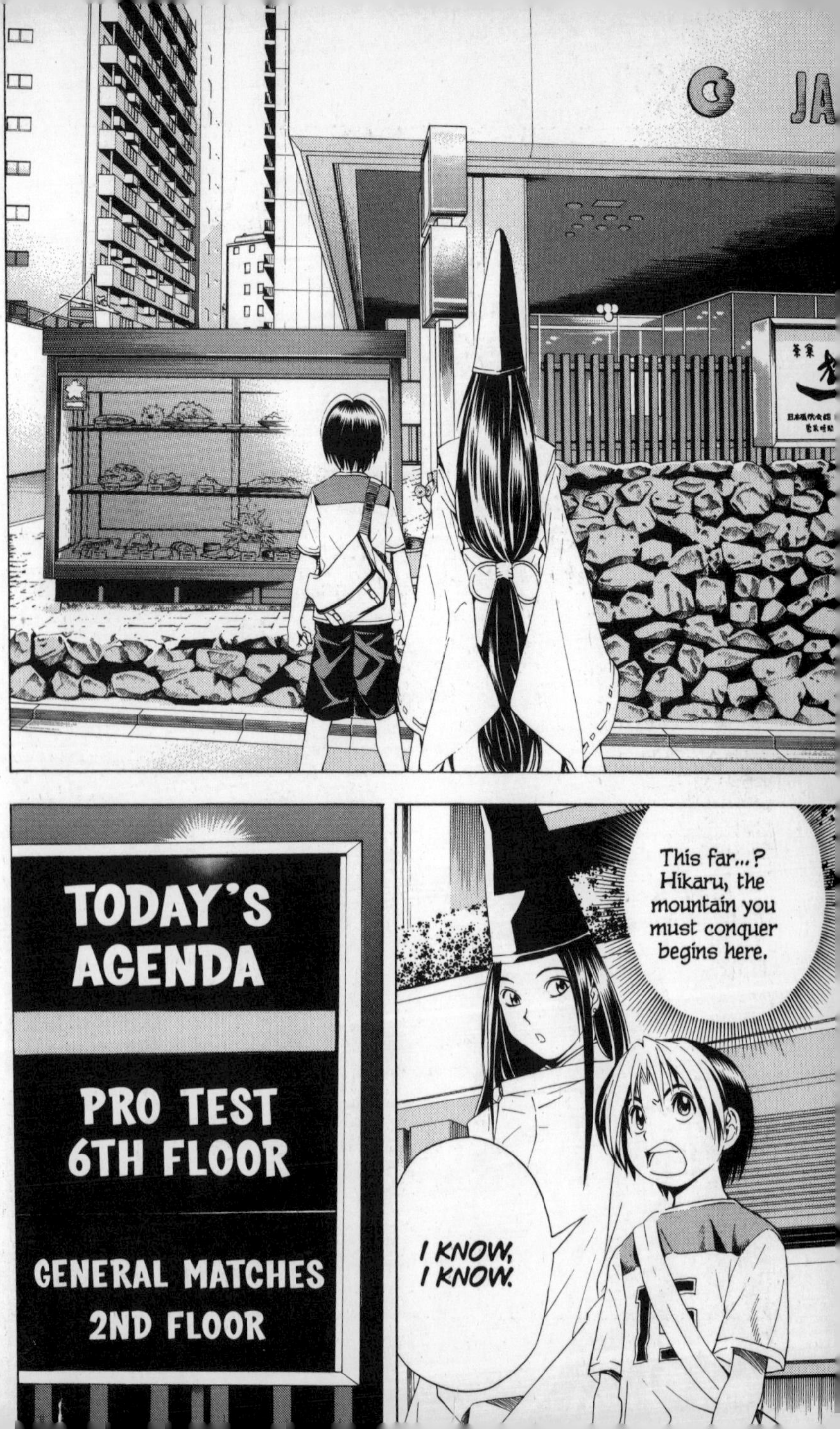
This far...? Hikaru, the mountain you must conquer begins here.
I KNOW, I KNOW.
TODAY'S AGENDA
PRO TEST 6TH FLOOR
GENERAL MATCHES 2ND FLOOR

READ THIS WAY

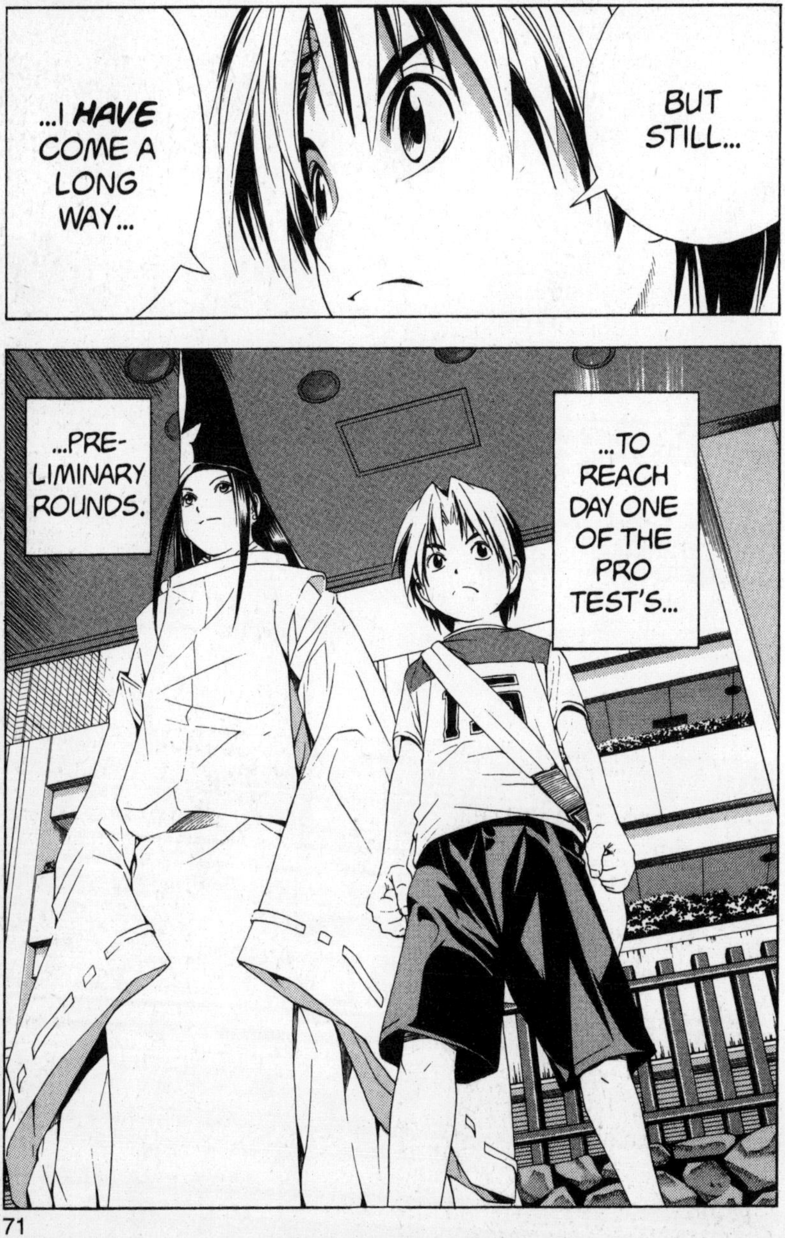
BUT STILL...
...I **HAVE** COME A LONG WAY...
...TO REACH DAY ONE OF THE PRO TEST'S...
...PRE-LIMINARY ROUNDS.

THE 1ST ALL-TIME GREATEST CHARACTER CONTEST SURVEY RESULTS!

(11TH-53RD ON P. 92)

This poll was conducted in Japan.

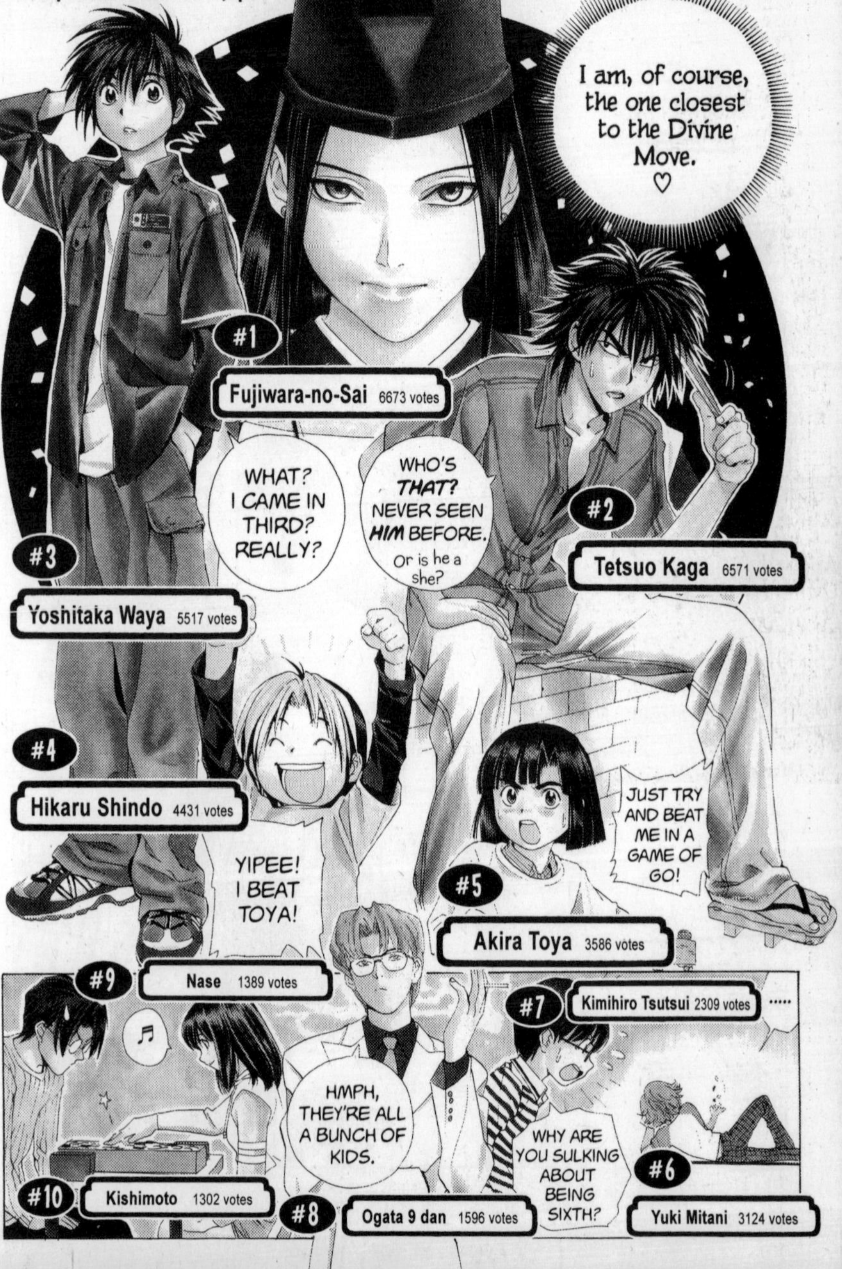
I am, of course, the one closest to the Divine Move. ♡
#1
Fujiwara-no-Sai 6673 votes
#2
Tetsuo Kaga 6571 votes
WHO'S *THAT?* NEVER SEEN *HIM* BEFORE.
Or is he a she?
WHAT? I CAME IN THIRD? REALLY?
#3
Yoshitaka Waya 5517 votes
#4
Hikaru Shindo 4431 votes
JUST TRY AND BEAT ME IN A GAME OF GO!
#5
Akira Toya 3586 votes
YIPEE! I BEAT TOYA!
#6
Yuki Mitani 3124 votes
WHY ARE YOU SULKING ABOUT BEING SIXTH?
#7
Kimihiro Tsutsui 2309 votes .....
#8
Ogata 9 dan 1596 votes
HMPH, THEY'RE ALL A BUNCH OF KIDS.
#9
Nase 1389 votes
♪
#10
Kishimoto 1302 votes

Game 64: "Pro Test Prelims, Day One: The Man with the Beard"

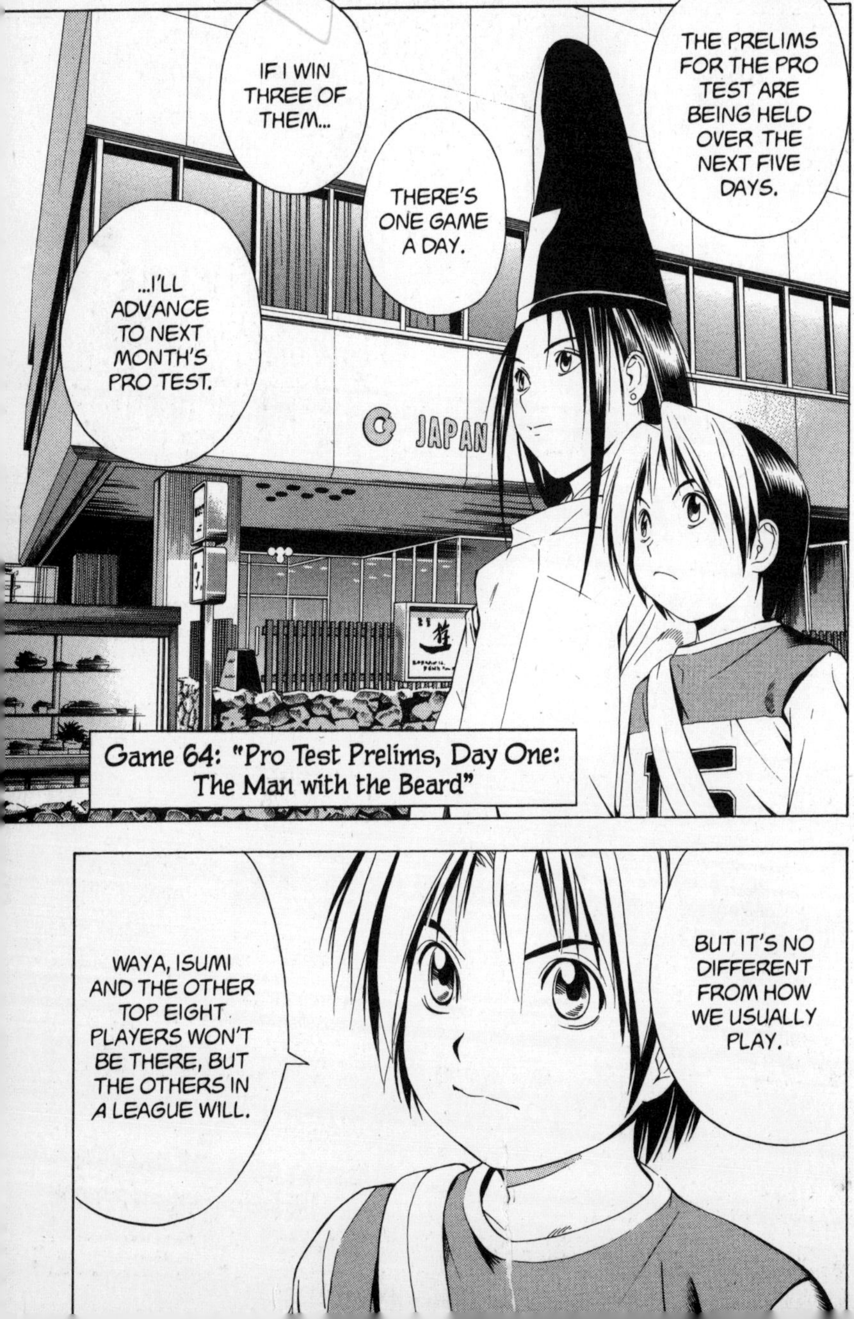
THE PRELIMS FOR THE PRO TEST ARE BEING HELD OVER THE NEXT FIVE DAYS.
THERE'S ONE GAME A DAY.
IF I WIN THREE OF THEM...
...I'LL ADVANCE TO NEXT MONTH'S PRO TEST.
JAPAN
BUT IT'S NO DIFFERENT FROM HOW WE USUALLY PLAY.
WAYA, ISUMI AND THE OTHER TOP EIGHT PLAYERS WON'T BE THERE, BUT THE OTHERS IN A LEAGUE WILL.

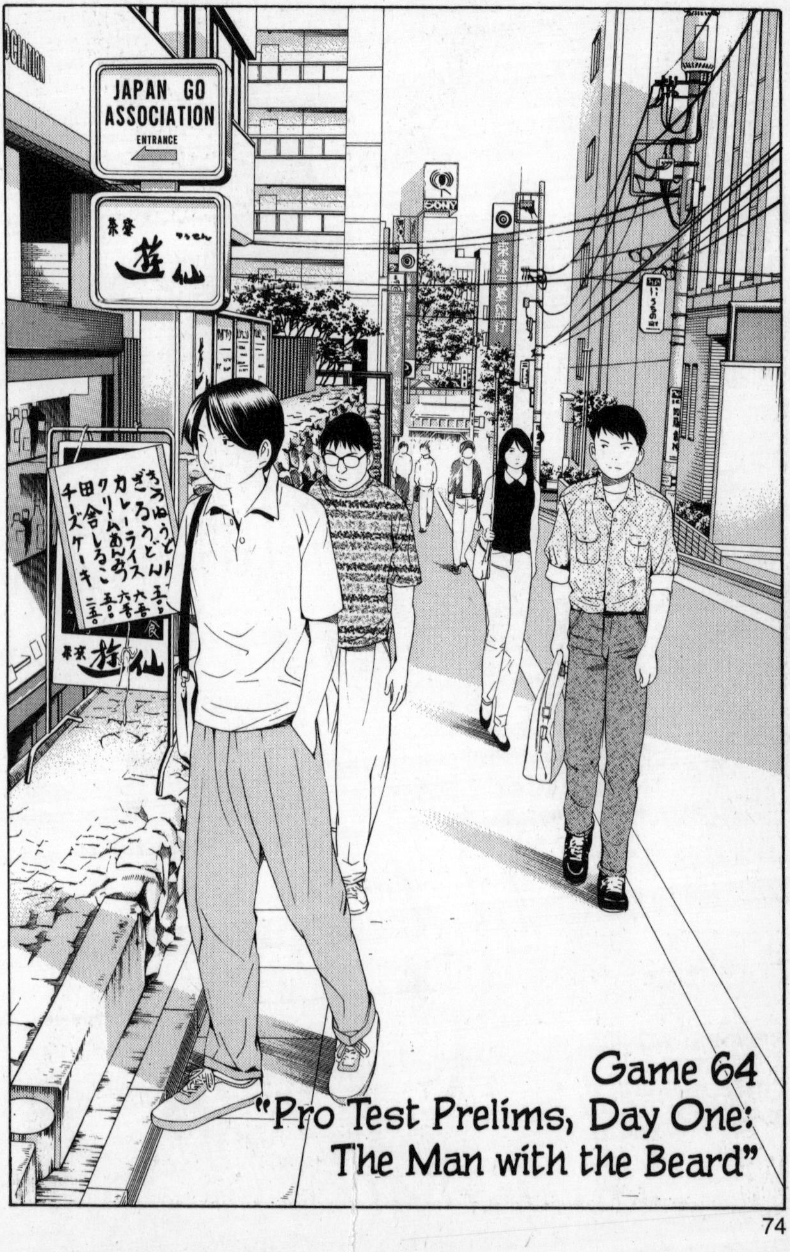
JAPAN GO ASSOCIATION
ENTRANCE
Game 64
"Pro Test Prelims, Day One: The Man with the Beard"

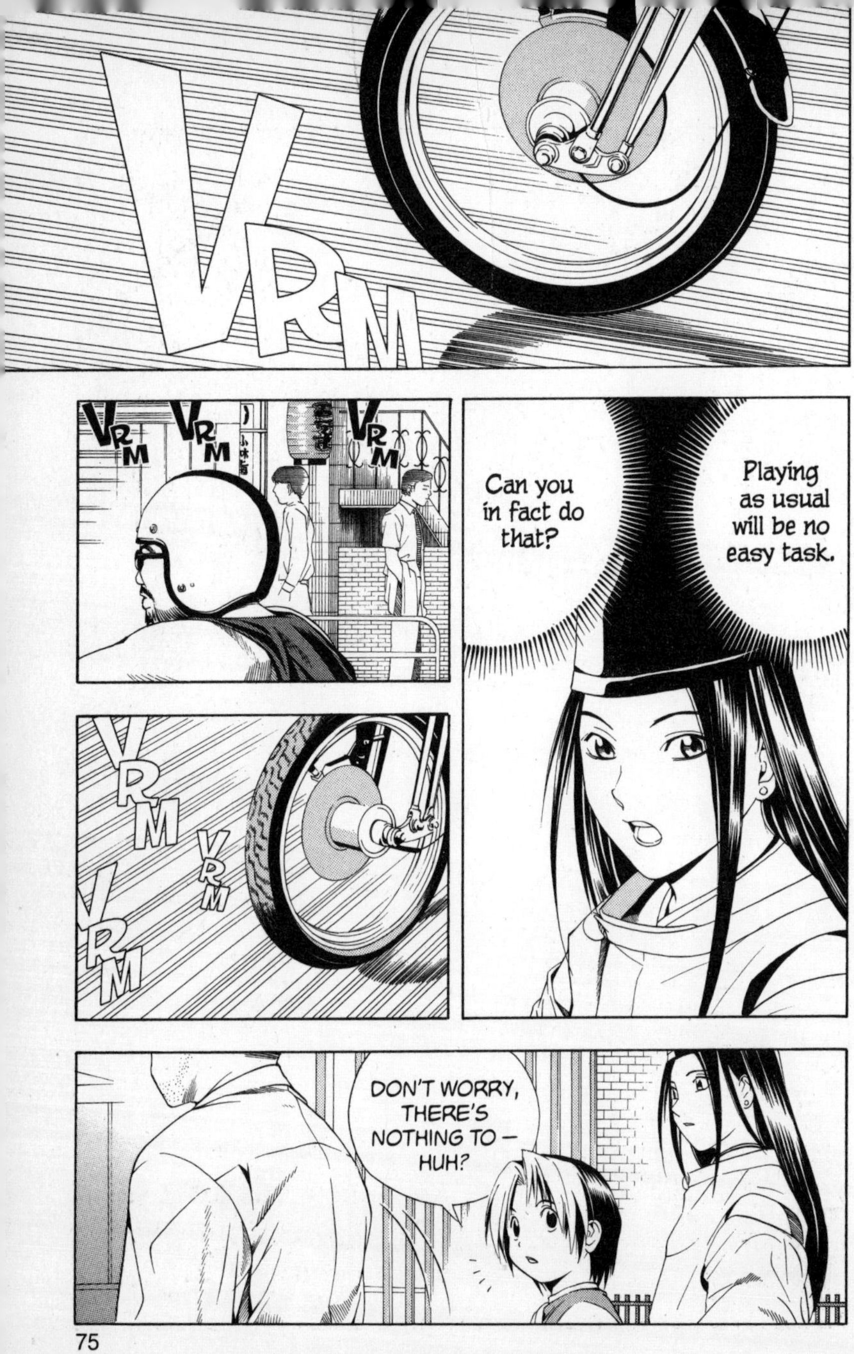
VRM
Playing as usual will be no easy task.
Can you in fact do that?
VRM
VRM
VRM
VRM
VRM
VRM
DON'T WORRY, THERE'S NOTHING TO— HUH?

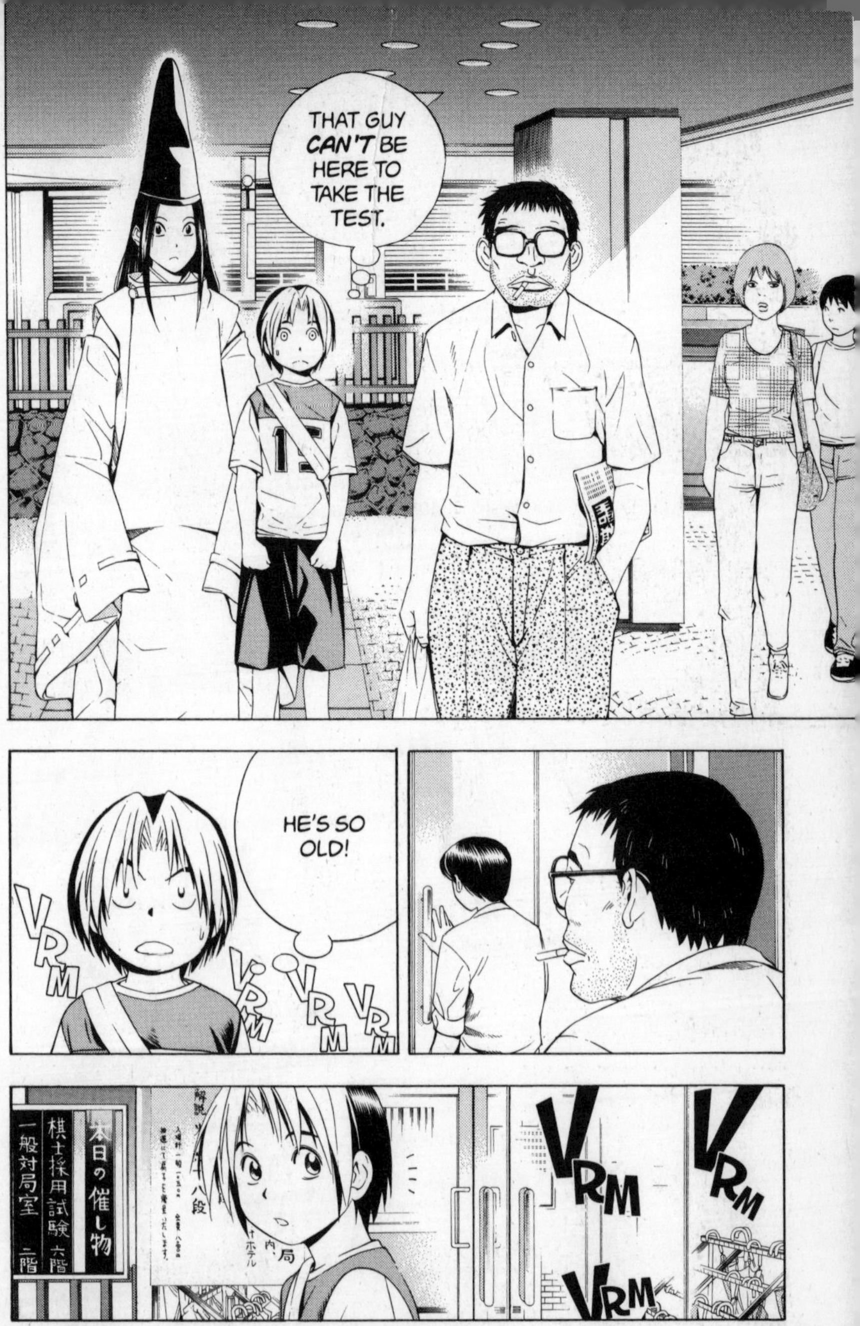
THAT GUY *CAN'T* BE HERE TO TAKE THE TEST.
HE'S SO OLD!
VRM
VRM
VRM
VRM
VRM
VRM
VRM
本日の催し物
棋士採用試験　六階
一般対局室　二階

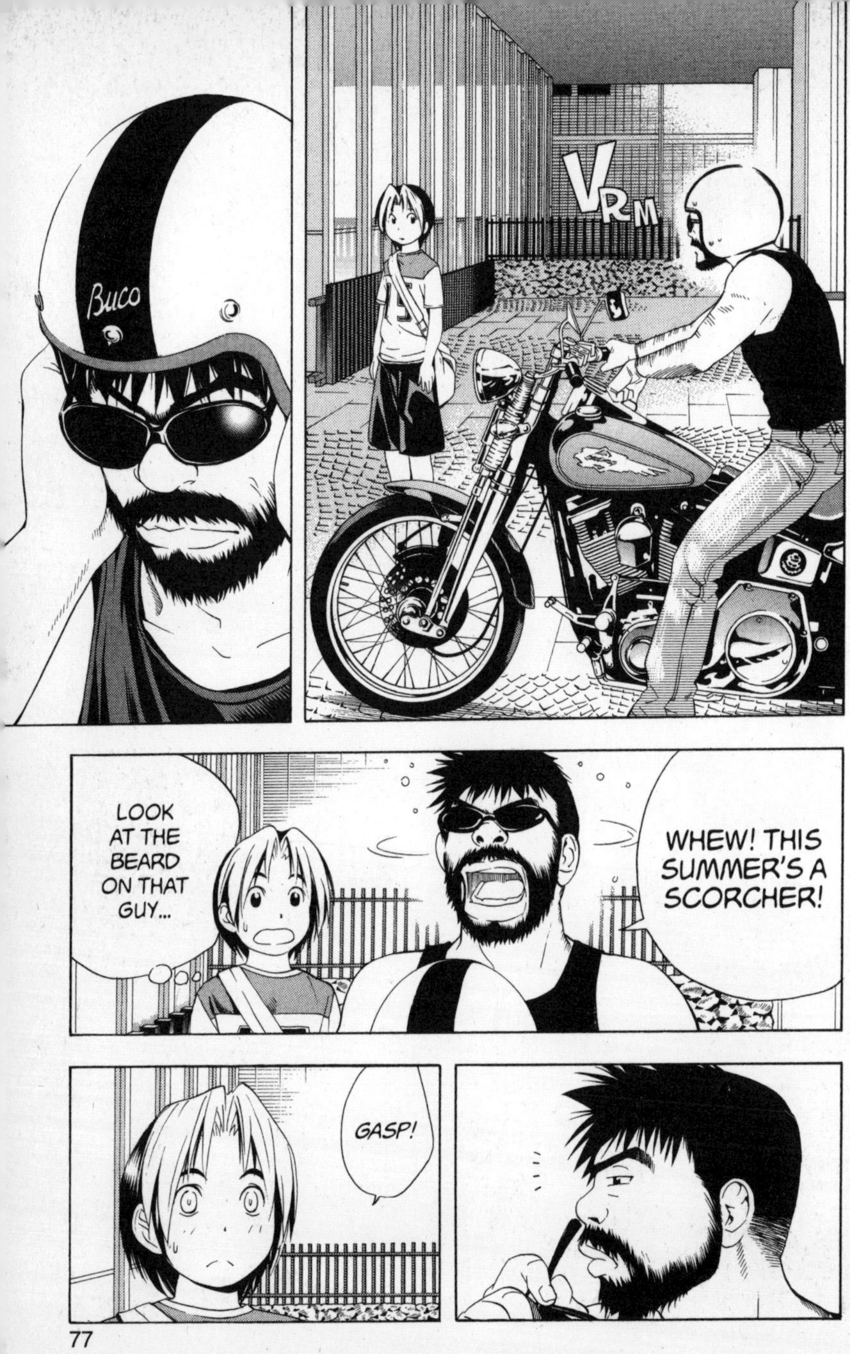
VRM
Buco
WHEW! THIS SUMMER'S A SCORCHER!
LOOK AT THE BEARD ON THAT GUY...
GASP!

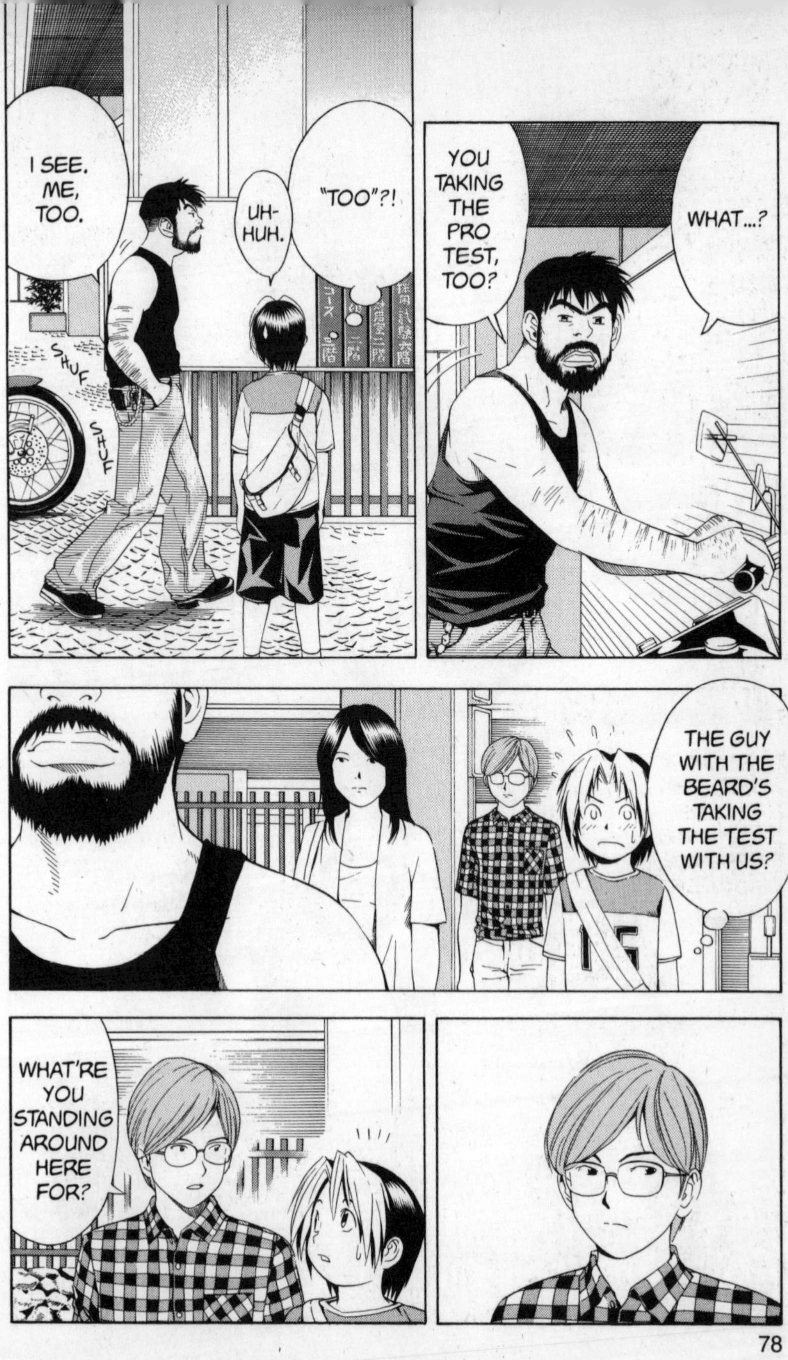
WHAT...?
YOU TAKING THE PRO TEST, TOO?
"TOO"?!
UH-HUH.
I SEE. ME, TOO.
SHUF
SHUF
THE GUY WITH THE BEARD'S TAKING THE TEST WITH US?
WHAT'RE YOU STANDING AROUND HERE FOR?

READ THIS WAY

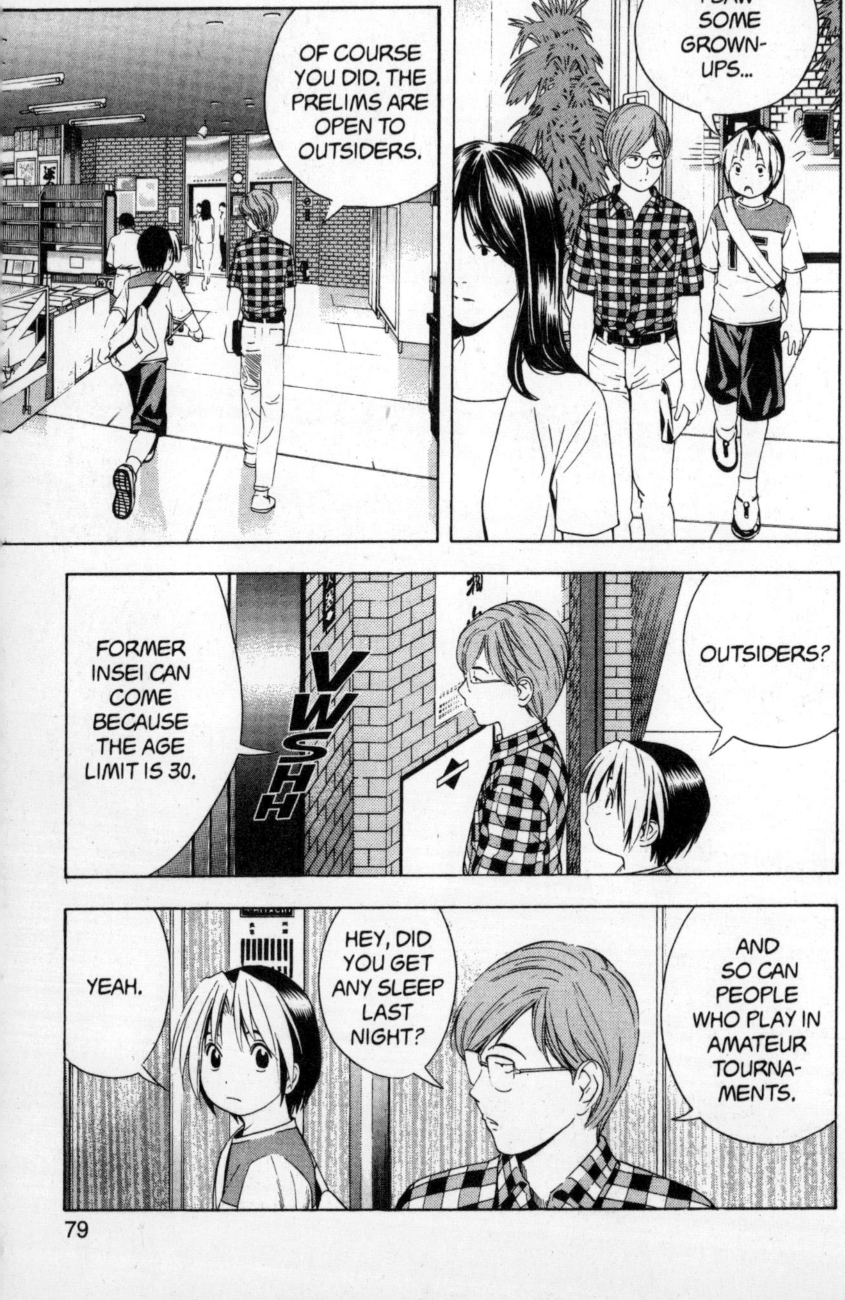
I SAW SOME GROWN-UPS...
OF COURSE YOU DID. THE PRELIMS ARE OPEN TO OUTSIDERS.
OUTSIDERS?
VWSHH
FORMER INSEI CAN COME BECAUSE THE AGE LIMIT IS 30.
AND SO CAN PEOPLE WHO PLAY IN AMATEUR TOURNAMENTS.
HEY, DID YOU GET ANY SLEEP LAST NIGHT?
YEAH.

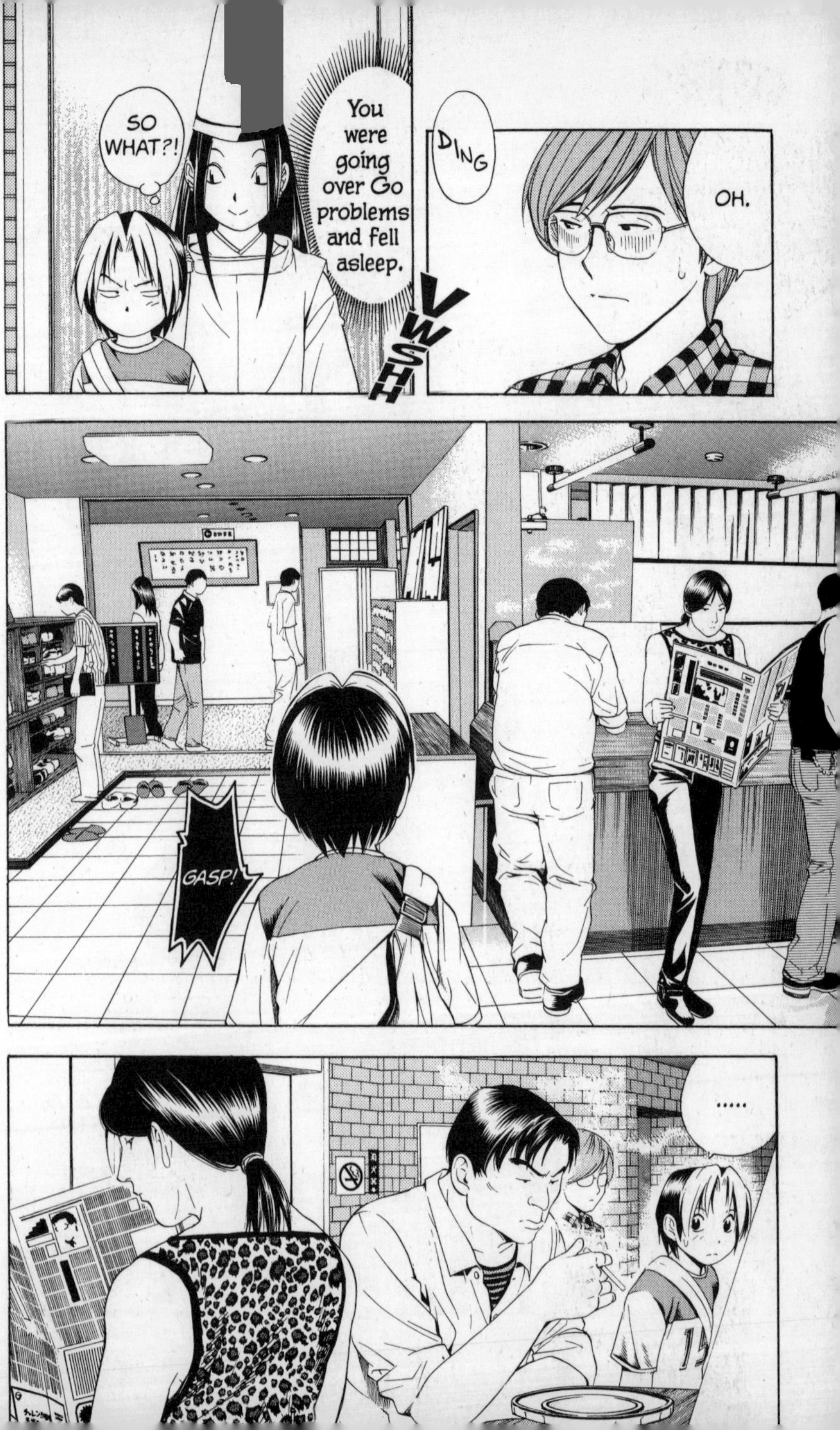
OH.
DING
You were going over Go problems and fell asleep.
VWSHH
SO WHAT?!
GASP!
......

READ THIS WAY

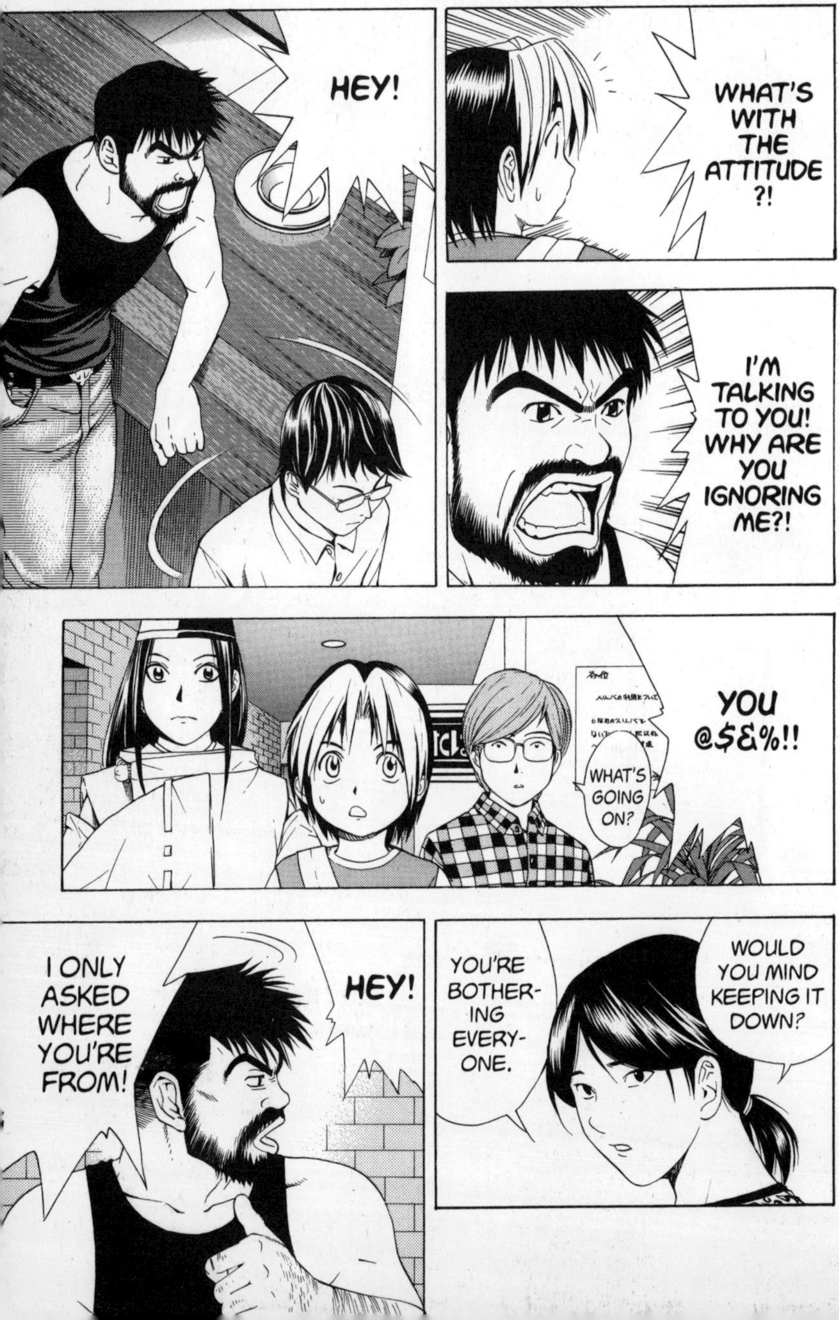
WHAT'S WITH THE ATTITUDE?!
I'M TALKING TO YOU! WHY ARE YOU IGNORING ME?!
HEY!
YOU @$&%!!
WHAT'S GOING ON?
WOULD YOU MIND KEEPING IT DOWN?
YOU'RE BOTHERING EVERYONE.
HEY!
I ONLY ASKED WHERE YOU'RE FROM!

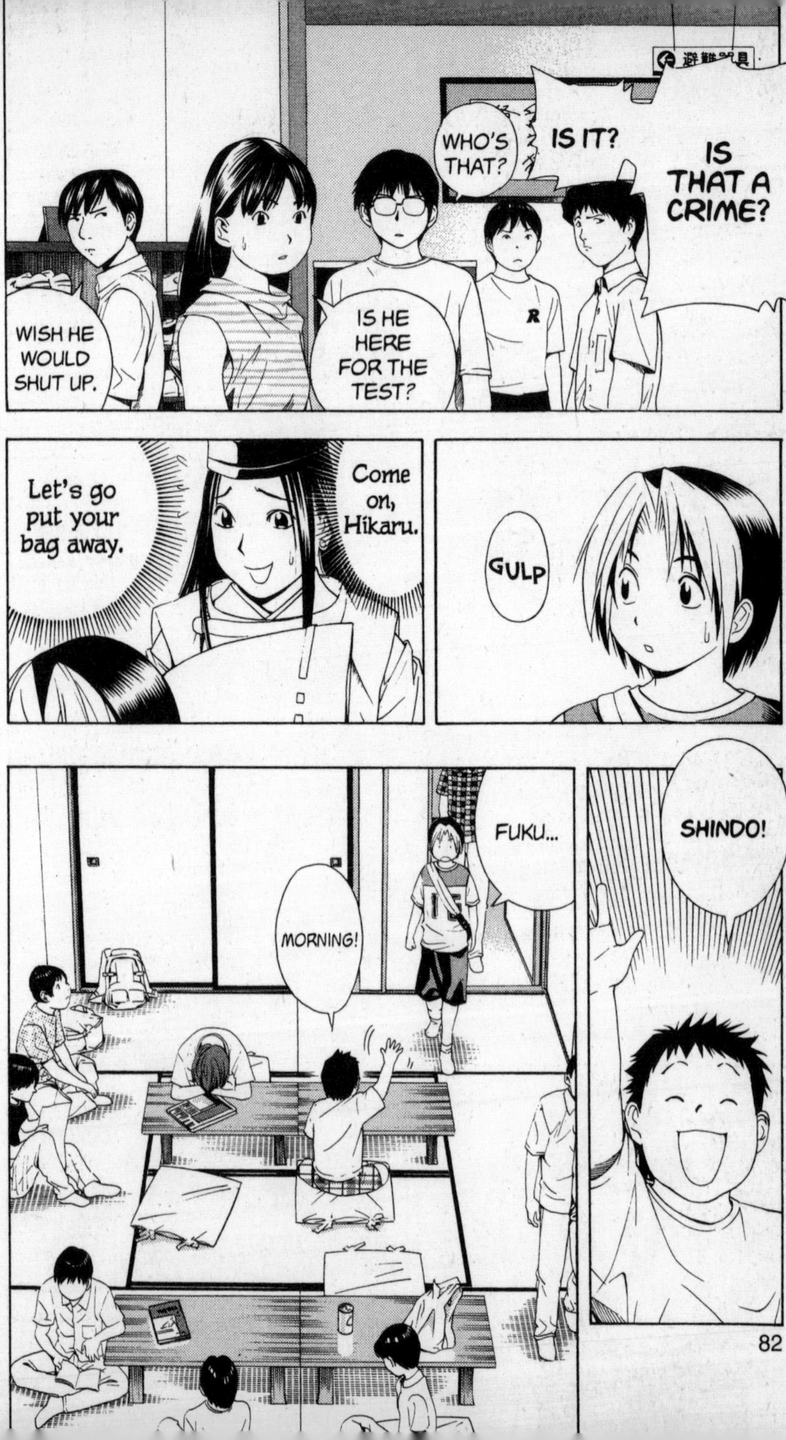
IS THAT A CRIME?
IS IT?
WHO'S THAT?
IS HE HERE FOR THE TEST?
WISH HE WOULD SHUT UP.
GULP
Come on, Hikaru.
Let's go put your bag away.
SHINDO!
FUKU...
MORNING!

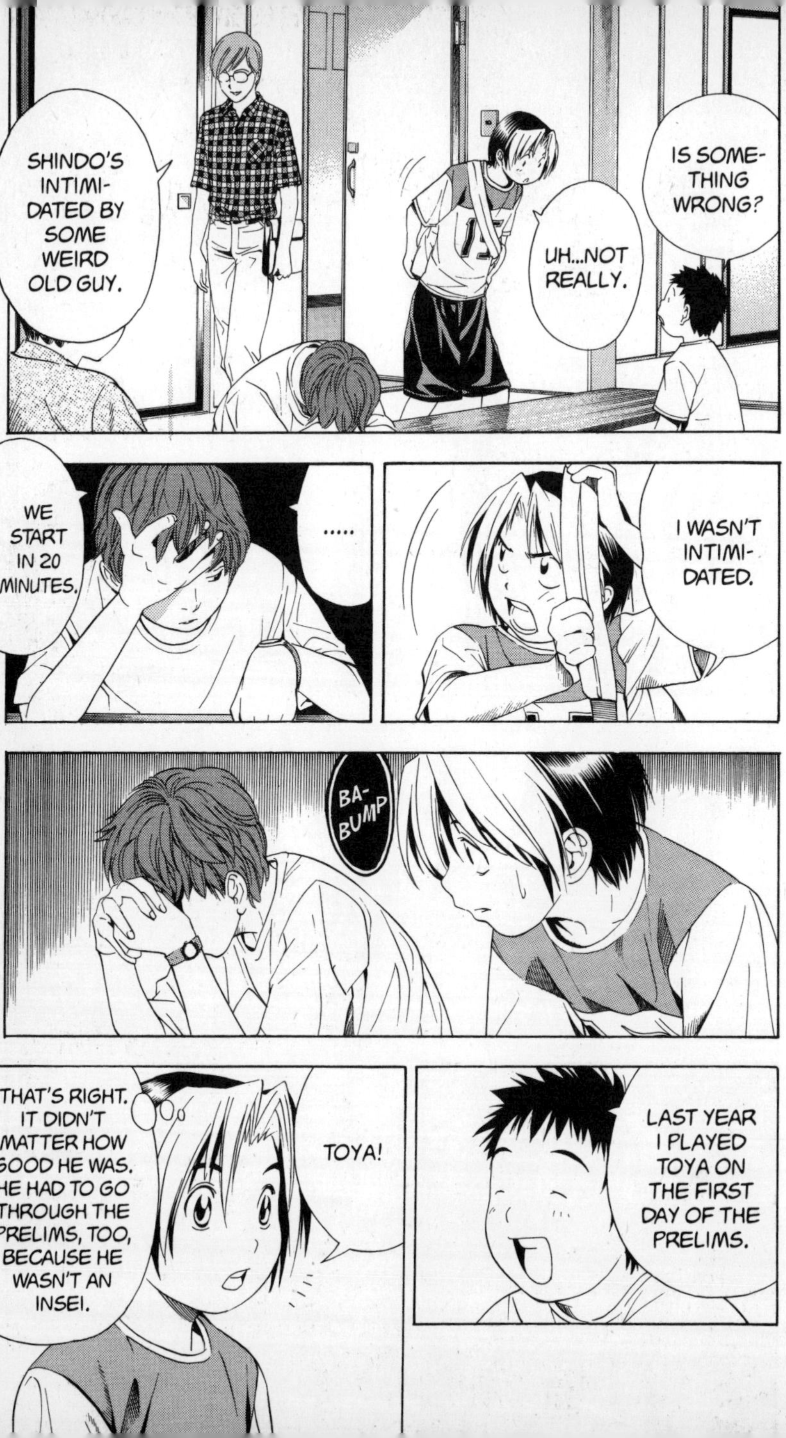
IS SOME-THING WRONG?
UH...NOT REALLY.
SHINDO'S INTIMI-DATED BY SOME WEIRD OLD GUY.
I WASN'T INTIMI-DATED.
.....
WE START IN 20 MINUTES.
BA-BUMP
LAST YEAR I PLAYED TOYA ON THE FIRST DAY OF THE PRELIMS.
TOYA!
THAT'S RIGHT. IT DIDN'T MATTER HOW GOOD HE WAS. HE HAD TO GO THROUGH THE PRELIMS, TOO, BECAUSE HE WASN'T AN INSEI.

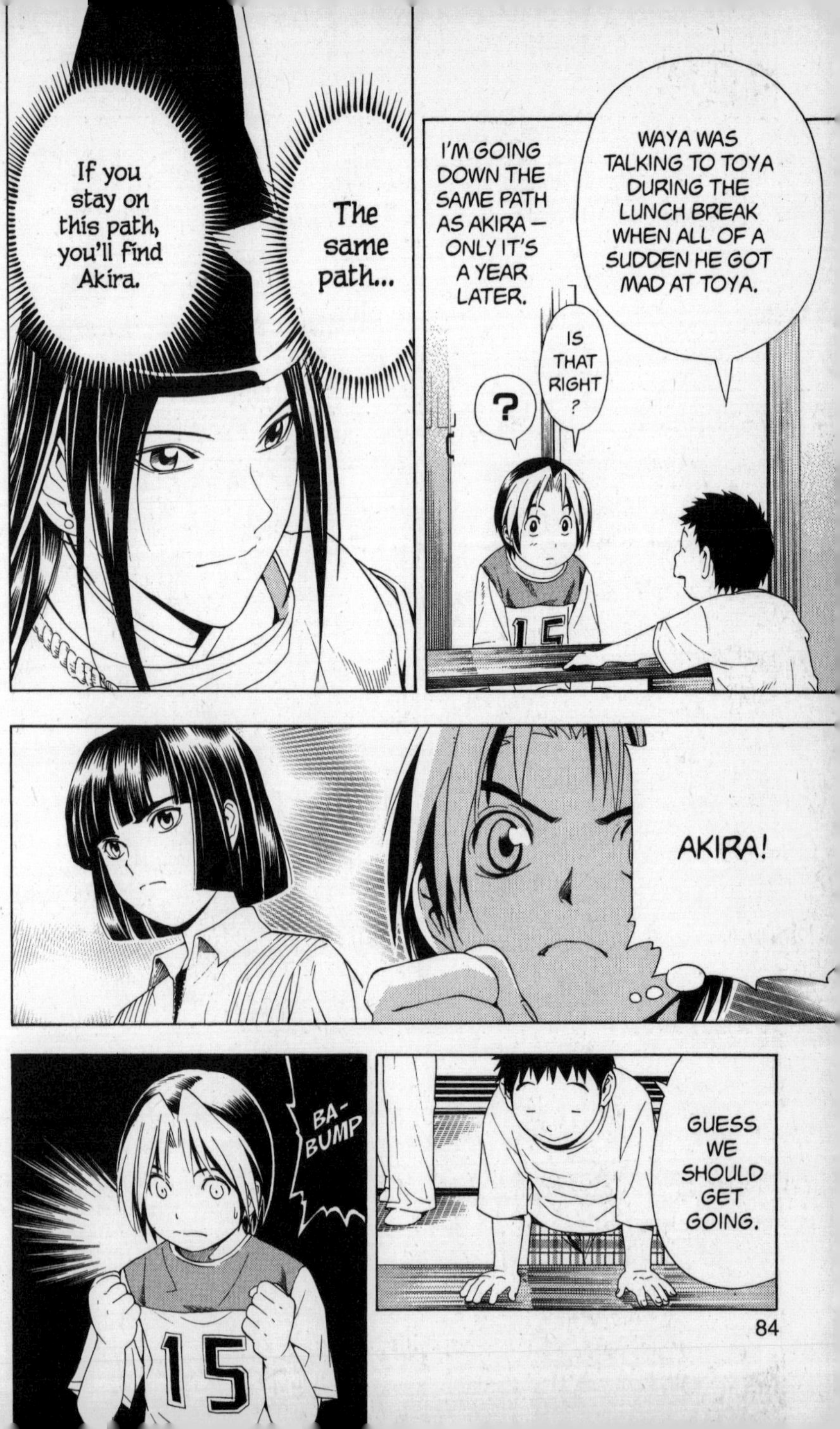
WAYA WAS TALKING TO TOYA DURING THE LUNCH BREAK WHEN ALL OF A SUDDEN HE GOT MAD AT TOYA.
I'M GOING DOWN THE SAME PATH AS AKIRA — ONLY IT'S A YEAR LATER.
IS THAT RIGHT?
?
The same path...
If you stay on this path, you'll find Akira.
AKIRA!
GUESS WE SHOULD GET GOING.
BA-BUMP

READ THIS WAY

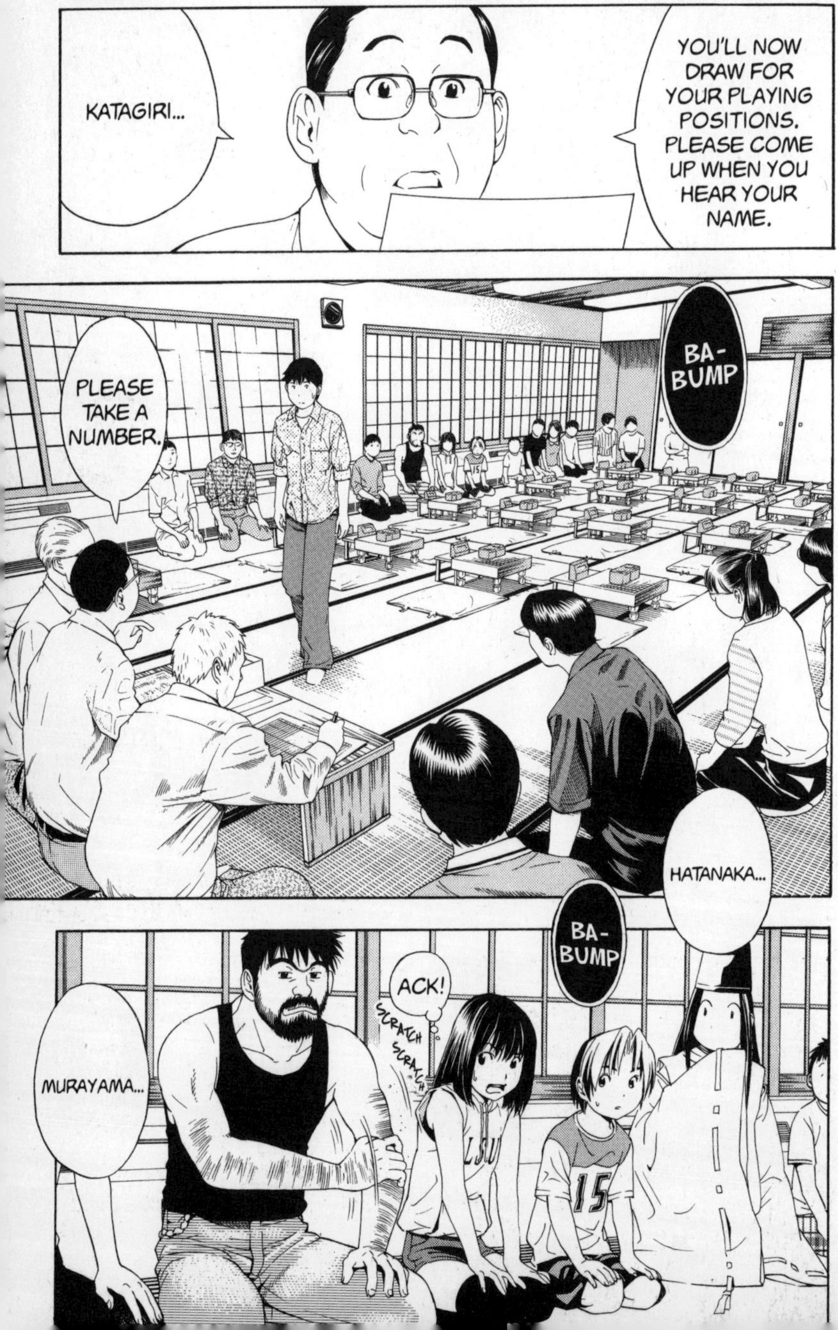
YOU'LL NOW DRAW FOR YOUR PLAYING POSITIONS. PLEASE COME UP WHEN YOU HEAR YOUR NAME.
KATAGIRI...
BA-BUMP
PLEASE TAKE A NUMBER.
HATANAKA...
BA-BUMP
ACK!
SCRATCH SCRATCH
MURAYAMA...

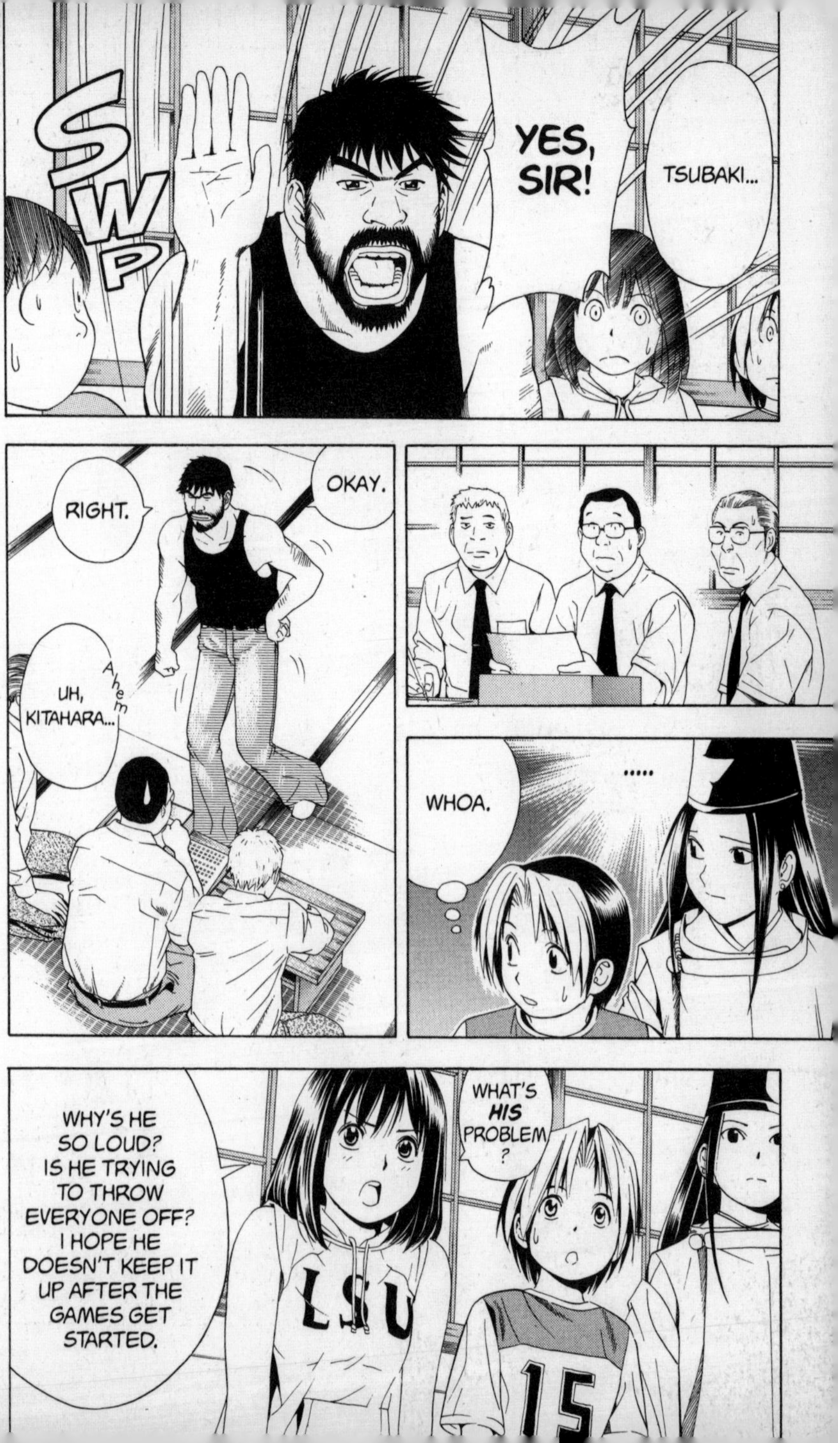
TSUBAKI...
YES, SIR!
SWP
.....
WHOA.
OKAY.
RIGHT.
Ahem
UH, KITAHARA...
WHAT'S **HIS** PROBLEM?
WHY'S HE SO LOUD? IS HE TRYING TO THROW EVERYONE OFF? I HOPE HE DOESN'T KEEP IT UP AFTER THE GAMES GET STARTED.
LSU
15

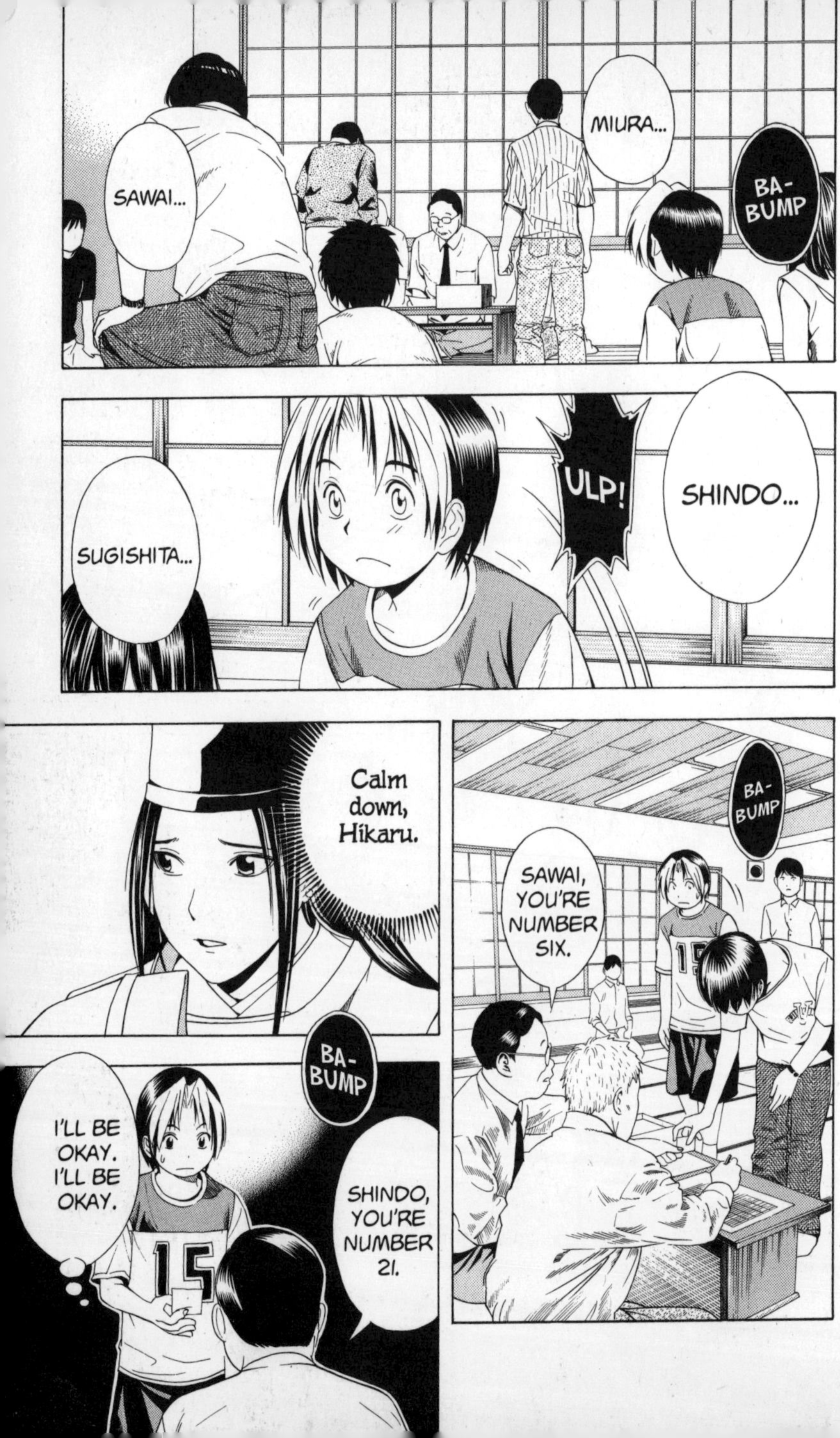
BA-BUMP
MIURA...
SAWAI...
SHINDO...
ULP!
SUGISHITA...
BA-BUMP
SAWAI, YOU'RE NUMBER SIX.
Calm down, Hikaru.
BA-BUMP
SHINDO, YOU'RE NUMBER 21.
I'LL BE OKAY. I'LL BE OKAY.

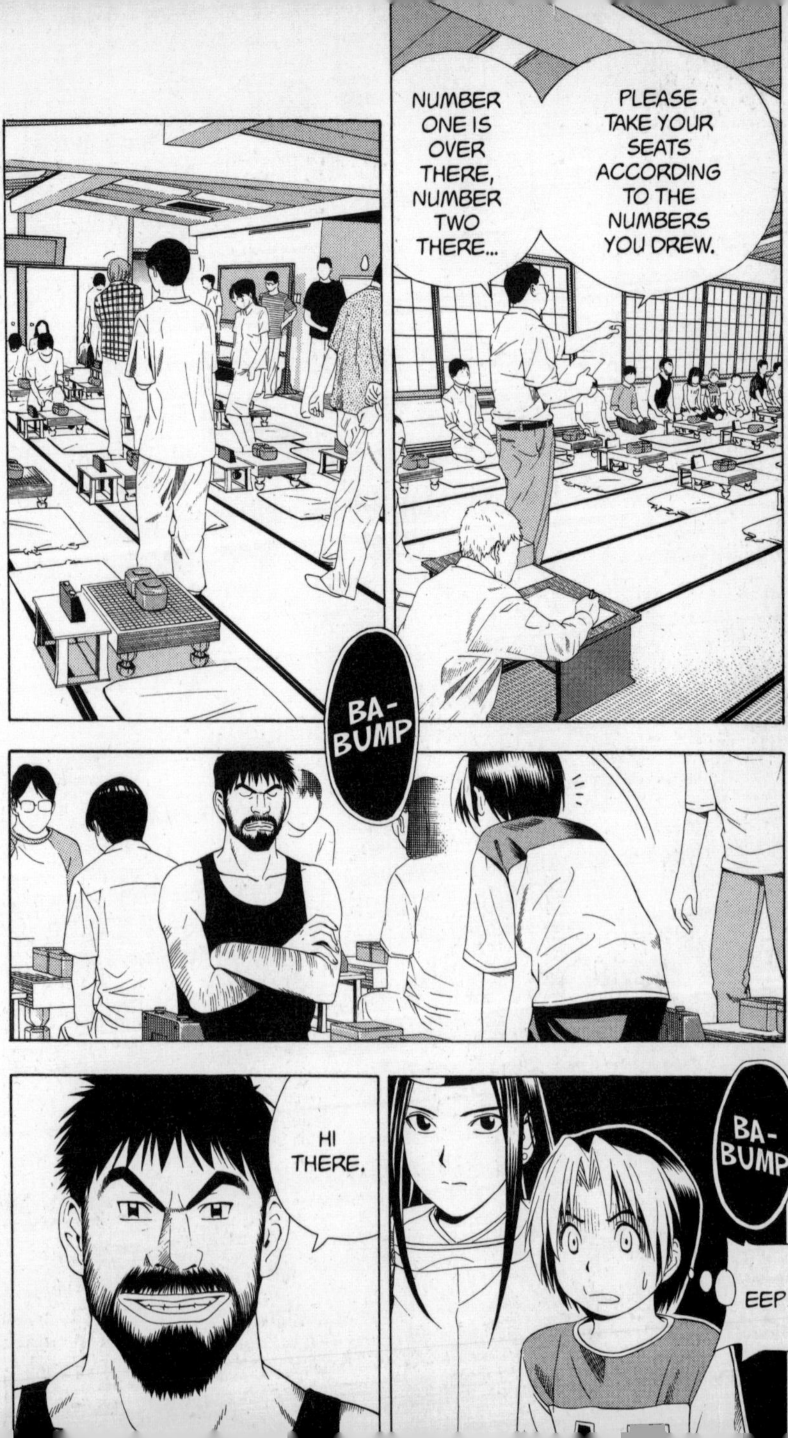
PLEASE TAKE YOUR SEATS ACCORDING TO THE NUMBERS YOU DREW.
NUMBER ONE IS OVER THERE, NUMBER TWO THERE...
BA-BUMP
BA-BUMP
EEP!
HI THERE.

READ THIS WAY

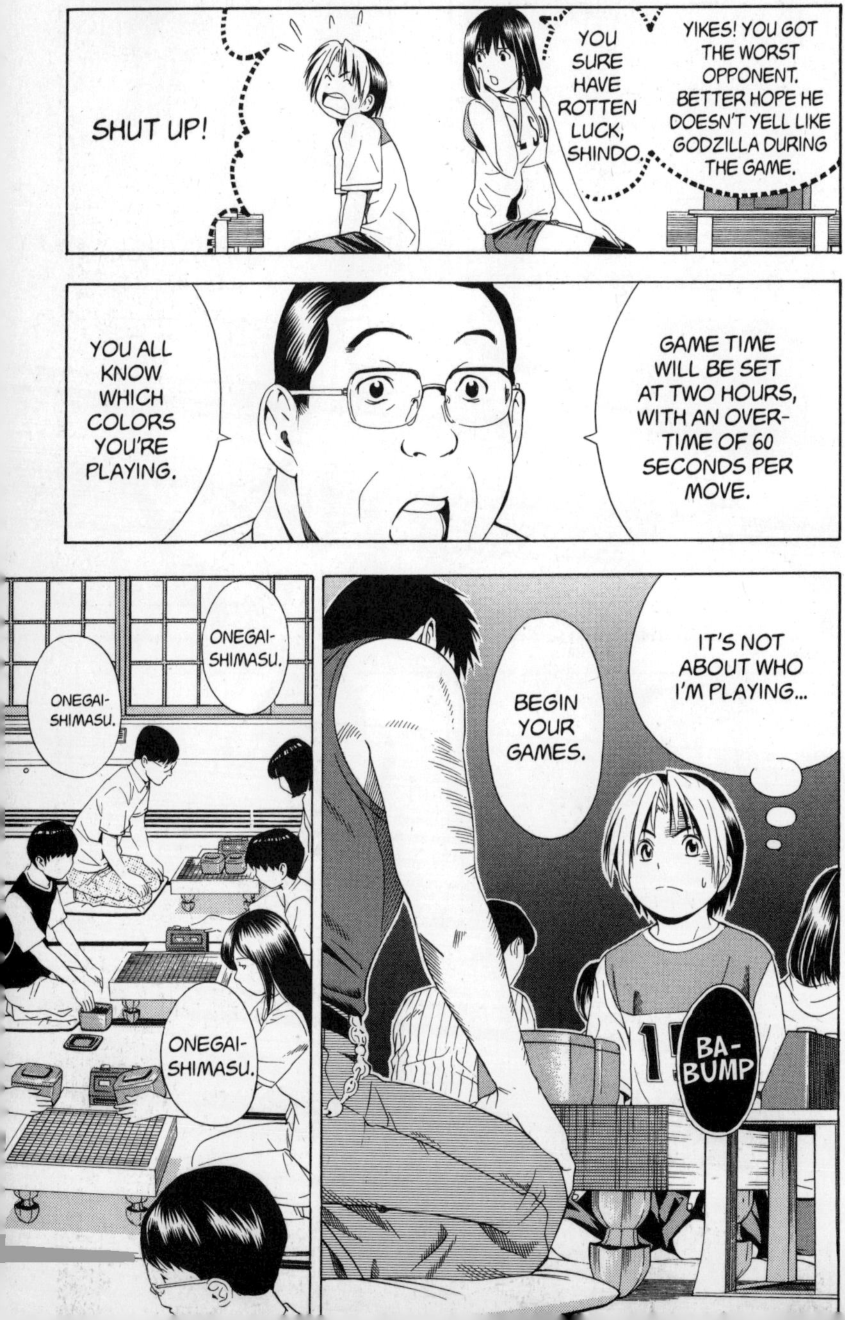
YIKES! YOU GOT THE WORST OPPONENT. BETTER HOPE HE DOESN'T YELL LIKE GODZILLA DURING THE GAME.
YOU SURE HAVE ROTTEN LUCK, SHINDO.
SHUT UP!
GAME TIME WILL BE SET AT TWO HOURS, WITH AN OVER-TIME OF 60 SECONDS PER MOVE.
YOU ALL KNOW WHICH COLORS YOU'RE PLAYING.
IT'S NOT ABOUT WHO I'M PLAYING...
BEGIN YOUR GAMES.
BA-BUMP
ONEGAI-SHIMASU.
ONEGAI-SHIMASU.
ONEGAI-SHIMASU.

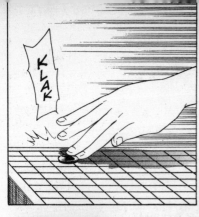

KLAK

OKAY!

......

KCHAK

HUH?

BOW

UH, EXCUSE ME.

READ THIS WAY

WHAT THE HECK?
1:59 1:29
IT'S BEEN 30 MINUTES...
...AND HE HASN'T PLAYED A SINGLE MOVE.

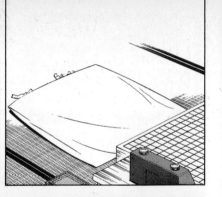

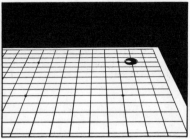

THE 1ST ALL-TIME GREATEST CHARACTER CONTEST
SURVEY RESULTS! (11TH THROUGH 53RD)

This poll was conducted in Japan.

11		Akari Fujisaki	932 votes
12		Yukari Umezawa 4 dan	883 votes
13		Shinichiro Isumi	691 votes
14		Toya Meijin	548 votes
15		Yumi Hotta	372 votes
16		Takeshi Obata	337 votes
17		Shirakawa 7 dan	327 votes
17		Yuri Hidaka	327 votes
19		Yuki's sister	297 votes
20		Fuku	150 votes
21		Ito	134 votes

22		Harumi Ichikawa
23		Female Kaio Go Club member # 2
24		Hon'inbo Shusaku
25		Mr. Akota
26		Mr. Dake
27		World Amateur Go Cup, U.S. rep.
28		Heihachi Shindo
29		Yun Sensei
30		Zama Oza
31		Masako Kaneko
32		Kosuke Ochi

33		Heian era Go instructor
34		Okumura
35		Kuwabara Sensei
36		Natsume
37		Mr. Shu
38		Tamako Sensei
39		Lee Rinshin
40		Insei instructor
40		Imanishi
42		Mitsuru Mashiba
43		Female Kaio Go Club member # 1

43		Mr. Hirose
45		Hikaru's mother
45		Morishita 9 dan
47		Ashiwara Sensei
48		Go software salesman
48		Takada
48		Go Weekly reporter
48		Kojima
48		Aoki
53		Community Center Go student
53		Kaio's principal
53		Kim

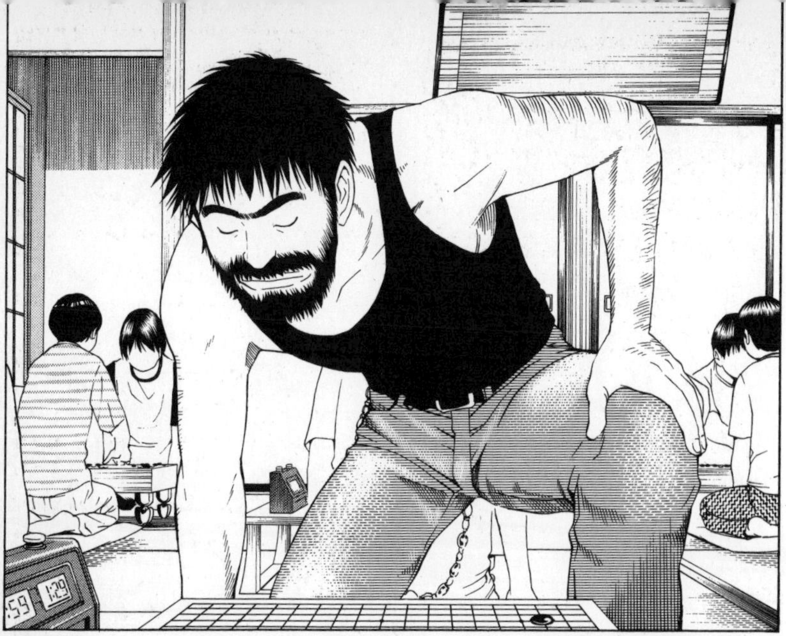
:59
1:29

Game 65 "Aim for Three Wins"

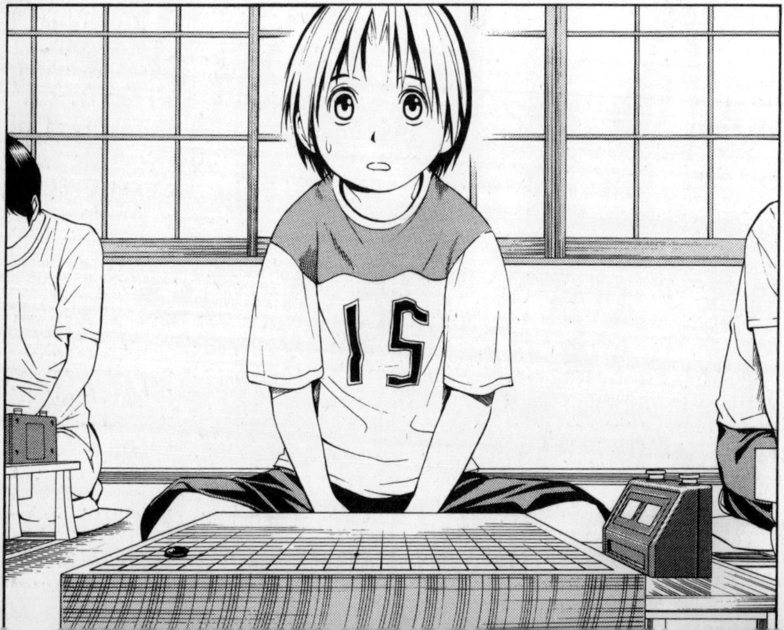
15

KCHK

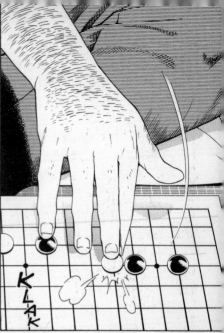

KLAK

KLAK

.....

SCRTCH

SCRTCH

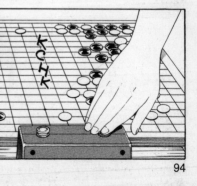

KCHK

94

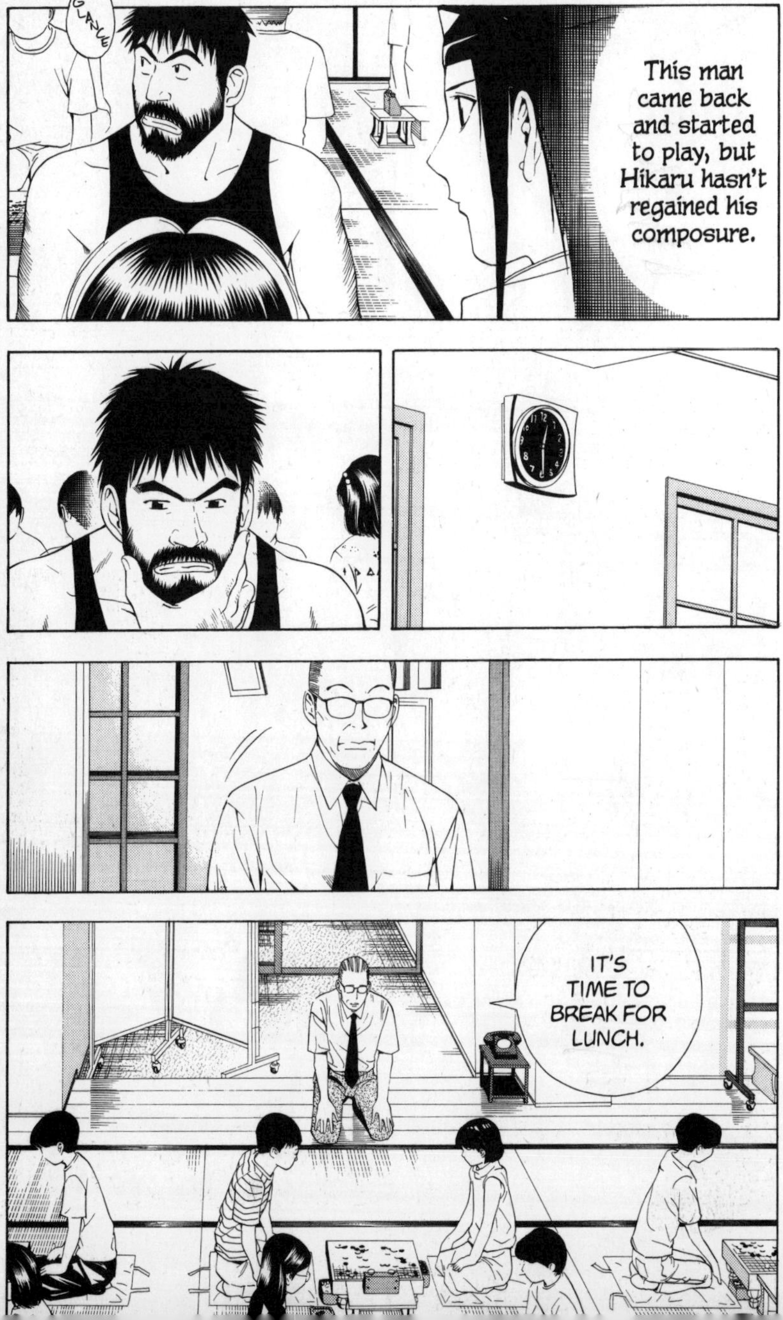
This man came back and started to play, but Hikaru hasn't regained his composure.
GLANCE
IT'S TIME TO BREAK FOR LUNCH.

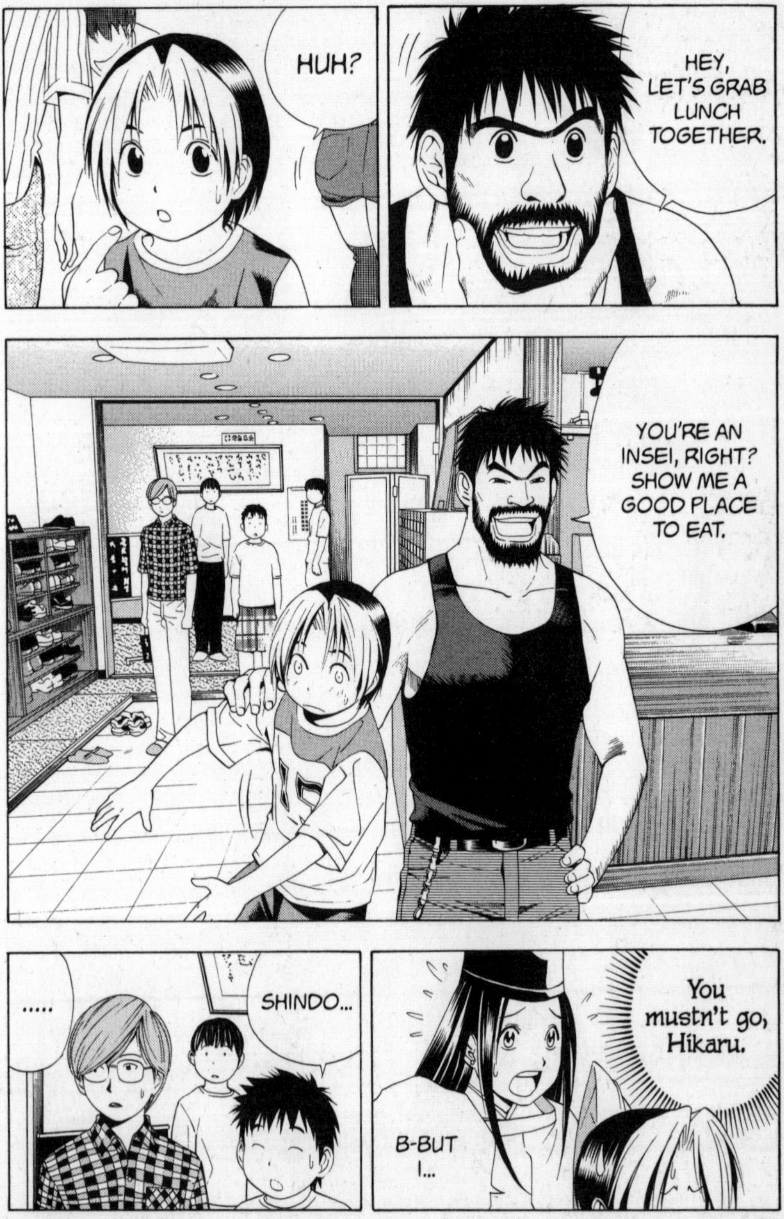

HEY, LET'S GRAB LUNCH TOGETHER.
HUH?
YOU'RE AN INSEI, RIGHT? SHOW ME A GOOD PLACE TO EAT.
You mustn't go, Hikaru.
B-BUT I...
SHINDO...
.....

READ THIS WAY

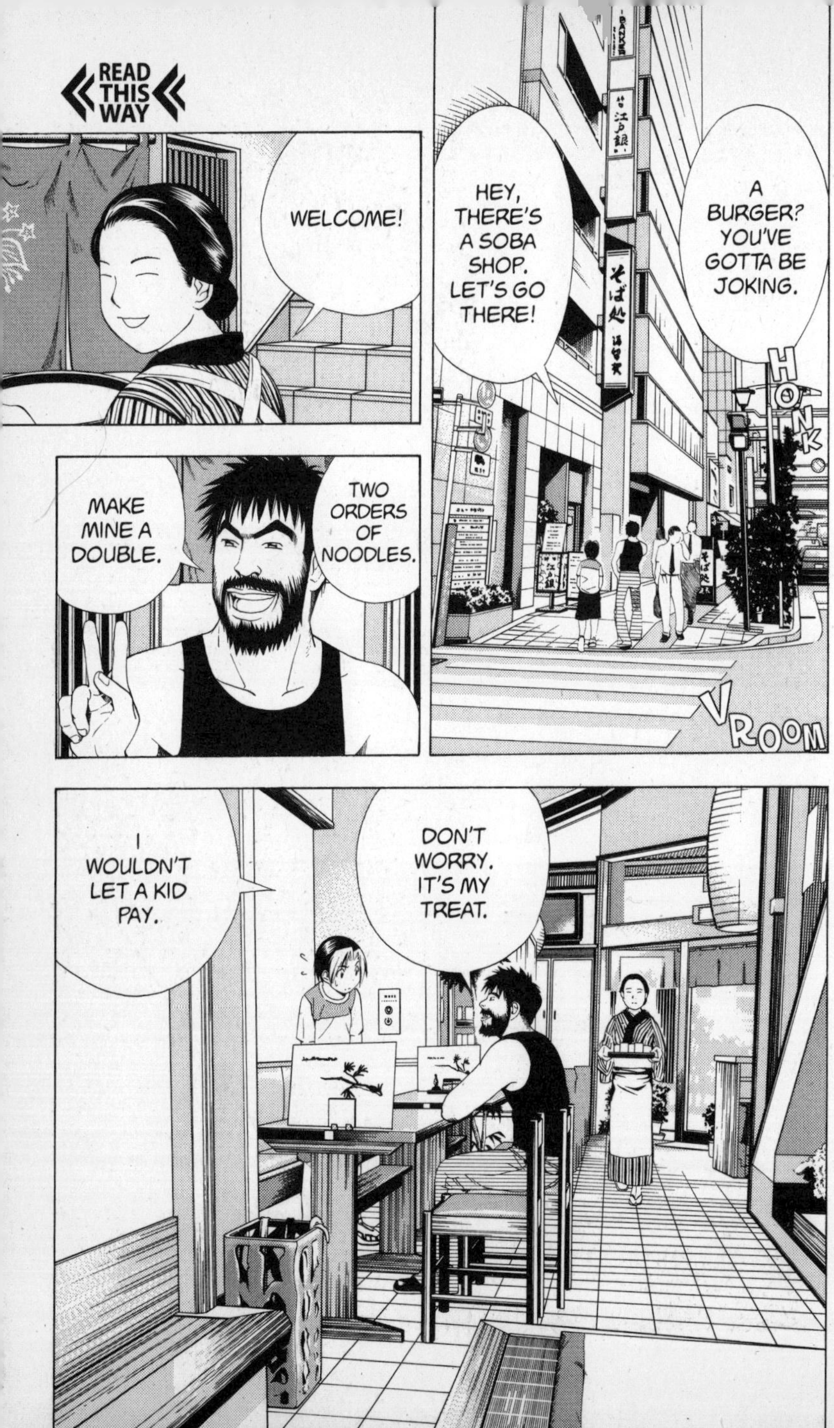

江戸銀
そば処
A BURGER? YOU'VE GOTTA BE JOKING.
HEY, THERE'S A SOBA SHOP. LET'S GO THERE!
HONK
VROOM
WELCOME!
TWO ORDERS OF NOODLES.
MAKE MINE A DOUBLE.
DON'T WORRY. IT'S MY TREAT.
I WOULDN'T LET A KID PAY.

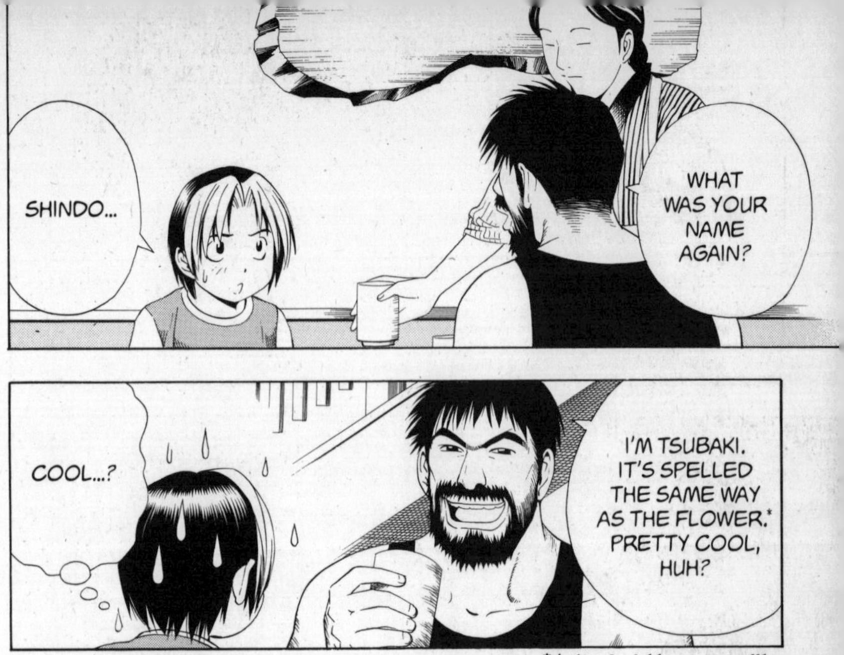
WHAT WAS YOUR NAME AGAIN?
SHINDO...
I'M TSUBAKI. IT'S SPELLED THE SAME WAY AS THE FLOWER.* PRETTY COOL, HUH?
COOL...?

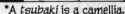

*A *tsubaki* is a camellia.

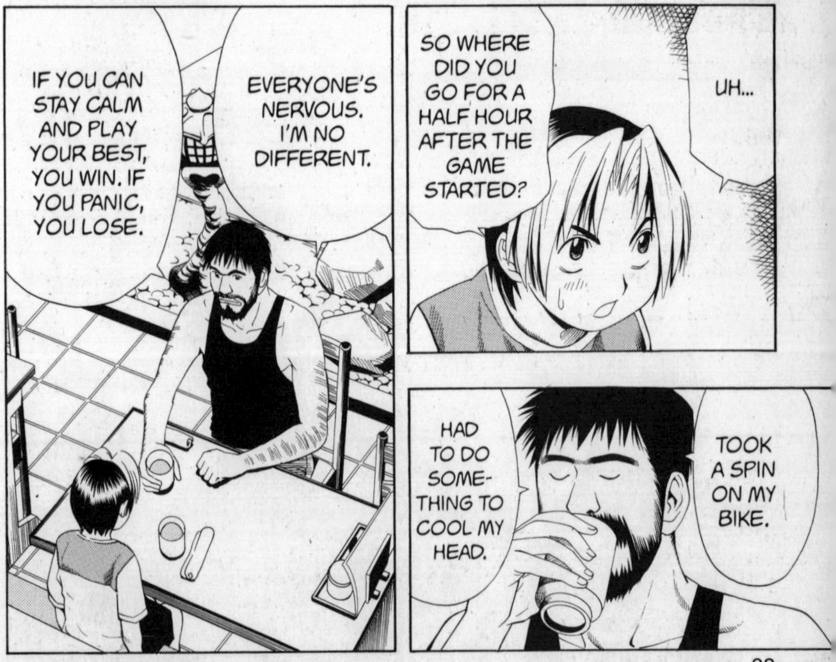
UH...
SO WHERE DID YOU GO FOR A HALF HOUR AFTER THE GAME STARTED?
TOOK A SPIN ON MY BIKE.
HAD TO DO SOME-THING TO COOL MY HEAD.
EVERYONE'S NERVOUS. I'M NO DIFFERENT.
IF YOU CAN STAY CALM AND PLAY YOUR BEST, YOU WIN. IF YOU PANIC, YOU LOSE.

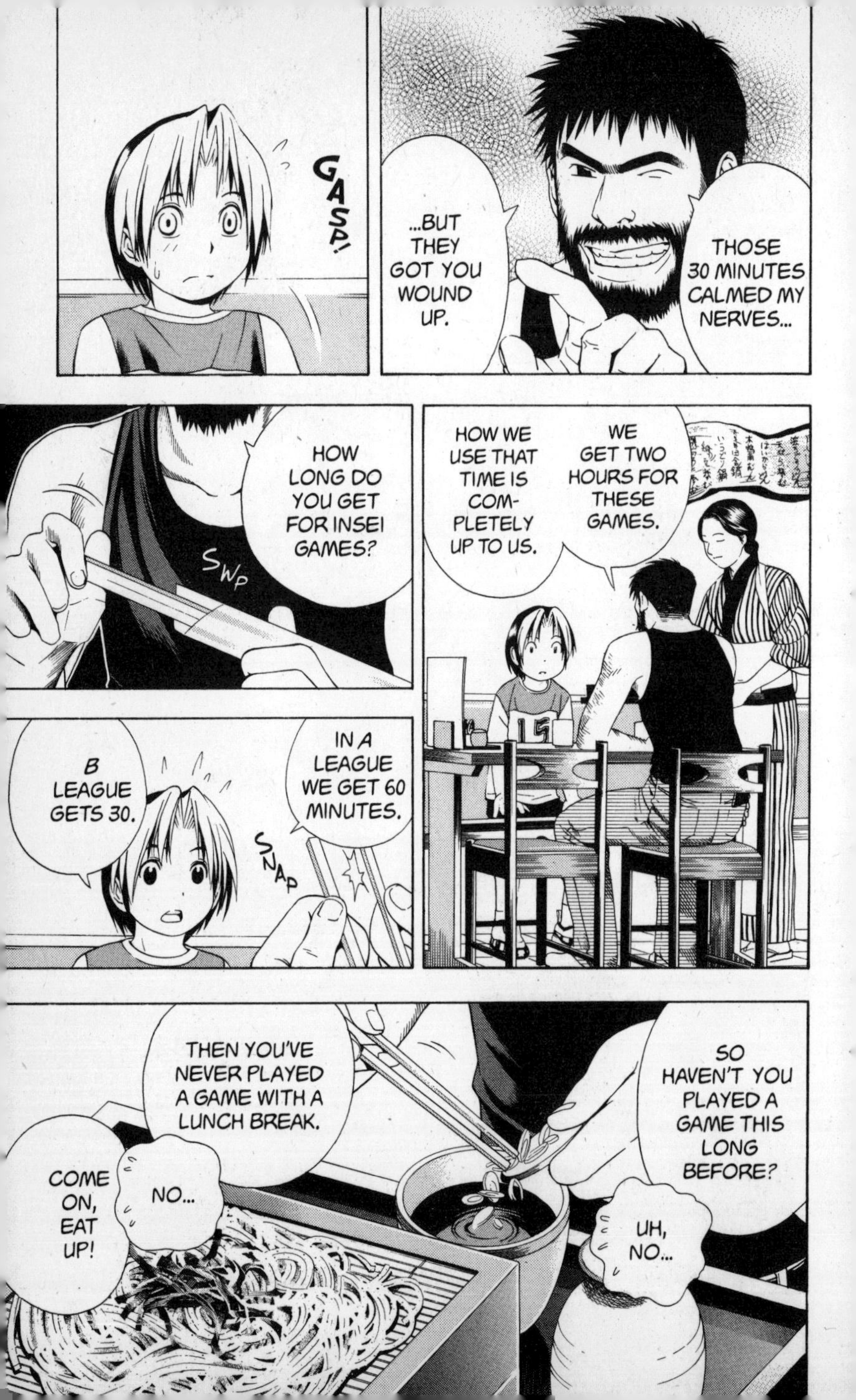
THOSE 30 MINUTES CALMED MY NERVES...
...BUT THEY GOT YOU WOUND UP.
GASP!
WE GET TWO HOURS FOR THESE GAMES.
HOW WE USE THAT TIME IS COM-PLETELY UP TO US.
HOW LONG DO YOU GET FOR INSEI GAMES?
SWP
IN A LEAGUE WE GET 60 MINUTES.
SNAP
B LEAGUE GETS 30.
SO HAVEN'T YOU PLAYED A GAME THIS LONG BEFORE?
UH, NO...
THEN YOU'VE NEVER PLAYED A GAME WITH A LUNCH BREAK.
NO...
COME ON, EAT UP!

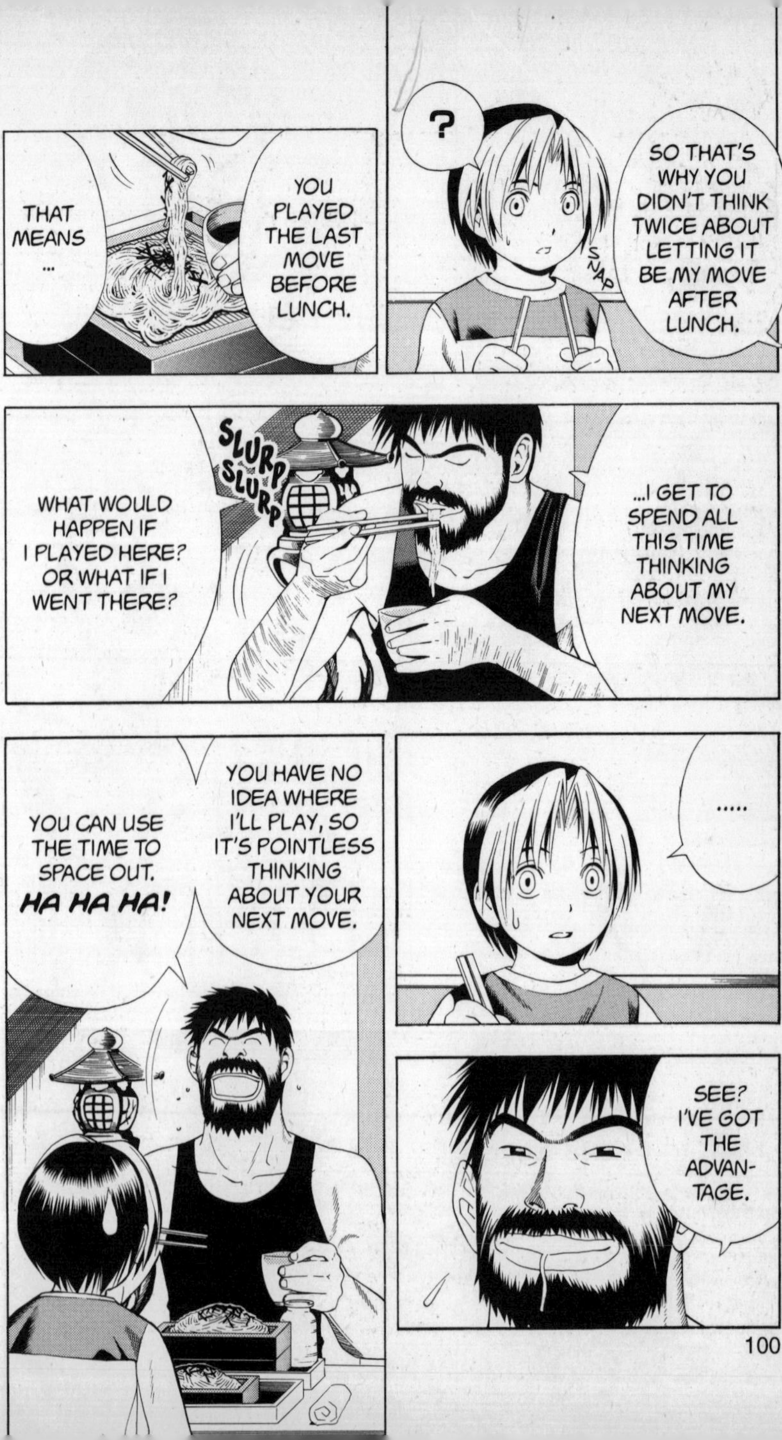
?
SO THAT'S WHY YOU DIDN'T THINK TWICE ABOUT LETTING IT BE MY MOVE AFTER LUNCH.
SNAP
YOU PLAYED THE LAST MOVE BEFORE LUNCH.
THAT MEANS ...
...I GET TO SPEND ALL THIS TIME THINKING ABOUT MY NEXT MOVE.
SLURP SLURP
WHAT WOULD HAPPEN IF I PLAYED HERE? OR WHAT IF I WENT THERE?
.....
SEE? I'VE GOT THE ADVAN-TAGE.
YOU HAVE NO IDEA WHERE I'LL PLAY, SO IT'S POINTLESS THINKING ABOUT YOUR NEXT MOVE.
YOU CAN USE THE TIME TO SPACE OUT. HA HA HA!

READ THIS WAY

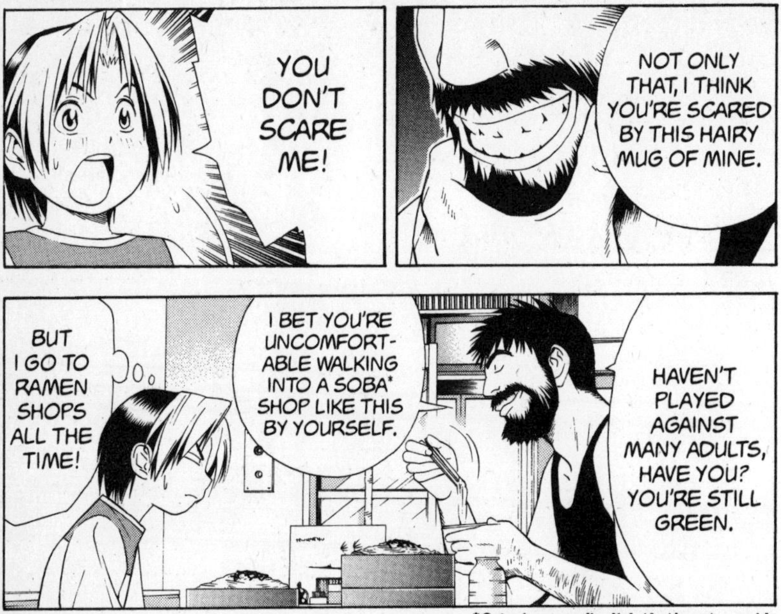
NOT ONLY THAT, I THINK YOU'RE SCARED BY THIS HAIRY MUG OF MINE.
YOU DON'T SCARE ME!
HAVEN'T PLAYED AGAINST MANY ADULTS, HAVE YOU? YOU'RE STILL GREEN.
I BET YOU'RE UNCOMFORTABLE WALKING INTO A SOBA* SHOP LIKE THIS BY YOURSELF.
BUT I GO TO RAMEN SHOPS ALL THE TIME!

*Soba is a noodle dish that's eaten cold.

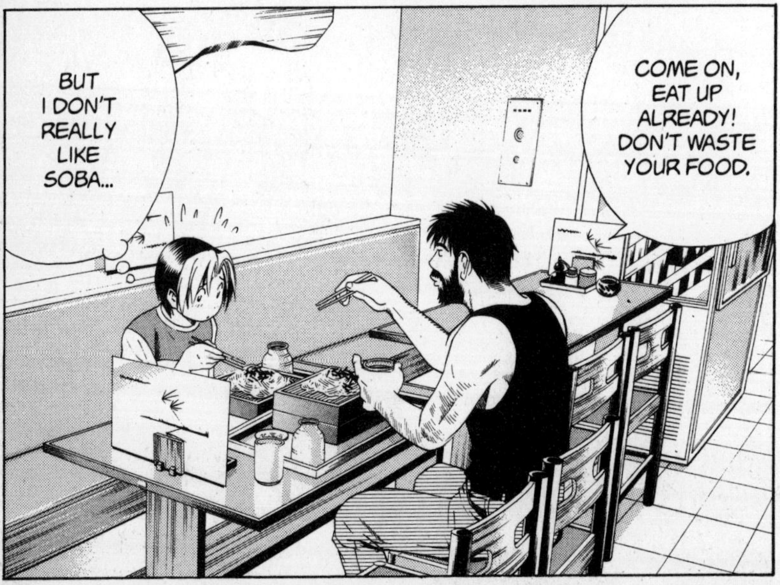
COME ON, EAT UP ALREADY! DON'T WASTE YOUR FOOD.
BUT I DON'T REALLY LIKE SOBA...

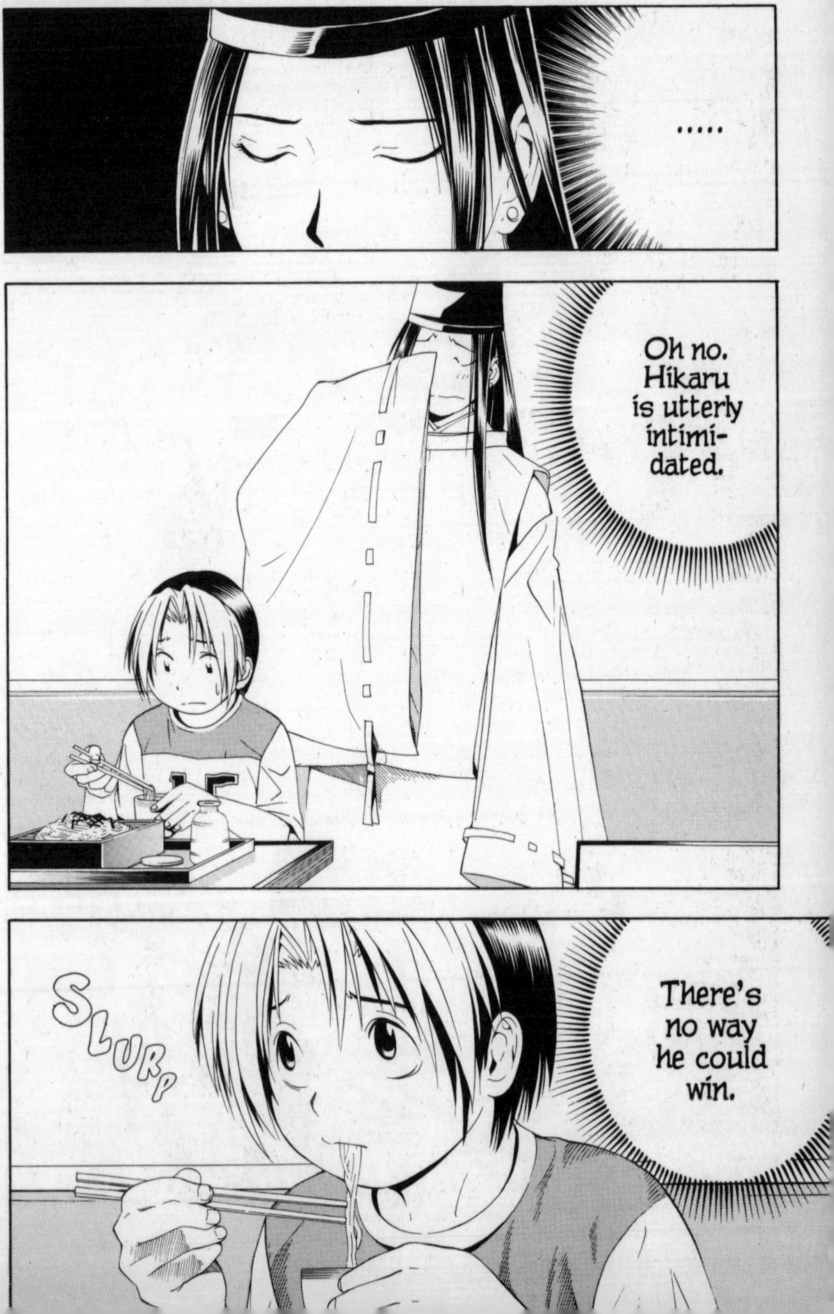
.....
Oh no. Hikaru is utterly intimidated.
There's no way he could win.
SLURP

READ THIS WAY

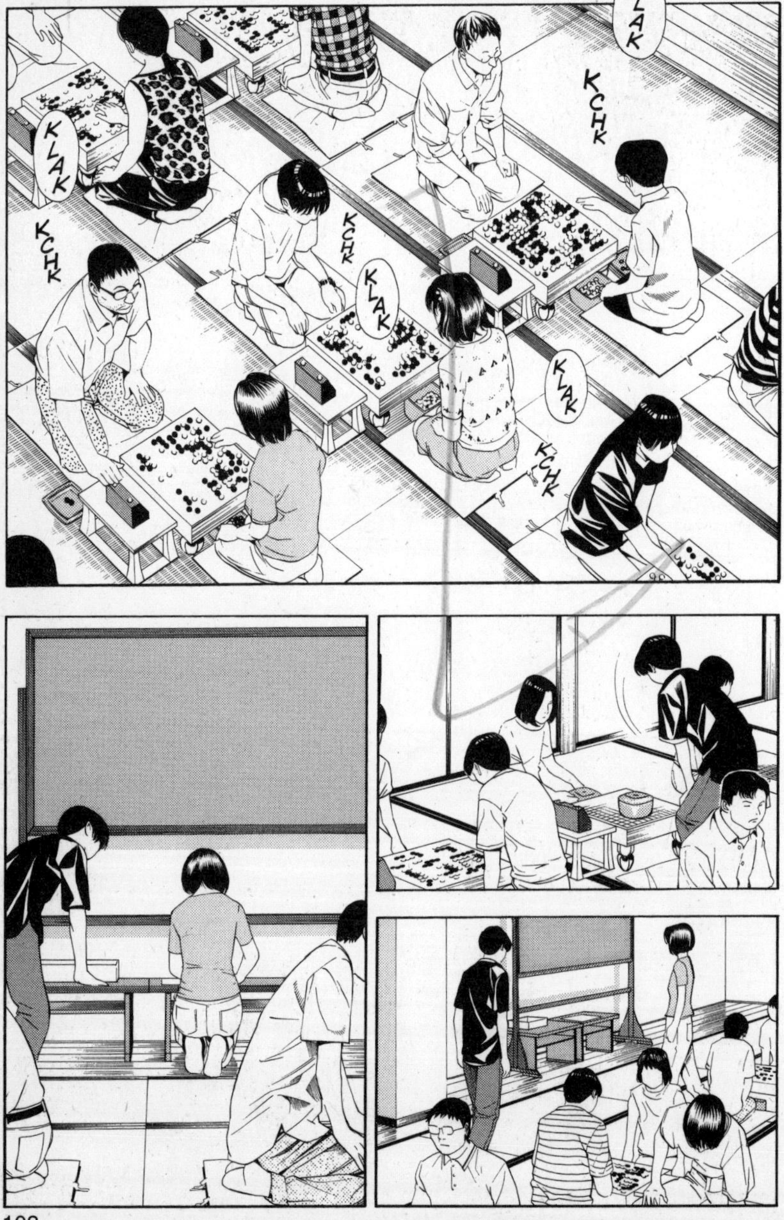
KLAK
KCHK
KLAK
KCHK
KLAK
KCHK
KLAK
KCHK

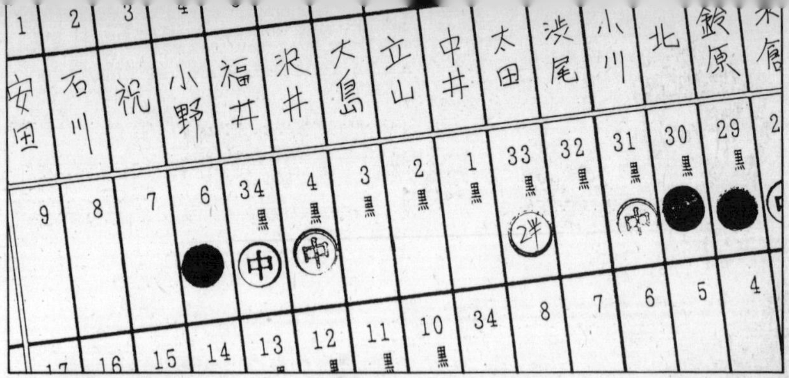
安田
石川
祝
小野
福井
沢井
大島
立山
中井
太田
渋尾
小川
北
鈴原

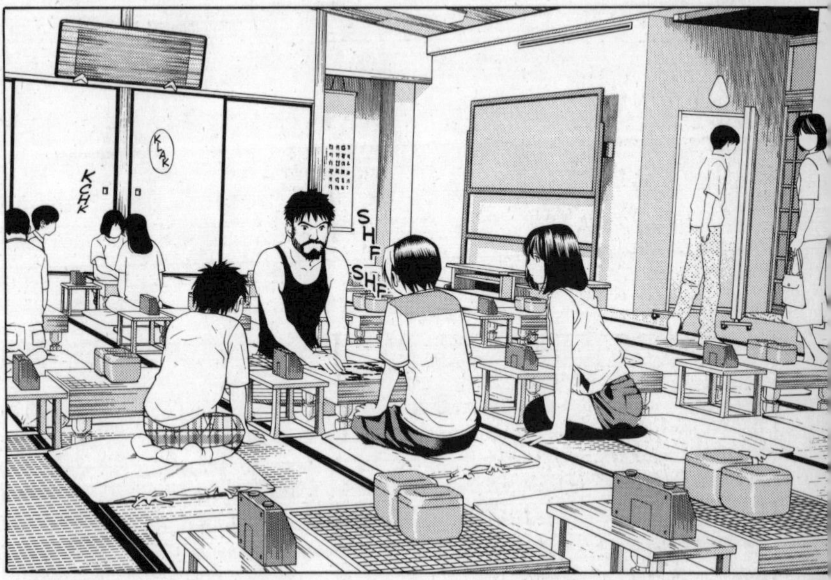
SHF
SHF
KLAK
KCHK

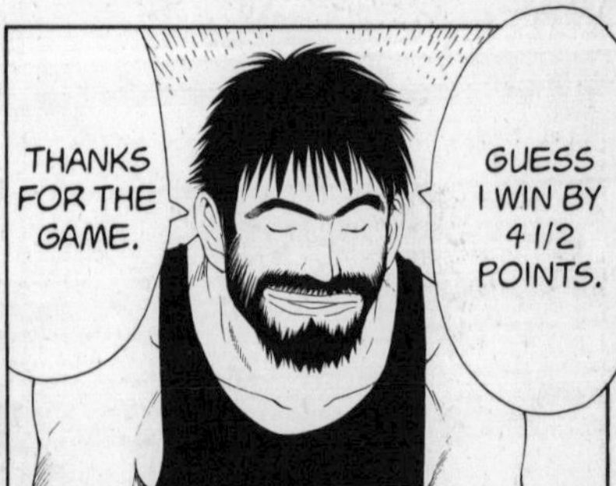
GUESS I WIN BY 4 1/2 POINTS.
THANKS FOR THE GAME.

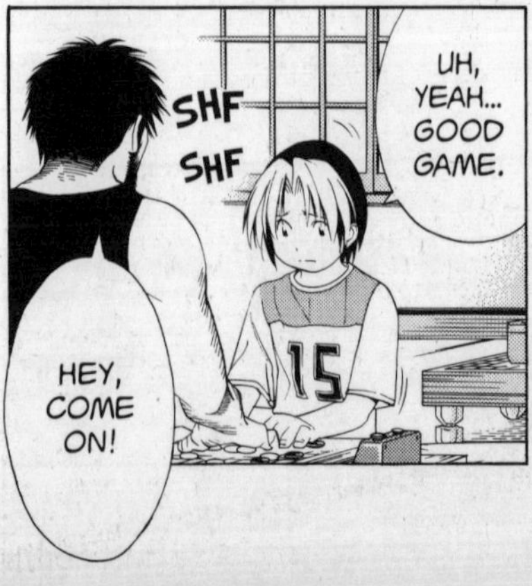
UH, YEAH... GOOD GAME.
SHF
SHF
HEY, COME ON!

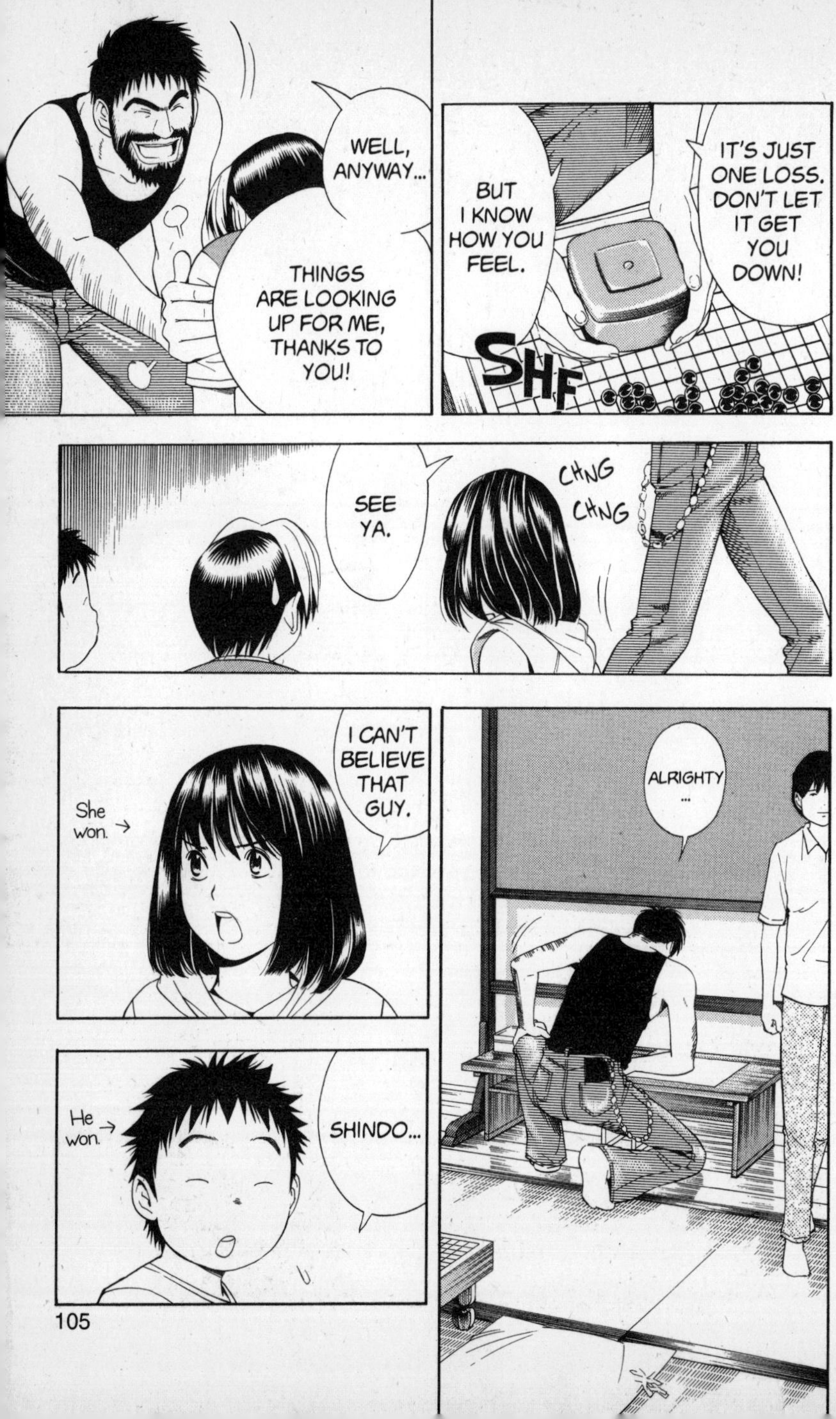
IT'S JUST ONE LOSS. DON'T LET IT GET YOU DOWN!
BUT I KNOW HOW YOU FEEL.
SHF
WELL, ANYWAY...
THINGS ARE LOOKING UP FOR ME, THANKS TO YOU!
CHNG CHNG
SEE YA.
ALRIGHTY ...
I CAN'T BELIEVE THAT GUY.
She won. →
SHINDO...
He won. →

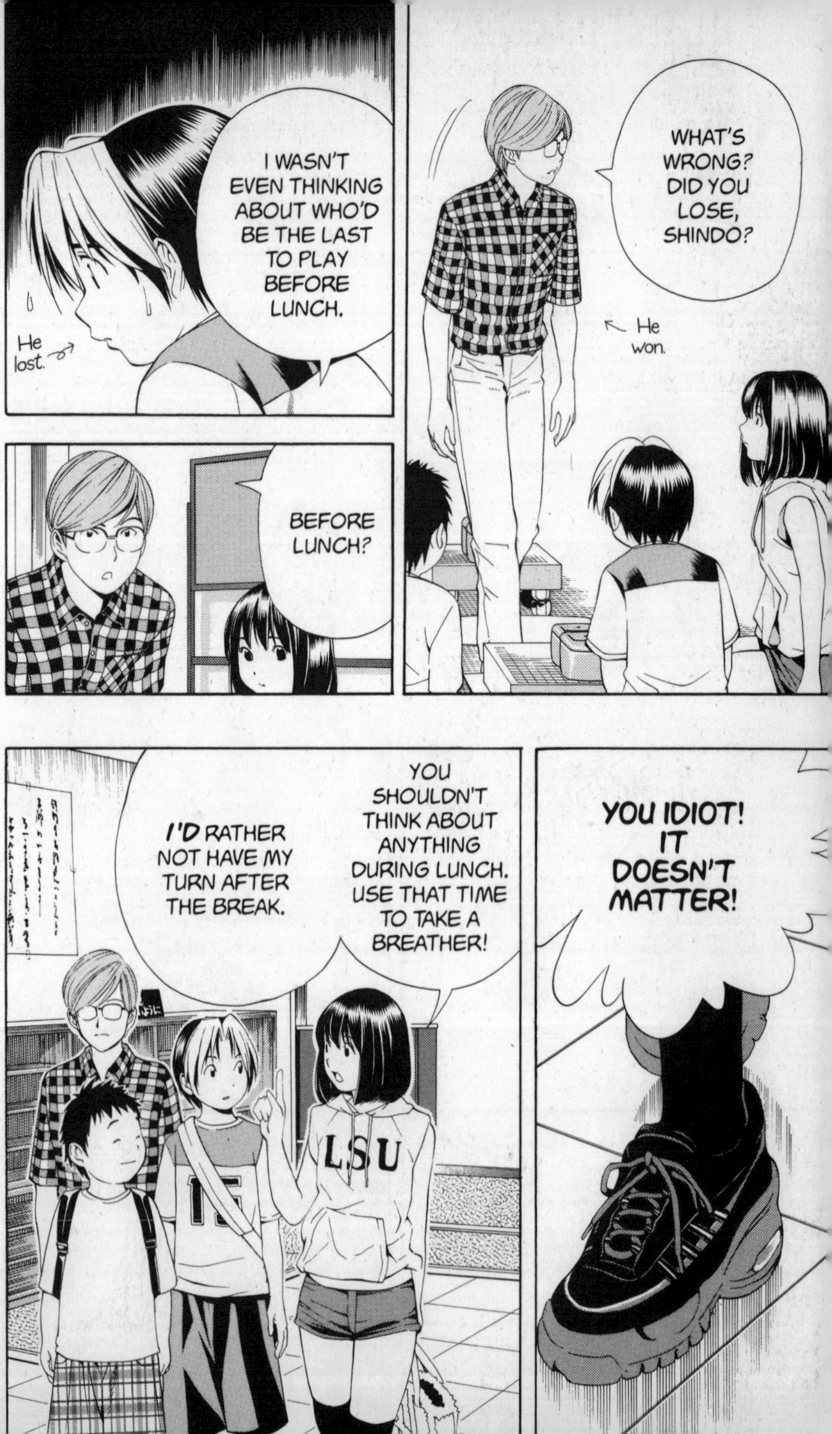
WHAT'S WRONG? DID YOU LOSE, SHINDO?
He won.
I WASN'T EVEN THINKING ABOUT WHO'D BE THE LAST TO PLAY BEFORE LUNCH.
He lost.
BEFORE LUNCH?
YOU IDIOT! IT DOESN'T MATTER!
YOU SHOULDN'T THINK ABOUT ANYTHING DURING LUNCH. USE THAT TIME TO TAKE A BREATHER!
I'D RATHER NOT HAVE MY TURN AFTER THE BREAK.
LSU

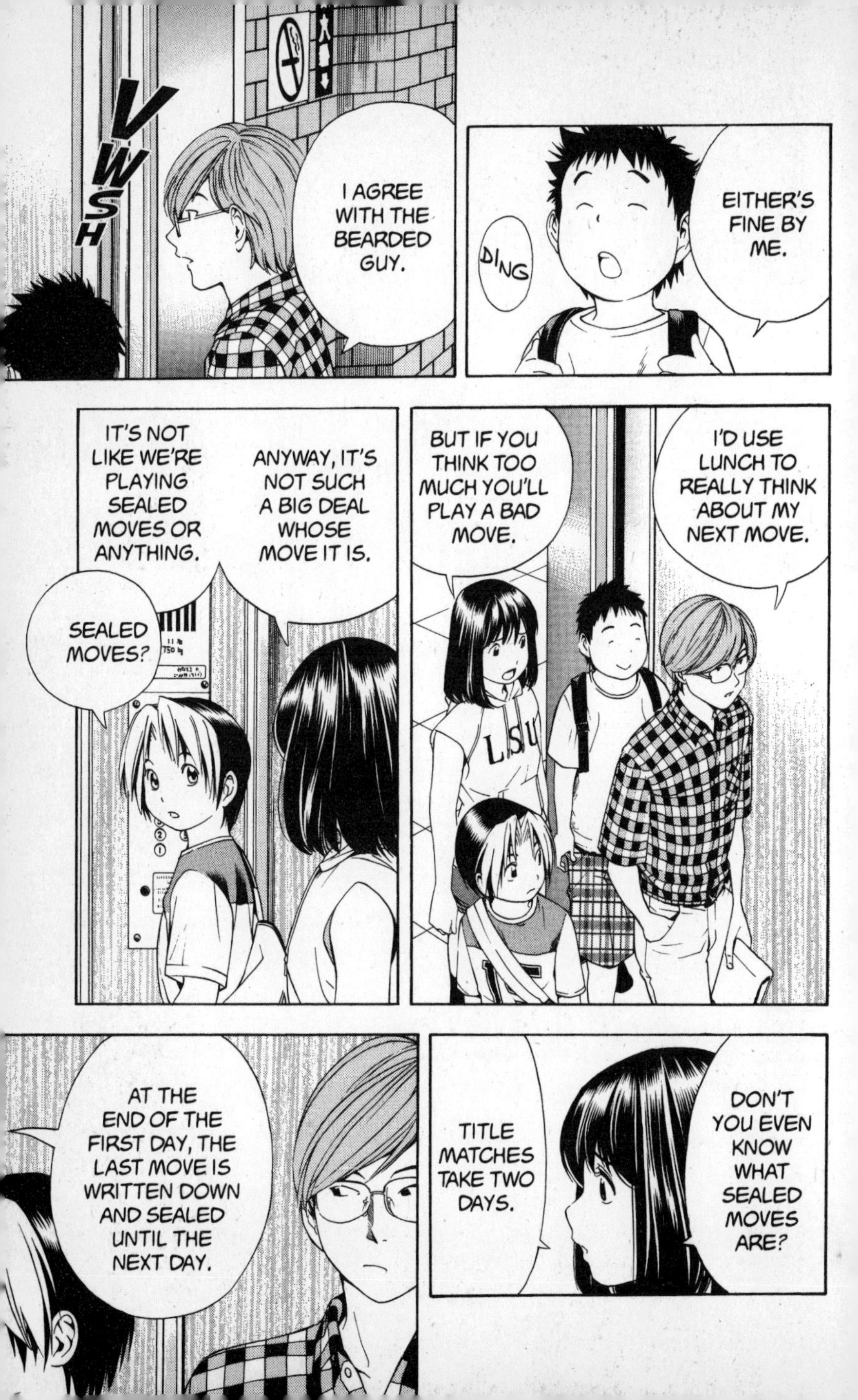
DING
EITHER'S FINE BY ME.
VWSH
I AGREE WITH THE BEARDED GUY.
I'D USE LUNCH TO REALLY THINK ABOUT MY NEXT MOVE.
BUT IF YOU THINK TOO MUCH YOU'LL PLAY A BAD MOVE.
LSU
ANYWAY, IT'S NOT SUCH A BIG DEAL WHOSE MOVE IT IS.
IT'S NOT LIKE WE'RE PLAYING SEALED MOVES OR ANYTHING.
SEALED MOVES?
DON'T YOU EVEN KNOW WHAT SEALED MOVES ARE?
TITLE MATCHES TAKE TWO DAYS.
AT THE END OF THE FIRST DAY, THE LAST MOVE IS WRITTEN DOWN AND SEALED UNTIL THE NEXT DAY.

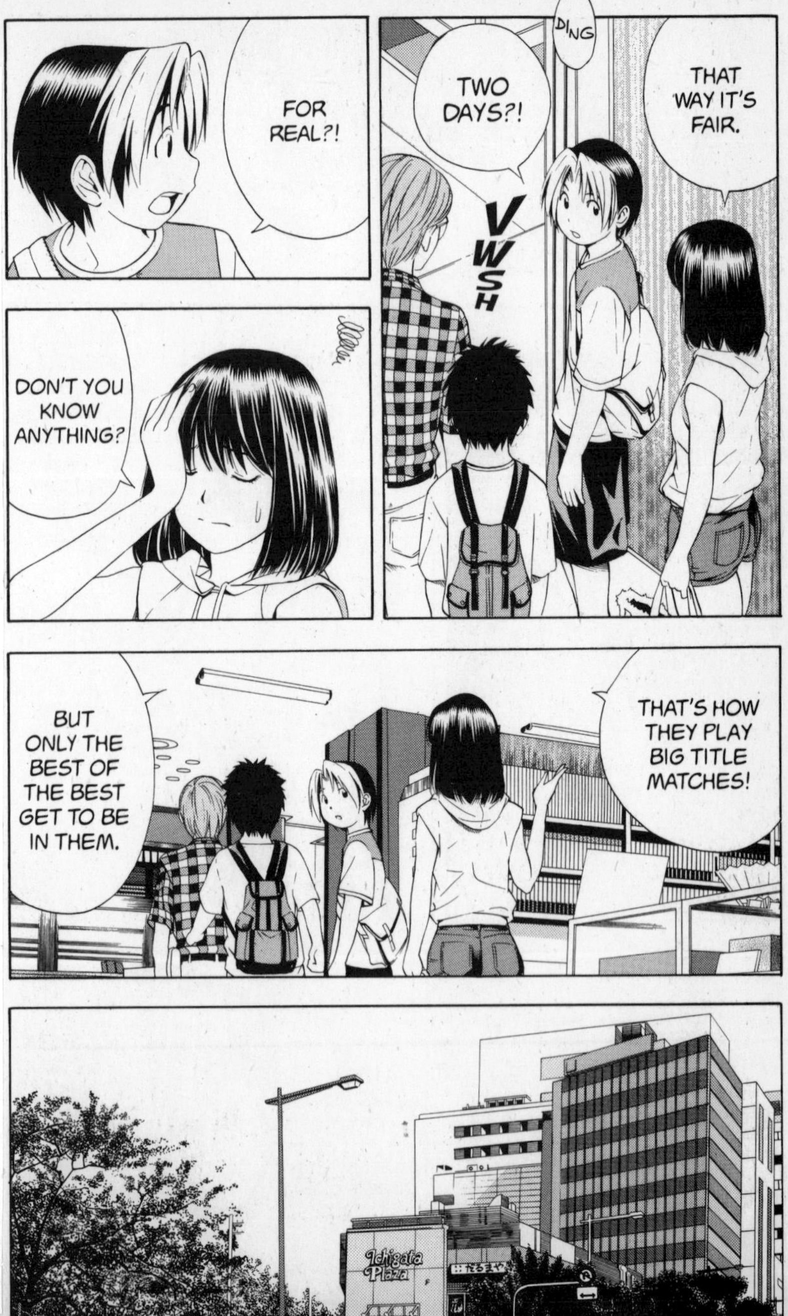
THAT WAY IT'S FAIR.
DING
TWO DAYS?!
VWSH
FOR REAL?!
DON'T YOU KNOW ANYTHING?
THAT'S HOW THEY PLAY BIG TITLE MATCHES!
BUT ONLY THE BEST OF THE BEST GET TO BE IN THEM.
Ichigata Plaza

READ THIS WAY

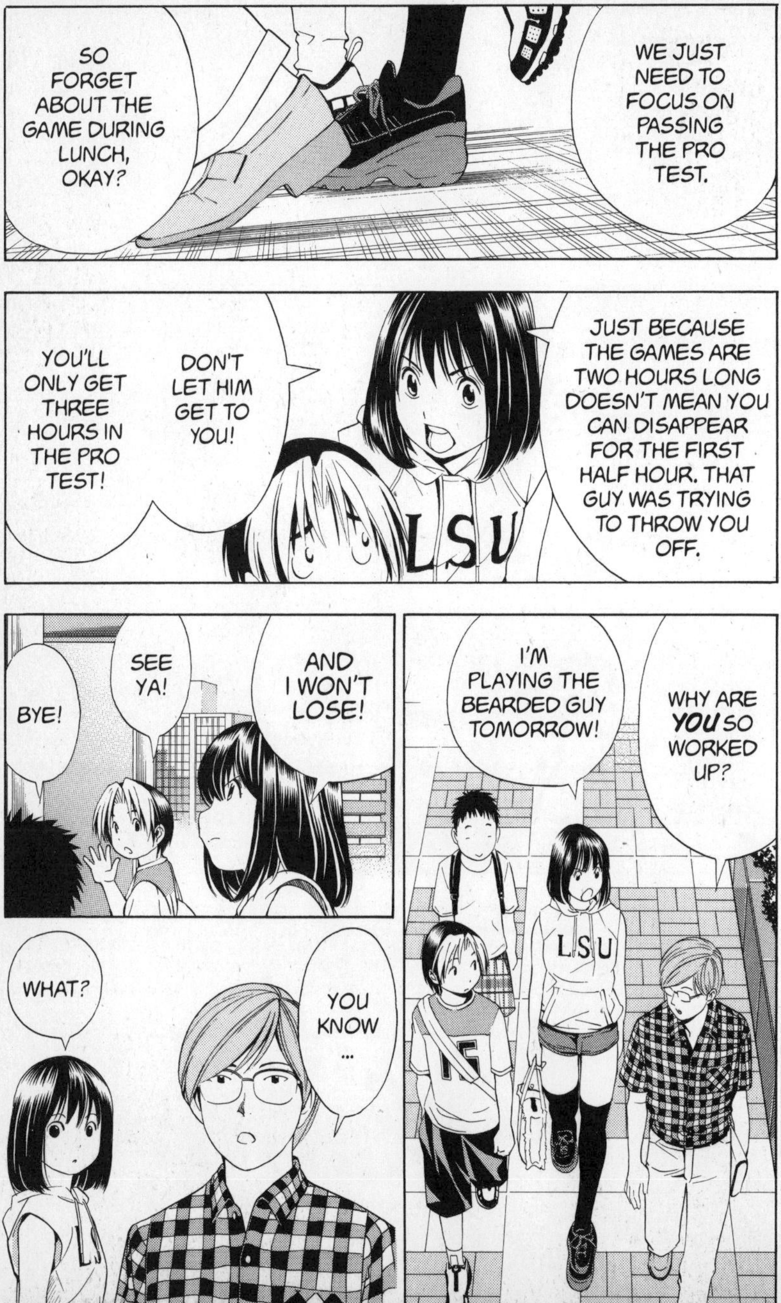

WE JUST NEED TO FOCUS ON PASSING THE PRO TEST.
SO FORGET ABOUT THE GAME DURING LUNCH, OKAY?
JUST BECAUSE THE GAMES ARE TWO HOURS LONG DOESN'T MEAN YOU CAN DISAPPEAR FOR THE FIRST HALF HOUR. THAT GUY WAS TRYING TO THROW YOU OFF.
DON'T LET HIM GET TO YOU!
YOU'LL ONLY GET THREE HOURS IN THE PRO TEST!
WHY ARE ***YOU*** SO WORKED UP?
I'M PLAYING THE BEARDED GUY TOMORROW!
AND I WON'T LOSE!
SEE YA!
BYE!
YOU KNOW ...
WHAT?

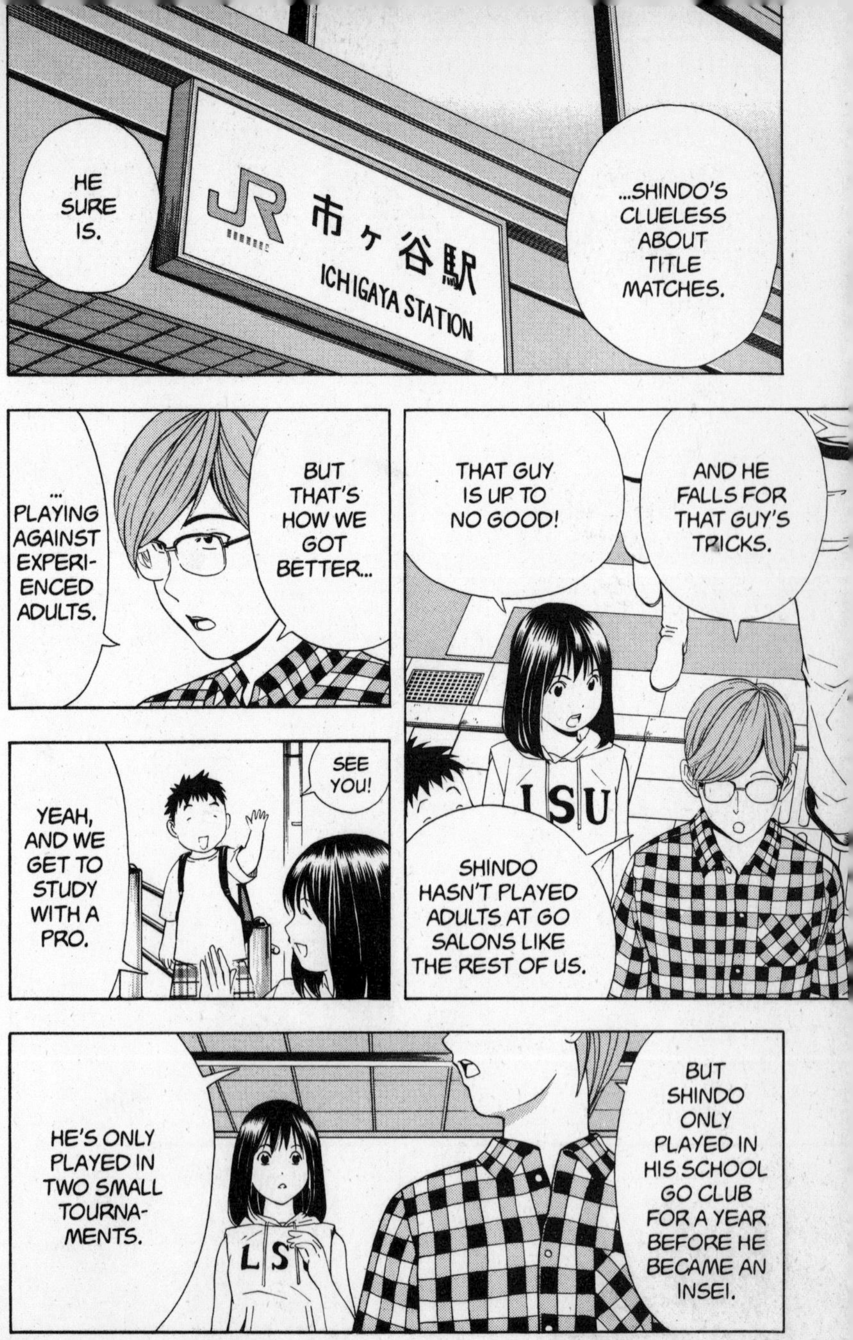
...SHINDO'S CLUELESS ABOUT TITLE MATCHES.
JR
市ヶ谷駅
ICHIGAYA STATION
HE SURE IS.
AND HE FALLS FOR THAT GUY'S TRICKS.
THAT GUY IS UP TO NO GOOD!
SHINDO HASN'T PLAYED ADULTS AT GO SALONS LIKE THE REST OF US.
BUT THAT'S HOW WE GOT BETTER...
...PLAYING AGAINST EXPERIENCED ADULTS.
SEE YOU!
YEAH, AND WE GET TO STUDY WITH A PRO.
BUT SHINDO ONLY PLAYED IN HIS SCHOOL GO CLUB FOR A YEAR BEFORE HE BECAME AN INSEI.
HE'S ONLY PLAYED IN TWO SMALL TOURNAMENTS.

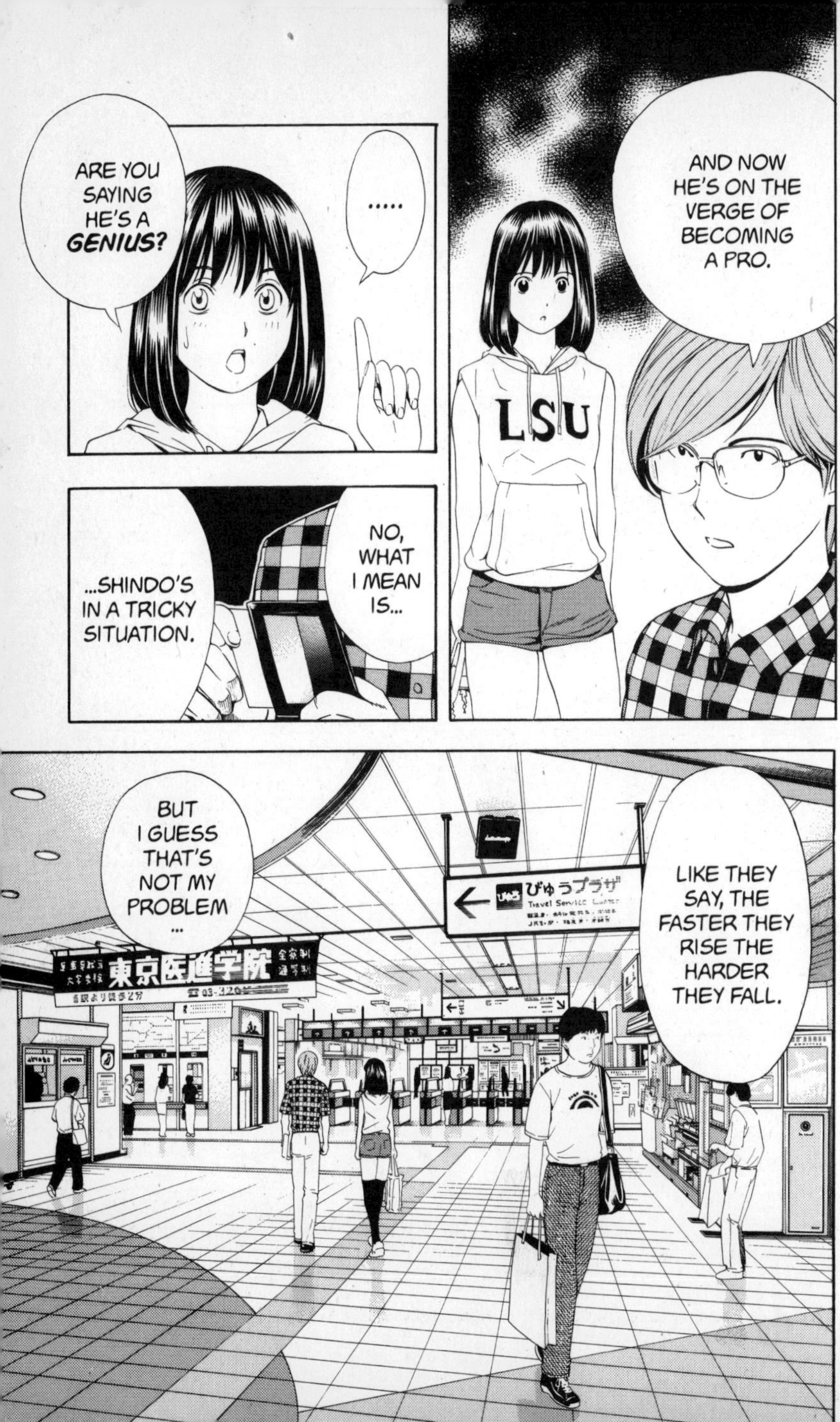
AND NOW HE'S ON THE VERGE OF BECOMING A PRO.
.....
ARE YOU SAYING HE'S A **GENIUS?**
NO, WHAT I MEAN IS...
...SHINDO'S IN A TRICKY SITUATION.
LSU
LIKE THEY SAY, THE FASTER THEY RISE THE HARDER THEY FALL.
BUT I GUESS THAT'S NOT MY PROBLEM ...
びゅうプラザ
東京医進学院

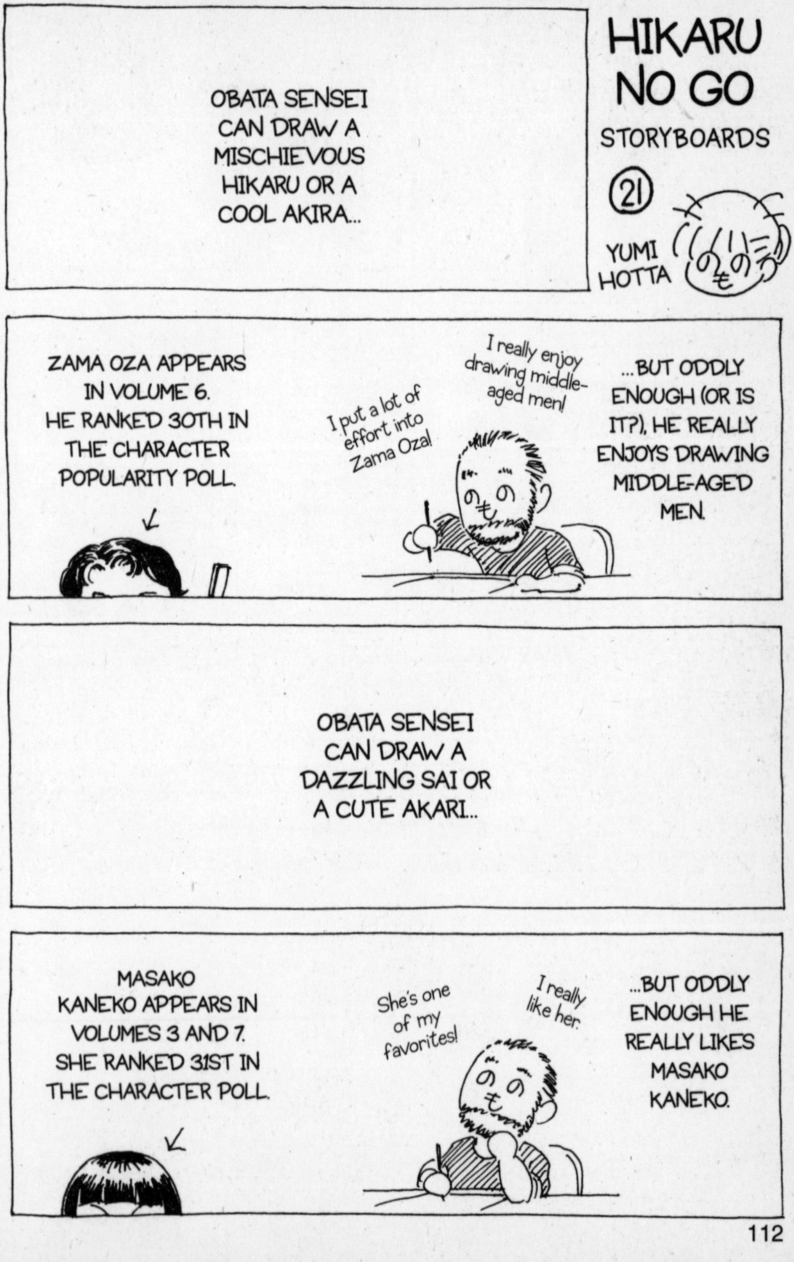
HIKARU NO GO
STORYBOARDS
21
YUMI HOTTA
OBATA SENSEI CAN DRAW A MISCHIEVOUS HIKARU OR A COOL AKIRA...
...BUT ODDLY ENOUGH (OR IS IT?), HE REALLY ENJOYS DRAWING MIDDLE-AGED MEN.
I really enjoy drawing middle-aged men!
I put a lot of effort into Zama Oza!
ZAMA OZA APPEARS IN VOLUME 6. HE RANKED 30TH IN THE CHARACTER POPULARITY POLL.
OBATA SENSEI CAN DRAW A DAZZLING SAI OR A CUTE AKARI...
...BUT ODDLY ENOUGH HE REALLY LIKES MASAKO KANEKO.
I really like her.
She's one of my favorites!
MASAKO KANEKO APPEARS IN VOLUMES 3 AND 7. SHE RANKED 31ST IN THE CHARACTER POLL.

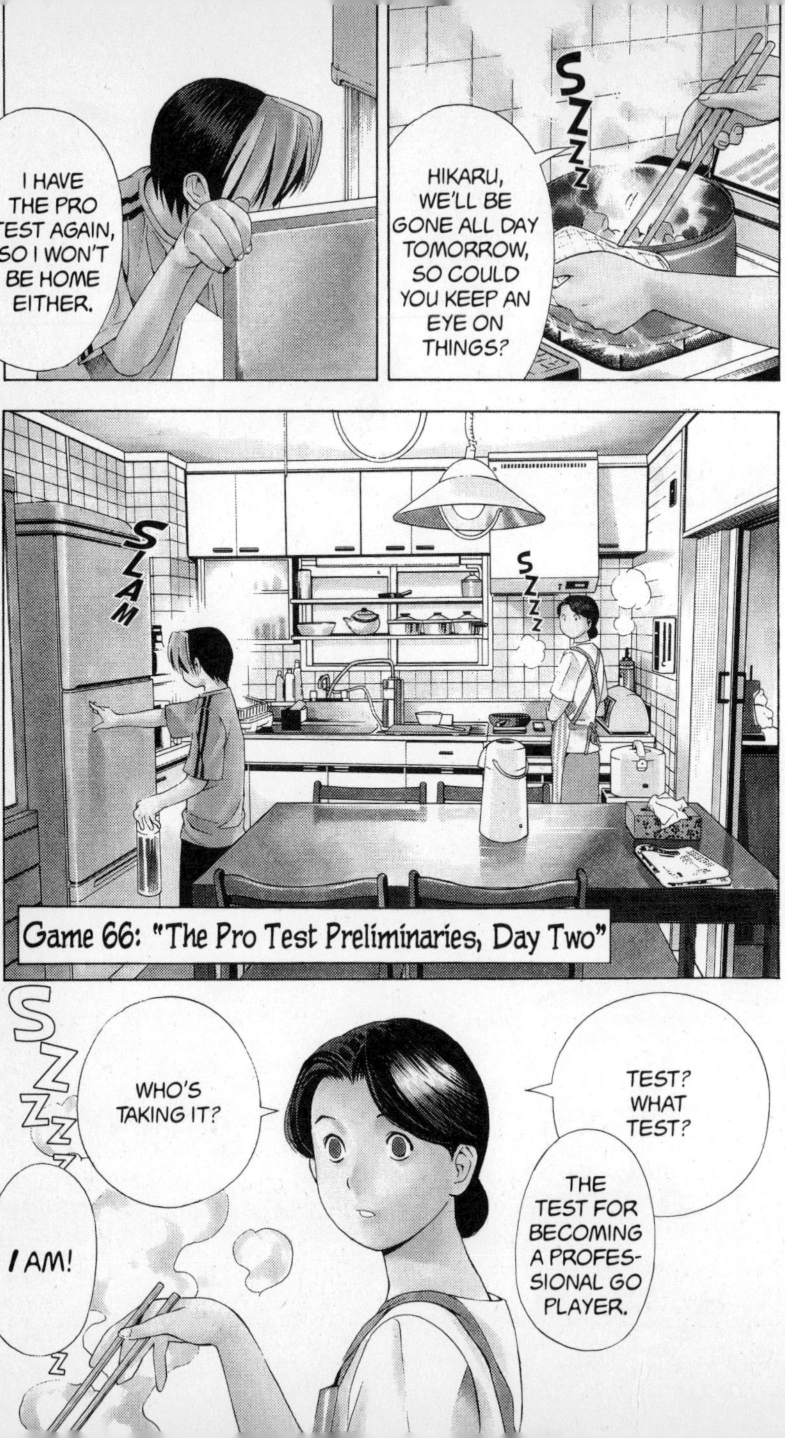
SZZZ
HIKARU, WE'LL BE GONE ALL DAY TOMORROW, SO COULD YOU KEEP AN EYE ON THINGS?
I HAVE THE PRO TEST AGAIN, SO I WON'T BE HOME EITHER.
SZZZ
SLAM
Game 66: "The Pro Test Preliminaries, Day Two"
SZZZ
TEST? WHAT TEST?
THE TEST FOR BECOMING A PROFES-SIONAL GO PLAYER.
WHO'S TAKING IT?
I AM!

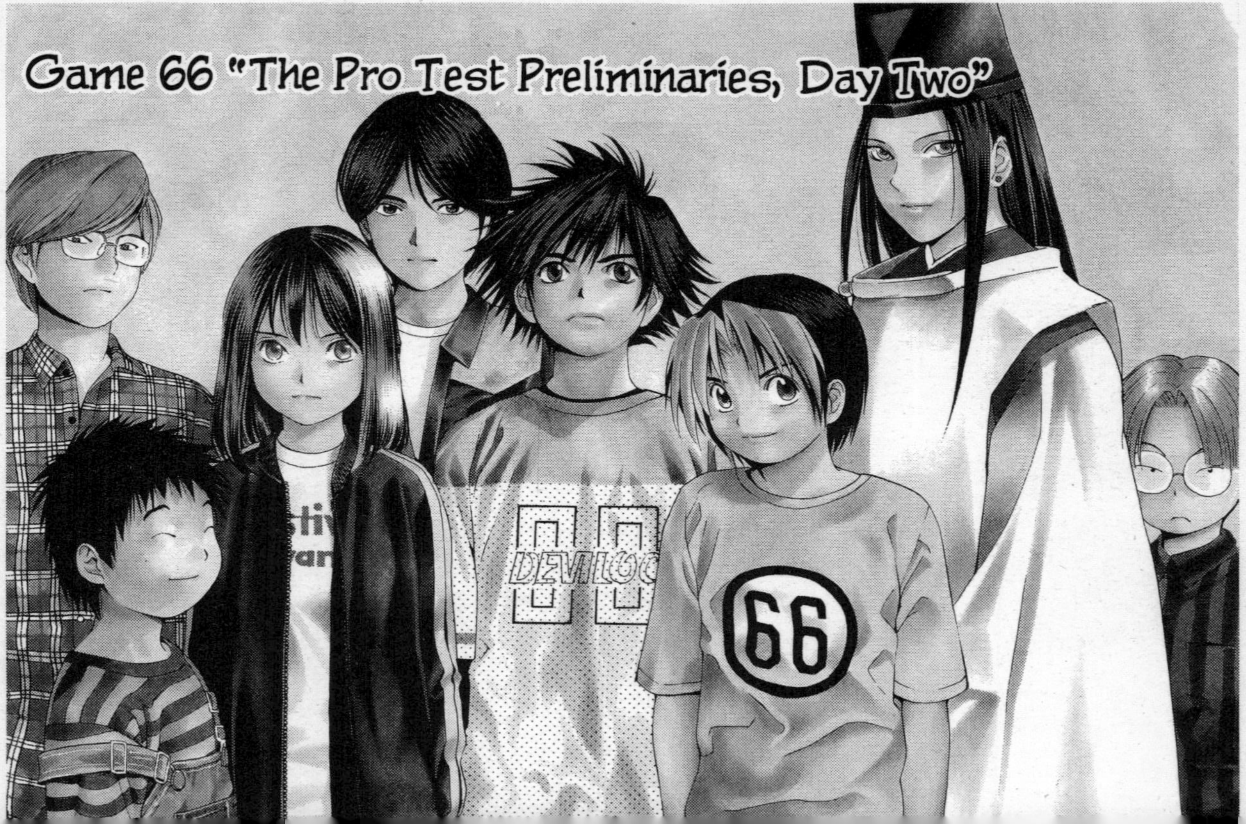
Game 66 "The Pro Test Preliminaries, Day Two"
66

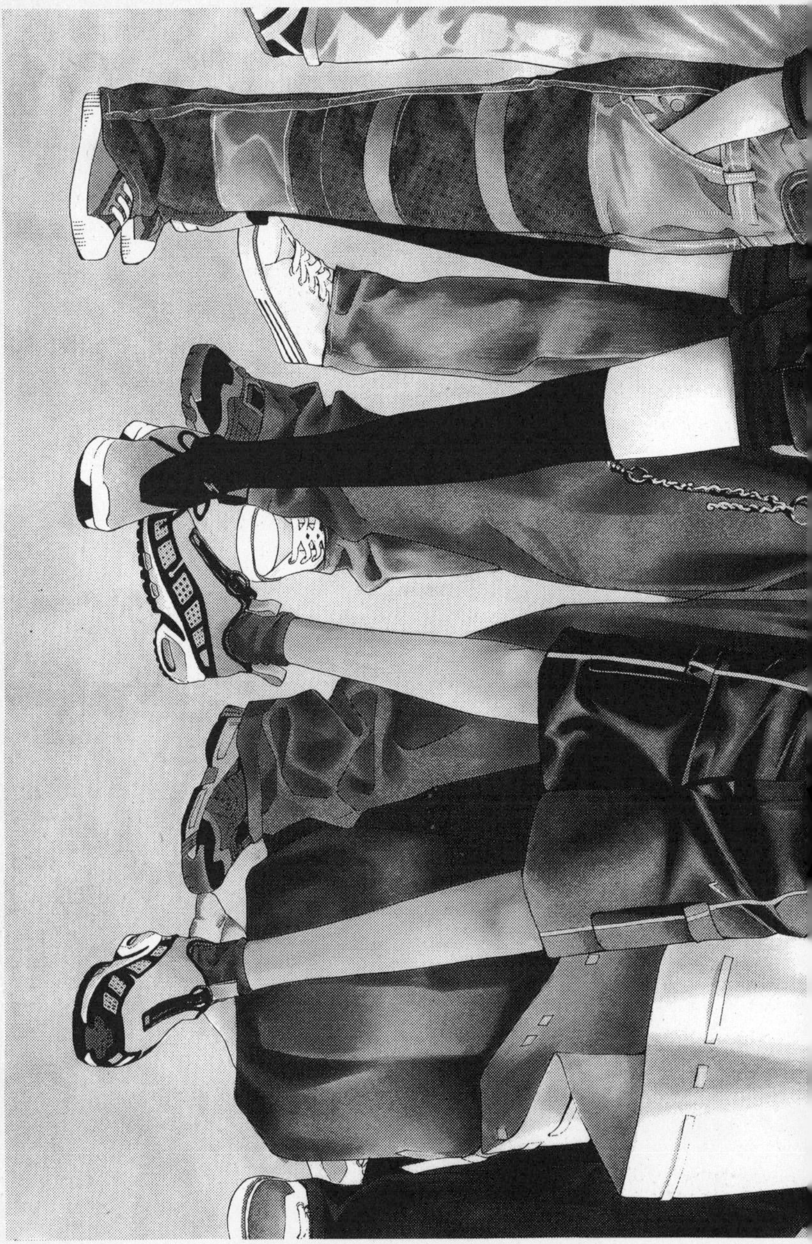

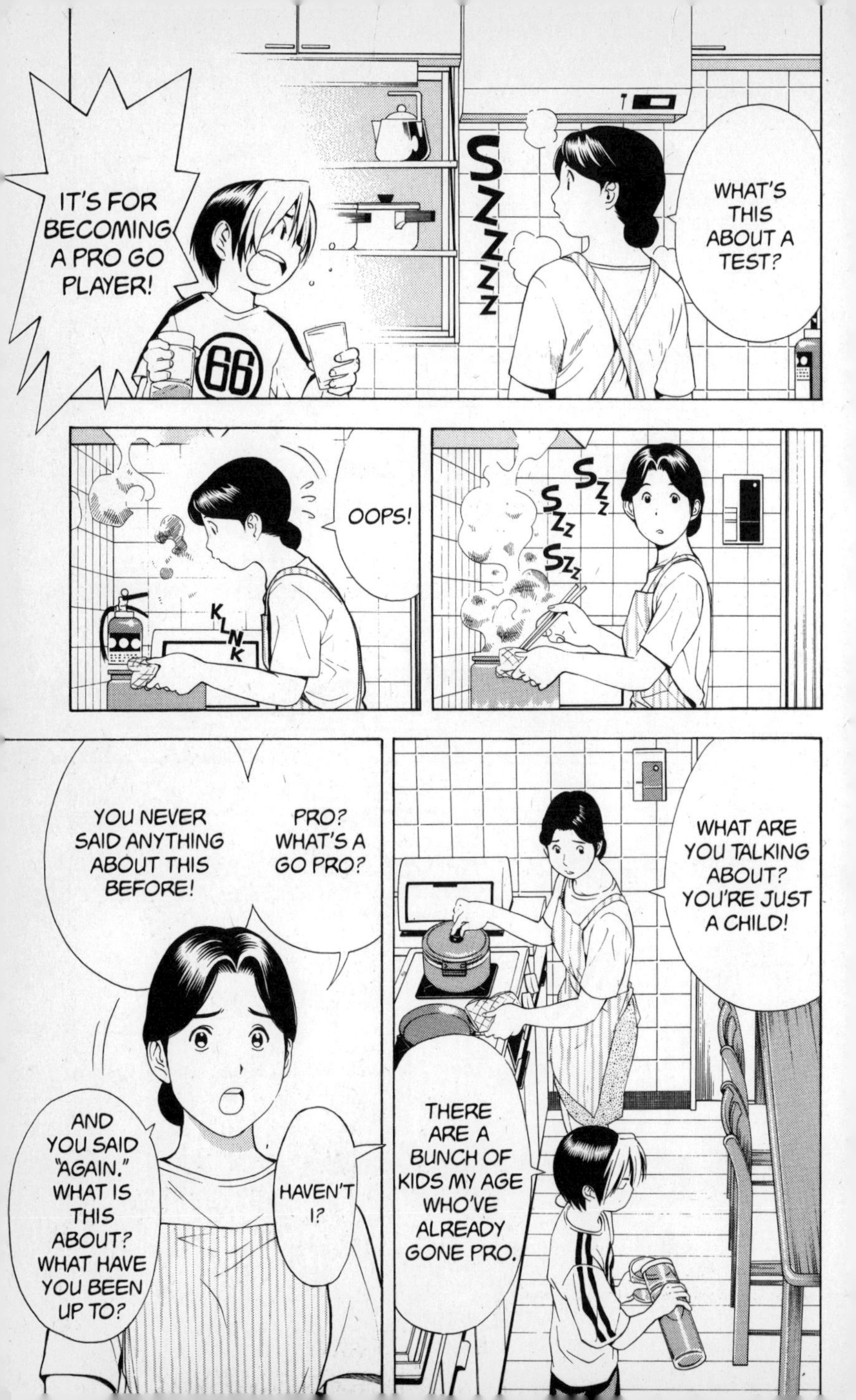
WHAT'S THIS ABOUT A TEST?
SZZZZZ
IT'S FOR BECOMING A PRO GO PLAYER!
SZZ SZZ SZZ
OOPS!
KLNK
WHAT ARE YOU TALKING ABOUT? YOU'RE JUST A CHILD!
THERE ARE A BUNCH OF KIDS MY AGE WHO'VE ALREADY GONE PRO.
PRO? WHAT'S A GO PRO?
YOU NEVER SAID ANYTHING ABOUT THIS BEFORE!
HAVEN'T I?
AND YOU SAID "AGAIN." WHAT IS THIS ABOUT? WHAT HAVE YOU BEEN UP TO?

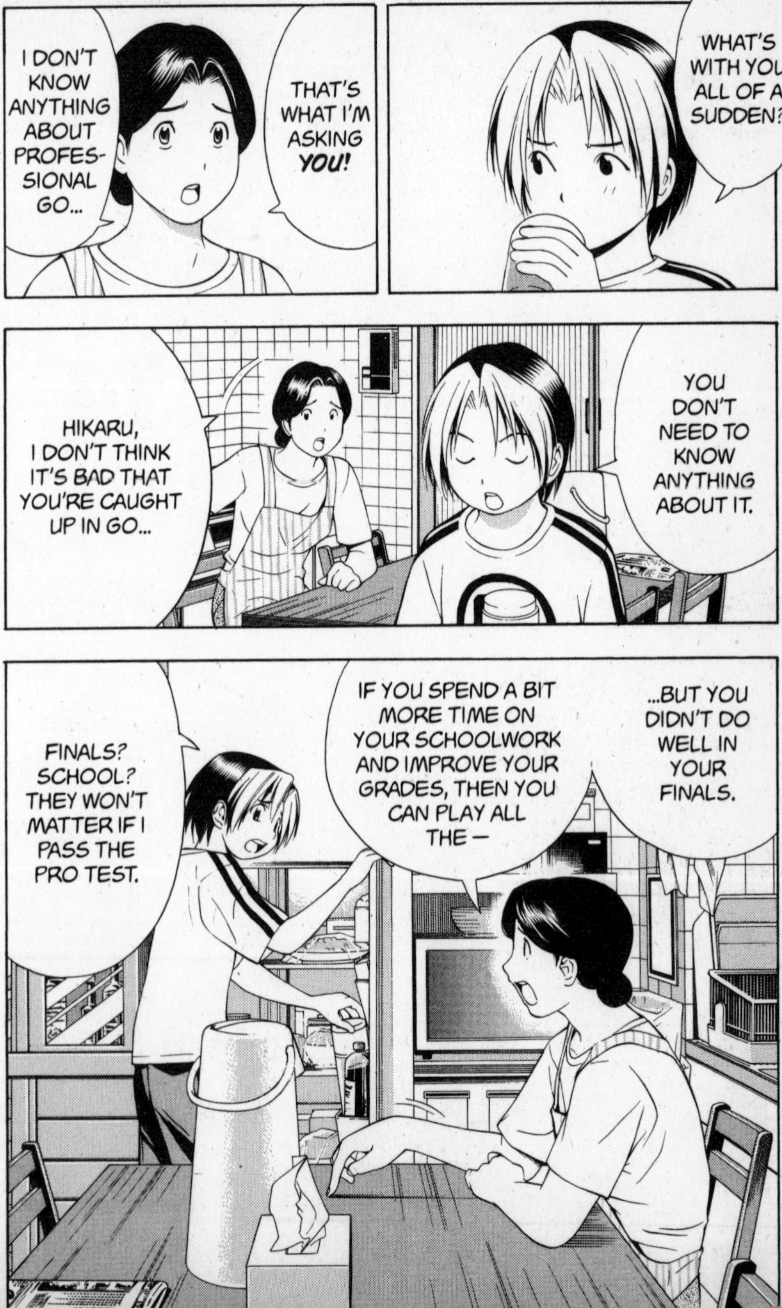
WHAT'S WITH YOU ALL OF A SUDDEN?
THAT'S WHAT I'M ASKING *YOU!*
I DON'T KNOW ANYTHING ABOUT PROFES-SIONAL GO...
YOU DON'T NEED TO KNOW ANYTHING ABOUT IT.
HIKARU, I DON'T THINK IT'S BAD THAT YOU'RE CAUGHT UP IN GO...
...BUT YOU DIDN'T DO WELL IN YOUR FINALS.
IF YOU SPEND A BIT MORE TIME ON YOUR SCHOOLWORK AND IMPROVE YOUR GRADES, THEN YOU CAN PLAY ALL THE —
FINALS? SCHOOL? THEY WON'T MATTER IF I PASS THE PRO TEST.

READ THIS WAY

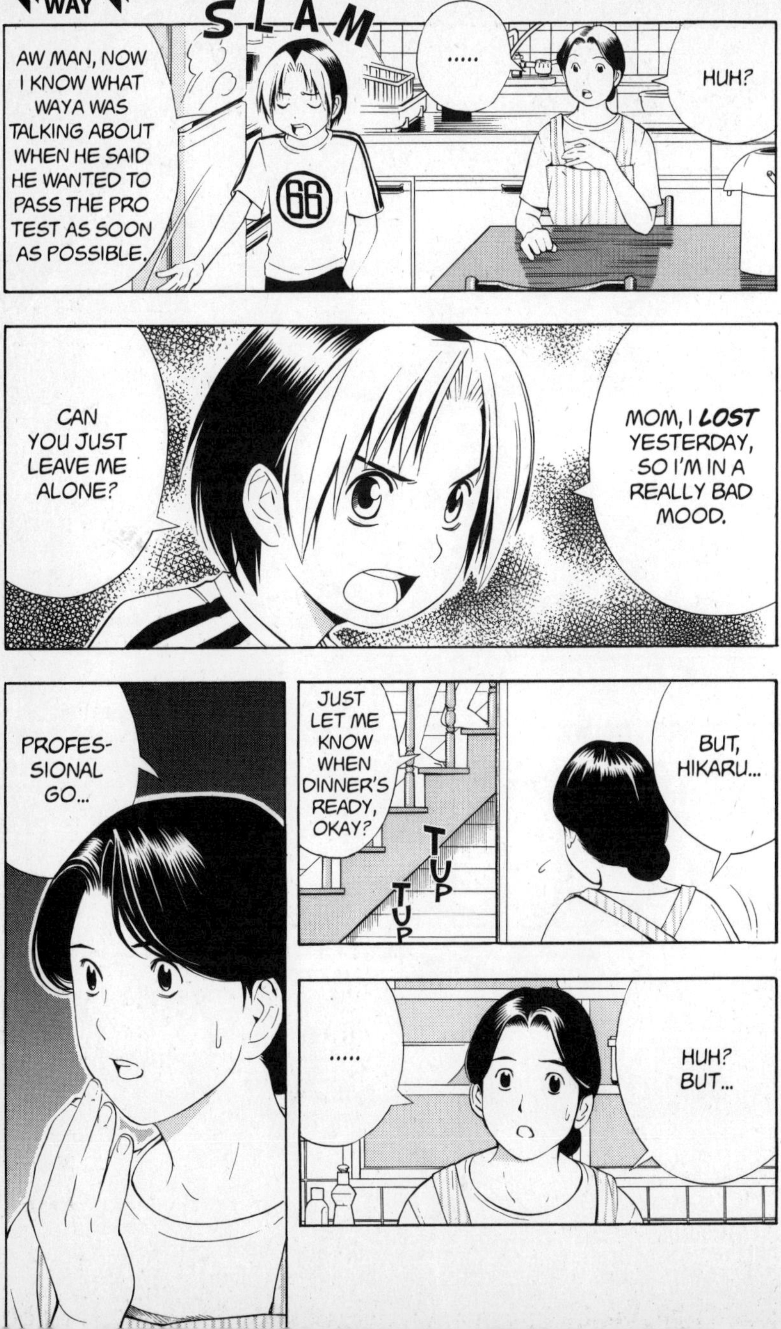
SLAM
HUH?
.....
AW MAN, NOW I KNOW WHAT WAYA WAS TALKING ABOUT WHEN HE SAID HE WANTED TO PASS THE PRO TEST AS SOON AS POSSIBLE.
MOM, I **LOST** YESTERDAY, SO I'M IN A REALLY BAD MOOD.
CAN YOU JUST LEAVE ME ALONE?
BUT, HIKARU...
JUST LET ME KNOW WHEN DINNER'S READY, OKAY?
TUP
TUP
HUH? BUT...
.....
PROFES- SIONAL GO...

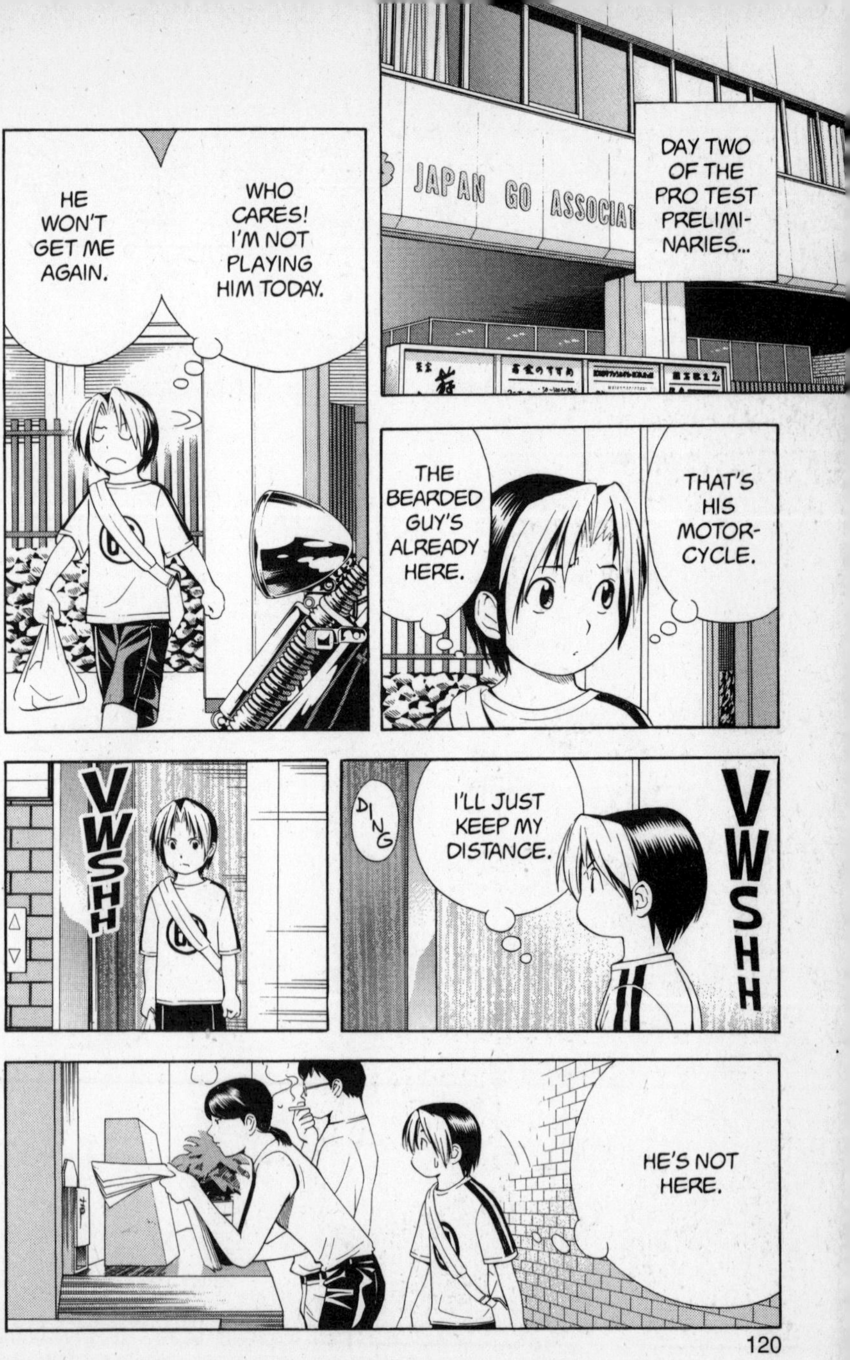
JAPAN GO ASSOCIAT
DAY TWO OF THE PRO TEST PRELIMINARIES...
THAT'S HIS MOTORCYCLE.
THE BEARDED GUY'S ALREADY HERE.
WHO CARES! I'M NOT PLAYING HIM TODAY.
HE WON'T GET ME AGAIN.
VWSHH
I'LL JUST KEEP MY DISTANCE.
DING
VWSHH
HE'S NOT HERE.

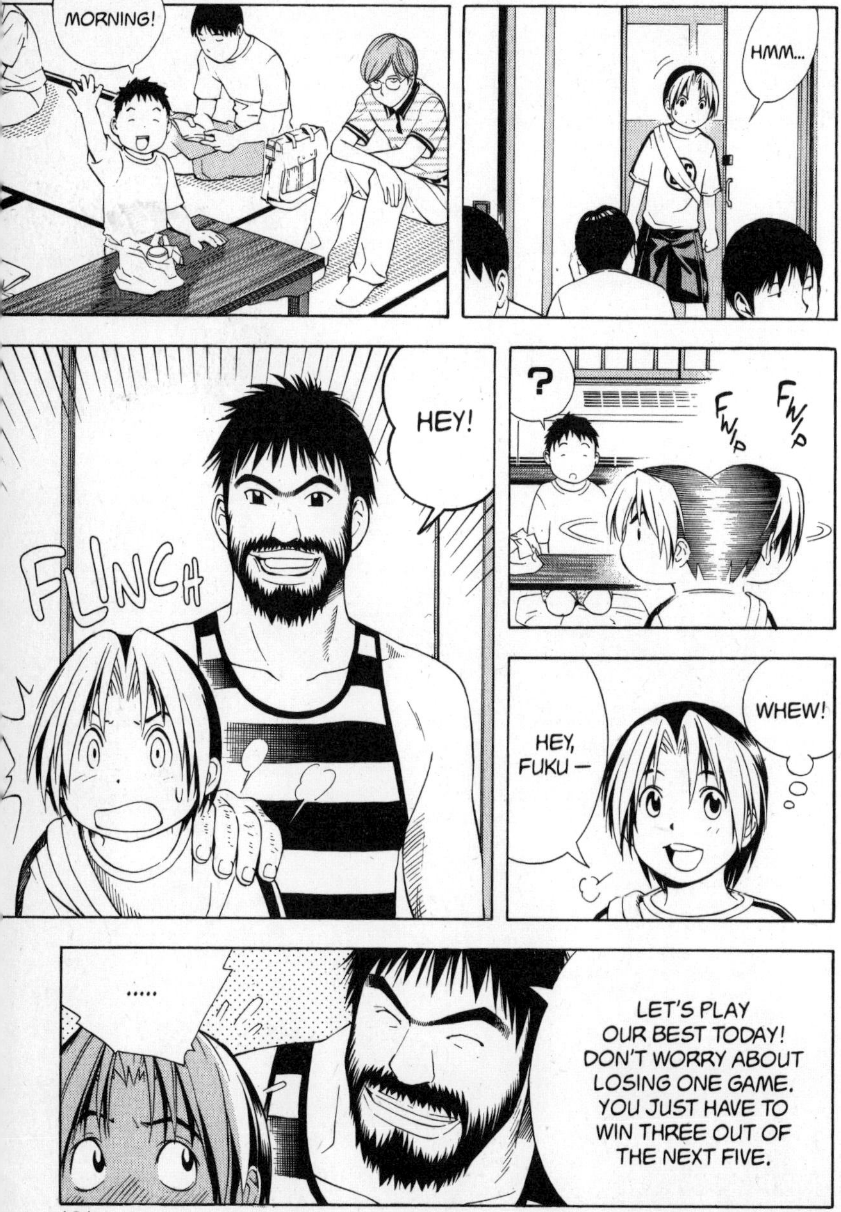
HMM...
MORNING!
?
FWIP
FWIP
WHEW!
HEY, FUKU—
HEY!
FLINCH
LET'S PLAY OUR BEST TODAY! DON'T WORRY ABOUT LOSING ONE GAME. YOU JUST HAVE TO WIN THREE OUT OF THE NEXT FIVE.
.....

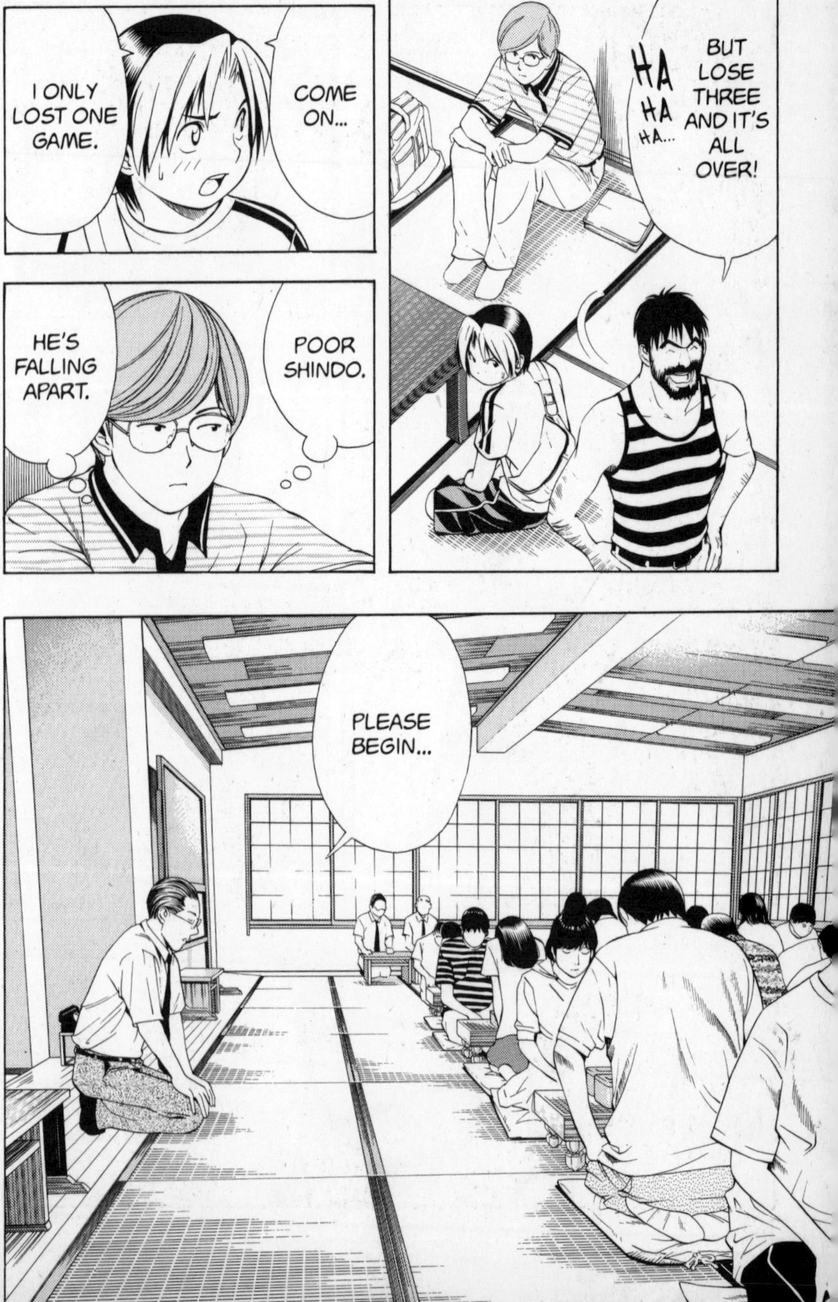
BUT LOSE THREE AND IT'S ALL OVER!
HA HA HA...
COME ON...
I ONLY LOST ONE GAME.
POOR SHINDO.
HE'S FALLING APART.
PLEASE BEGIN...

READ THIS WAY

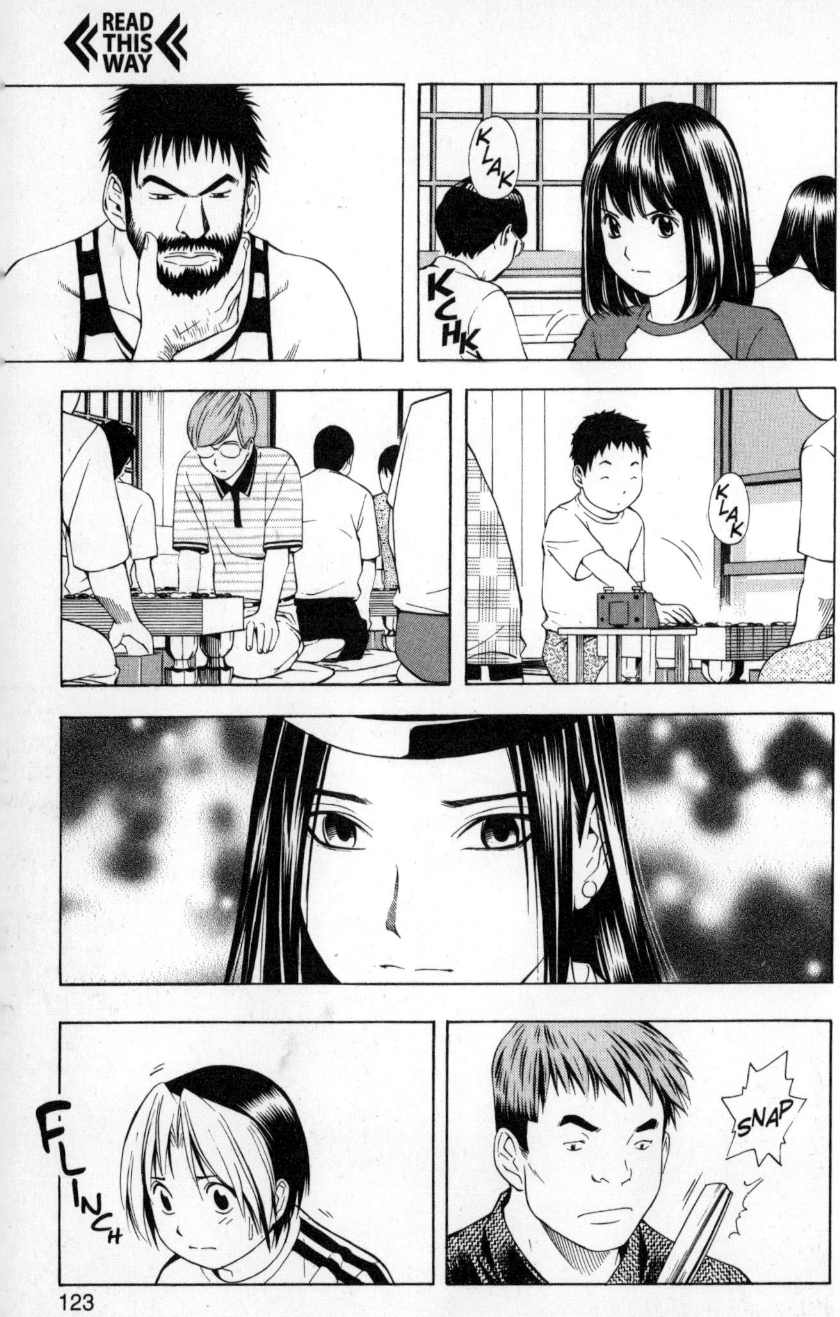
KLAK
KCHK
KLAK
SNAP
FLINCH

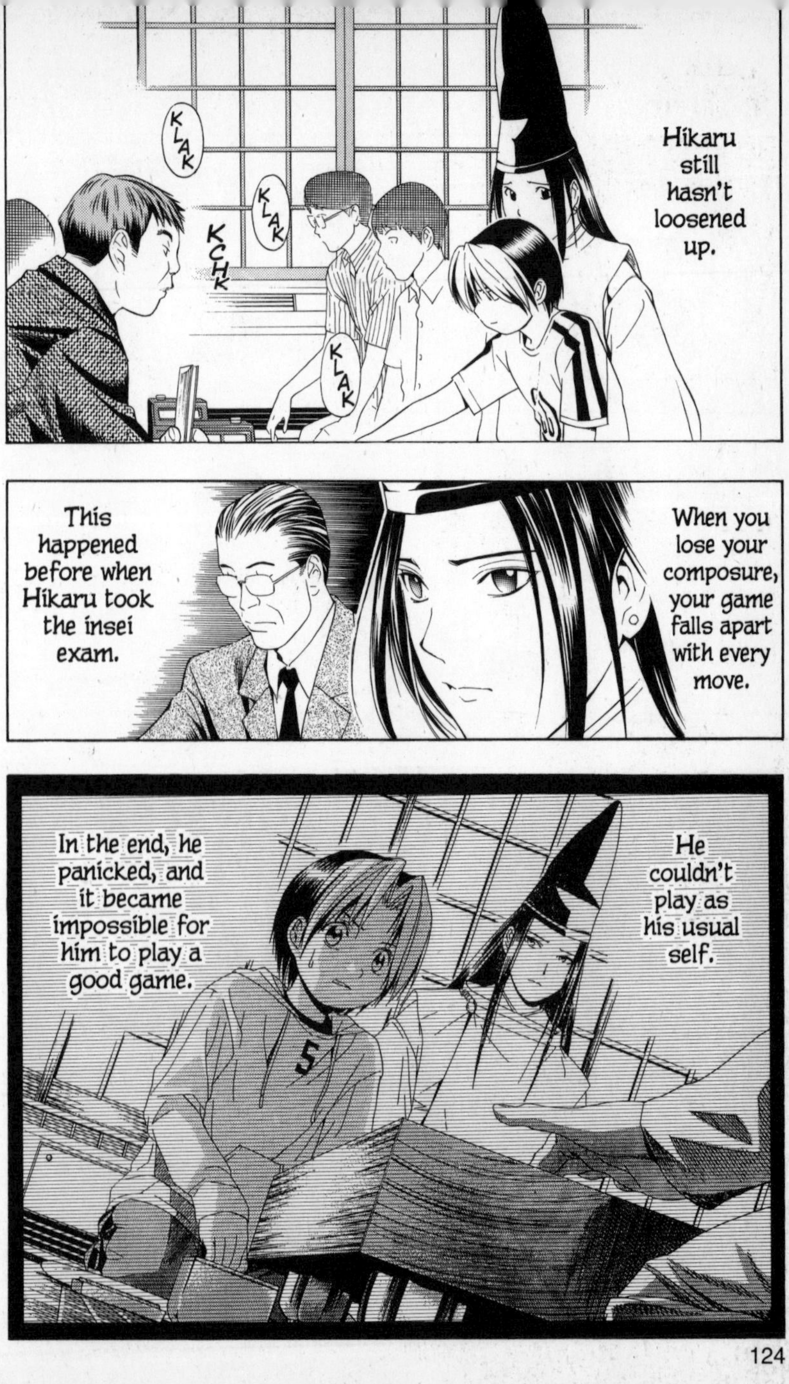
Hikaru still hasn't loosened up.
KLAK
KLAK
KCHK
KLAK
When you lose your composure, your game falls apart with every move.
This happened before when Hikaru took the insei exam.
He couldn't play as his usual self.
In the end, he panicked, and it became impossible for him to play a good game.

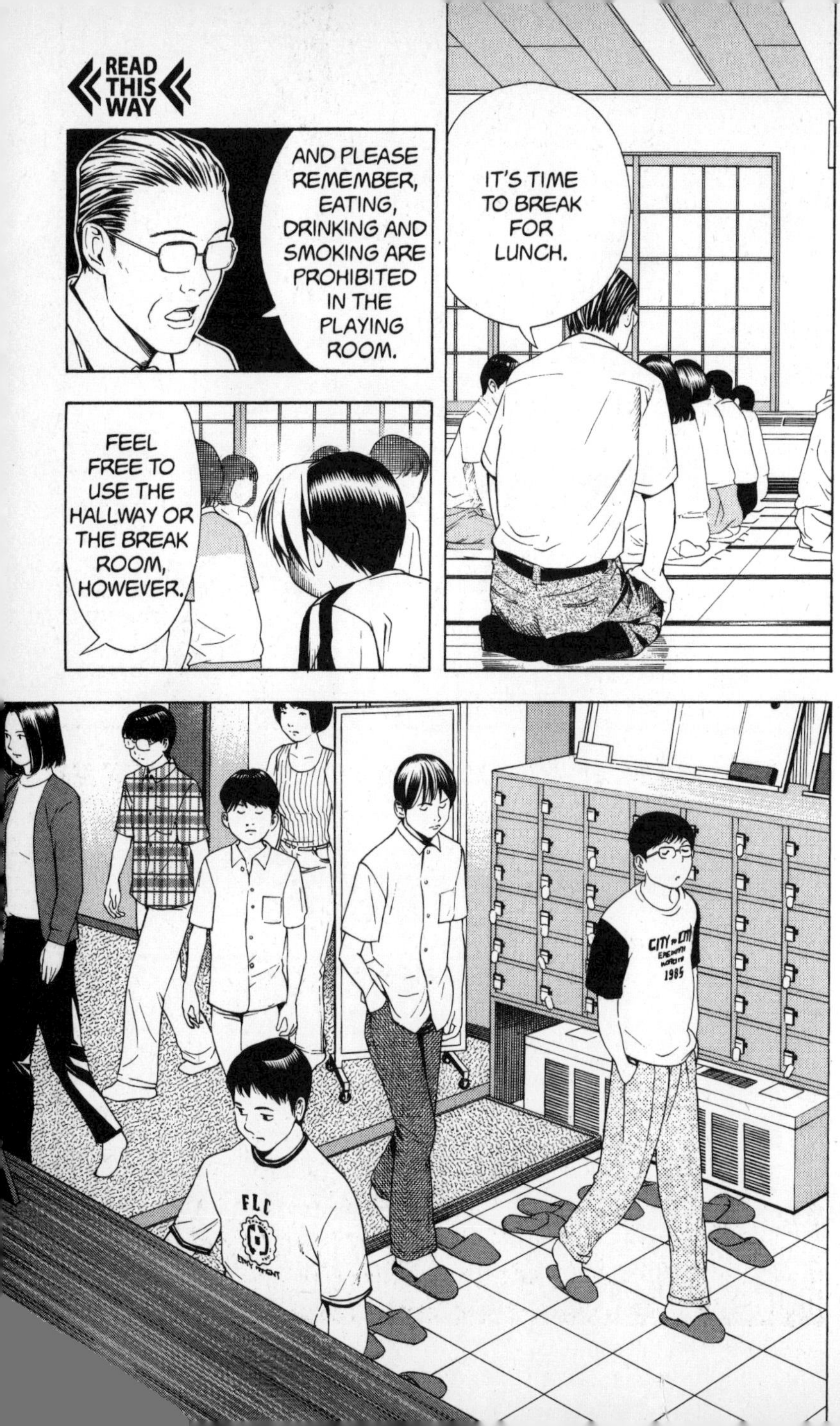
READ THIS WAY
IT'S TIME TO BREAK FOR LUNCH.
AND PLEASE REMEMBER, EATING, DRINKING AND SMOKING ARE PROHIBITED IN THE PLAYING ROOM.
FEEL FREE TO USE THE HALLWAY OR THE BREAK ROOM, HOWEVER.

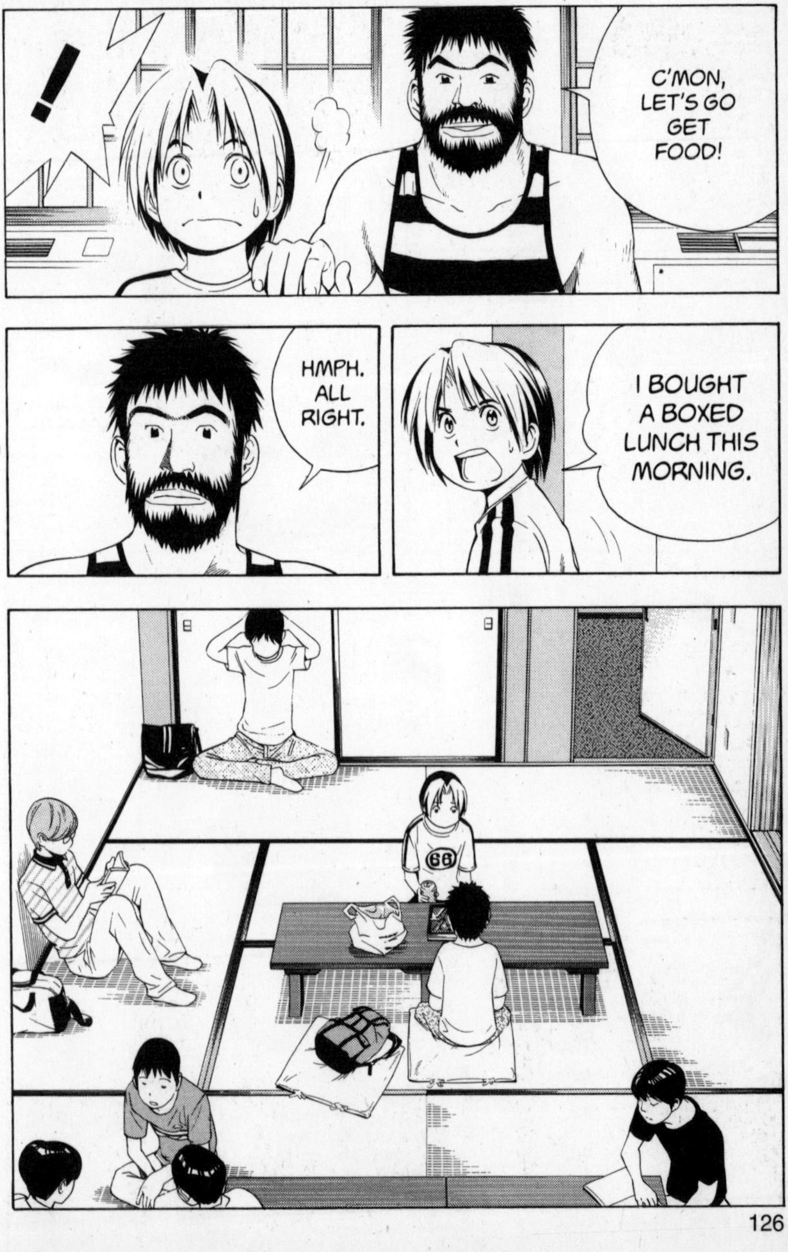
C'MON, LET'S GO GET FOOD!
!
I BOUGHT A BOXED LUNCH THIS MORNING.
HMPH. ALL RIGHT.
66

READ THIS WAY

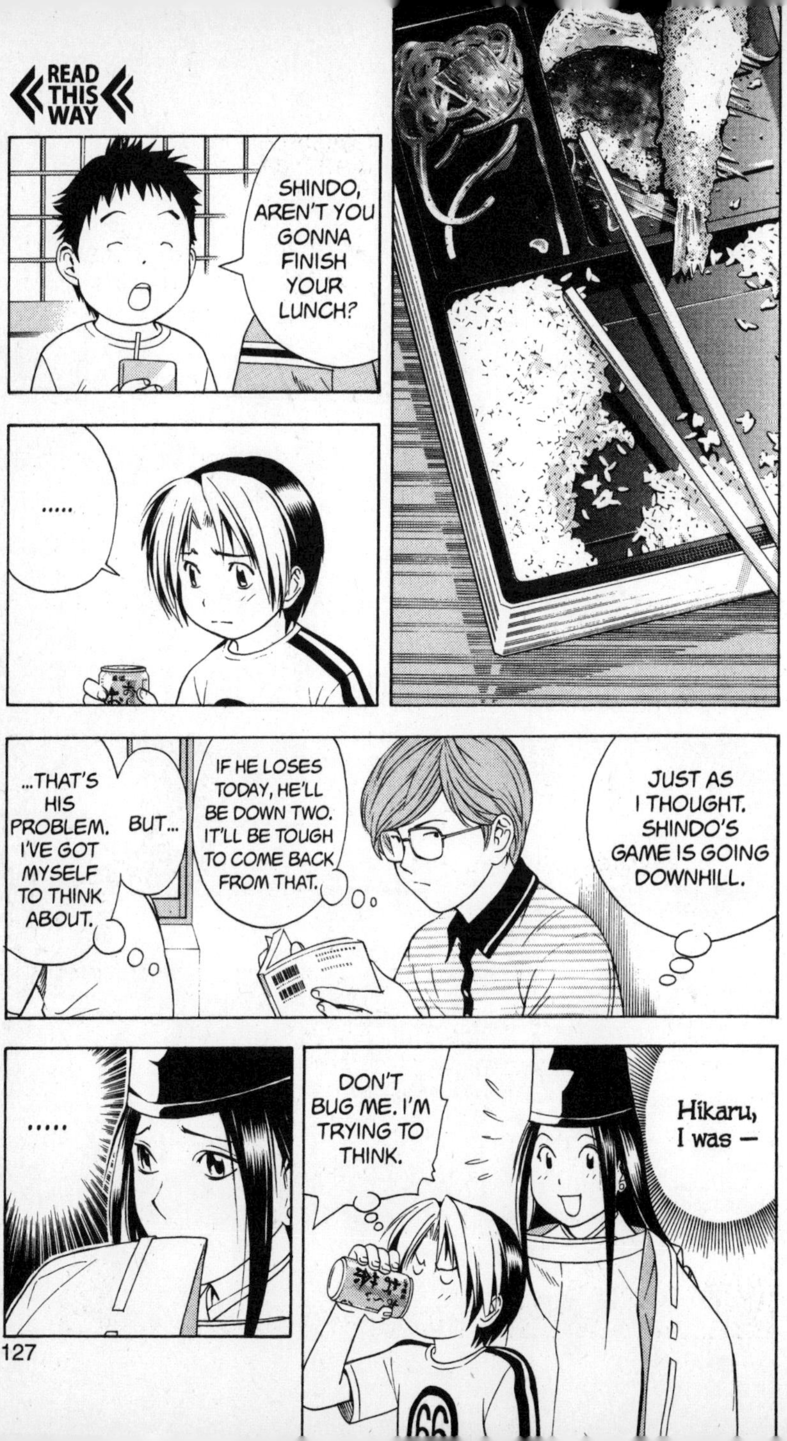
SHINDO, AREN'T YOU GONNA FINISH YOUR LUNCH?
......
JUST AS I THOUGHT. SHINDO'S GAME IS GOING DOWNHILL.
IF HE LOSES TODAY, HE'LL BE DOWN TWO. IT'LL BE TOUGH TO COME BACK FROM THAT.
BUT...
...THAT'S HIS PROBLEM. I'VE GOT MYSELF TO THINK ABOUT.
Hikaru, I was —
DON'T BUG ME. I'M TRYING TO THINK.
.....

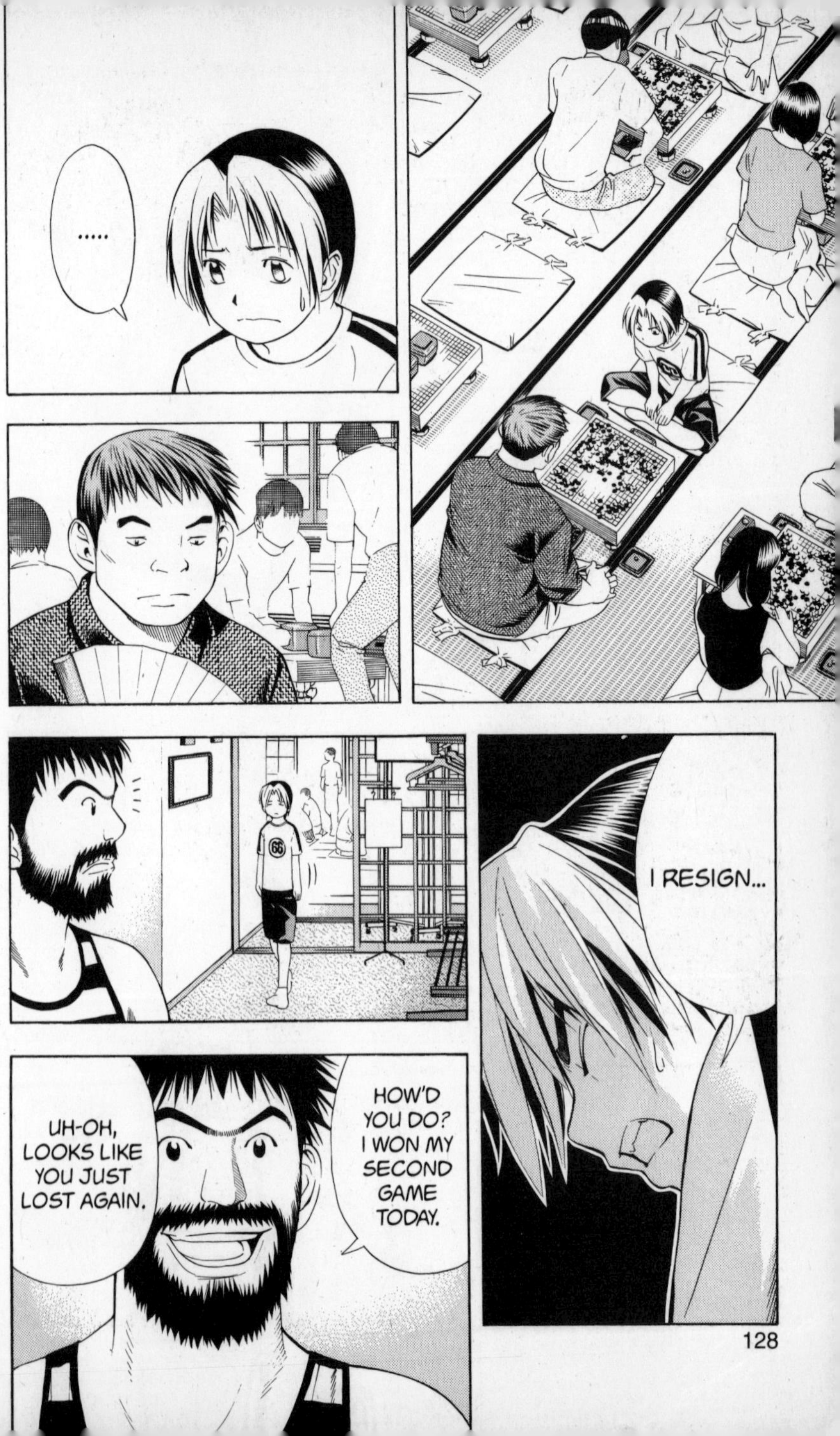
.....
I RESIGN...
HOW'D YOU DO? I WON MY SECOND GAME TODAY.
UH-OH, LOOKS LIKE YOU JUST LOST AGAIN.

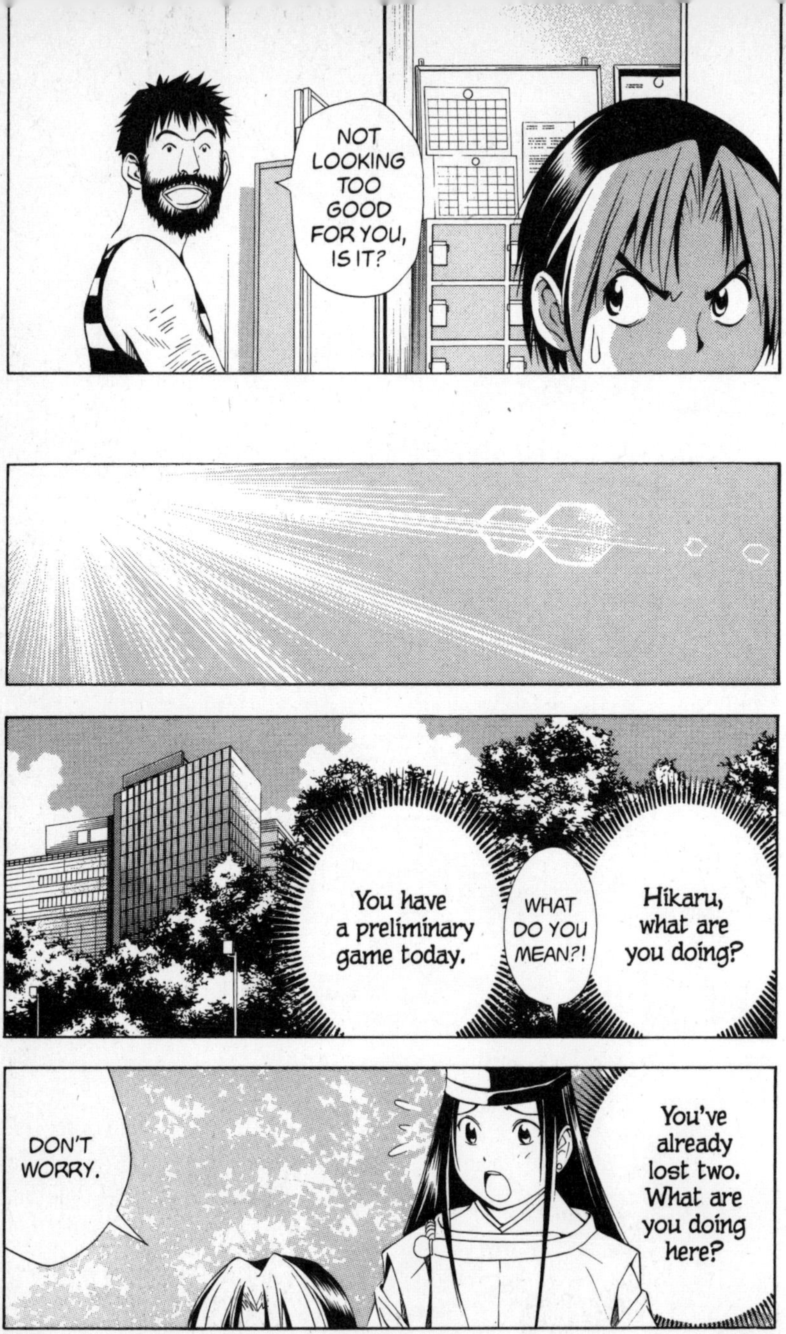
NOT LOOKING TOO GOOD FOR YOU, IS IT?
Hikaru, what are you doing?
WHAT DO YOU MEAN?!
You have a preliminary game today.
You've already lost two. What are you doing here?
DON'T WORRY.

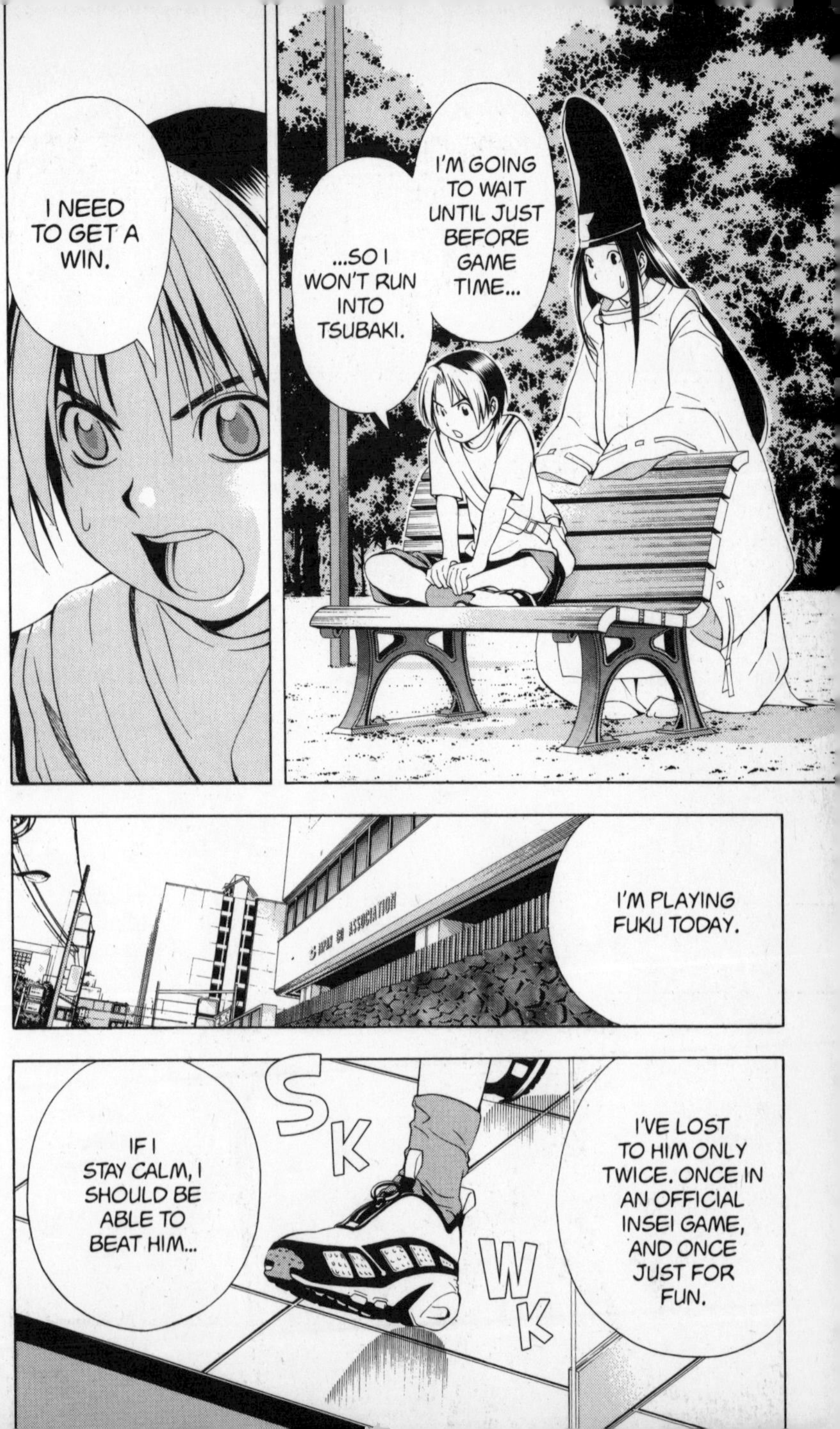
I'M GOING TO WAIT UNTIL JUST BEFORE GAME TIME...
...SO I WON'T RUN INTO TSUBAKI.
I NEED TO GET A WIN.
I'M PLAYING FUKU TODAY.
I'VE LOST TO HIM ONLY TWICE. ONCE IN AN OFFICIAL INSEI GAME, AND ONCE JUST FOR FUN.
SK WK
IF I STAY CALM, I SHOULD BE ABLE TO BEAT HIM...

READ THIS WAY

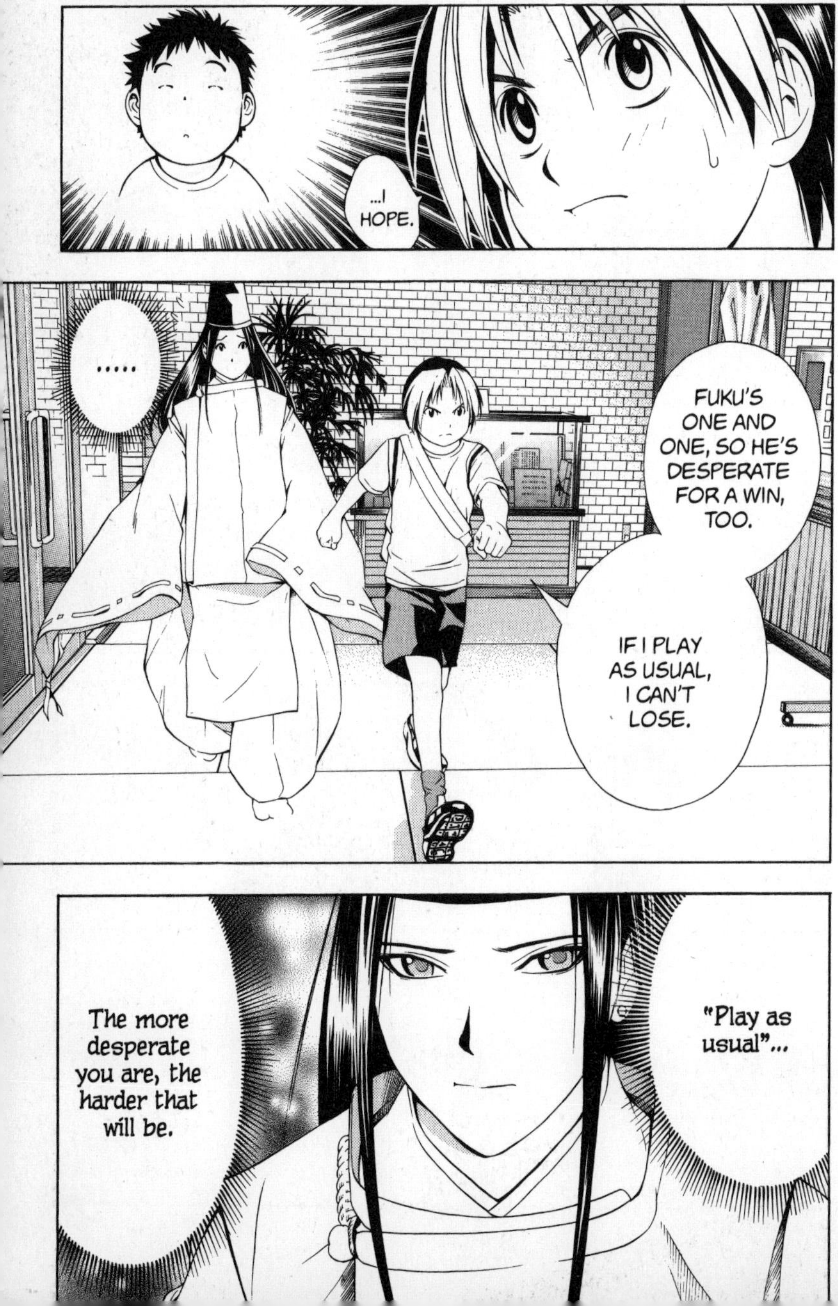
...I HOPE.
FUKU'S ONE AND ONE, SO HE'S DESPERATE FOR A WIN, TOO.
IF I PLAY AS USUAL, I CAN'T LOSE.
.....
"Play as usual"...
The more desperate you are, the harder that will be.

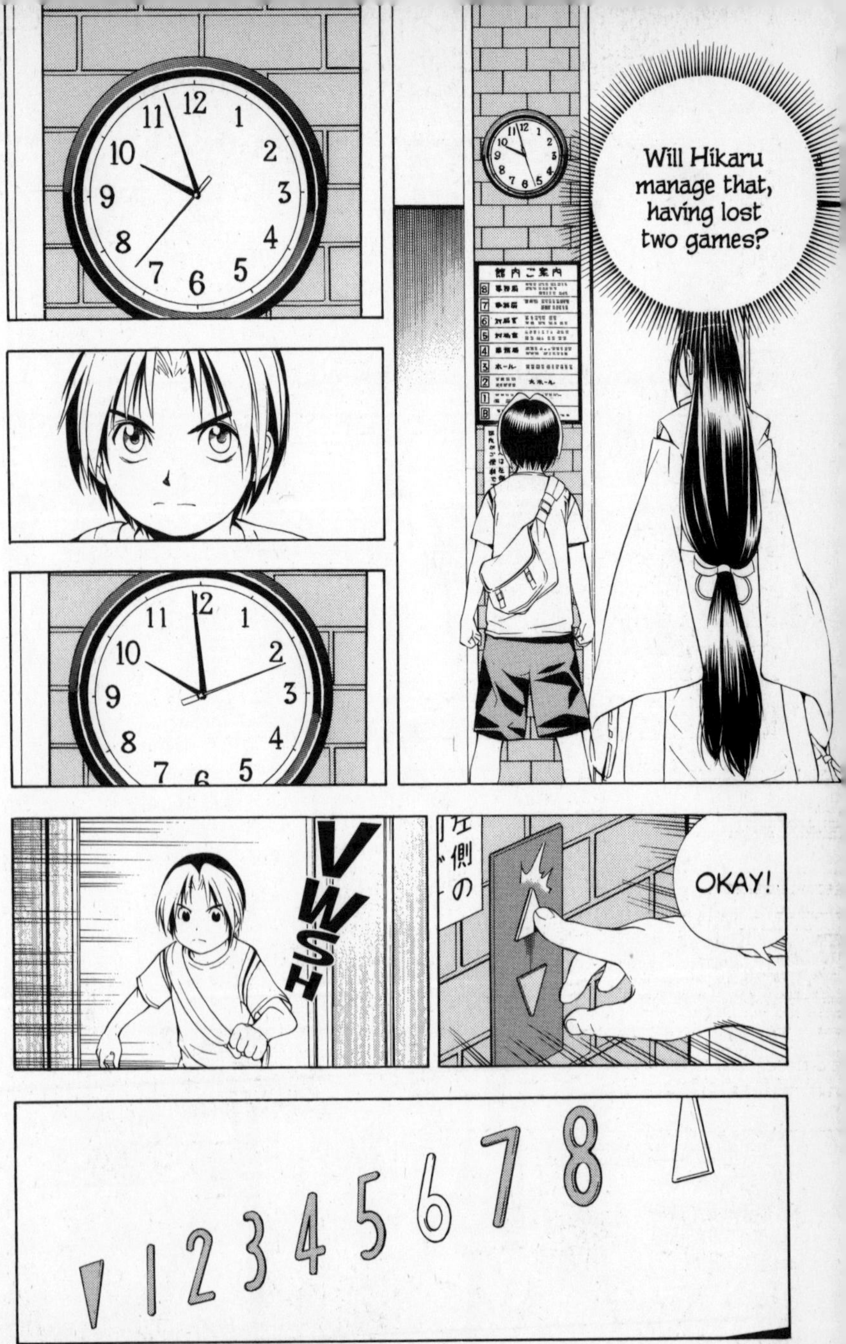
Will Hikaru manage that, having lost two games?
左側の
OKAY!
VWSH
12345678

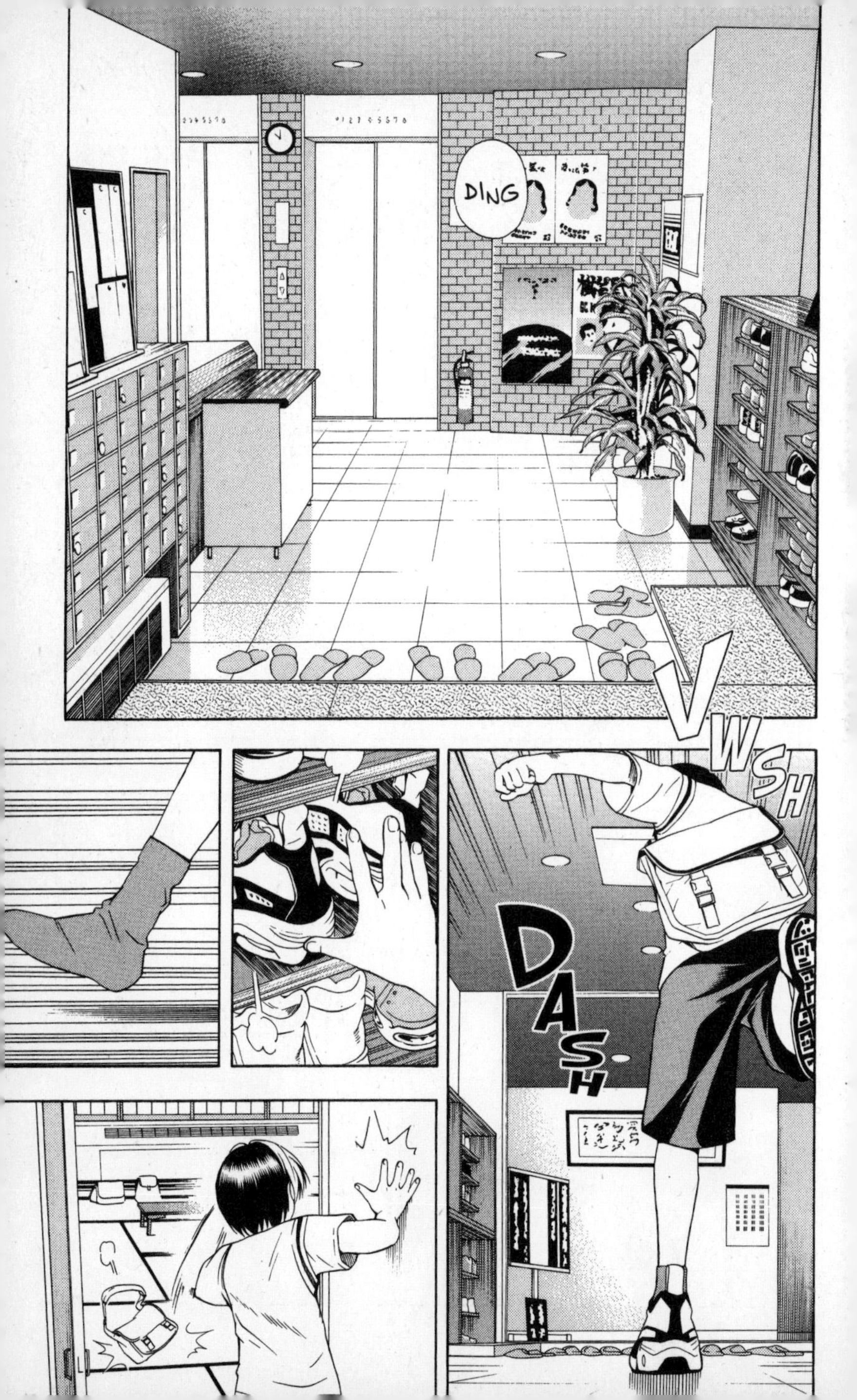
DING
VWSH
DASH

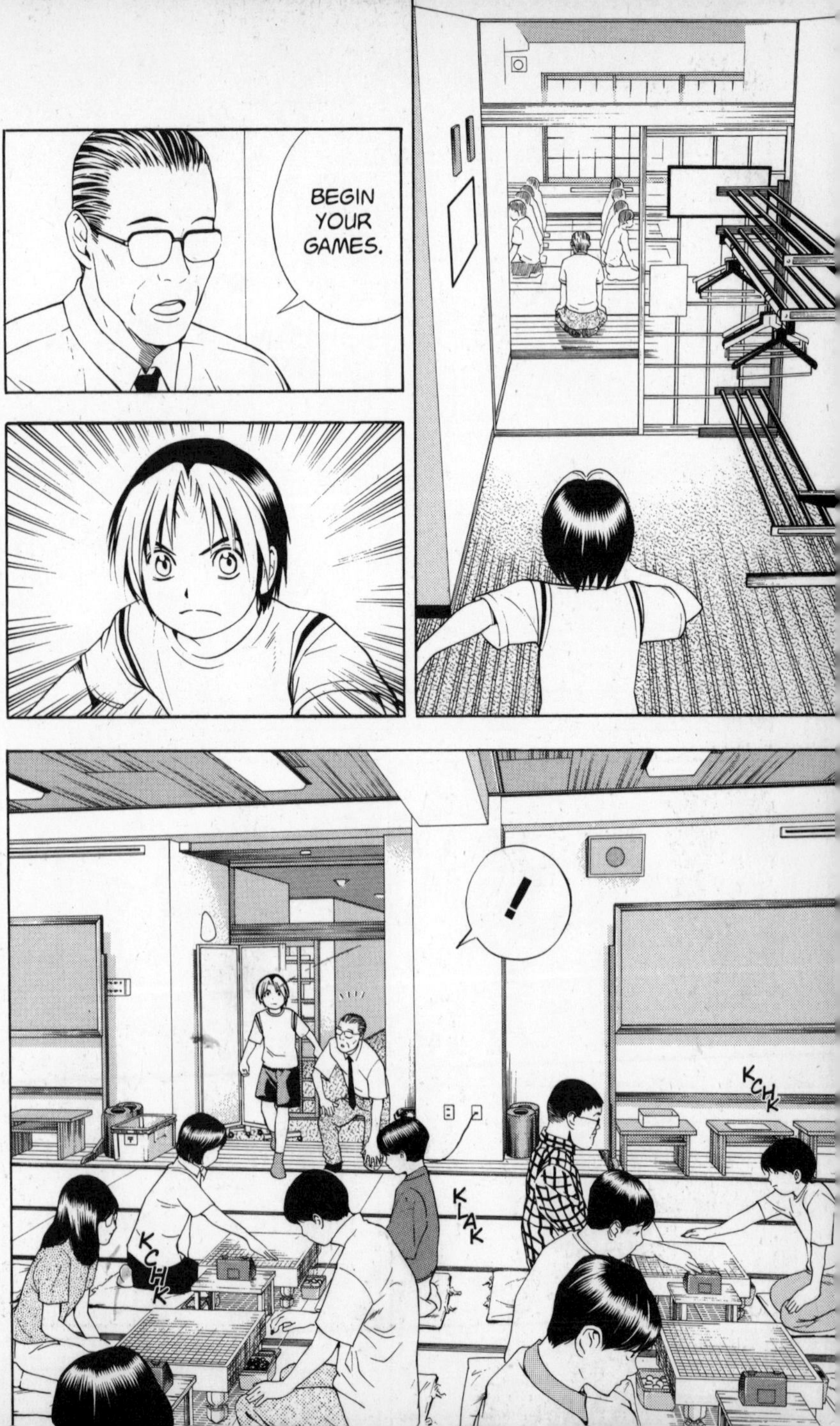
BEGIN YOUR GAMES.
!
KCHK
KLAK
KCHK

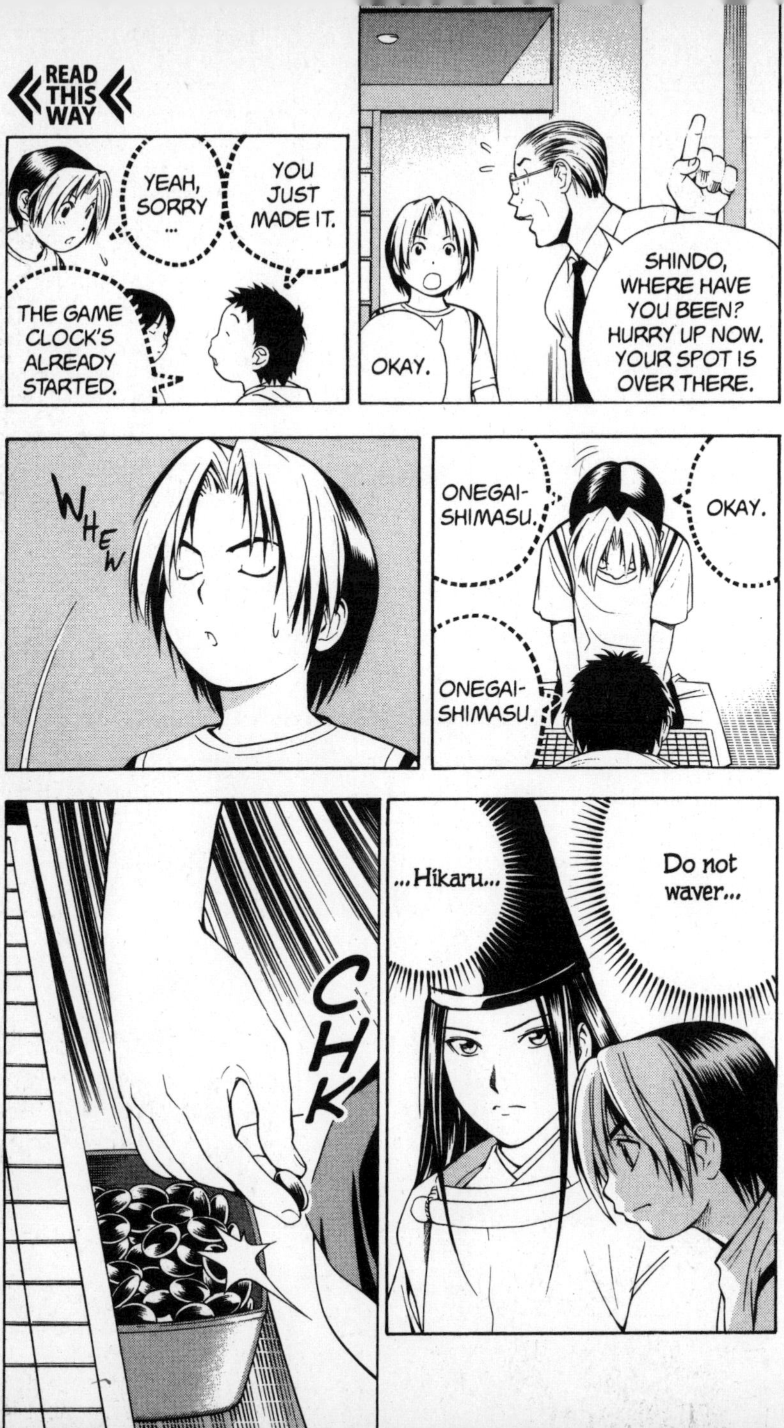
READ THIS WAY
SHINDO, WHERE HAVE YOU BEEN? HURRY UP NOW. YOUR SPOT IS OVER THERE.
OKAY.
YOU JUST MADE IT.
YEAH, SORRY ...
THE GAME CLOCK'S ALREADY STARTED.
OKAY.
ONEGAI-SHIMASU.
ONEGAI-SHIMASU.
WHEW
Do not waver...
...Hikaru...
CHK

Game 67

"The Pro Test Preliminaries:
Day Three"

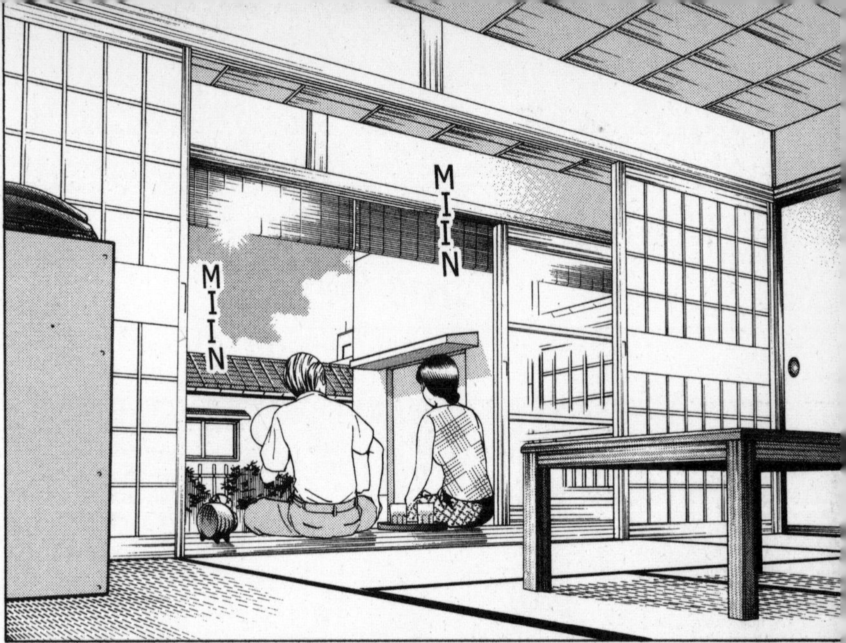
MIIN
MIIN

Miin = sound of cicadas

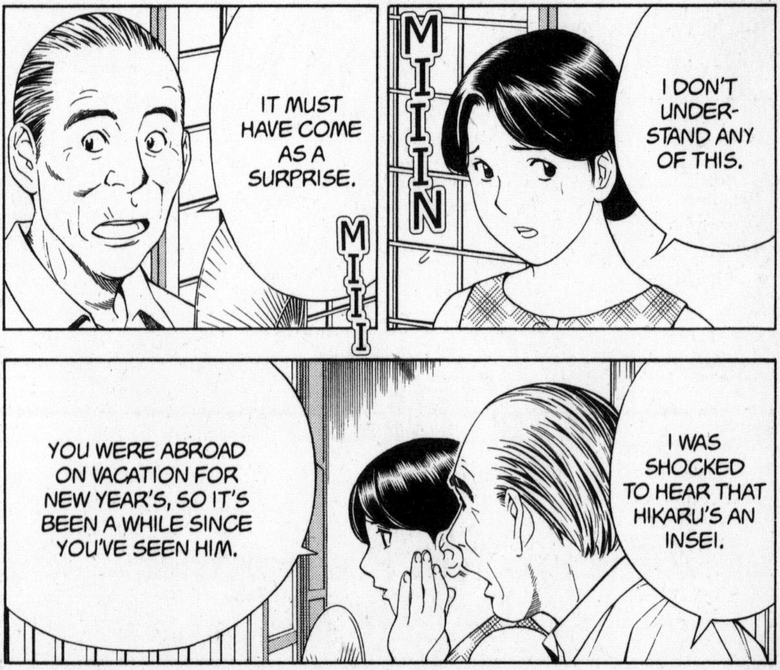
MIIIN
I DON'T UNDER-STAND ANY OF THIS.
IT MUST HAVE COME AS A SURPRISE.
MIIII
I WAS SHOCKED TO HEAR THAT HIKARU'S AN INSEI.
YOU WERE ABROAD ON VACATION FOR NEW YEAR'S, SO IT'S BEEN A WHILE SINCE YOU'VE SEEN HIM.

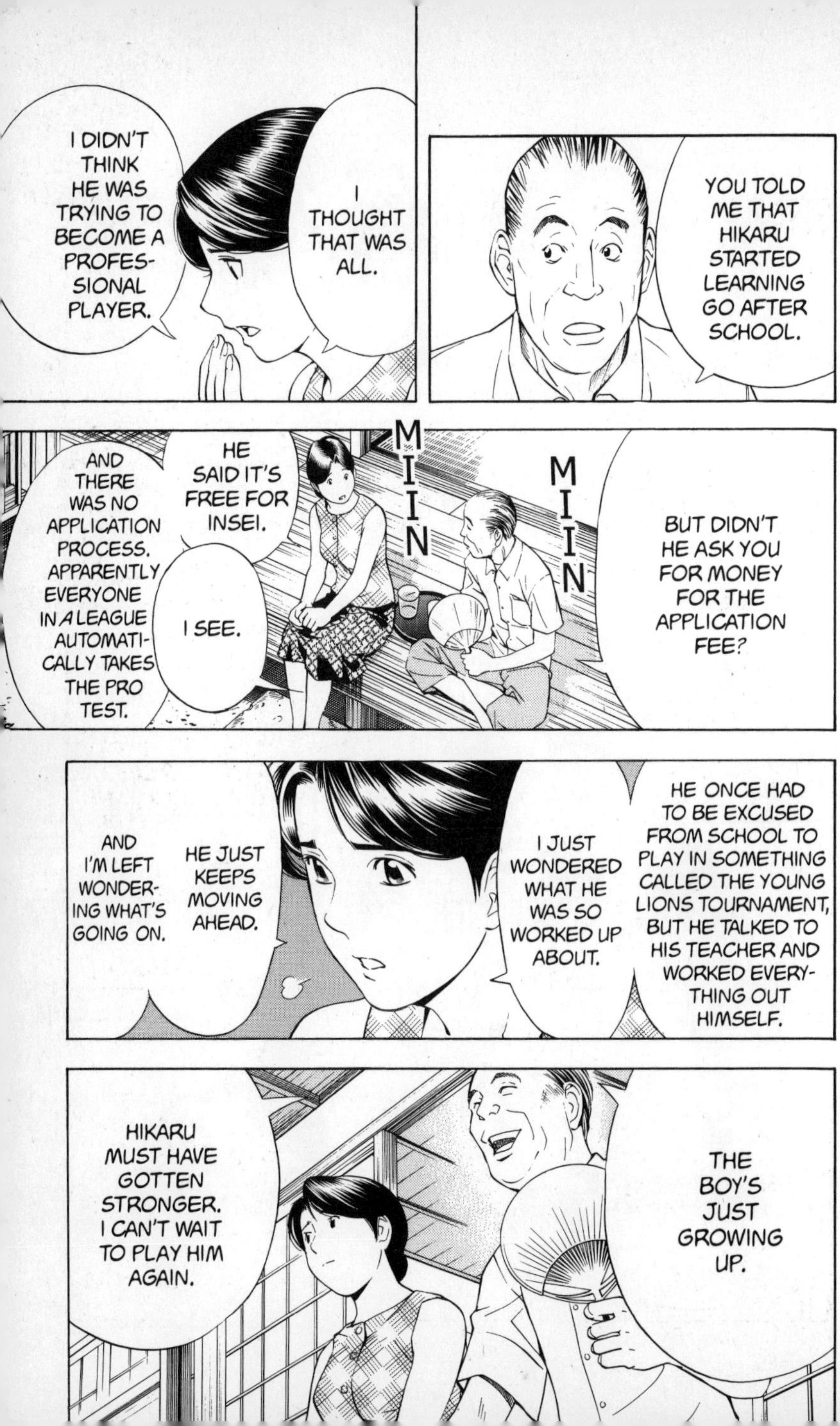
YOU TOLD ME THAT HIKARU STARTED LEARNING GO AFTER SCHOOL.
I THOUGHT THAT WAS ALL.
I DIDN'T THINK HE WAS TRYING TO BECOME A PROFES-SIONAL PLAYER.
BUT DIDN'T HE ASK YOU FOR MONEY FOR THE APPLICATION FEE?
MIIN
MIIN
HE SAID IT'S FREE FOR INSEI.
AND THERE WAS NO APPLICATION PROCESS. APPARENTLY EVERYONE IN A LEAGUE AUTOMATI-CALLY TAKES THE PRO TEST.
I SEE.
HE ONCE HAD TO BE EXCUSED FROM SCHOOL TO PLAY IN SOMETHING CALLED THE YOUNG LIONS TOURNAMENT, BUT HE TALKED TO HIS TEACHER AND WORKED EVERY-THING OUT HIMSELF.
I JUST WONDERED WHAT HE WAS SO WORKED UP ABOUT.
HE JUST KEEPS MOVING AHEAD.
AND I'M LEFT WONDER-ING WHAT'S GOING ON.
THE BOY'S JUST GROWING UP.
HIKARU MUST HAVE GOTTEN STRONGER. I CAN'T WAIT TO PLAY HIM AGAIN.

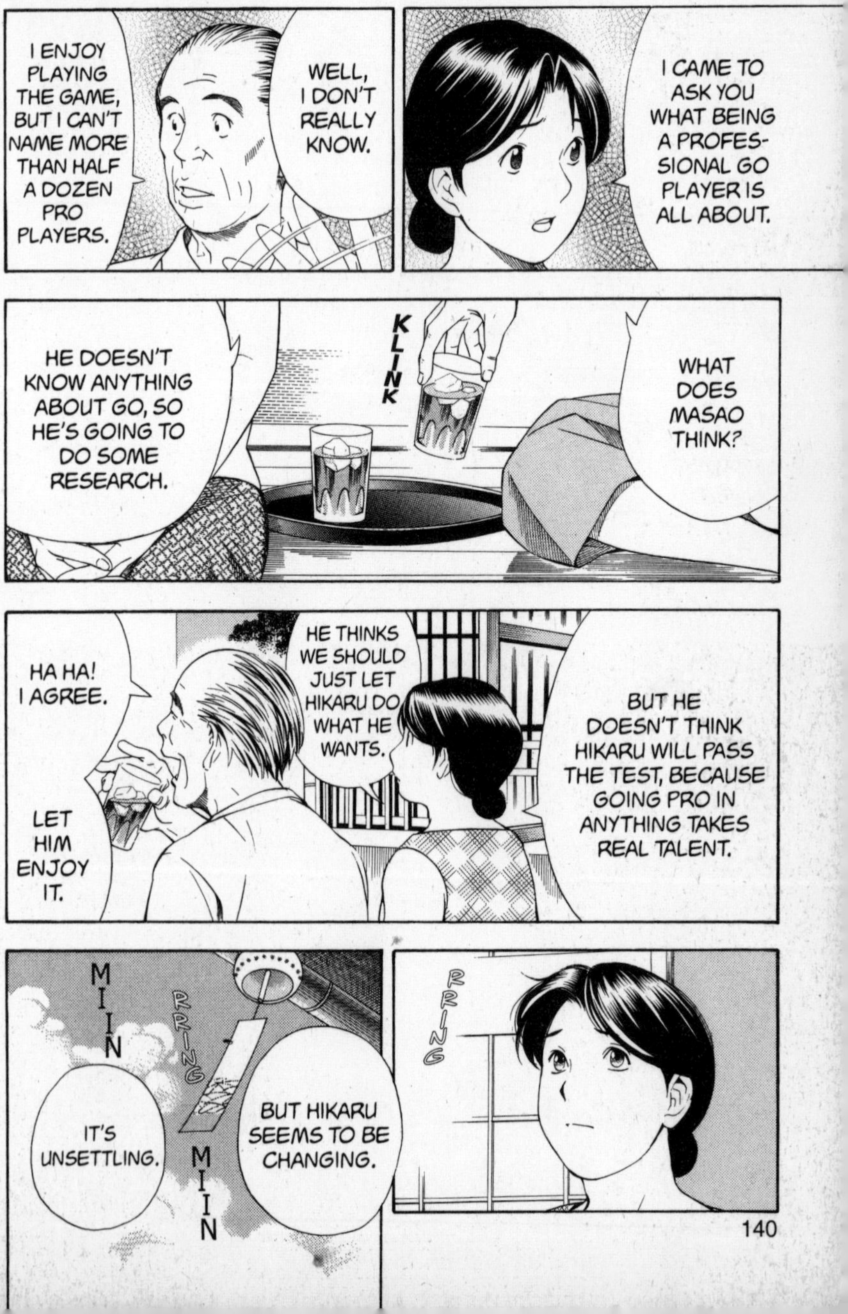
I CAME TO ASK YOU WHAT BEING A PROFES-SIONAL GO PLAYER IS ALL ABOUT.
WELL, I DON'T REALLY KNOW.
I ENJOY PLAYING THE GAME, BUT I CAN'T NAME MORE THAN HALF A DOZEN PRO PLAYERS.
WHAT DOES MASAO THINK?
KLINK
HE DOESN'T KNOW ANYTHING ABOUT GO, SO HE'S GOING TO DO SOME RESEARCH.
BUT HE DOESN'T THINK HIKARU WILL PASS THE TEST, BECAUSE GOING PRO IN ANYTHING TAKES REAL TALENT.
HE THINKS WE SHOULD JUST LET HIKARU DO WHAT HE WANTS.
HA HA! I AGREE.
LET HIM ENJOY IT.
RRING
BUT HIKARU SEEMS TO BE CHANGING.
MIIN
RRING
MIIN
IT'S UNSETTLING.

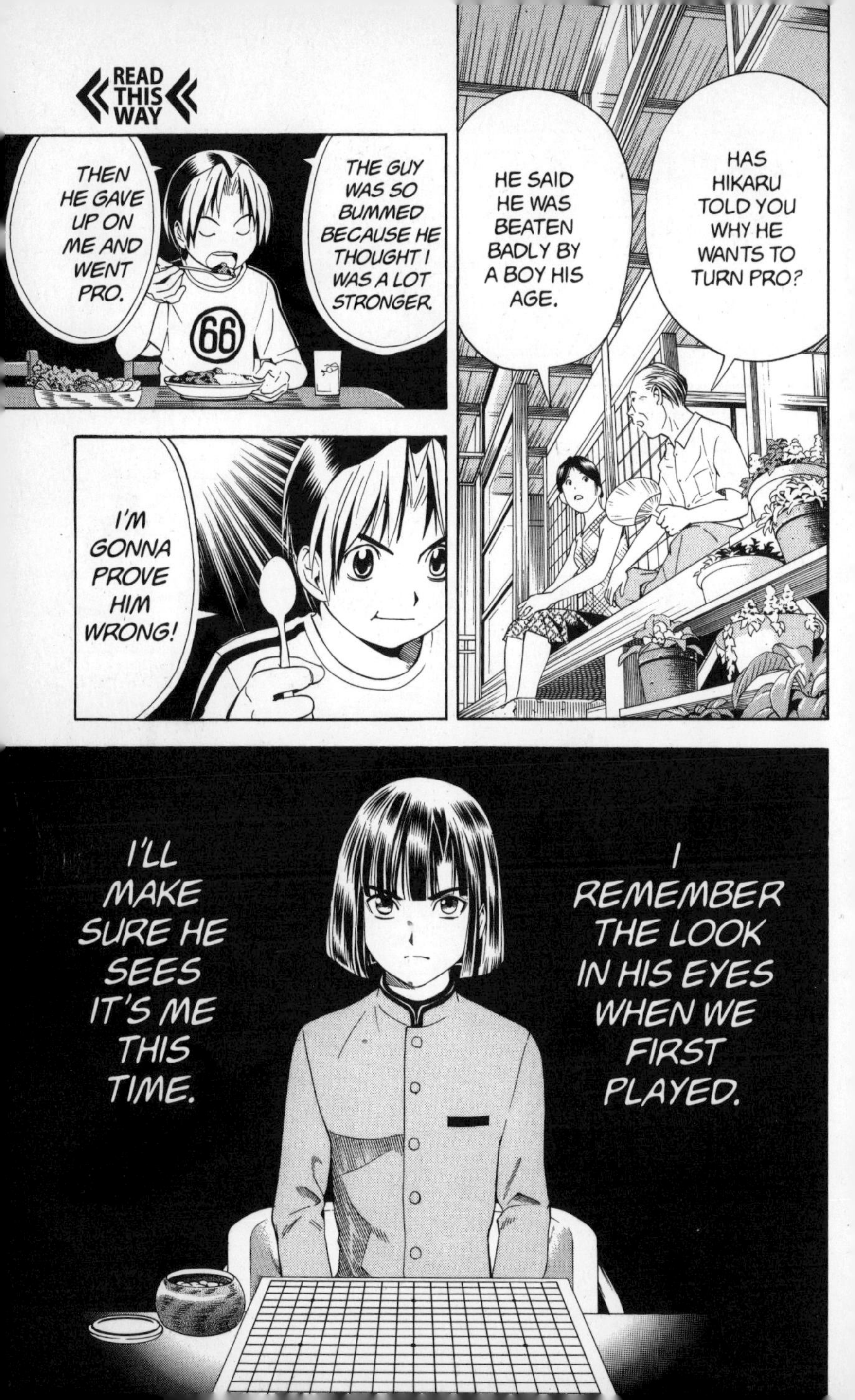
READ THIS WAY
HAS HIKARU TOLD YOU WHY HE WANTS TO TURN PRO?
HE SAID HE WAS BEATEN BADLY BY A BOY HIS AGE.
THE GUY WAS SO BUMMED BECAUSE HE THOUGHT I WAS A LOT STRONGER.
THEN HE GAVE UP ON ME AND WENT PRO.
66
I'M GONNA PROVE HIM WRONG!
I REMEMBER THE LOOK IN HIS EYES WHEN WE FIRST PLAYED.
I'LL MAKE SURE HE SEES IT'S ME THIS TIME.

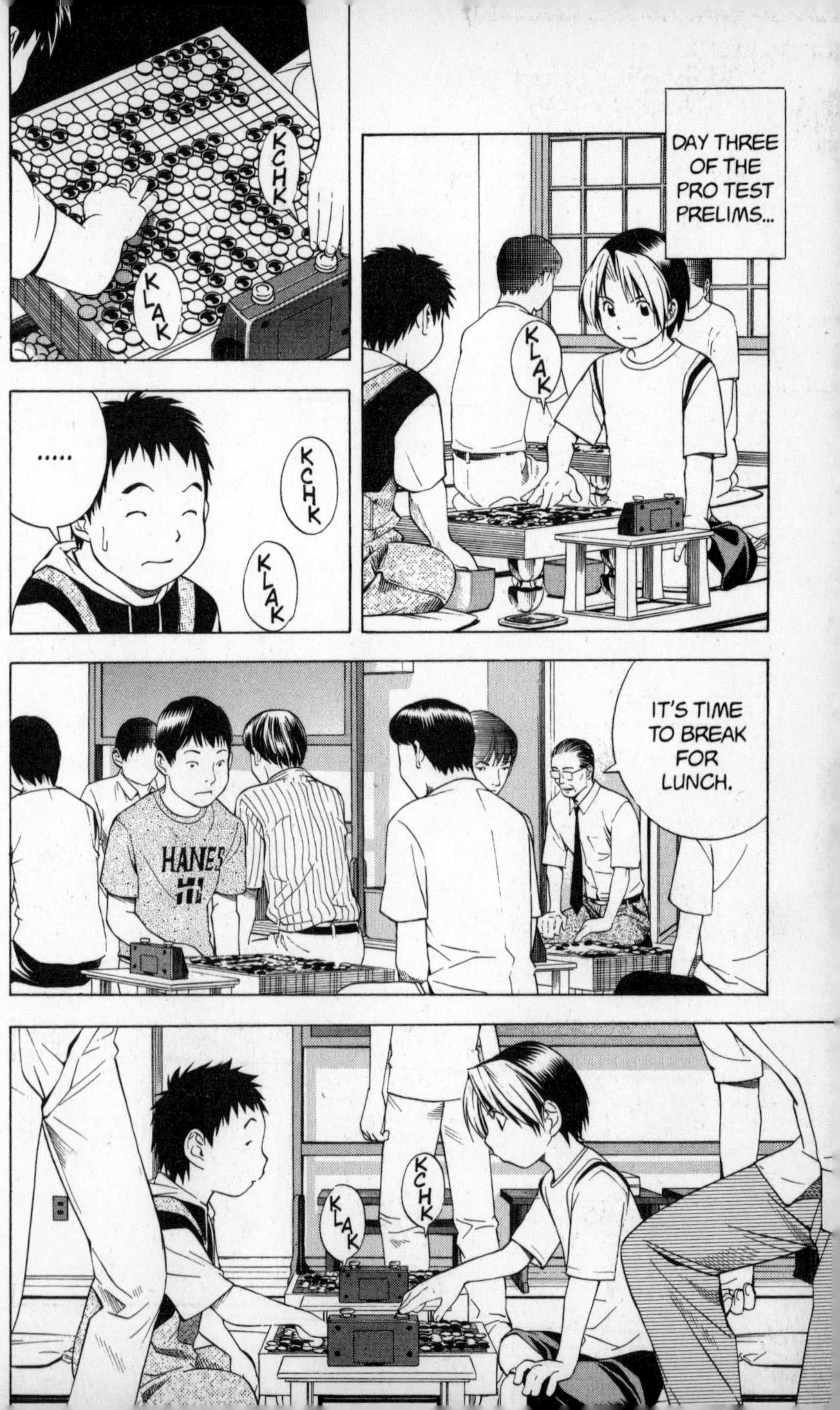
DAY THREE OF THE PRO TEST PRELIMS...
KLAK
KCHK
KLAK
KCHK
KLAK
.....
IT'S TIME TO BREAK FOR LUNCH.
HANES
KCHK
KLAK

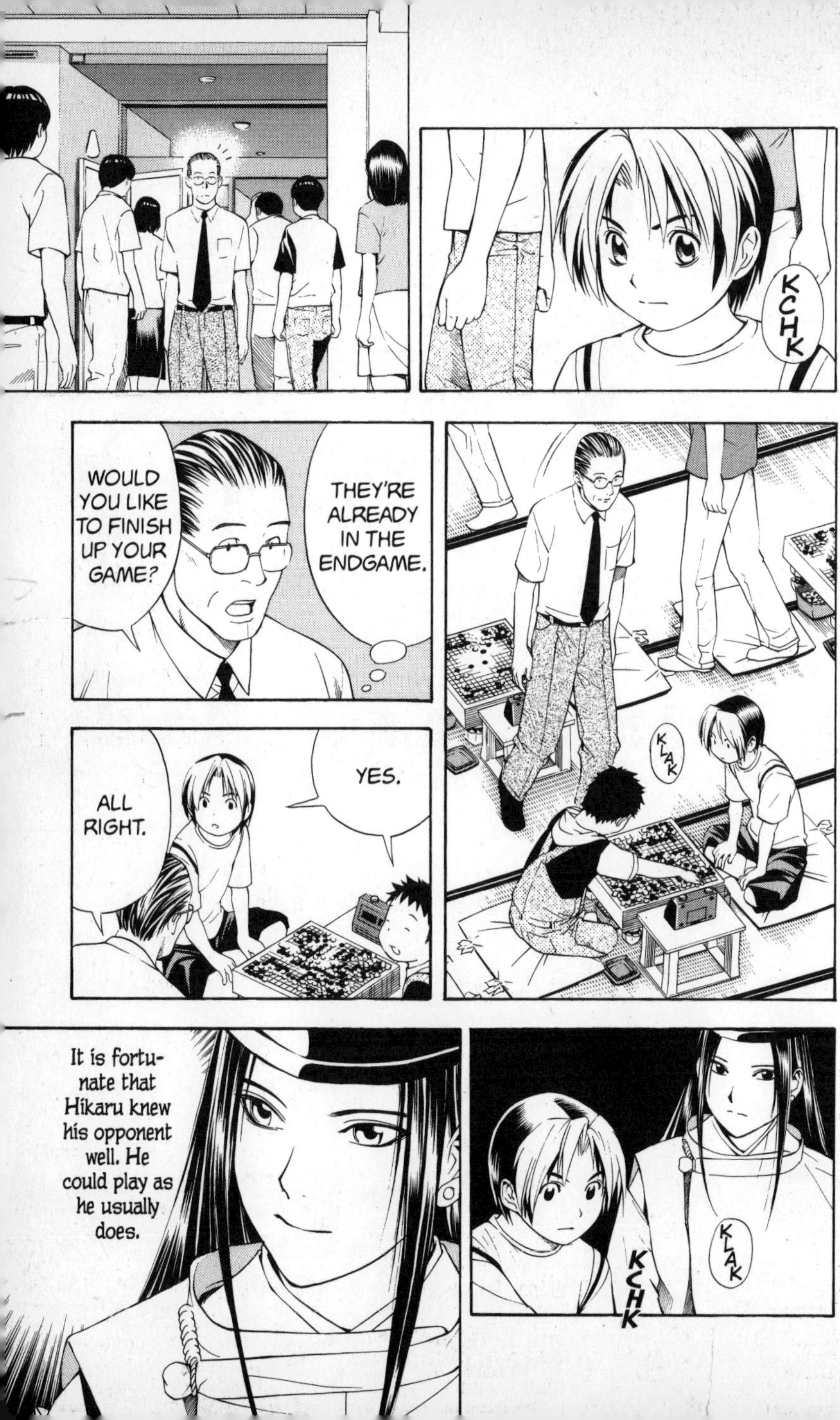
KCHK
KLAK
THEY'RE ALREADY IN THE ENDGAME.
WOULD YOU LIKE TO FINISH UP YOUR GAME?
YES.
ALL RIGHT.
KLAK
KCHK
It is fortunate that Hikaru knew his opponent well. He could play as he usually does.

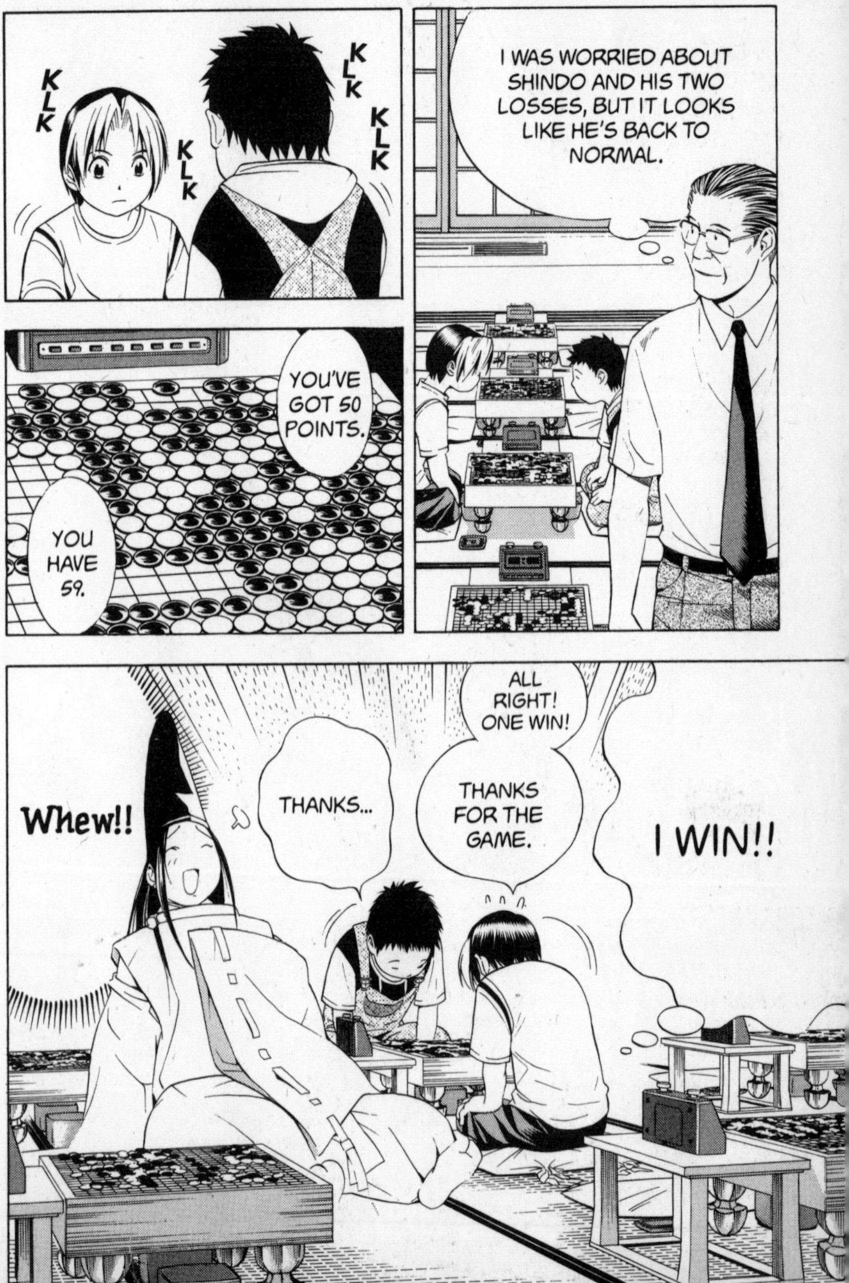

I WAS WORRIED ABOUT SHINDO AND HIS TWO LOSSES, BUT IT LOOKS LIKE HE'S BACK TO NORMAL.
KLK
KLK
KLK
KLK
YOU'VE GOT 50 POINTS.
YOU HAVE 59.
I WIN!!
ALL RIGHT! ONE WIN!
THANKS FOR THE GAME.
THANKS...
Whew!!

READ THIS WAY

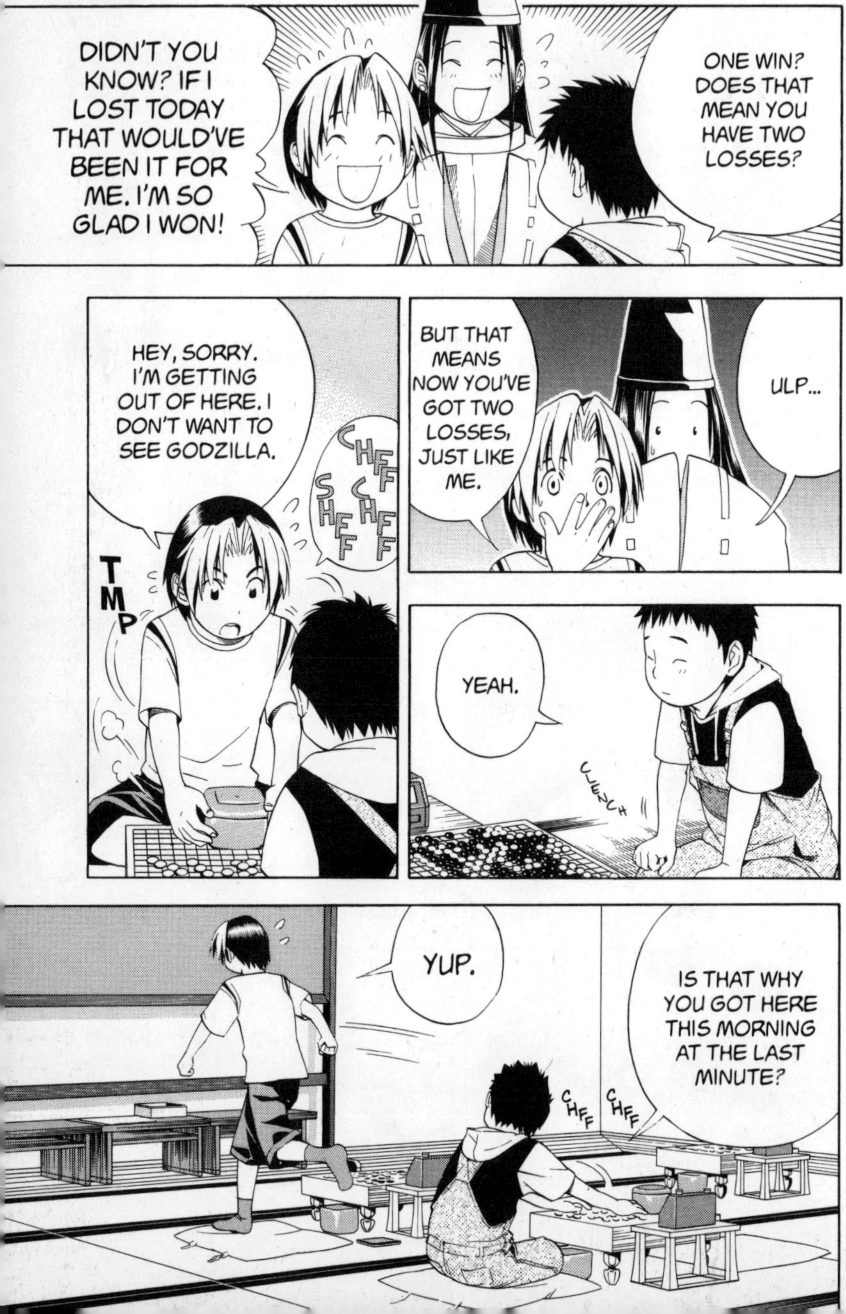
ONE WIN? DOES THAT MEAN YOU HAVE TWO LOSSES?
DIDN'T YOU KNOW? IF I LOST TODAY THAT WOULD'VE BEEN IT FOR ME. I'M SO GLAD I WON!
ULP...
BUT THAT MEANS NOW YOU'VE GOT TWO LOSSES, JUST LIKE ME.
YEAH.
CLENCH
HEY, SORRY. I'M GETTING OUT OF HERE. I DON'T WANT TO SEE GODZILLA.
CHFF SHFF CHFF SHFF
TMP
IS THAT WHY YOU GOT HERE THIS MORNING AT THE LAST MINUTE?
YUP.
CHFF CHFF

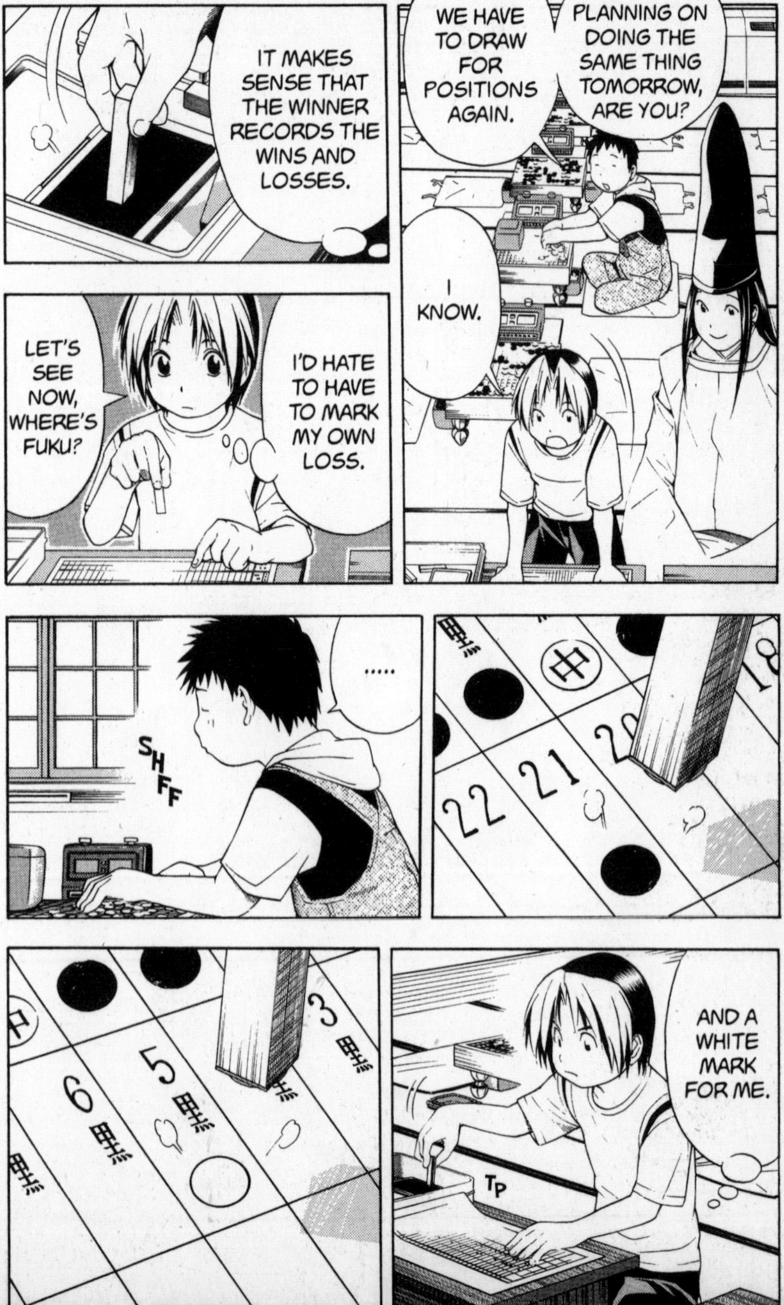
YOU AREN'T PLANNING ON DOING THE SAME THING TOMORROW, ARE YOU?
WE HAVE TO DRAW FOR POSITIONS AGAIN.
I KNOW.
IT MAKES SENSE THAT THE WINNER RECORDS THE WINS AND LOSSES.
I'D HATE TO HAVE TO MARK MY OWN LOSS.
LET'S SEE NOW, WHERE'S FUKU?
.....
SHFF
AND A WHITE MARK FOR ME.
TP

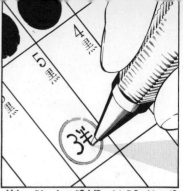

AND ONE MORE...

He's writing down "3 1/2 points" for himself.

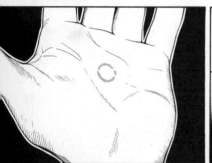

HEH HEH!

CLENCH

I'M GOING TO GET ME ANOTHER WHITE MARK TOMORROW!

Tomorrow ...

... you will still bear the burden of two losses.

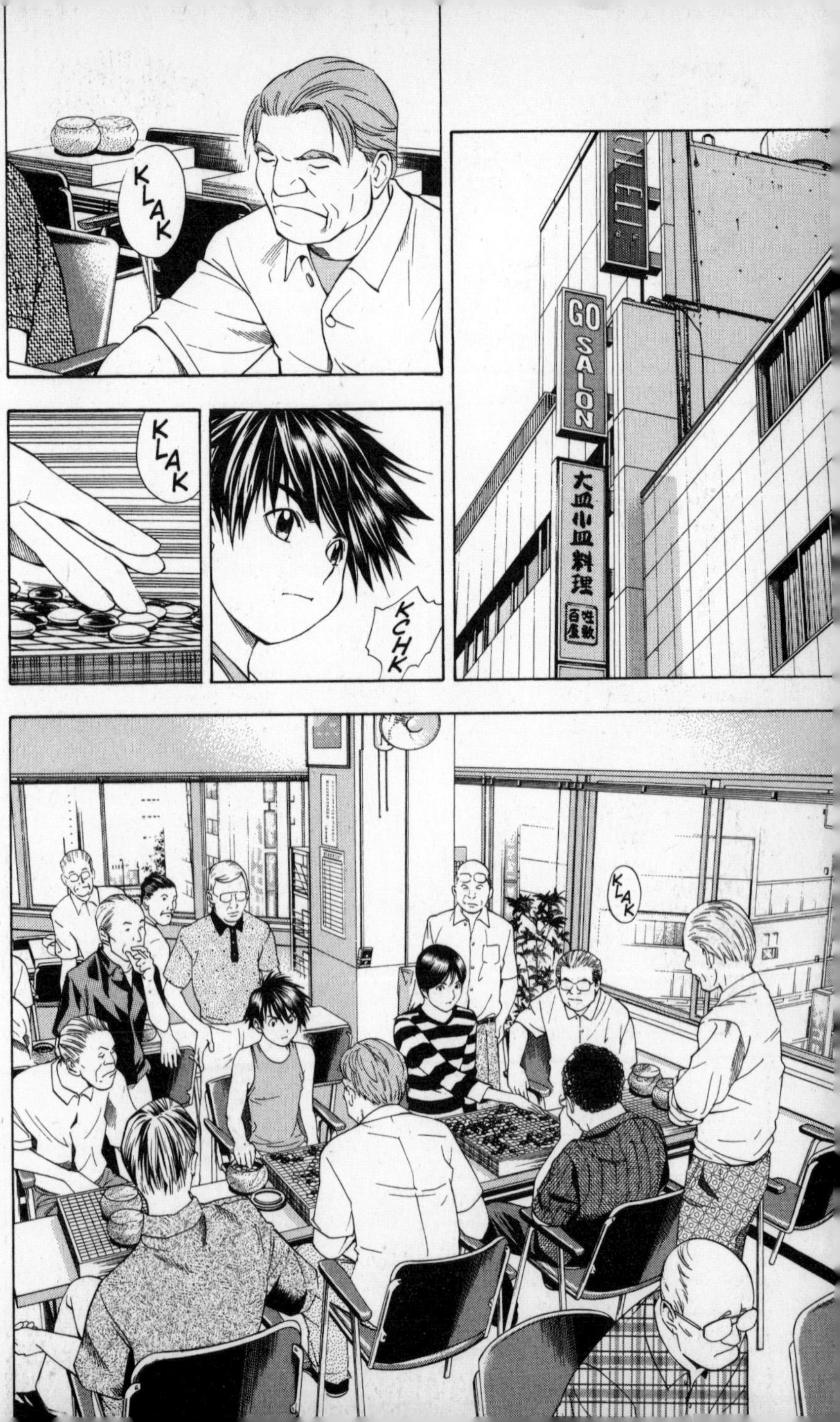
GO SALON
大皿小皿料理
KLAK
KCHK
KLAK
KLAK

READ THIS WAY

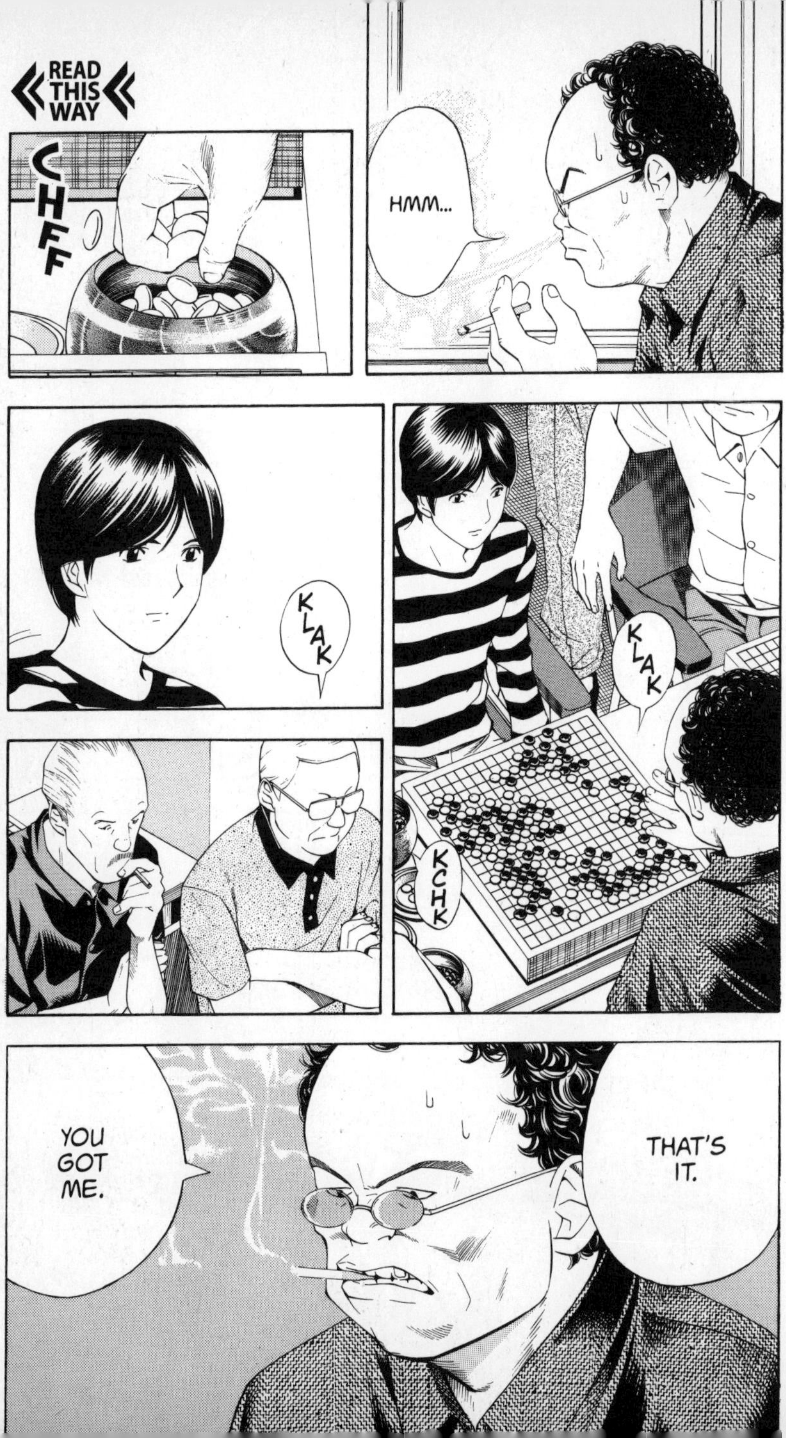
HMM...
CHFF
KLAK
KCHK
KLAK
THAT'S IT.
YOU GOT ME.

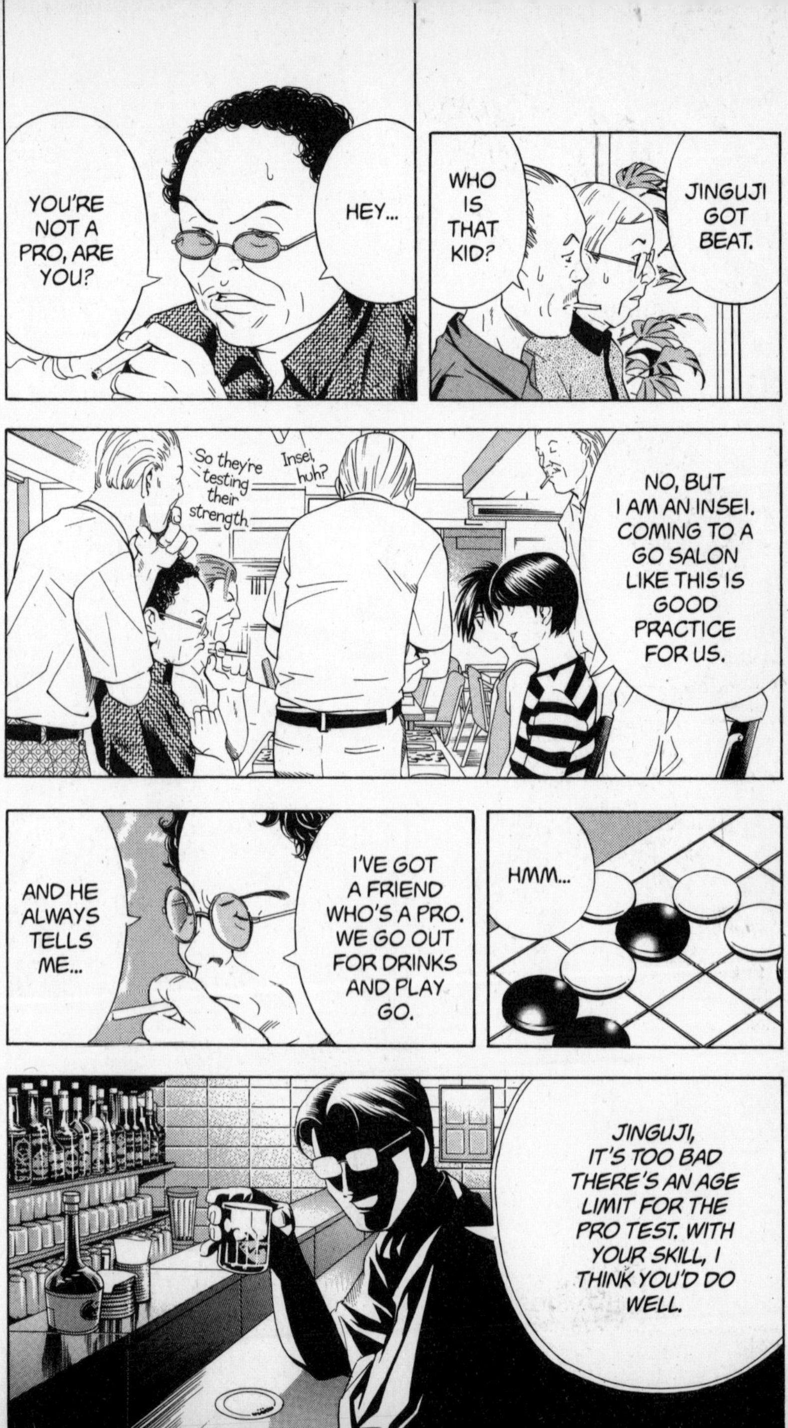
JINGUJI GOT BEAT.
WHO IS THAT KID?
HEY...
YOU'RE NOT A PRO, ARE YOU?
NO, BUT I AM AN INSEI. COMING TO A GO SALON LIKE THIS IS GOOD PRACTICE FOR US.
Insei, huh?
So they're testing their strength.
HMM...
I'VE GOT A FRIEND WHO'S A PRO. WE GO OUT FOR DRINKS AND PLAY GO.
AND HE ALWAYS TELLS ME...
JINGUJI, IT'S TOO BAD THERE'S AN AGE LIMIT FOR THE PRO TEST. WITH YOUR SKILL, I THINK YOU'D DO WELL.

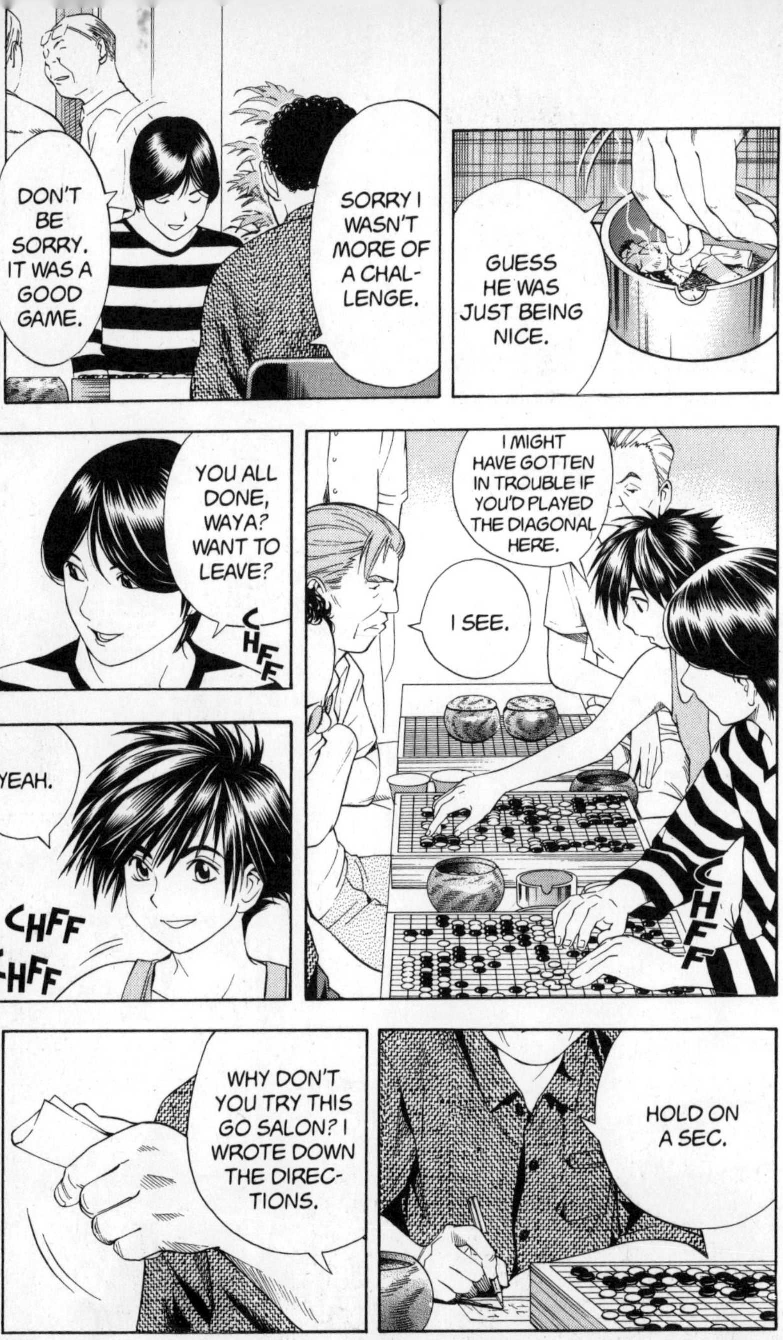
GUESS HE WAS JUST BEING NICE.
SORRY I WASN'T MORE OF A CHAL-LENGE.
DON'T BE SORRY. IT WAS A GOOD GAME.
I MIGHT HAVE GOTTEN IN TROUBLE IF YOU'D PLAYED THE DIAGONAL HERE.
I SEE.
CHFF
YOU ALL DONE, WAYA? WANT TO LEAVE?
CHFF
YEAH.
CHFF CHFF
HOLD ON A SEC.
WHY DON'T YOU TRY THIS GO SALON? I WROTE DOWN THE DIREC-TIONS.

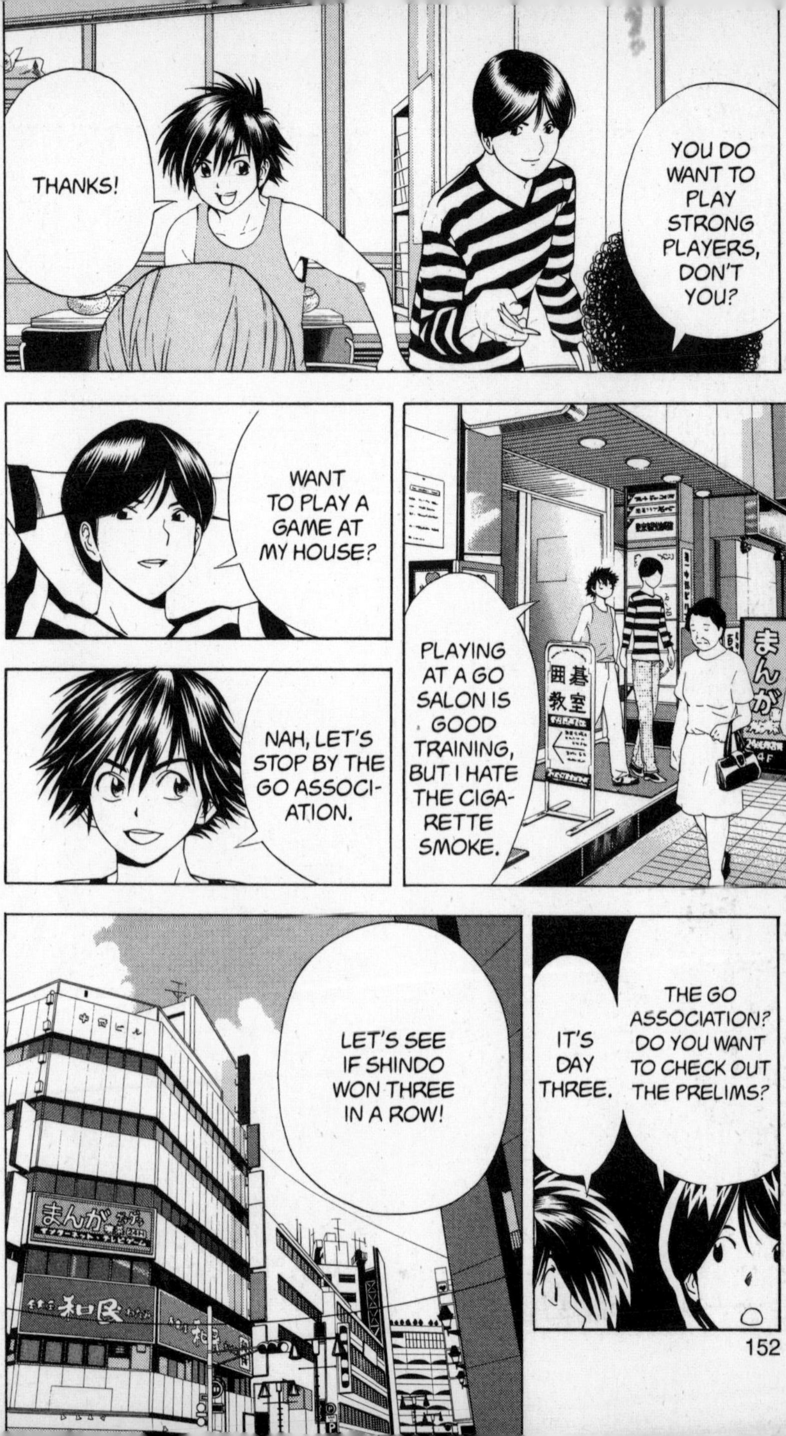
YOU DO WANT TO PLAY STRONG PLAYERS, DON'T YOU?
THANKS!
PLAYING AT A GO SALON IS GOOD TRAINING, BUT I HATE THE CIGARETTE SMOKE.
囲碁教室
まんが
WANT TO PLAY A GAME AT MY HOUSE?
NAH, LET'S STOP BY THE GO ASSOCIATION.
THE GO ASSOCIATION? DO YOU WANT TO CHECK OUT THE PRELIMS?
IT'S DAY THREE.
LET'S SEE IF SHINDO WON THREE IN A ROW!
まんが
和民

READ THIS WAY

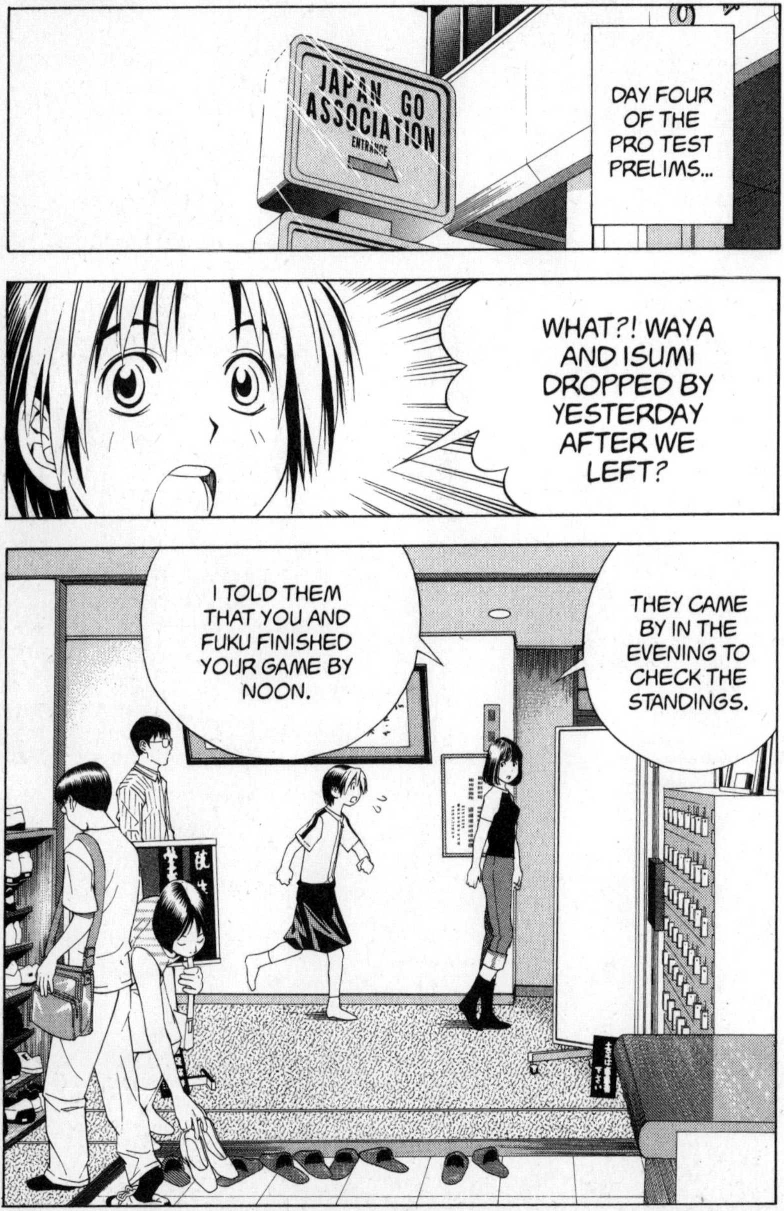
JAPAN GO ASSOCIATION
ENTRANCE
DAY FOUR OF THE PRO TEST PRELIMS...
WHAT?! WAYA AND ISUMI DROPPED BY YESTERDAY AFTER WE LEFT?
THEY CAME BY IN THE EVENING TO CHECK THE STANDINGS.
I TOLD THEM THAT YOU AND FUKU FINISHED YOUR GAME BY NOON.

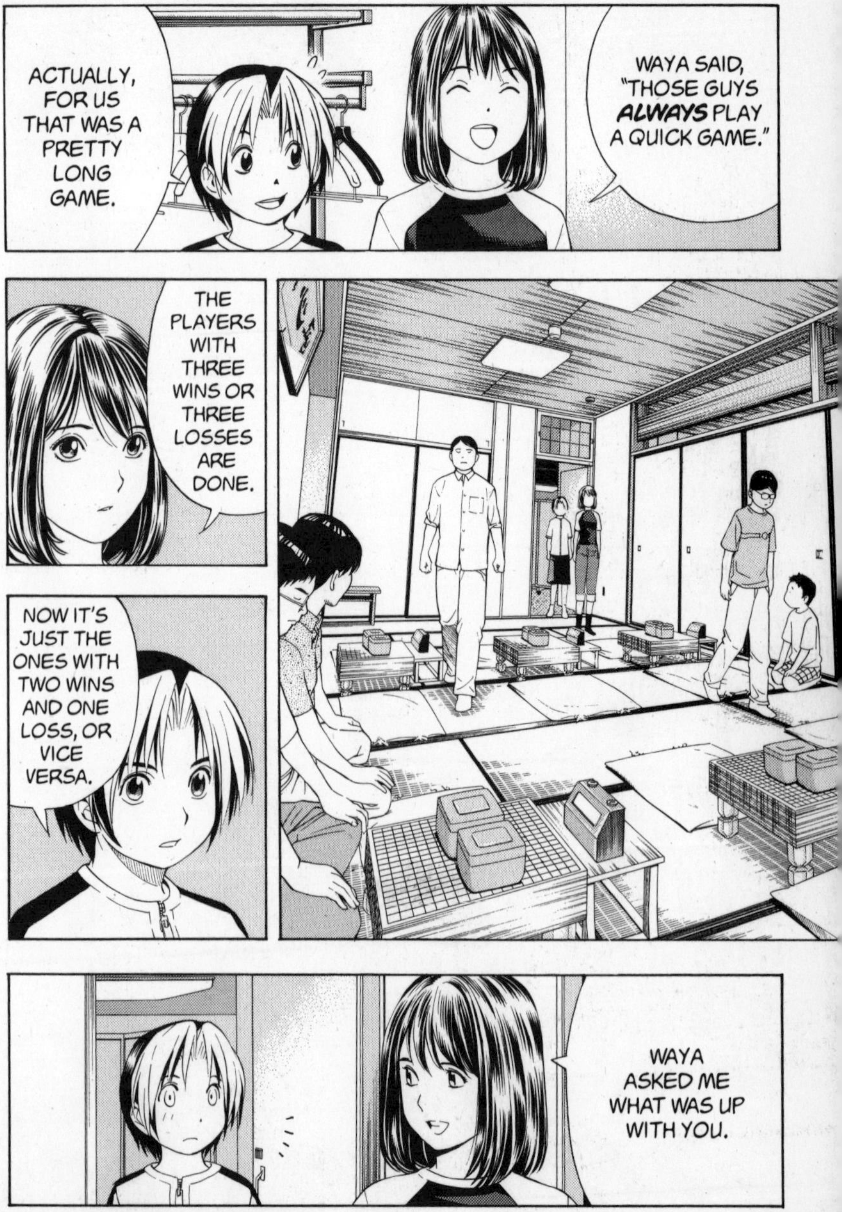
WAYA SAID, "THOSE GUYS ALWAYS PLAY A QUICK GAME."
ACTUALLY, FOR US THAT WAS A PRETTY LONG GAME.
THE PLAYERS WITH THREE WINS OR THREE LOSSES ARE DONE.
NOW IT'S JUST THE ONES WITH TWO WINS AND ONE LOSS, OR VICE VERSA.
WAYA ASKED ME WHAT WAS UP WITH YOU.

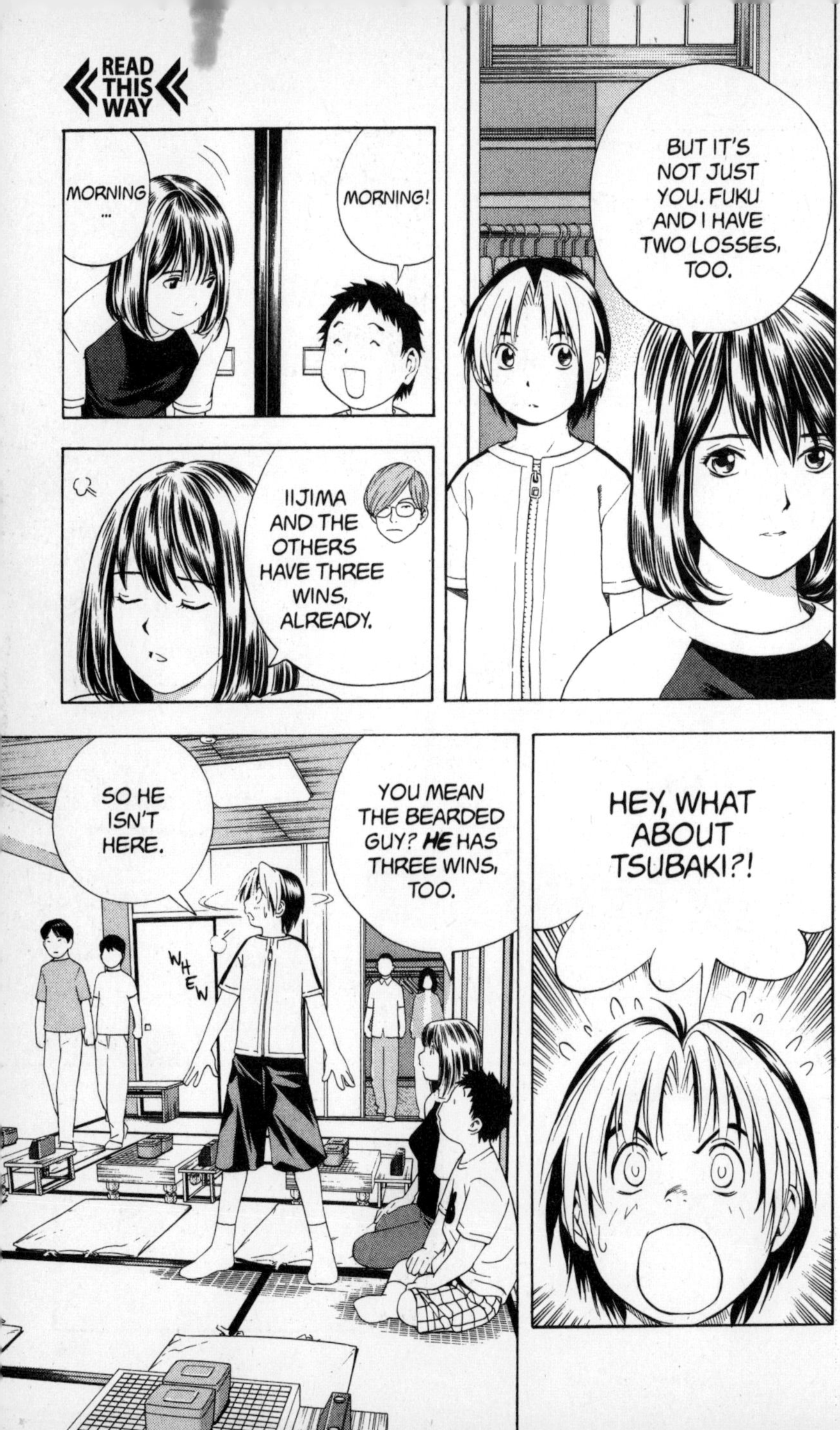
READ THIS WAY
BUT IT'S NOT JUST YOU. FUKU AND I HAVE TWO LOSSES, TOO.
MORNING!
MORNING ...
IIJIMA AND THE OTHERS HAVE THREE WINS, ALREADY.
HEY, WHAT ABOUT TSUBAKI?!
YOU MEAN THE BEARDED GUY? ***HE*** HAS THREE WINS, TOO.
SO HE ISN'T HERE.
WHEW

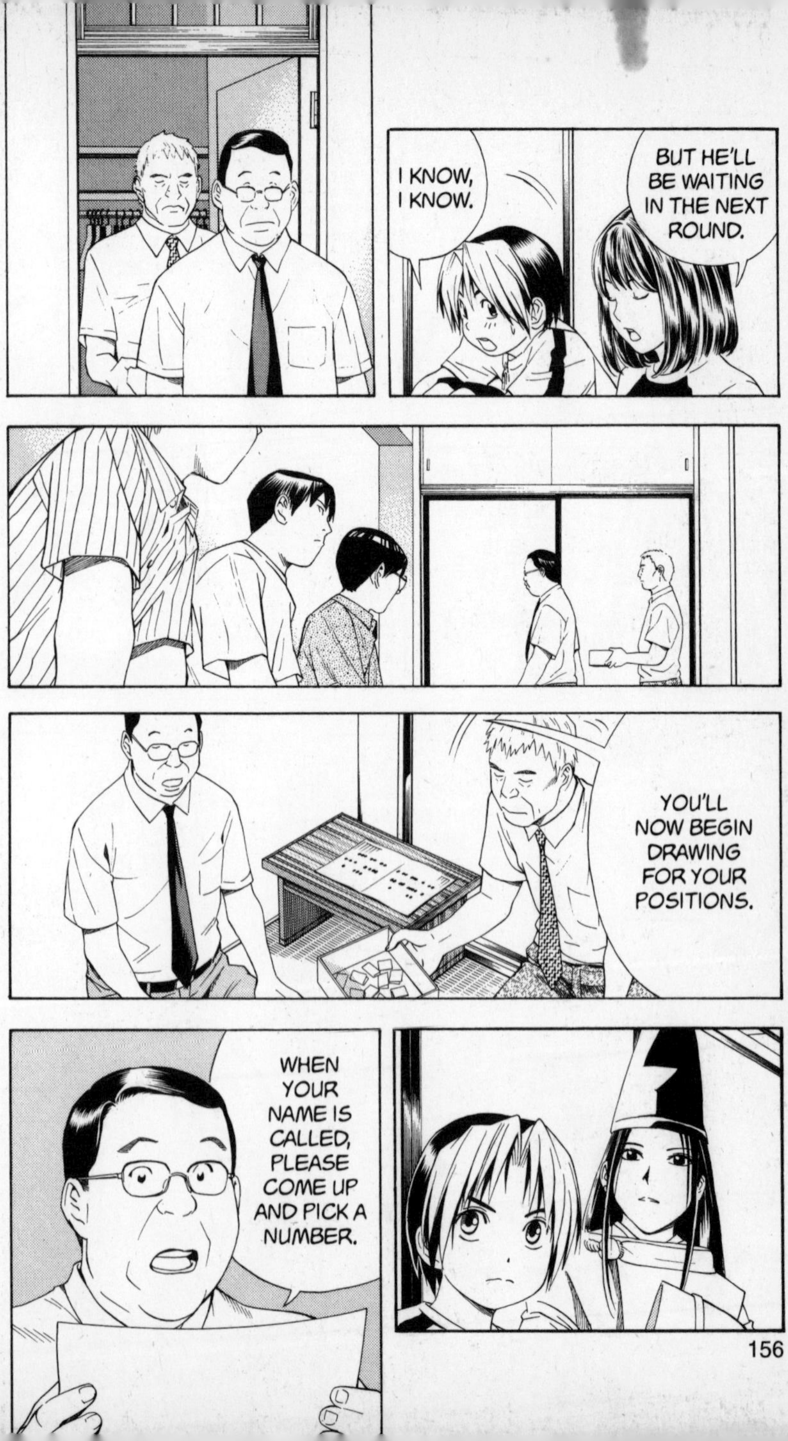
BUT HE'LL BE WAITING IN THE NEXT ROUND.
I KNOW, I KNOW.
YOU'LL NOW BEGIN DRAWING FOR YOUR POSITIONS.
WHEN YOUR NAME IS CALLED, PLEASE COME UP AND PICK A NUMBER.

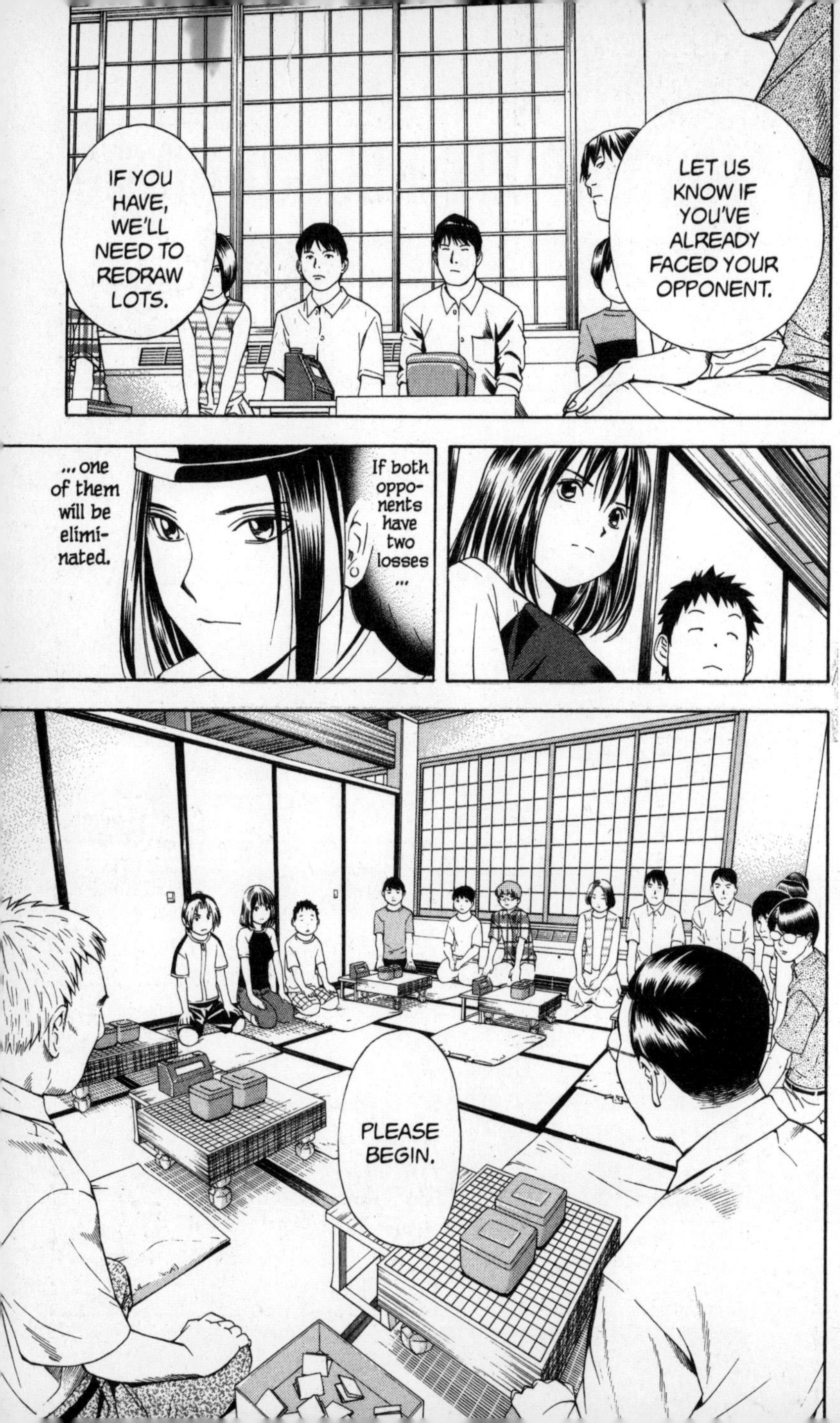
LET US KNOW IF YOU'VE ALREADY FACED YOUR OPPONENT.
IF YOU HAVE, WE'LL NEED TO REDRAW LOTS.
If both oppo-nents have two losses ...
... one of them will be elimi-nated.
PLEASE BEGIN.

A WORD ABOUT HIKARU NO GO

JAPAN GO ASSOCIATION, 2ND FLOOR

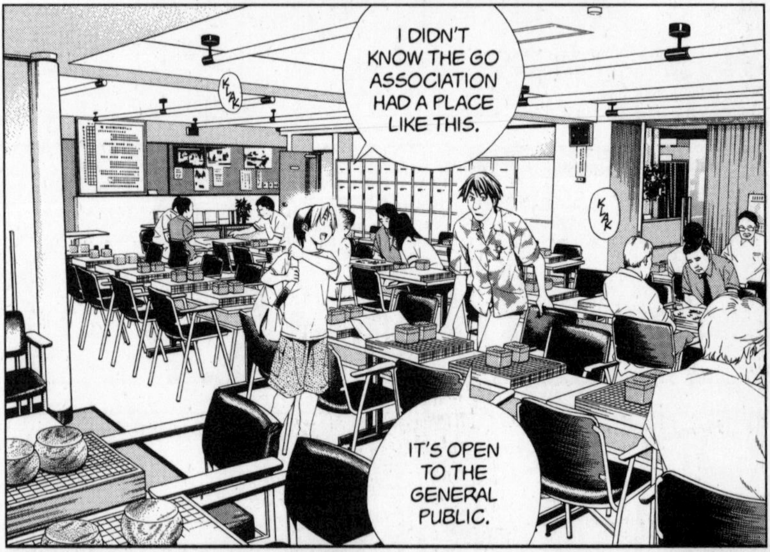
I DIDN'T KNOW THE GO ASSOCIATION HAD A PLACE LIKE THIS.
KLAK
KLAK
IT'S OPEN TO THE GENERAL PUBLIC.

ANYONE CAN PLAY GO HERE, JUST LIKE AT A GO SALON. THERE ARE EVEN DAYS THAT ARE SET ASIDE FOR BEGINNERS.

THE PUBLIC HAS ACCESS TO THE FIRST THREE FLOORS.

IT MIGHT BE FUN TO VISIT AND SEE HOW ACCURATE THE SCENES ARE IN THE MANGA!

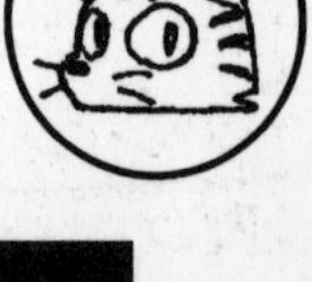

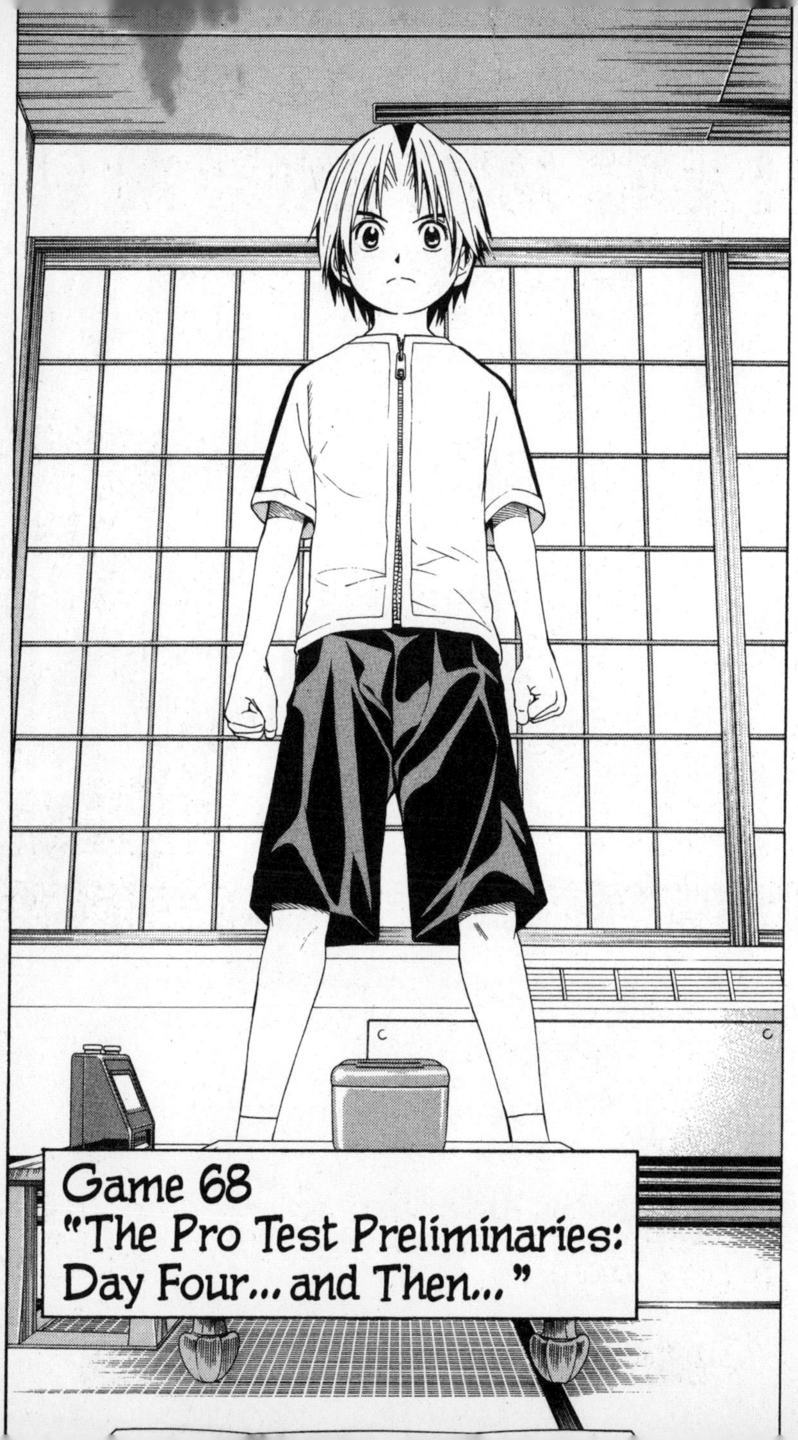
Game 68
"The Pro Test Preliminaries: Day Four... and Then..."

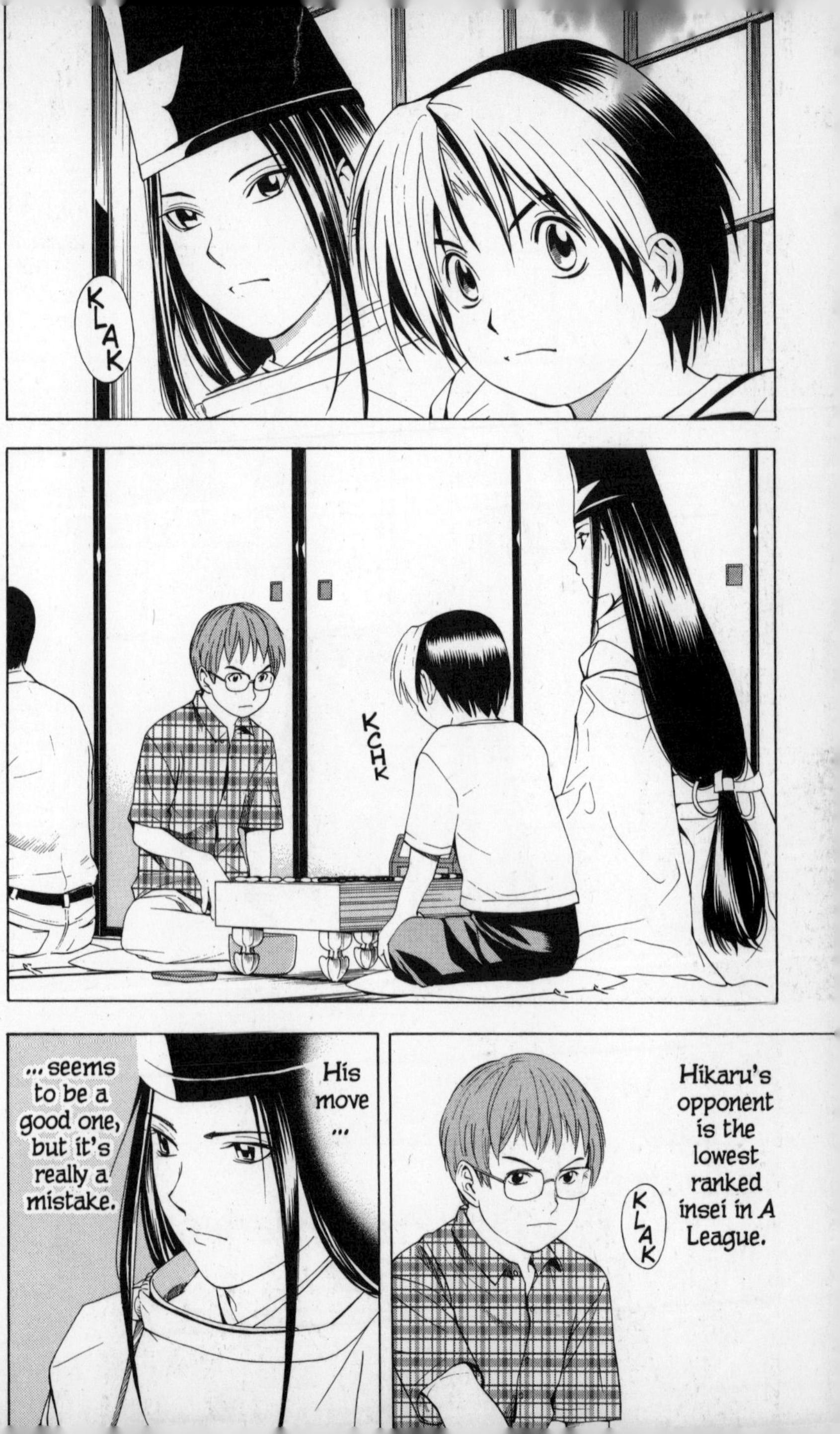
KLAK
KCHK
Hikaru's opponent is the lowest ranked insei in A League.
KLAK
His move ...
... seems to be a good one, but it's really a mistake.

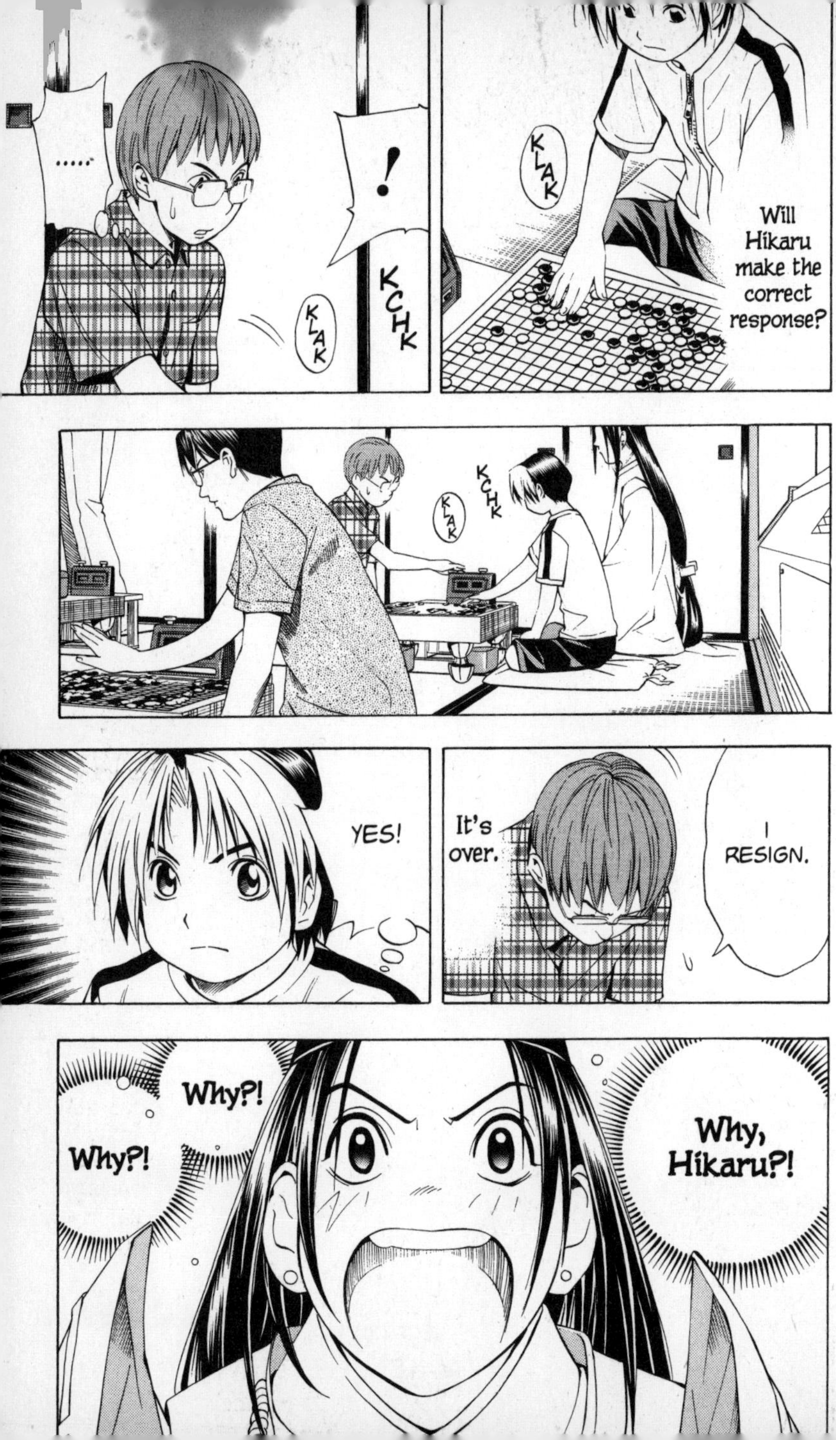
KLAK
Will Hikaru make the correct response?
!
KCHK
KLAK
......
KCHK
KLAK
I RESIGN.
It's over.
YES!
Why, Hikaru?!
Why?!
Why?!

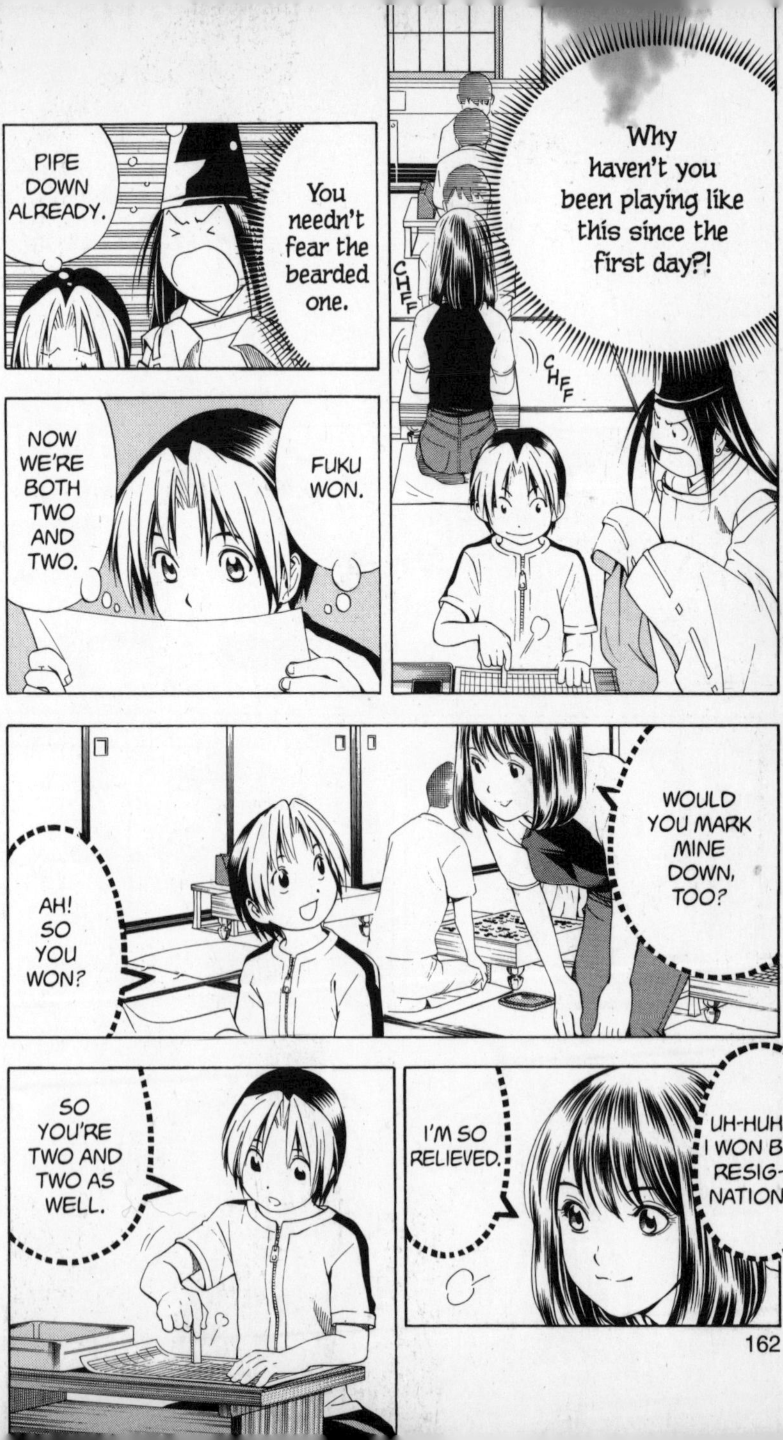

Why haven't you been playing like this since the first day?!
CHFF
CHFF
You needn't fear the bearded one.
PIPE DOWN ALREADY.
FUKU WON.
NOW WE'RE BOTH TWO AND TWO.
WOULD YOU MARK MINE DOWN, TOO?
AH! SO YOU WON?
UH-HUH. I WON BY RESIG-NATION.
I'M SO RELIEVED.
SO YOU'RE TWO AND TWO AS WELL.

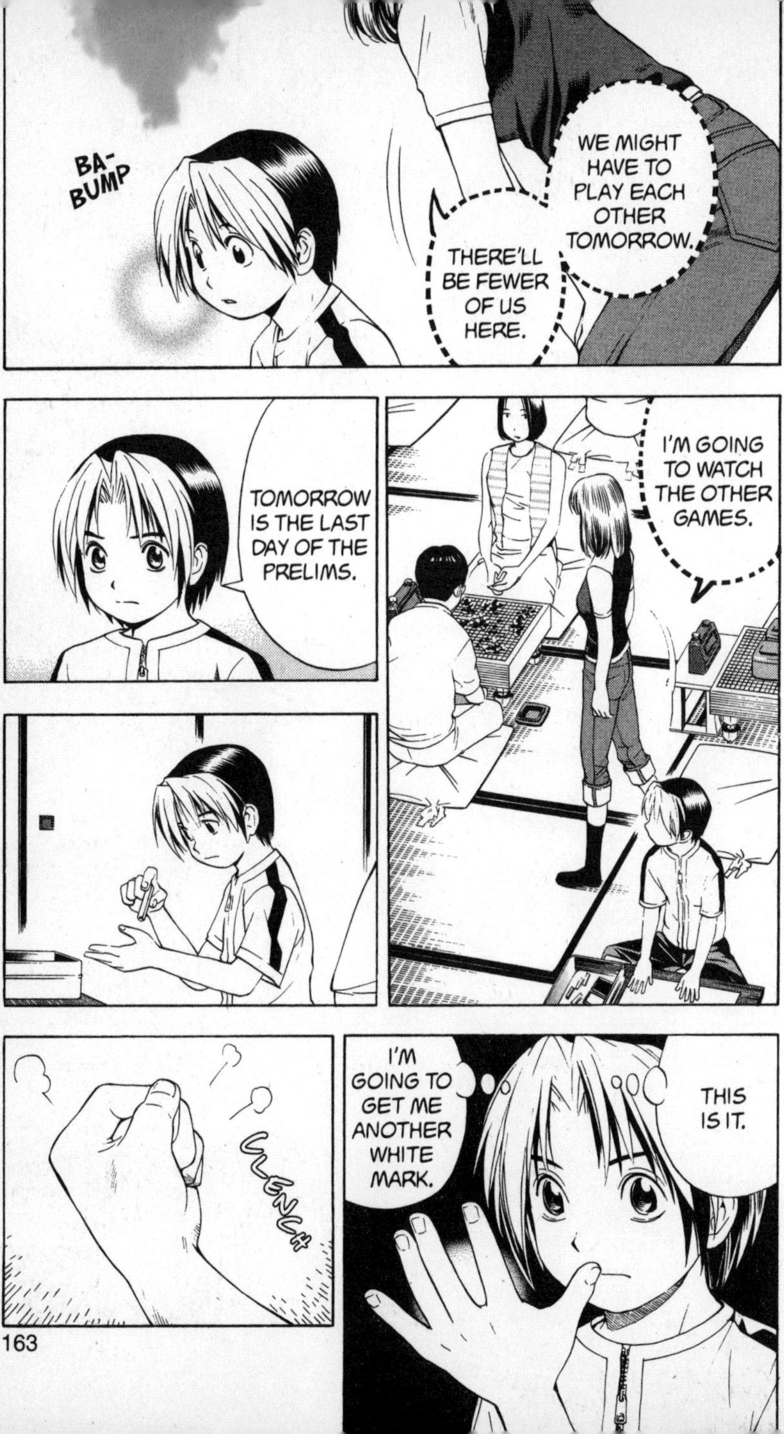
BA-BUMP
WE MIGHT HAVE TO PLAY EACH OTHER TOMORROW.
THERE'LL BE FEWER OF US HERE.
I'M GOING TO WATCH THE OTHER GAMES.
TOMORROW IS THE LAST DAY OF THE PRELIMS.
THIS IS IT.
I'M GOING TO GET ME ANOTHER WHITE MARK.
CLENCH

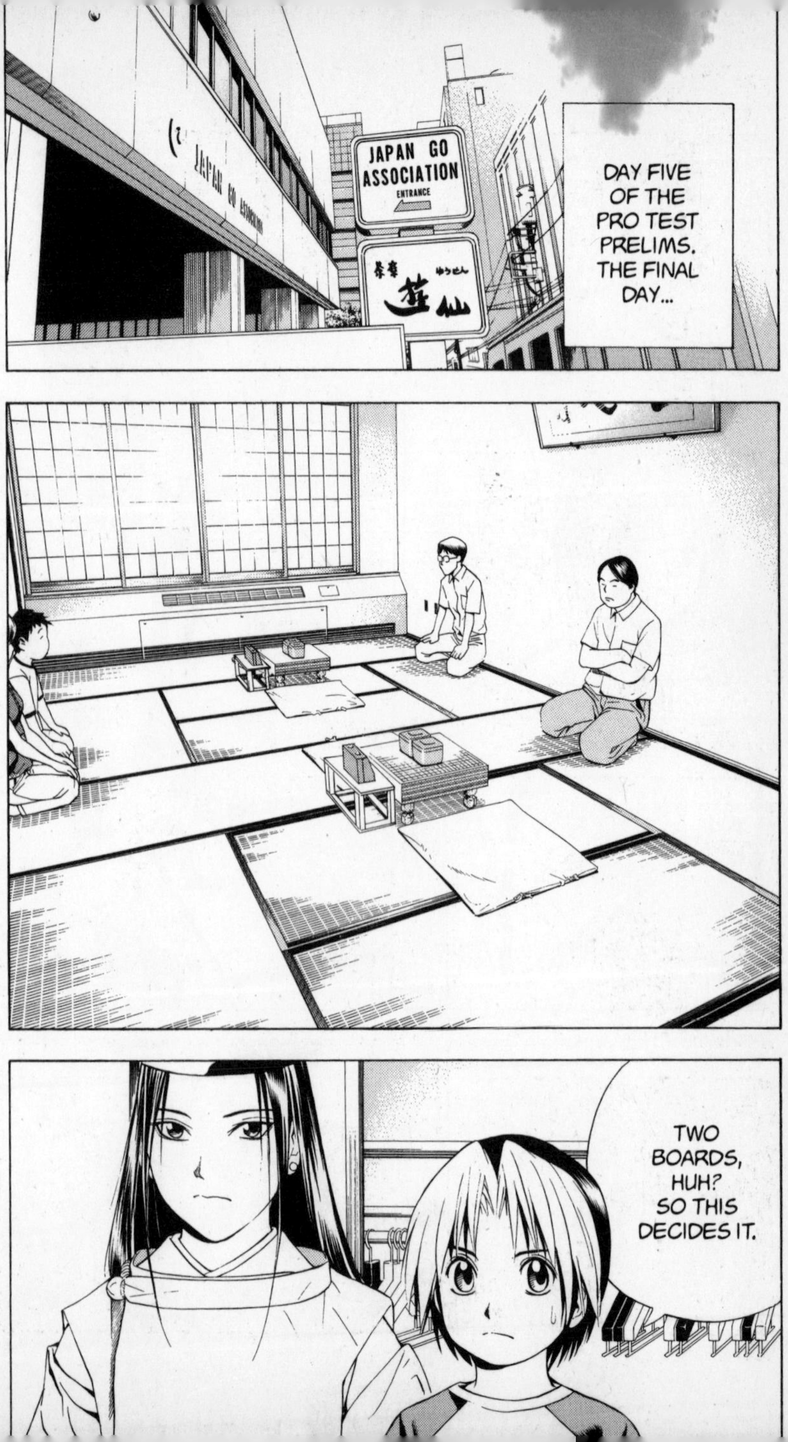
DAY FIVE OF THE PRO TEST PRELIMS. THE FINAL DAY...
JAPAN GO ASSOCIATION
ENTRANCE
TWO BOARDS, HUH? SO THIS DECIDES IT.

READ THIS WAY

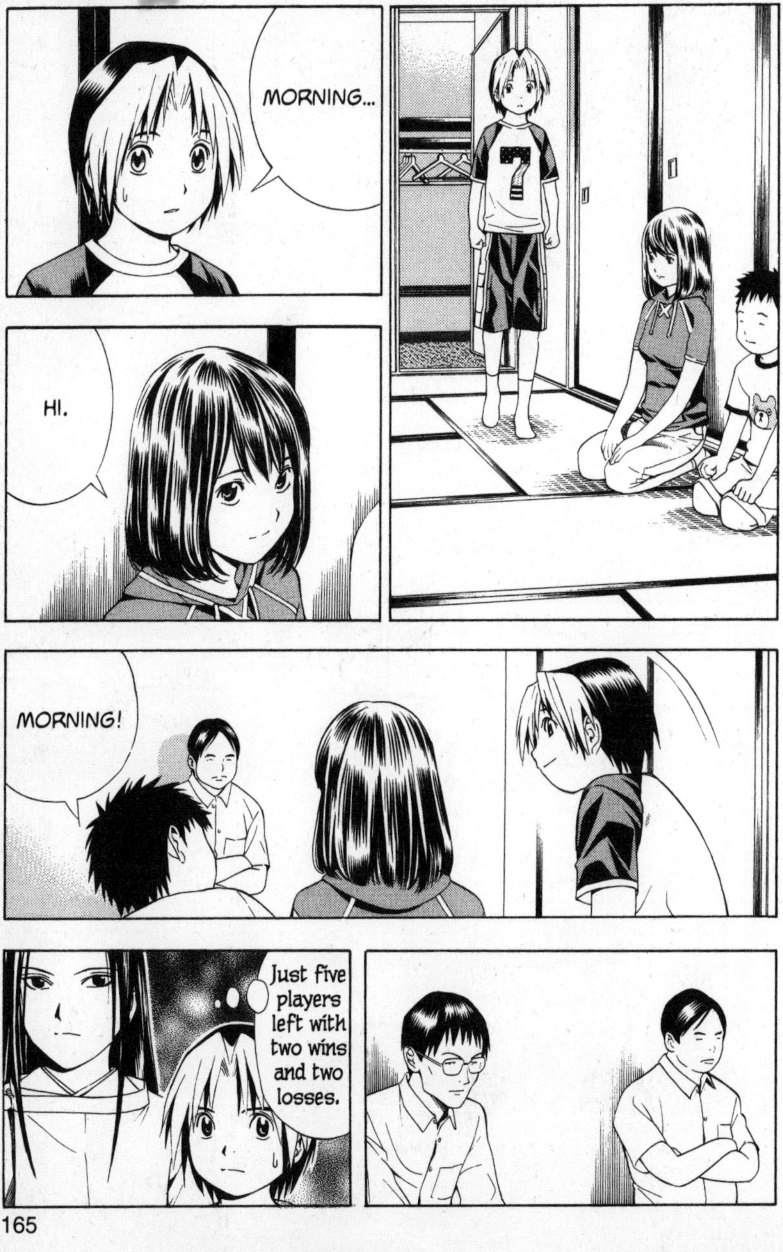
MORNING...
HI.
MORNING!
Just five players left with two wins and two losses.

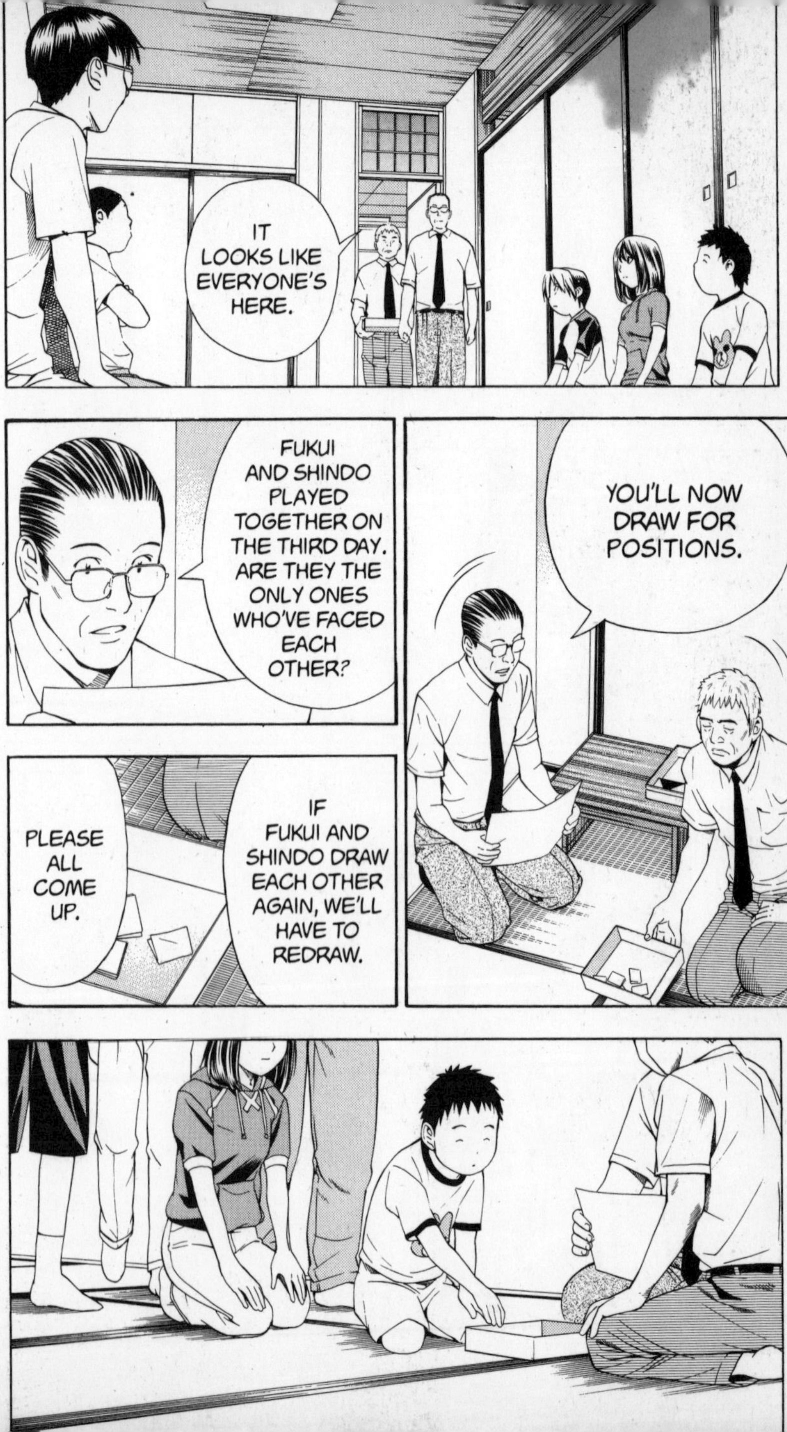
IT LOOKS LIKE EVERYONE'S HERE.
YOU'LL NOW DRAW FOR POSITIONS.
FUKUI AND SHINDO PLAYED TOGETHER ON THE THIRD DAY. ARE THEY THE ONLY ONES WHO'VE FACED EACH OTHER?
IF FUKUI AND SHINDO DRAW EACH OTHER AGAIN, WE'LL HAVE TO REDRAW.
PLEASE ALL COME UP.

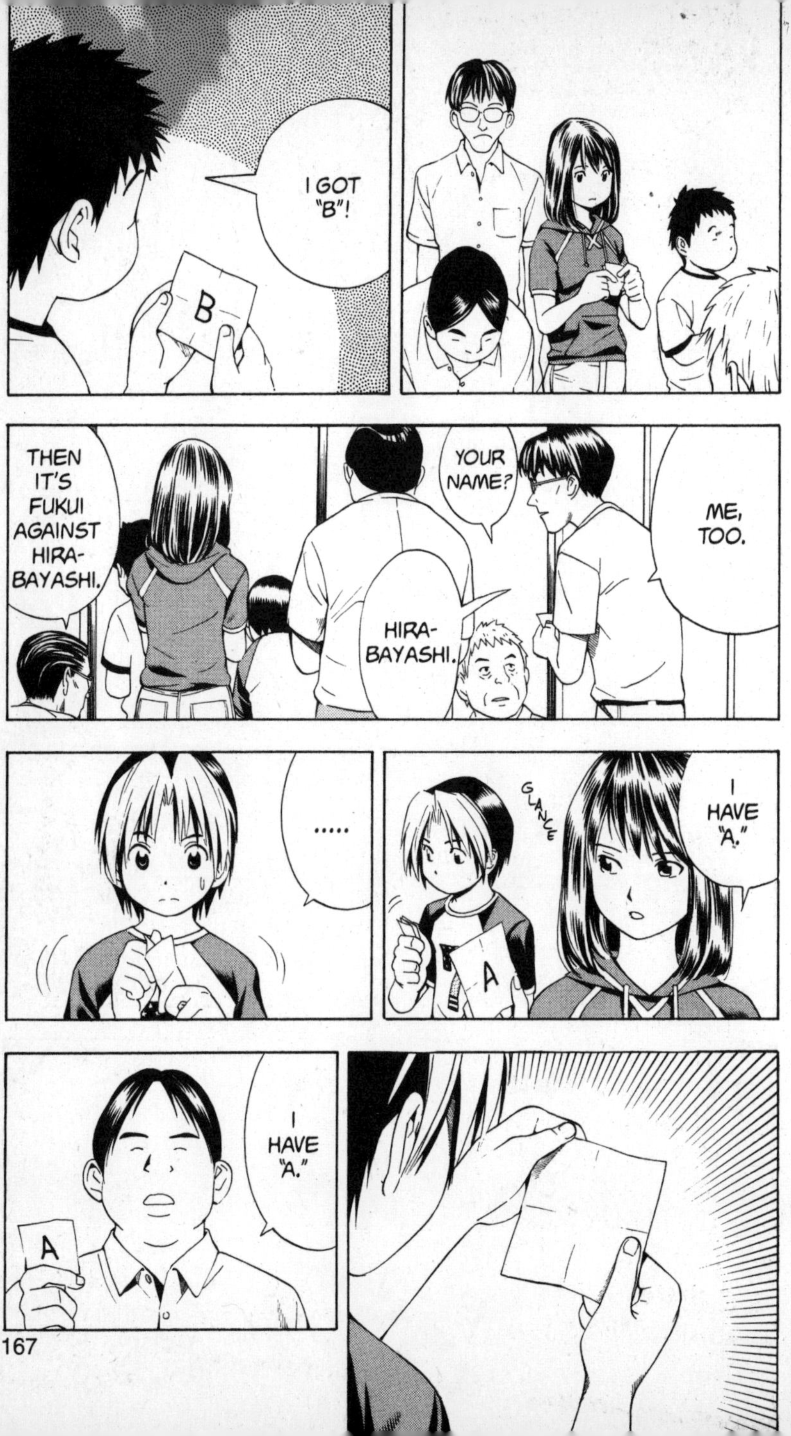
I GOT "B"!
ME, TOO.
YOUR NAME?
HIRA-BAYASHI.
THEN IT'S FUKUI AGAINST HIRA-BAYASHI.
I HAVE "A."
GLANCE
.....
I HAVE "A."

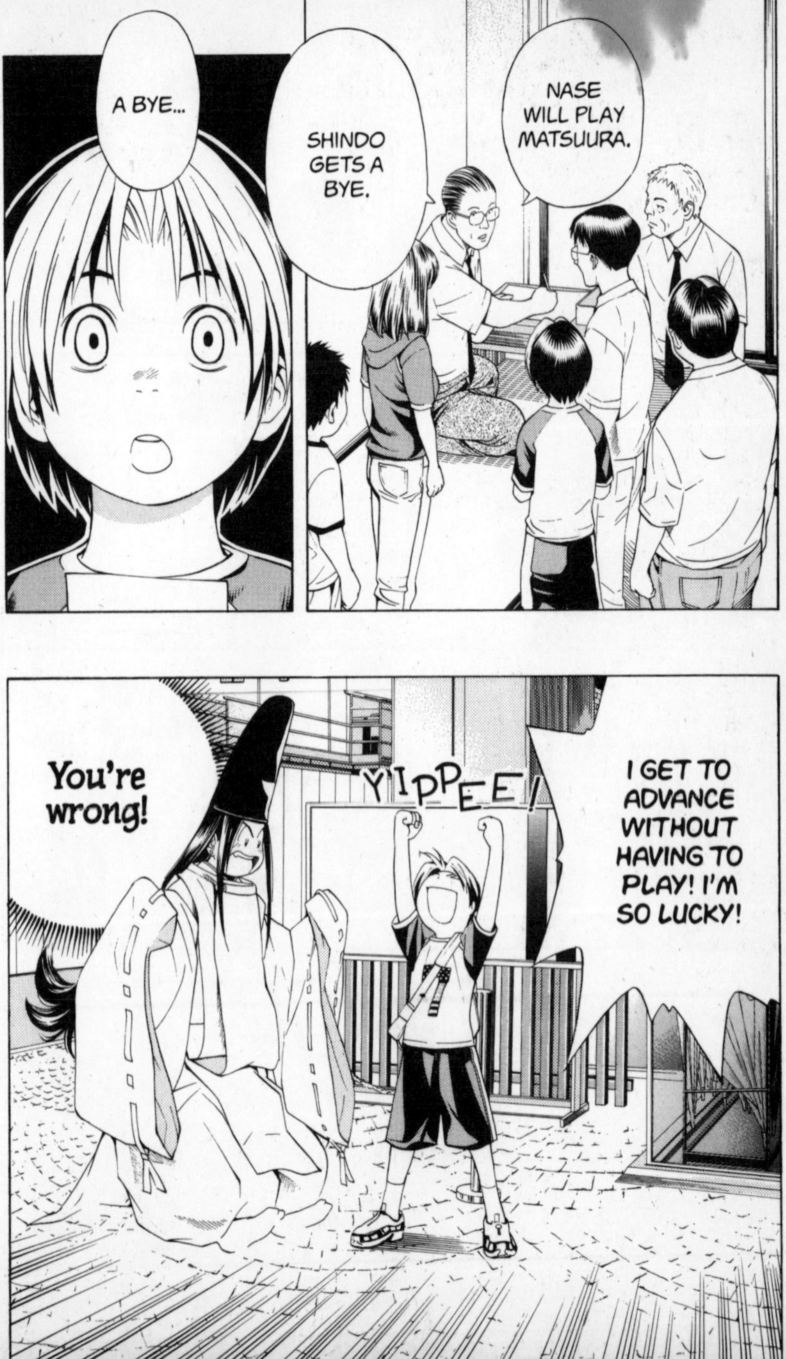
NASE WILL PLAY MATSUURA.
SHINDO GETS A BYE.
A BYE...
I GET TO ADVANCE WITHOUT HAVING TO PLAY! I'M SO LUCKY!
YIPPEE!
You're wrong!

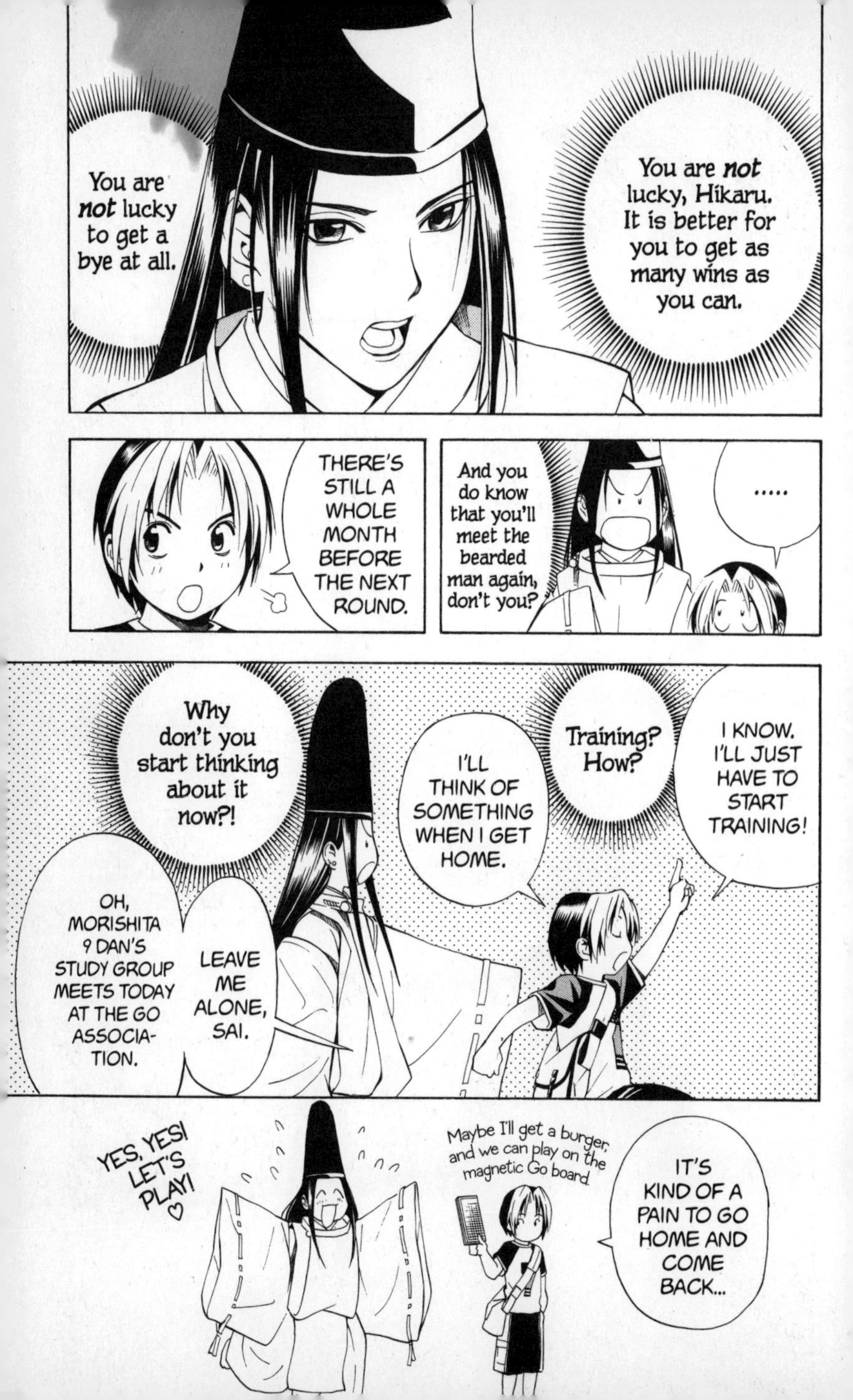
You are *not* lucky, Hikaru. It is better for you to get as many wins as you can.
You are *not* lucky to get a bye at all.
.....
And you do know that you'll meet the bearded man again, don't you?
THERE'S STILL A WHOLE MONTH BEFORE THE NEXT ROUND.
I KNOW. I'LL JUST HAVE TO START TRAINING!
Training? How?
I'LL THINK OF SOMETHING WHEN I GET HOME.
Why don't you start thinking about it now?!
LEAVE ME ALONE, SAI.
OH, MORISHITA 9 DAN'S STUDY GROUP MEETS TODAY AT THE GO ASSOCIA-TION.
IT'S KIND OF A PAIN TO GO HOME AND COME BACK...
Maybe I'll get a burger, and we can play on the magnetic Go board.
YES, YES! LET'S PLAY! ♡

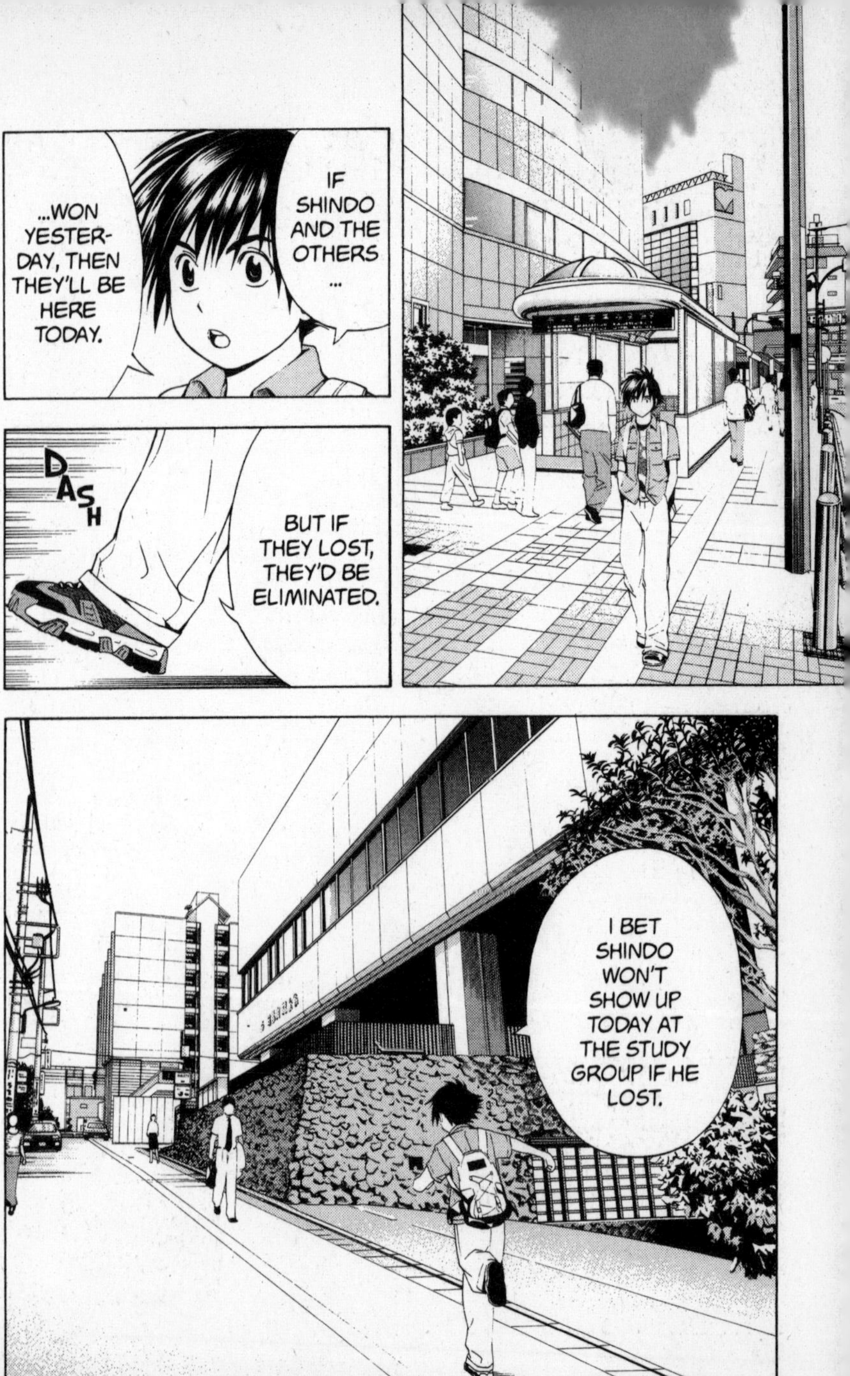
IF SHINDO AND THE OTHERS ...
...WON YESTER-DAY, THEN THEY'LL BE HERE TODAY.
DASH
BUT IF THEY LOST, THEY'D BE ELIMINATED.
I BET SHINDO WON'T SHOW UP TODAY AT THE STUDY GROUP IF HE LOST.

READ THIS WAY

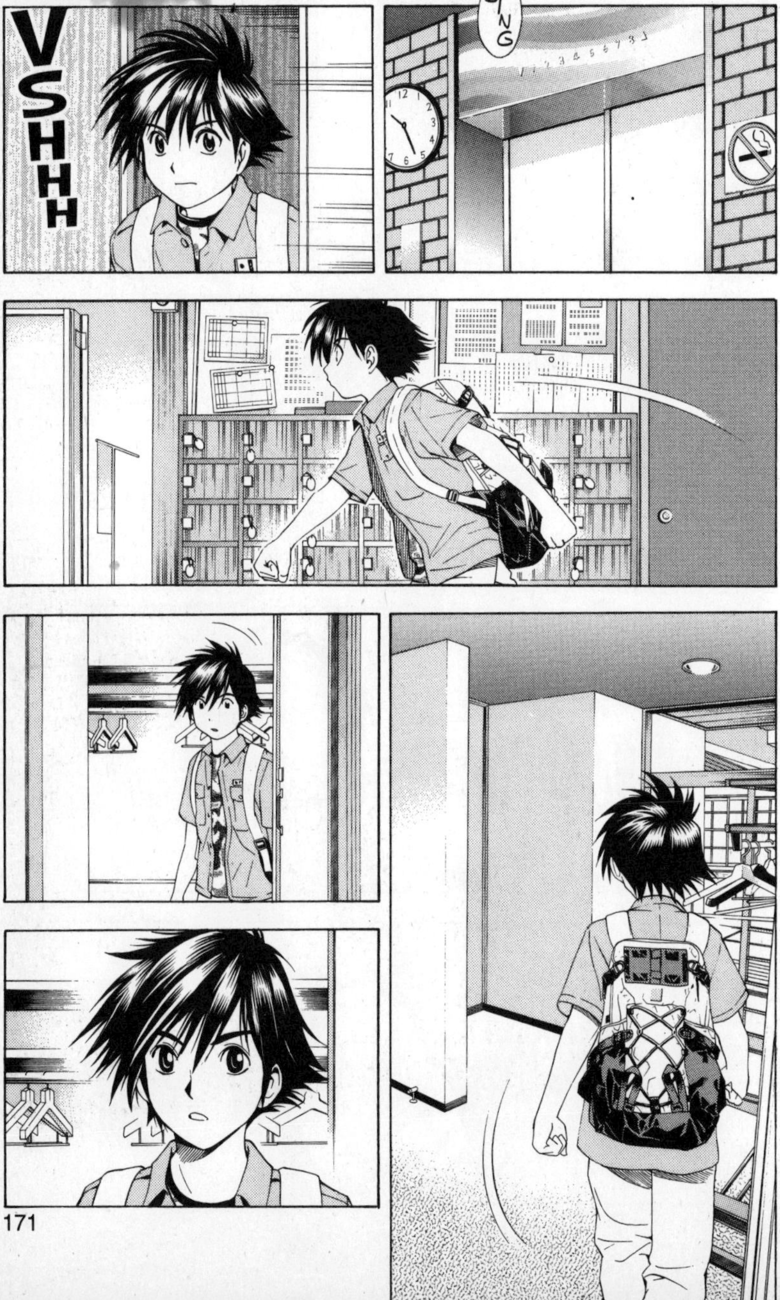
DING
VSHHH

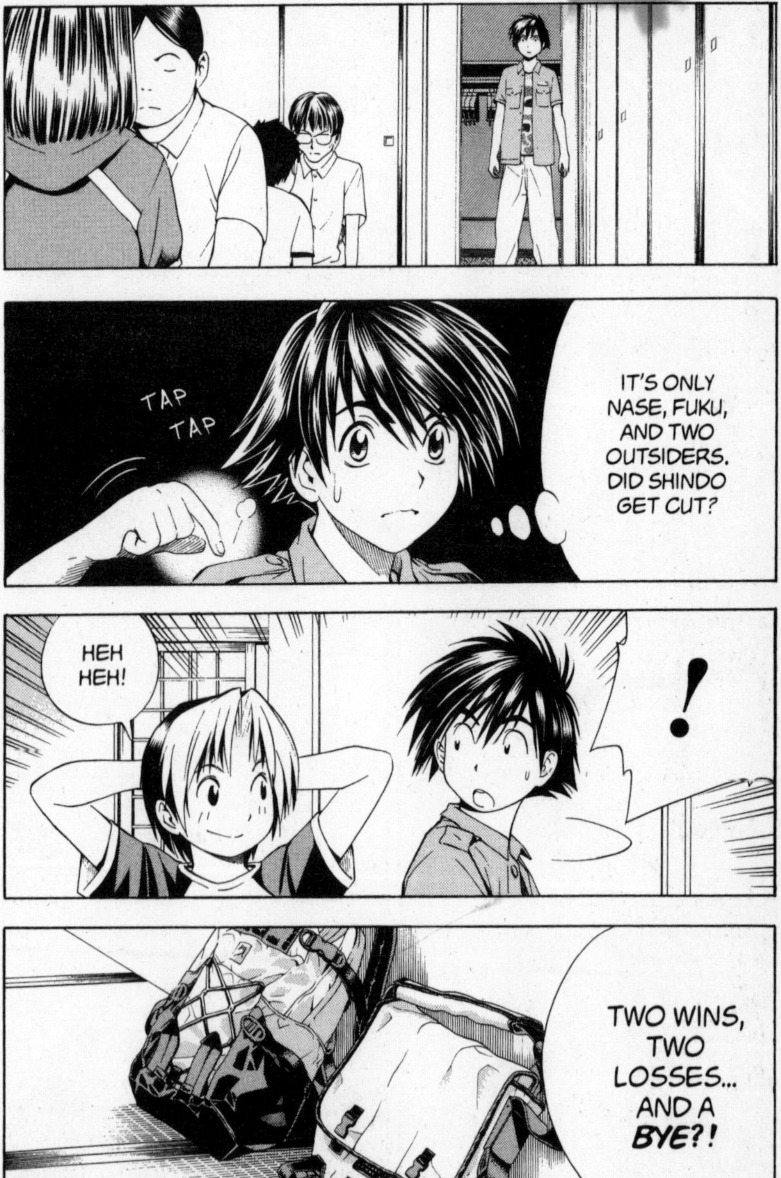
IT'S ONLY NASE, FUKU, AND TWO OUTSIDERS. DID SHINDO GET CUT?
TAP TAP
!
HEH HEH!
TWO WINS, TWO LOSSES... AND A *BYE*?!

READ THIS WAY

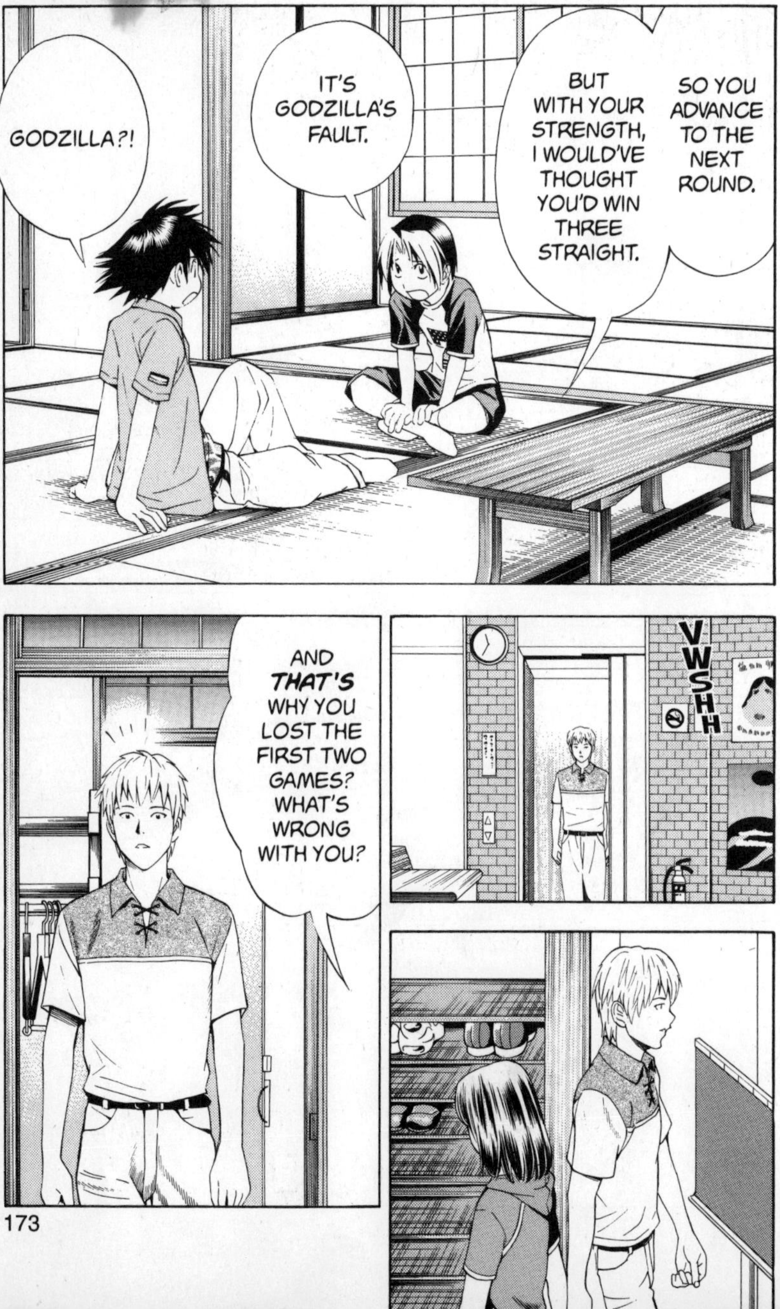

SO YOU ADVANCE TO THE NEXT ROUND.
BUT WITH YOUR STRENGTH, I WOULD'VE THOUGHT YOU'D WIN THREE STRAIGHT.
IT'S GODZILLA'S FAULT.
GODZILLA?!
VWSHH
AND *THAT'S* WHY YOU LOST THE FIRST TWO GAMES? WHAT'S WRONG WITH YOU?

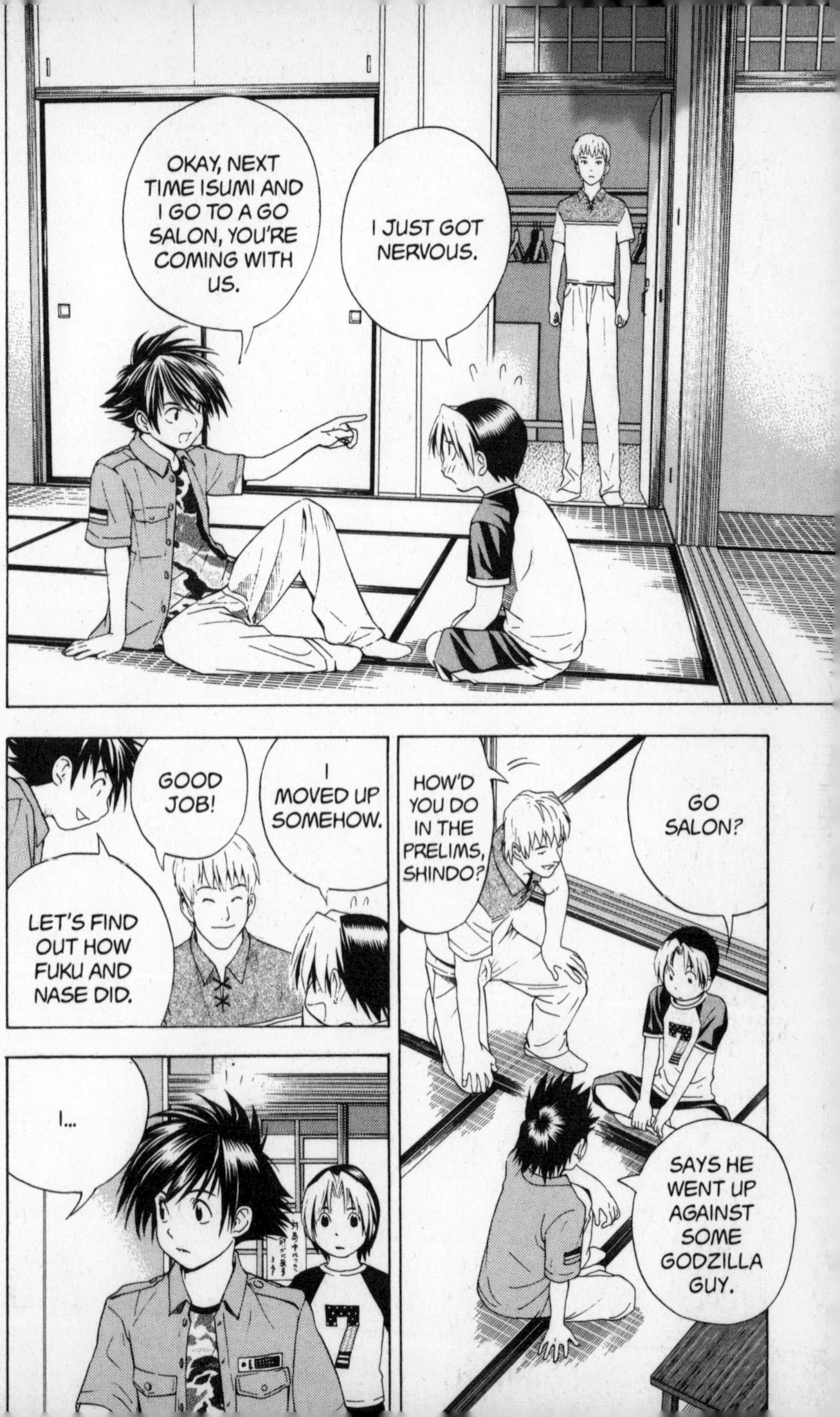
I JUST GOT NERVOUS.
OKAY, NEXT TIME ISUMI AND I GO TO A GO SALON, YOU'RE COMING WITH US.
GO SALON?
HOW'D YOU DO IN THE PRELIMS, SHINDO?
SAYS HE WENT UP AGAINST SOME GODZILLA GUY.
I MOVED UP SOMEHOW.
GOOD JOB!
LET'S FIND OUT HOW FUKU AND NASE DID.
I...

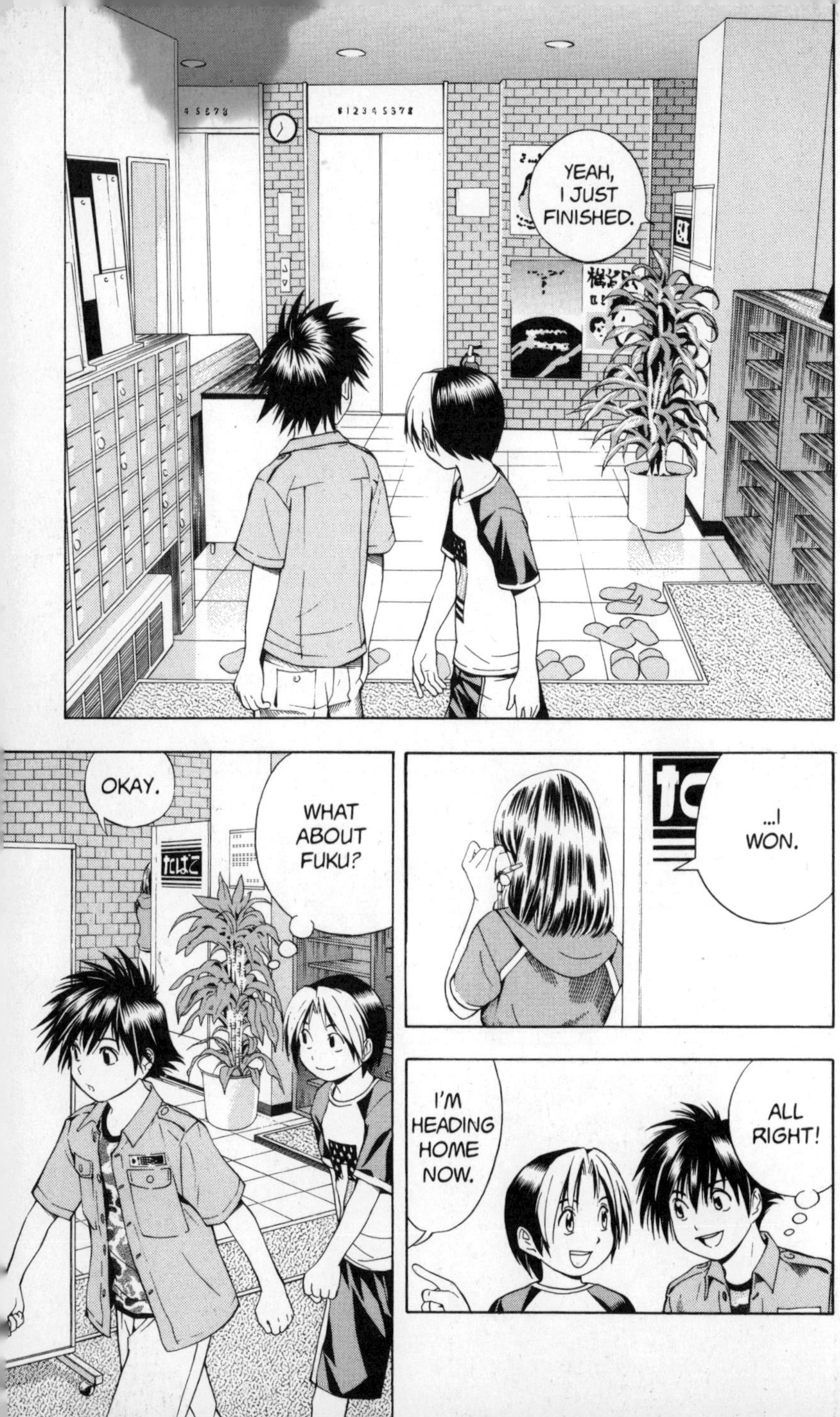
YEAH, I JUST FINISHED.
...I WON.
ALL RIGHT!
I'M HEADING HOME NOW.
WHAT ABOUT FUKU?
OKAY.
たばこ

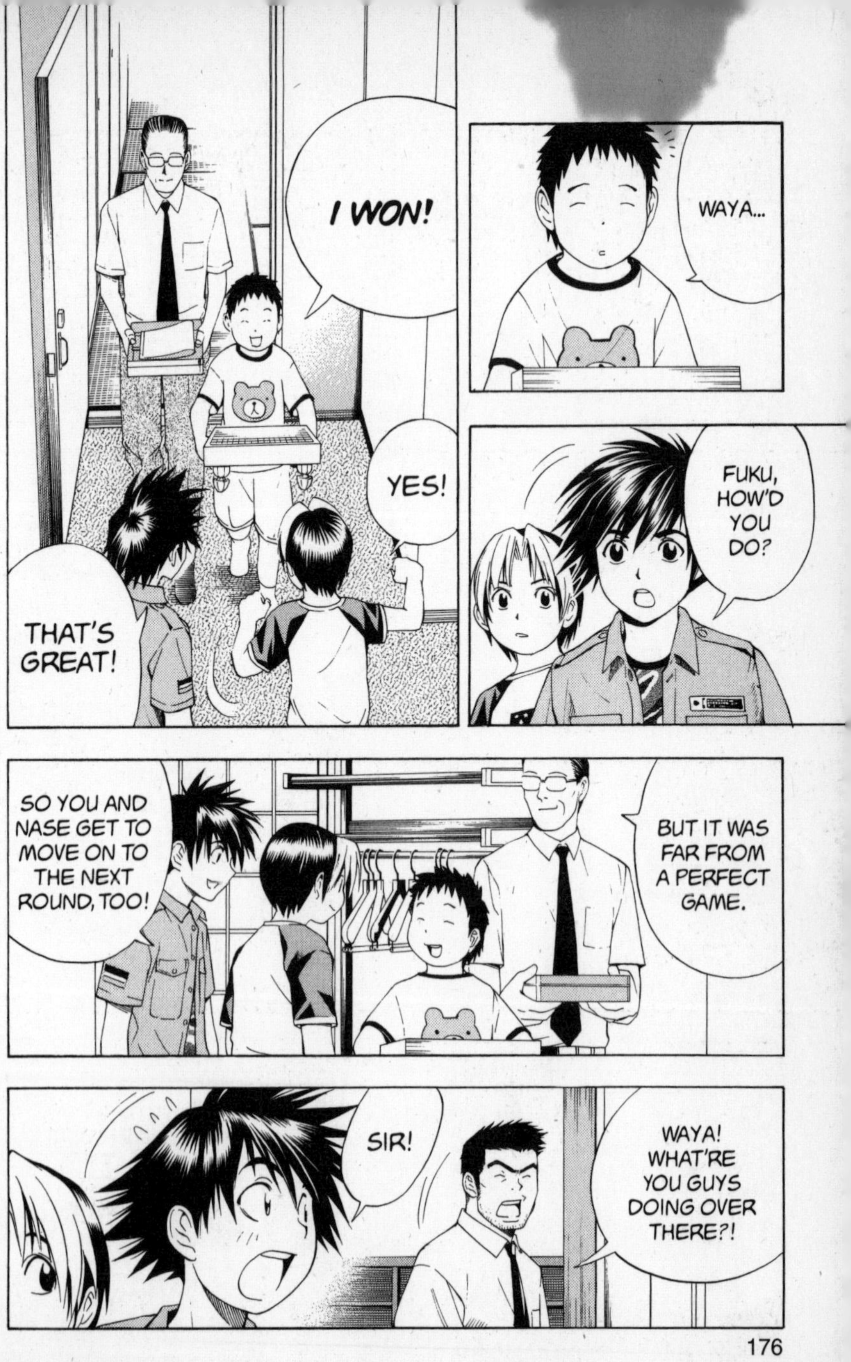
WAYA...
FUKU, HOW'D YOU DO?
I WON!
YES!
THAT'S GREAT!
BUT IT WAS FAR FROM A PERFECT GAME.
SO YOU AND NASE GET TO MOVE ON TO THE NEXT ROUND, TOO!
WAYA! WHAT'RE YOU GUYS DOING OVER THERE?!
SIR!

READ THIS WAY

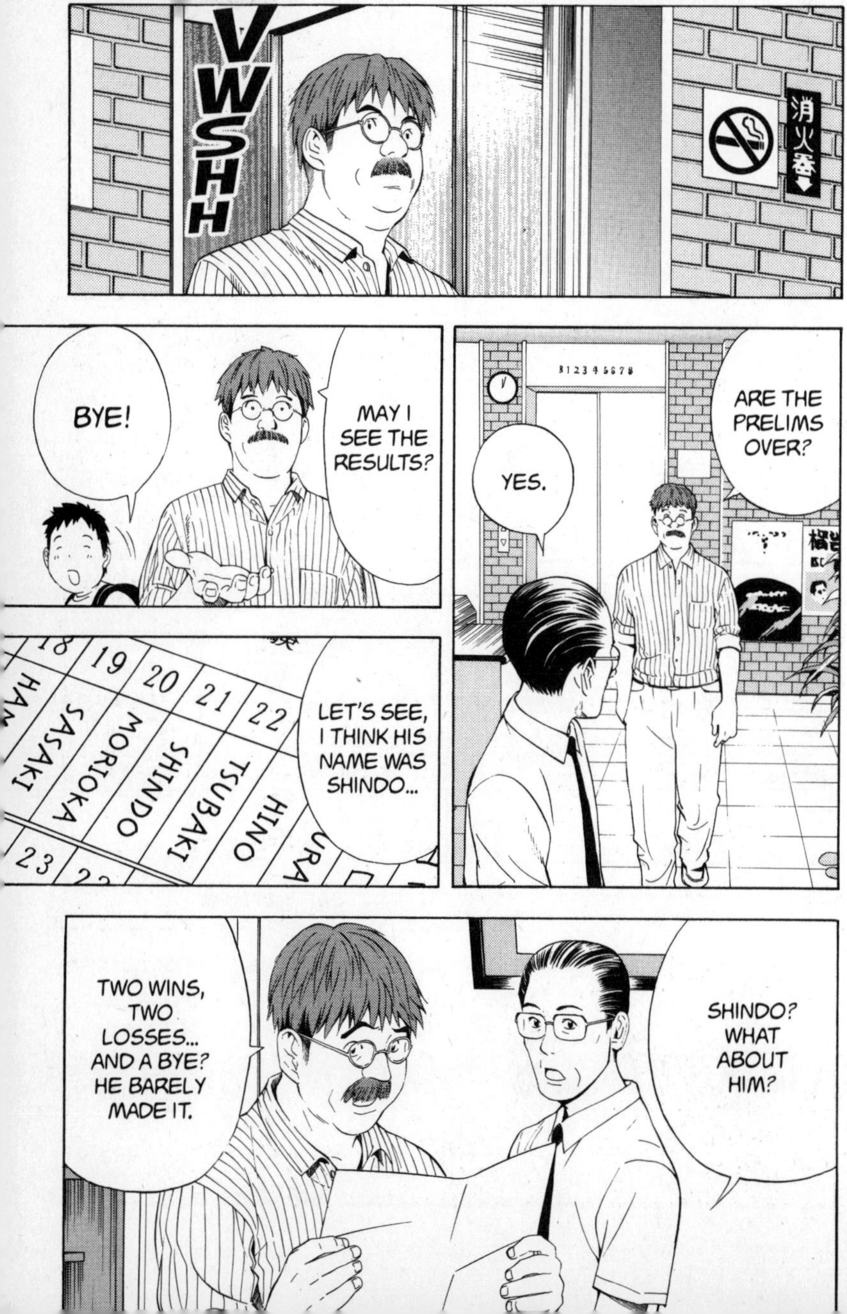

VWSHH
消火器
ARE THE PRELIMS OVER?
YES.
MAY I SEE THE RESULTS?
BYE!
LET'S SEE, I THINK HIS NAME WAS SHINDO...
18 19 20 21 22
HINO
TSUBAKI
SHINDO
MORIOKA
SASAKI
23
SHINDO? WHAT ABOUT HIM?
TWO WINS, TWO LOSSES... AND A BYE? HE BARELY MADE IT.

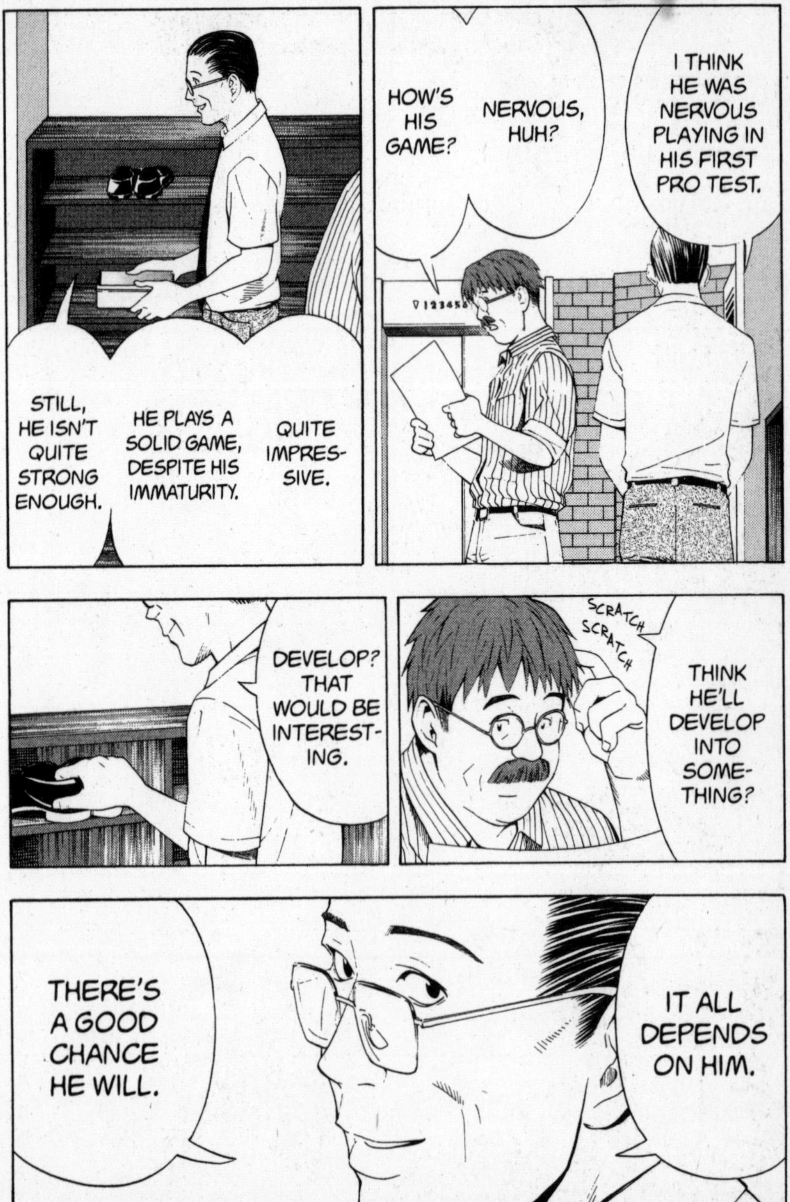
I THINK HE WAS NERVOUS PLAYING IN HIS FIRST PRO TEST.
NERVOUS, HUH?
HOW'S HIS GAME?
QUITE IMPRESSIVE.
HE PLAYS A SOLID GAME, DESPITE HIS IMMATURITY.
STILL, HE ISN'T QUITE STRONG ENOUGH.
SCRATCH SCRATCH
THINK HE'LL DEVELOP INTO SOMETHING?
DEVELOP? THAT WOULD BE INTERESTING.
IT ALL DEPENDS ON HIM.
THERE'S A GOOD CHANCE HE WILL.

I DON'T GET IT. COMPARED TO HIM, AKIRA TOYA HAS WON EIGHT STRAIGHT GAMES SINCE HIS DEBUT.

HMM.

KLAK

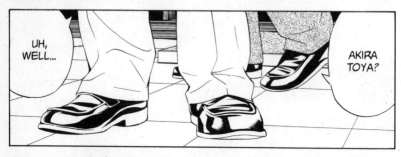

UH, WELL...

AKIRA TOYA?

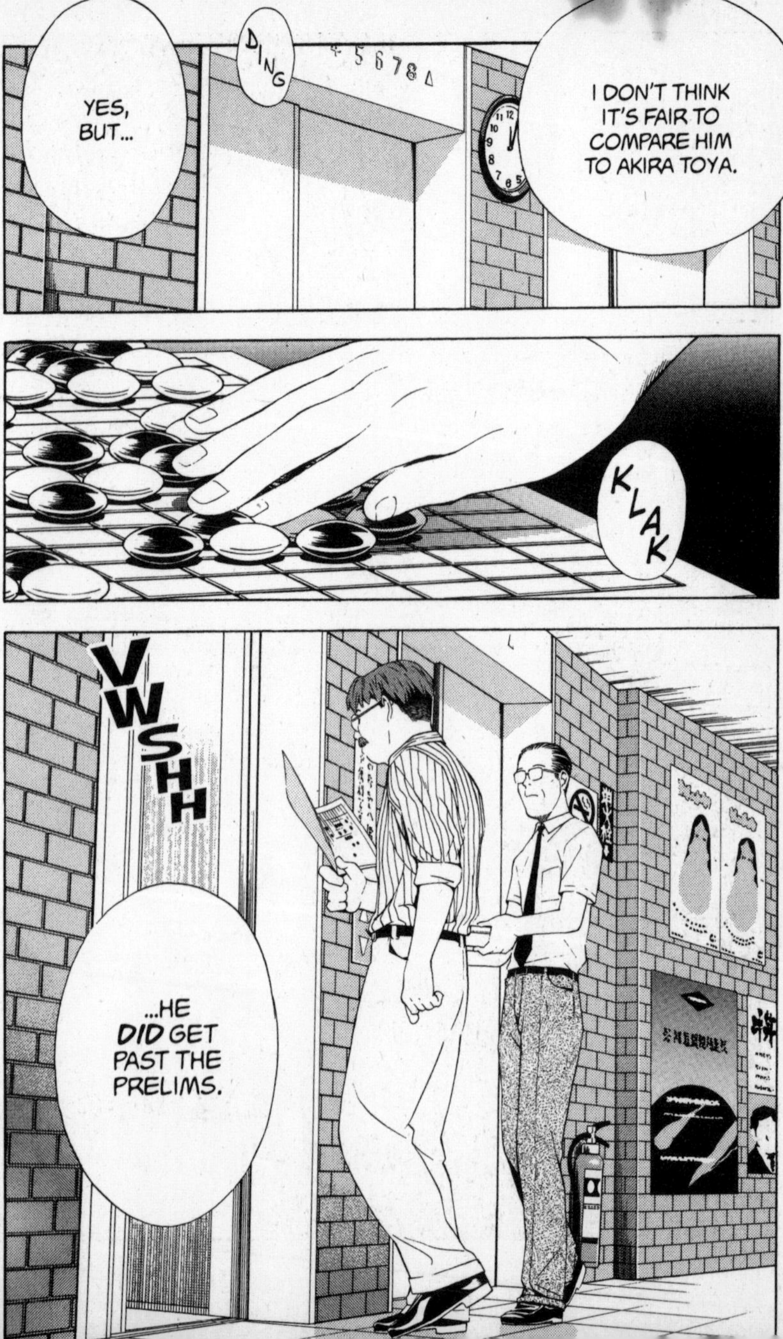
I DON'T THINK IT'S FAIR TO COMPARE HIM TO AKIRA TOYA.
DING
YES, BUT...
KLAK
VWSHH
...HE *DID* GET PAST THE PRELIMS.

READ THIS WAY

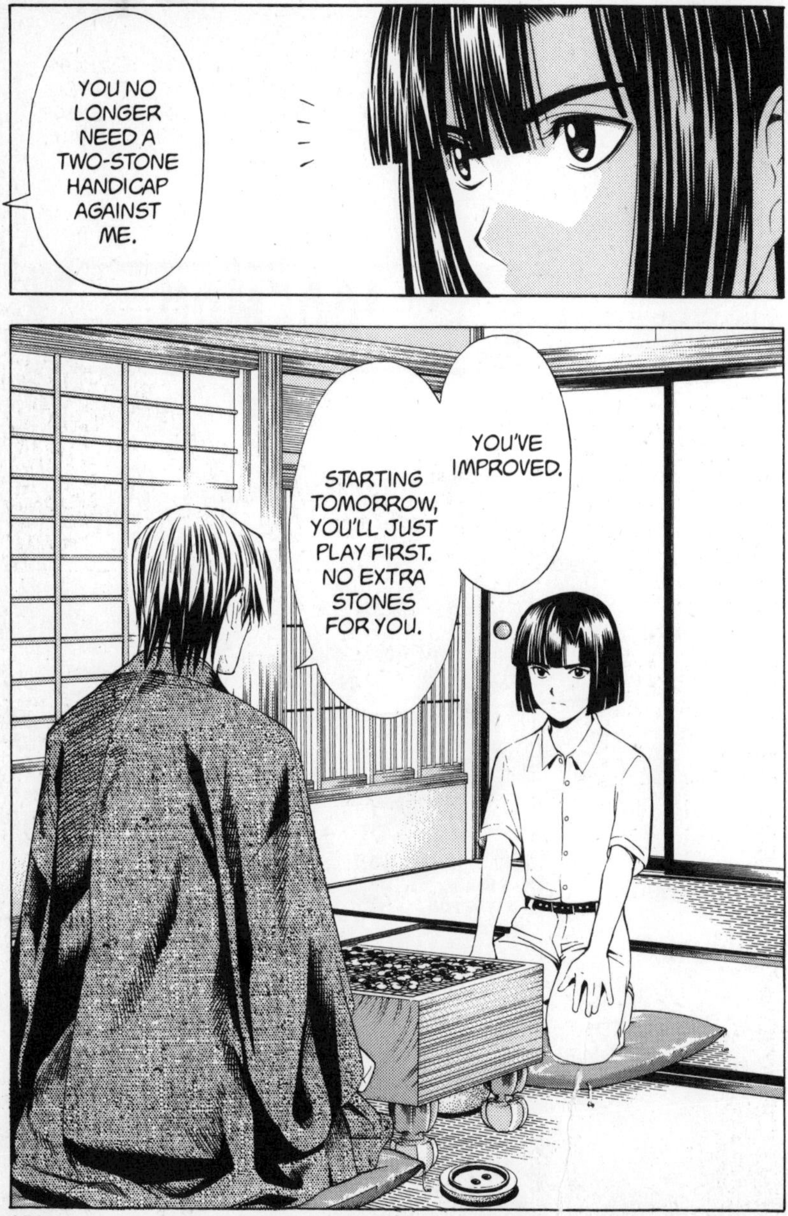
YOU NO LONGER NEED A TWO-STONE HANDICAP AGAINST ME.
YOU'VE IMPROVED.
STARTING TOMORROW, YOU'LL JUST PLAY FIRST. NO EXTRA STONES FOR YOU.

IGOEMON

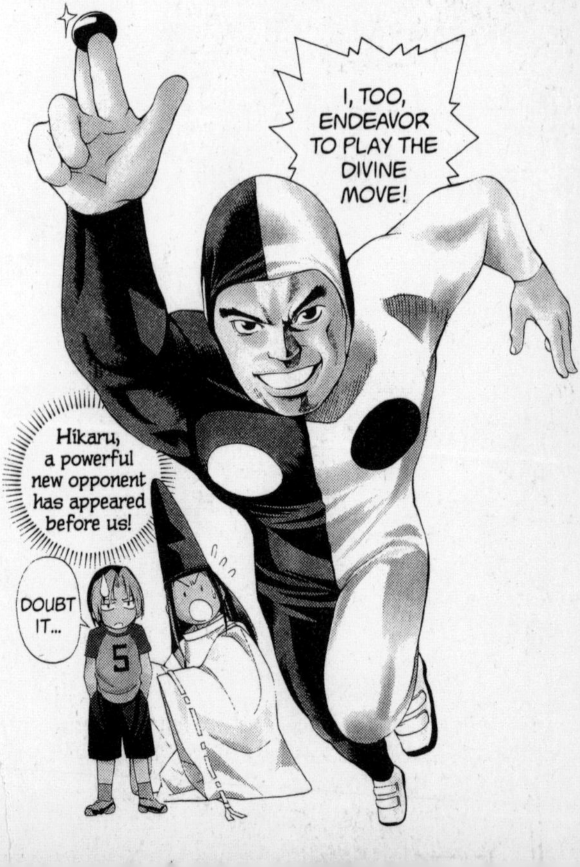
I, TOO, ENDEAVOR TO PLAY THE DIVINE MOVE!
Hikaru, a powerful new opponent has appeared before us!
DOUBT IT...

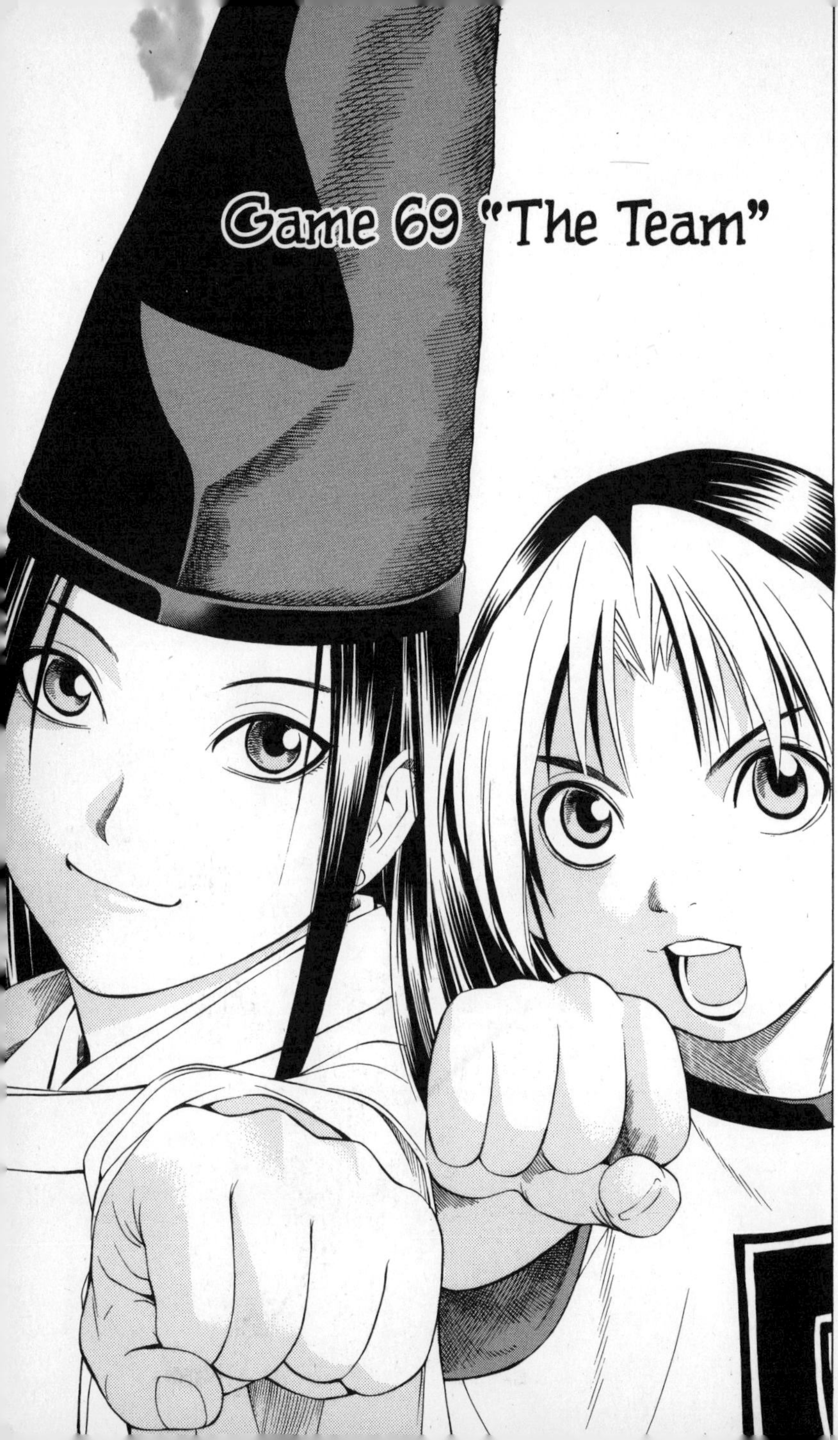
Game 69 "The Team"

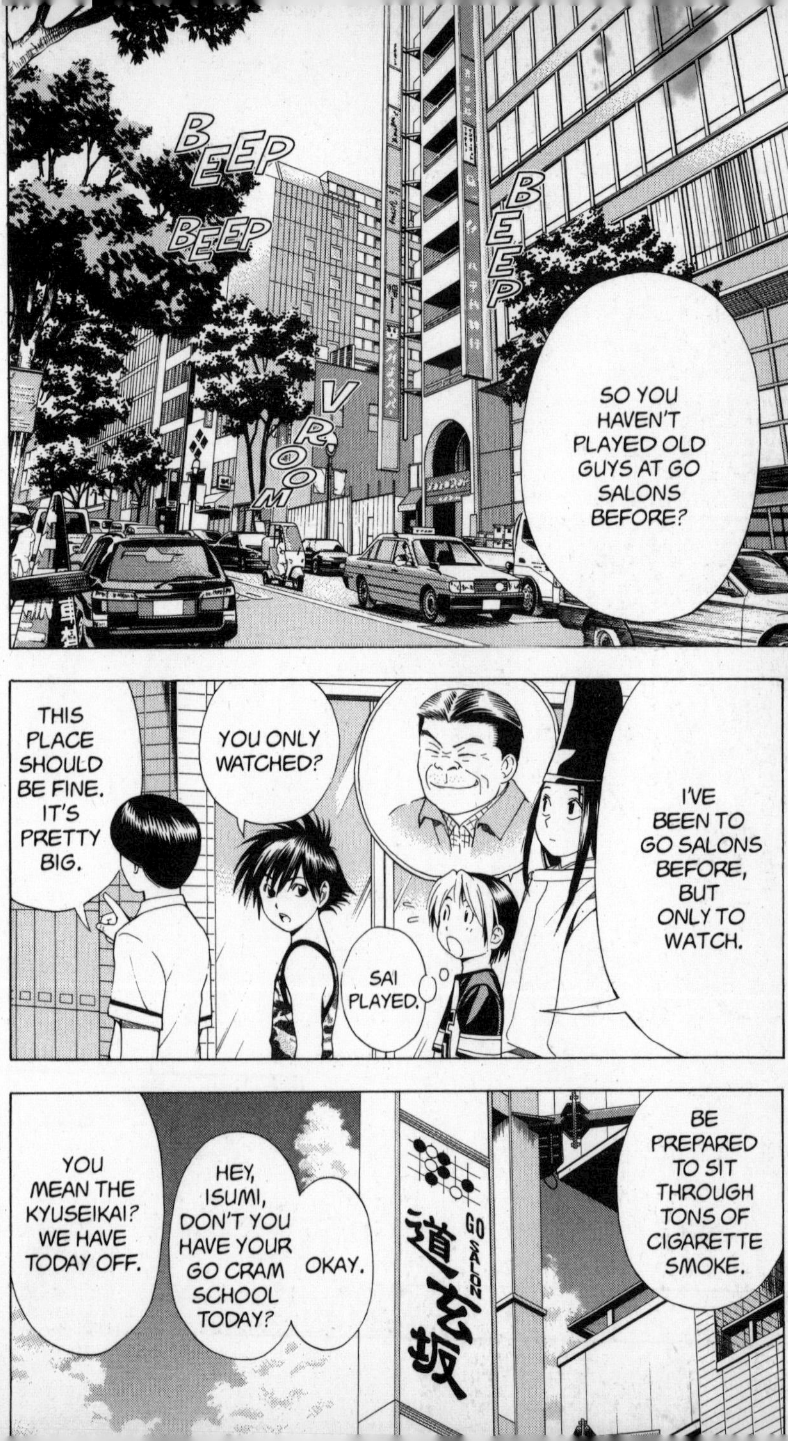
BEEP
BEEP
BEEP
SO YOU HAVEN'T PLAYED OLD GUYS AT GO SALONS BEFORE?
VROOM
I'VE BEEN TO GO SALONS BEFORE, BUT ONLY TO WATCH.
YOU ONLY WATCHED?
SAI PLAYED.
THIS PLACE SHOULD BE FINE. IT'S PRETTY BIG.
BE PREPARED TO SIT THROUGH TONS OF CIGARETTE SMOKE.
道玄坂
GO SALON
OKAY.
HEY, ISUMI, DON'T YOU HAVE YOUR GO CRAM SCHOOL TODAY?
YOU MEAN THE KYUSEIKAI? WE HAVE TODAY OFF.

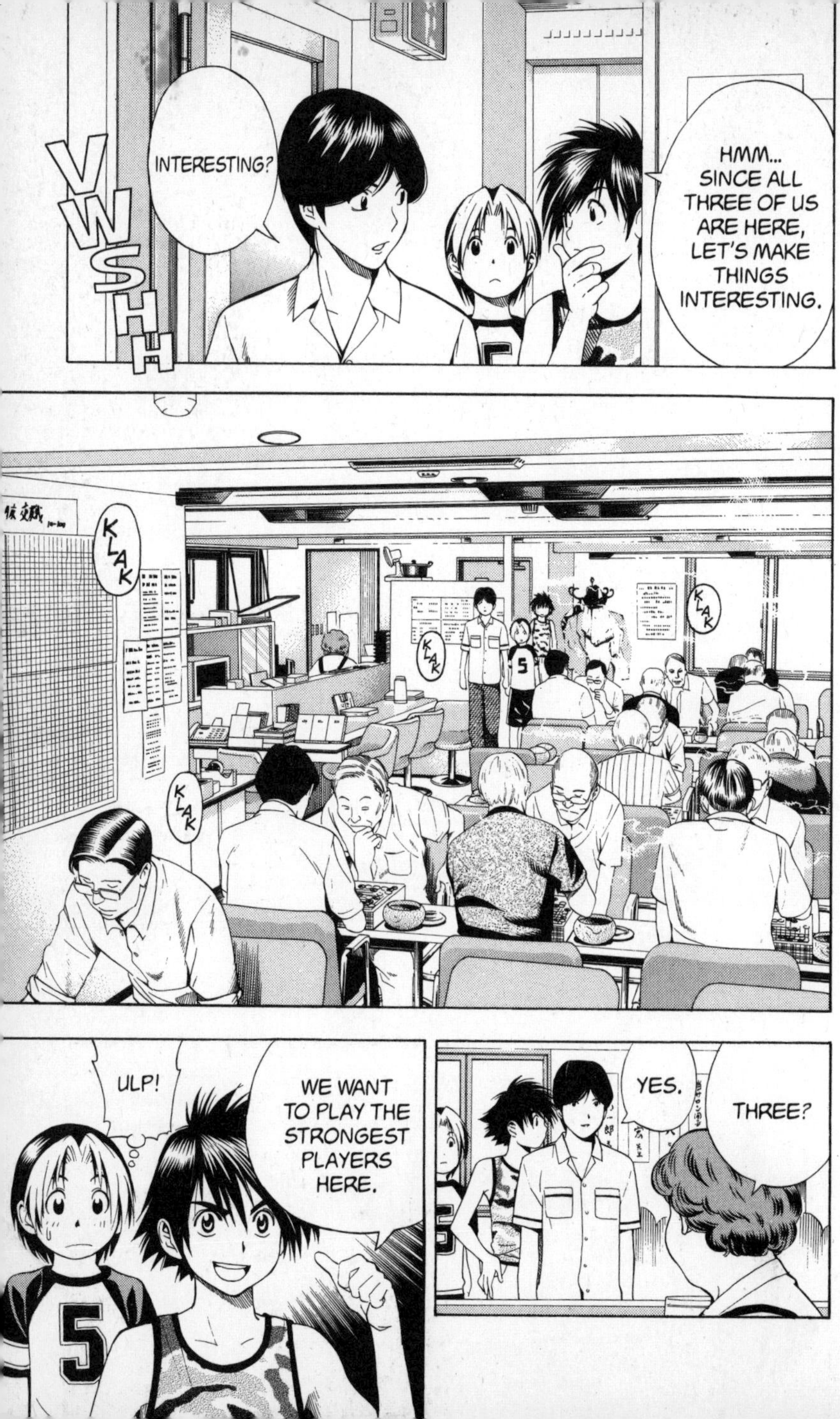
HMM... SINCE ALL THREE OF US ARE HERE, LET'S MAKE THINGS INTERESTING.
INTERESTING?
VWSHH
KLAK
KLAK
KLAK
KLAK
THREE?
YES.
WE WANT TO PLAY THE STRONGEST PLAYERS HERE.
ULP!

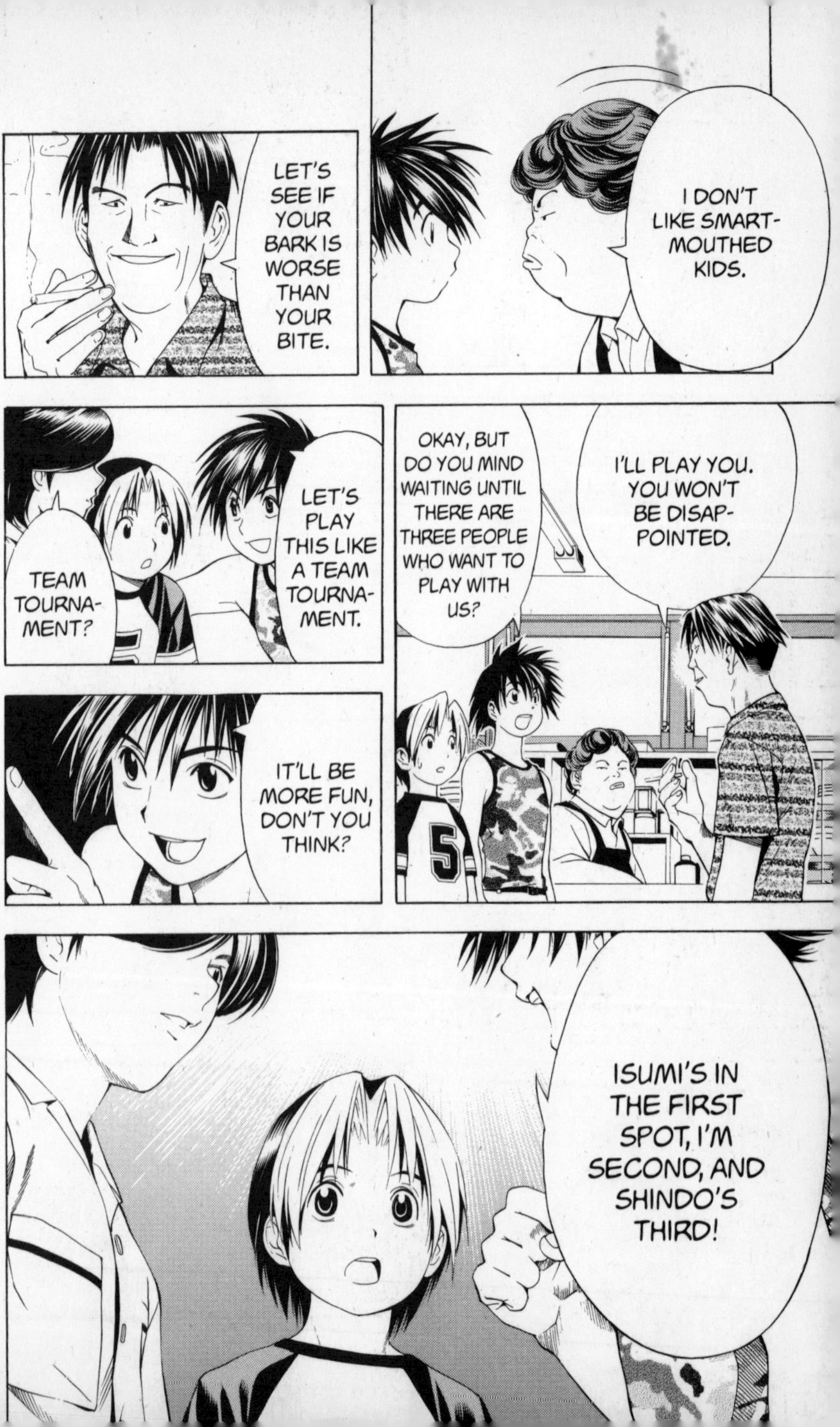
I DON'T LIKE SMART-MOUTHED KIDS.
LET'S SEE IF YOUR BARK IS WORSE THAN YOUR BITE.
I'LL PLAY YOU. YOU WON'T BE DISAPPOINTED.
OKAY, BUT DO YOU MIND WAITING UNTIL THERE ARE THREE PEOPLE WHO WANT TO PLAY WITH US?
LET'S PLAY THIS LIKE A TEAM TOURNAMENT.
TEAM TOURNAMENT?
IT'LL BE MORE FUN, DON'T YOU THINK?
ISUMI'S IN THE FIRST SPOT, I'M SECOND, AND SHINDO'S THIRD!

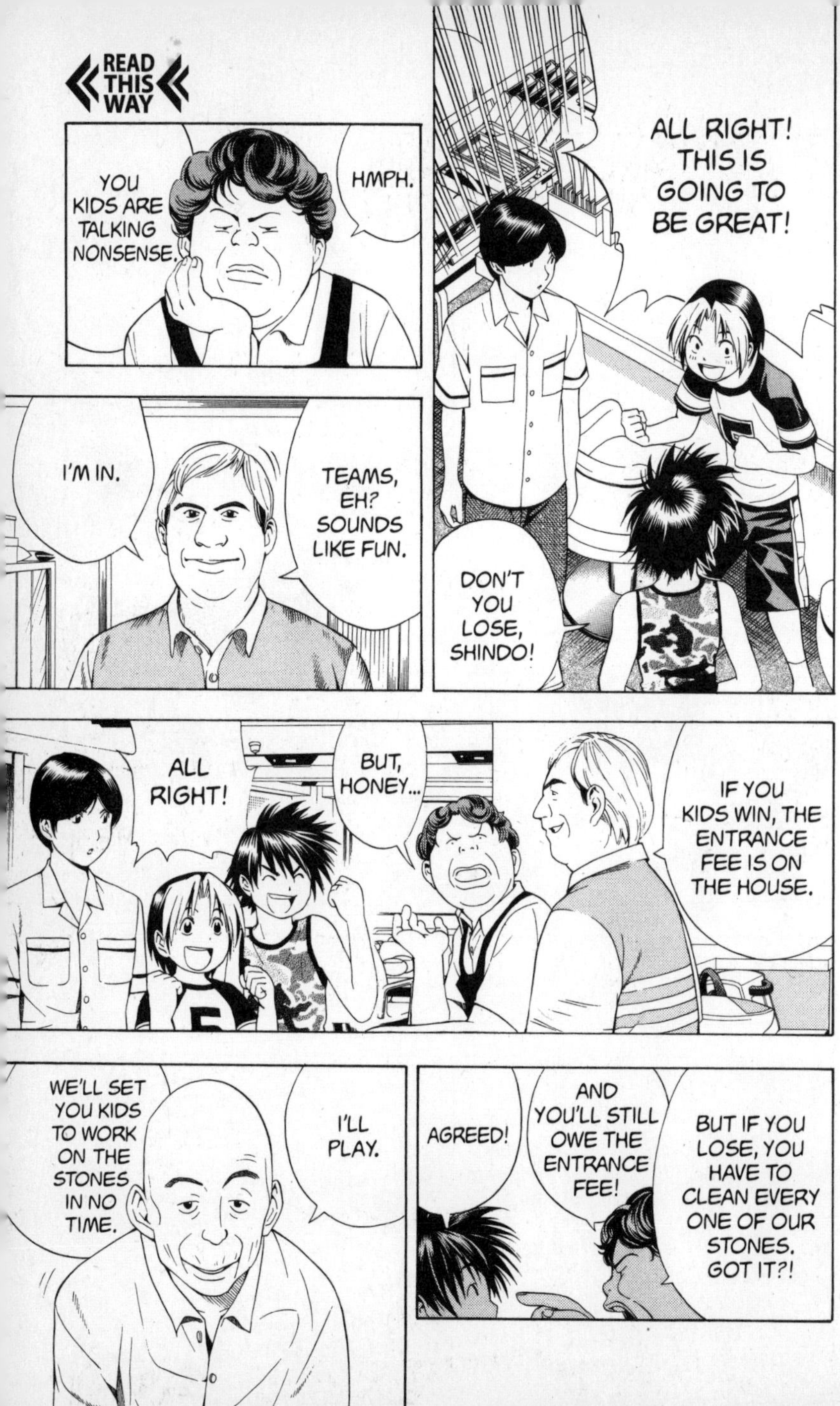
READ THIS WAY
ALL RIGHT! THIS IS GOING TO BE GREAT!
DON'T YOU LOSE, SHINDO!
HMPH.
YOU KIDS ARE TALKING NONSENSE.
TEAMS, EH? SOUNDS LIKE FUN.
I'M IN.
IF YOU KIDS WIN, THE ENTRANCE FEE IS ON THE HOUSE.
BUT, HONEY...
ALL RIGHT!
BUT IF YOU LOSE, YOU HAVE TO CLEAN EVERY ONE OF OUR STONES. GOT IT?!
AND YOU'LL STILL OWE THE ENTRANCE FEE!
AGREED!
I'LL PLAY.
WE'LL SET YOU KIDS TO WORK ON THE STONES IN NO TIME.

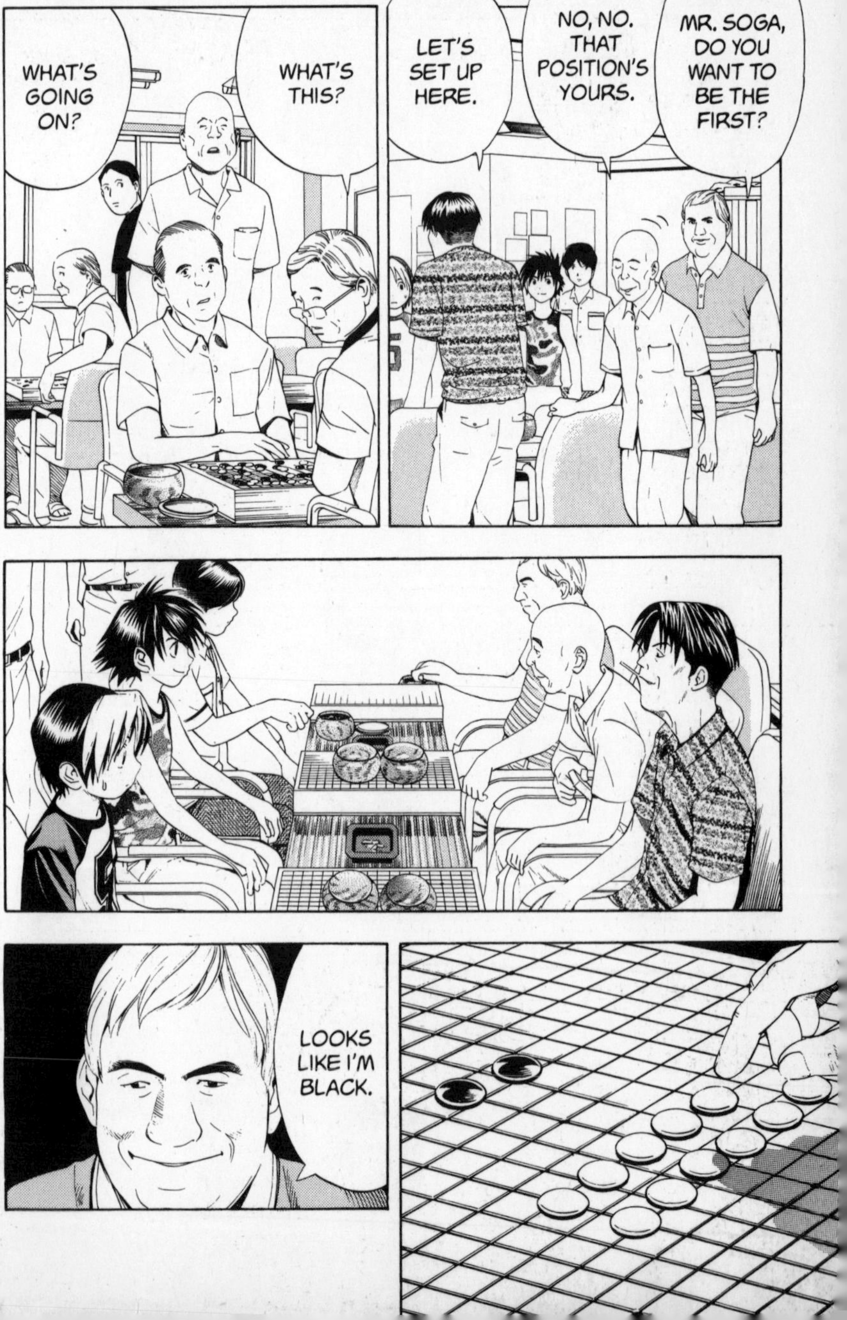
MR. SOGA, DO YOU WANT TO BE THE FIRST?
NO, NO. THAT POSITION'S YOURS.
LET'S SET UP HERE.
WHAT'S THIS?
WHAT'S GOING ON?
LOOKS LIKE I'M BLACK.

READ THIS WAY

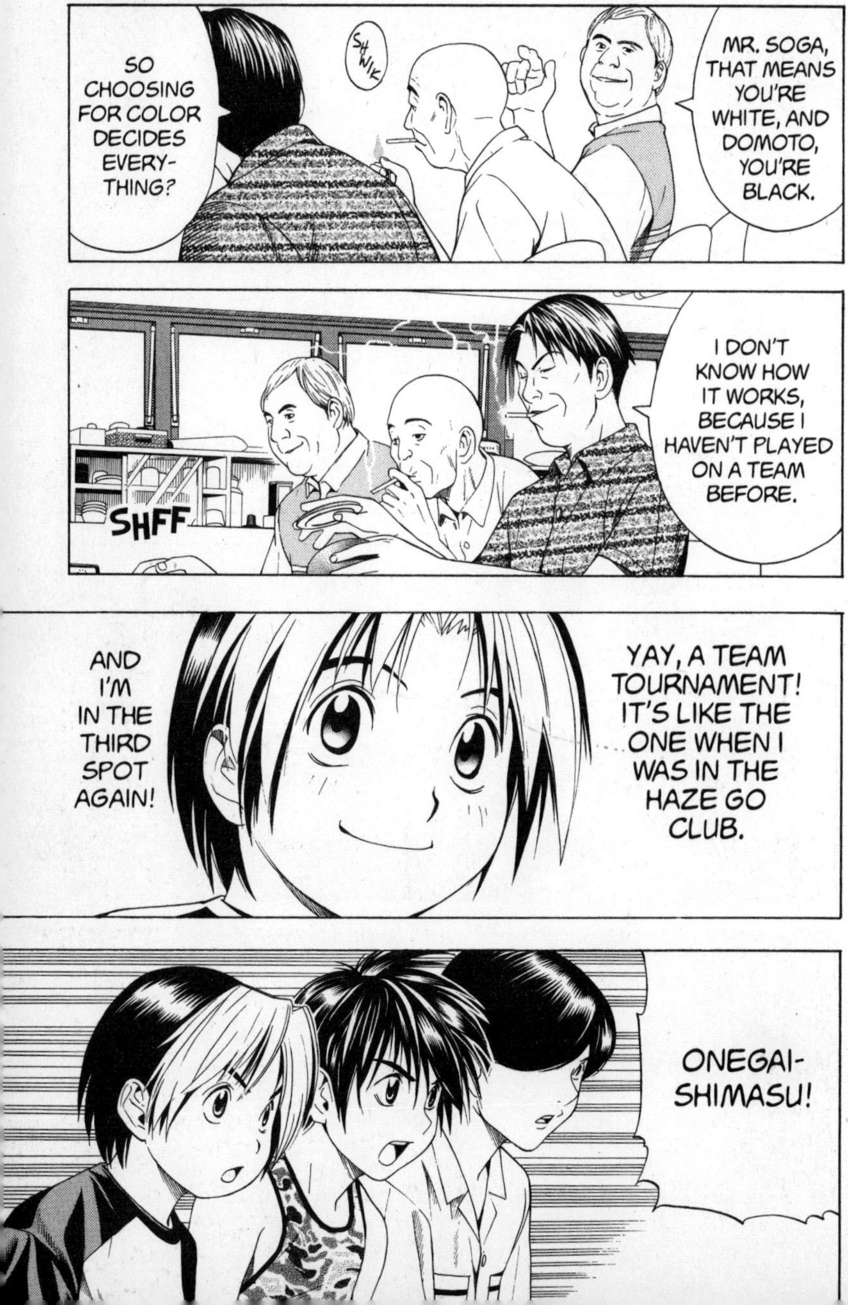
MR. SOGA, THAT MEANS YOU'RE WHITE, AND DOMOTO, YOU'RE BLACK.
SHWIK
SO CHOOSING FOR COLOR DECIDES EVERY-THING?
I DON'T KNOW HOW IT WORKS, BECAUSE I HAVEN'T PLAYED ON A TEAM BEFORE.
SHFF
YAY, A TEAM TOURNAMENT! IT'S LIKE THE ONE WHEN I WAS IN THE HAZE GO CLUB.
AND I'M IN THE THIRD SPOT AGAIN!
ONEGAI-SHIMASU!

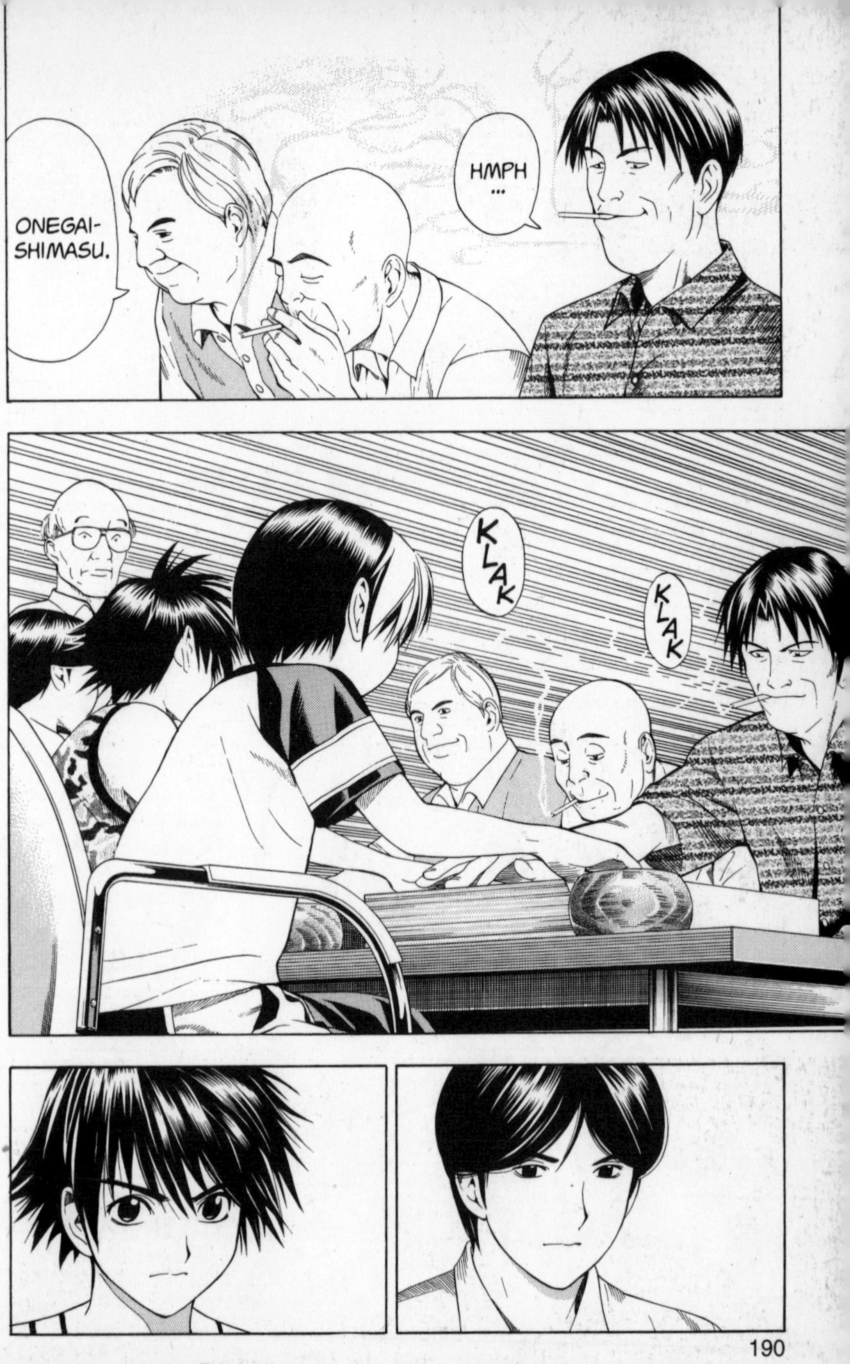
HMPH ...
ONEGAI-SHIMASU.
KLAK
KLAK

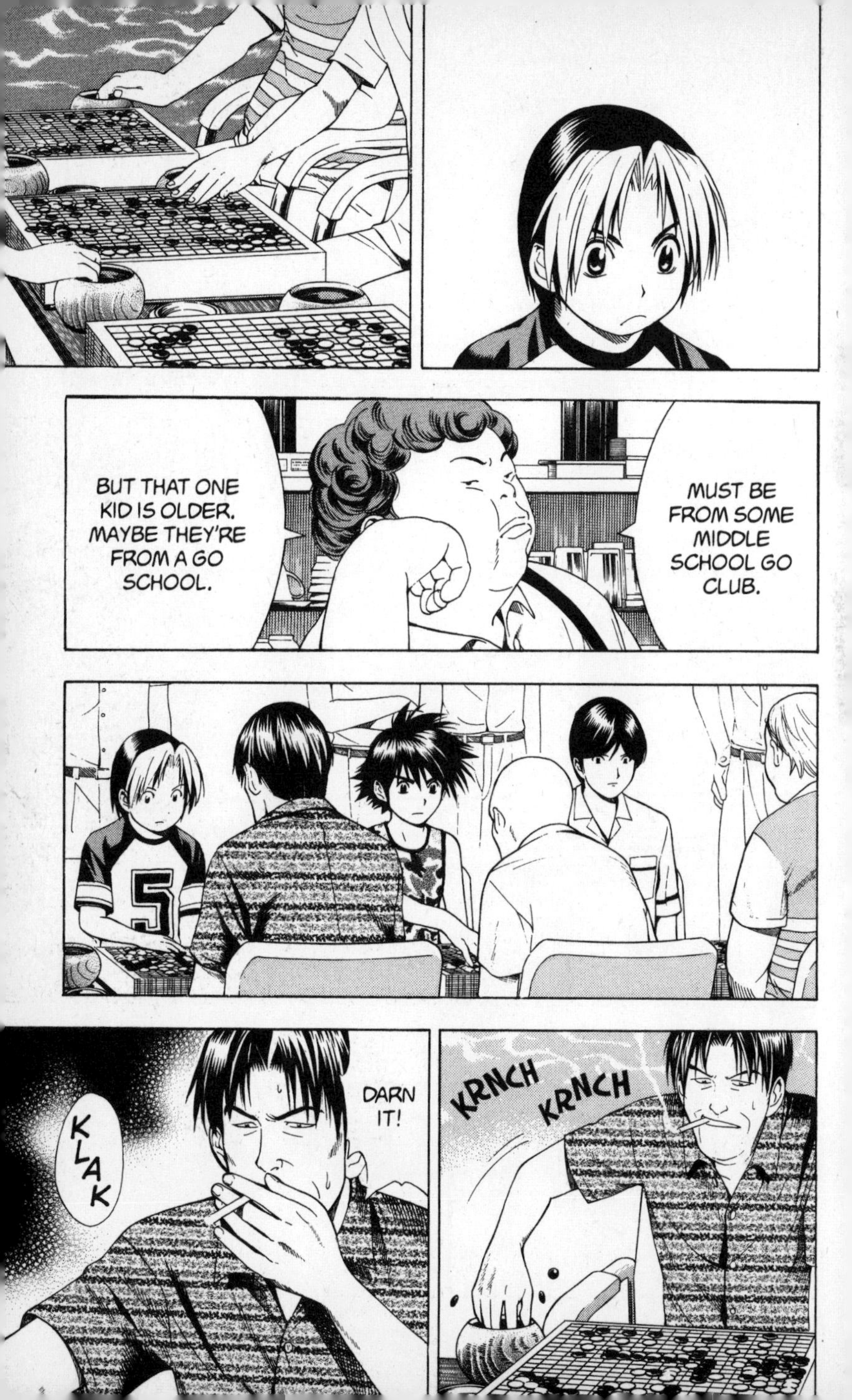
MUST BE FROM SOME MIDDLE SCHOOL GO CLUB.
BUT THAT ONE KID IS OLDER. MAYBE THEY'RE FROM A GO SCHOOL.
KRNCH KRNCH
DARN IT!
KLAK

IT'S OKAY.

I'LL BEAT HIM IF I STAY CALM.

LOOKS LIKE I GOT THE FIRST WIN!

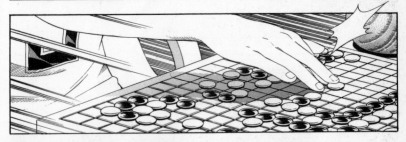

I RESIGN.

I LOST.

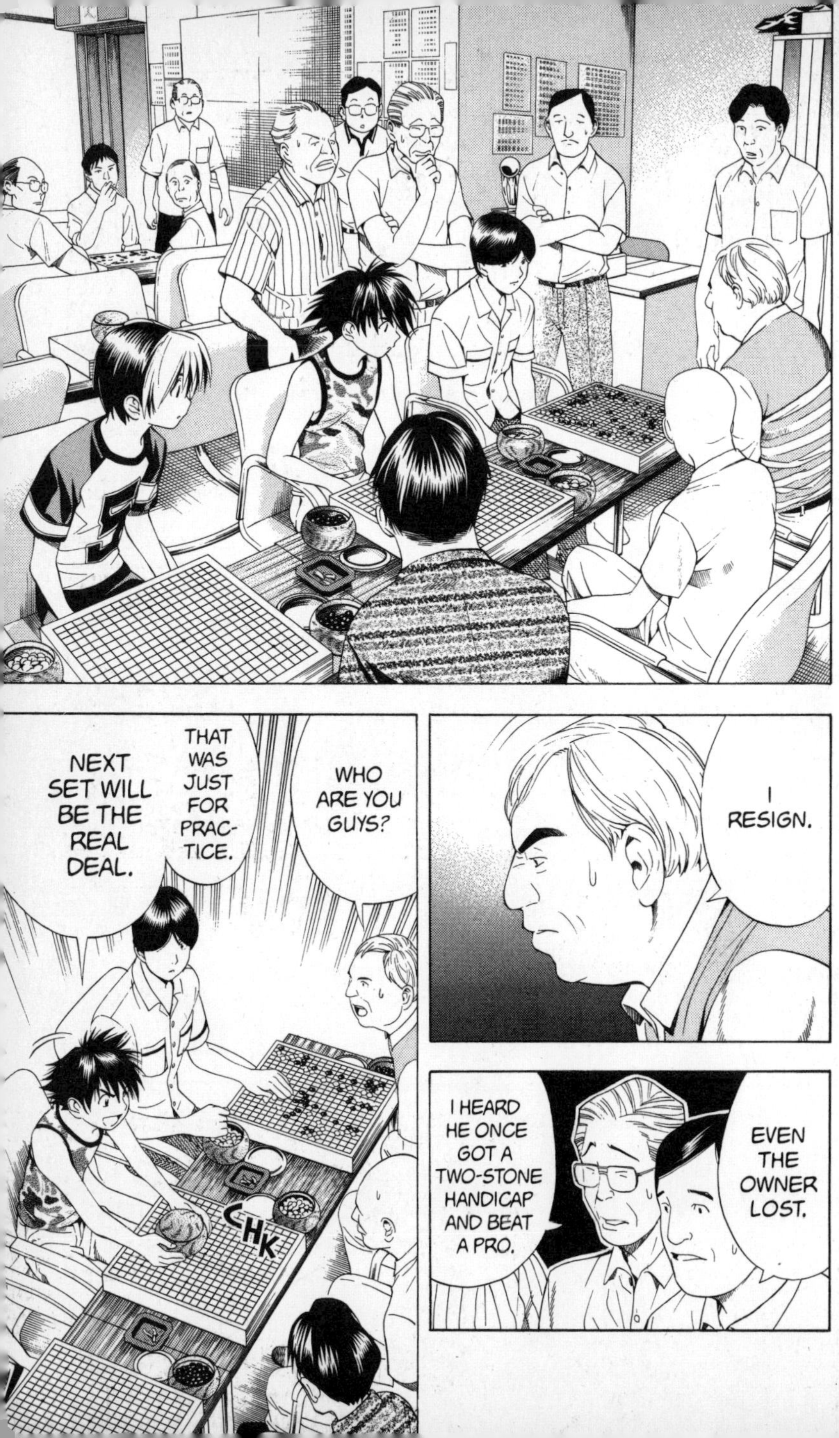
I RESIGN.
EVEN THE OWNER LOST.
I HEARD HE ONCE GOT A TWO-STONE HANDICAP AND BEAT A PRO.
WHO ARE YOU GUYS?
THAT WAS JUST FOR PRAC-TICE.
NEXT SET WILL BE THE REAL DEAL.
CHK

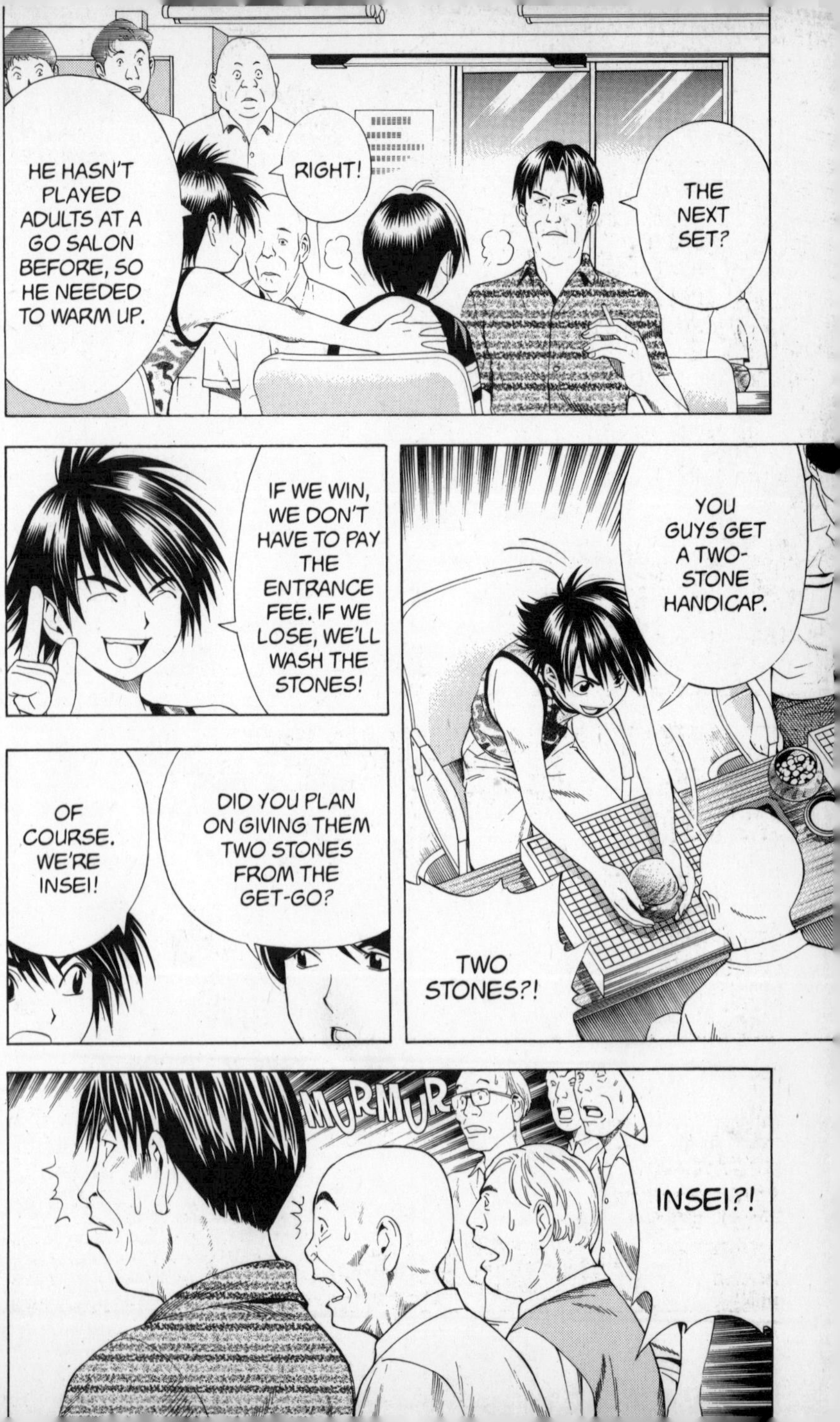
THE NEXT SET?
RIGHT!
HE HASN'T PLAYED ADULTS AT A GO SALON BEFORE, SO HE NEEDED TO WARM UP.
YOU GUYS GET A TWO-STONE HANDICAP.
TWO STONES?!
IF WE WIN, WE DON'T HAVE TO PAY THE ENTRANCE FEE. IF WE LOSE, WE'LL WASH THE STONES!
DID YOU PLAN ON GIVING THEM TWO STONES FROM THE GET-GO?
OF COURSE. WE'RE INSEI!
MURMUR
INSEI?!

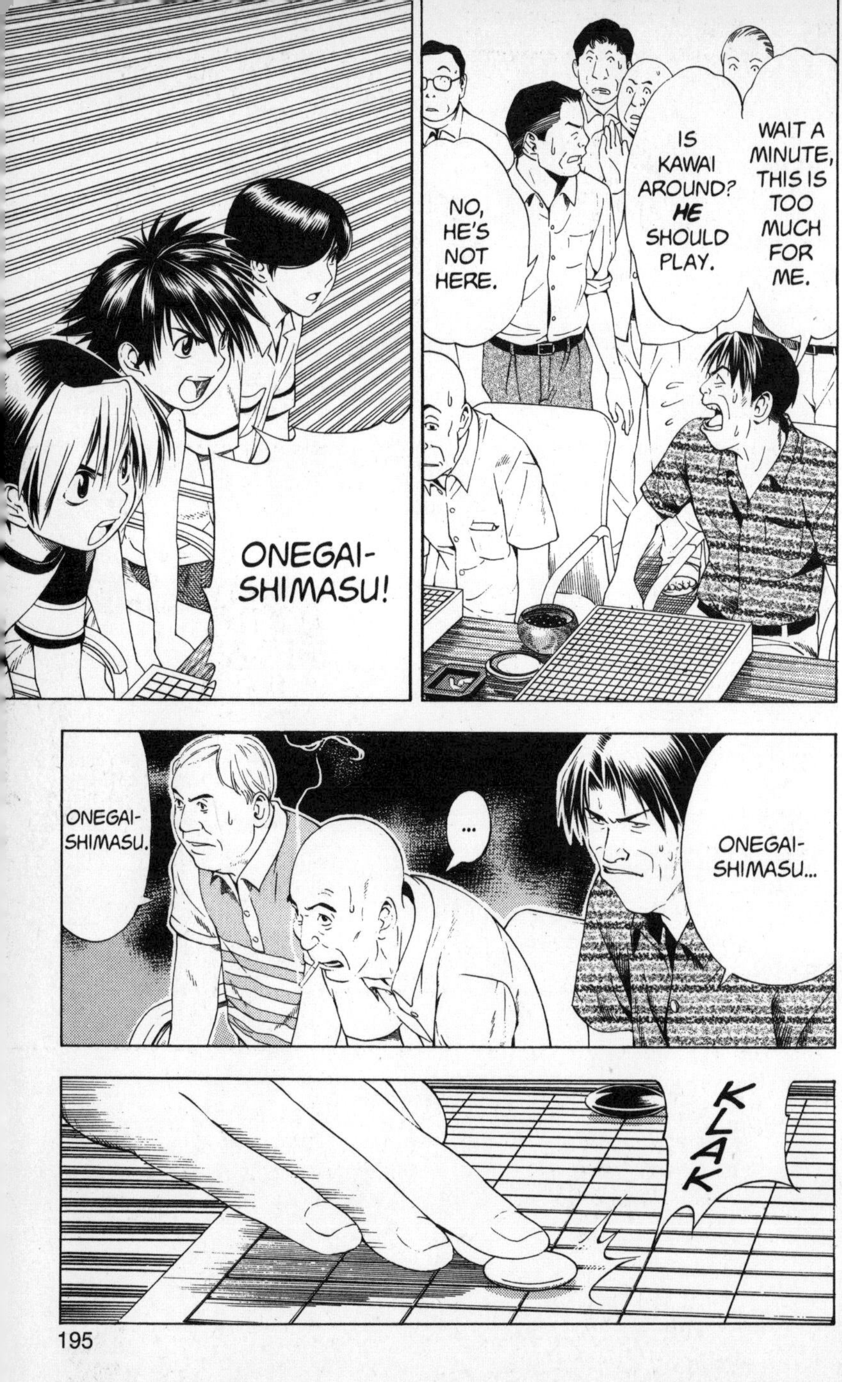
WAIT A MINUTE, THIS IS TOO MUCH FOR ME.
IS KAWAI AROUND? HE SHOULD PLAY.
NO, HE'S NOT HERE.
ONEGAI-SHIMASU!
ONEGAI-SHIMASU...
...
ONEGAI-SHIMASU.
KLAK

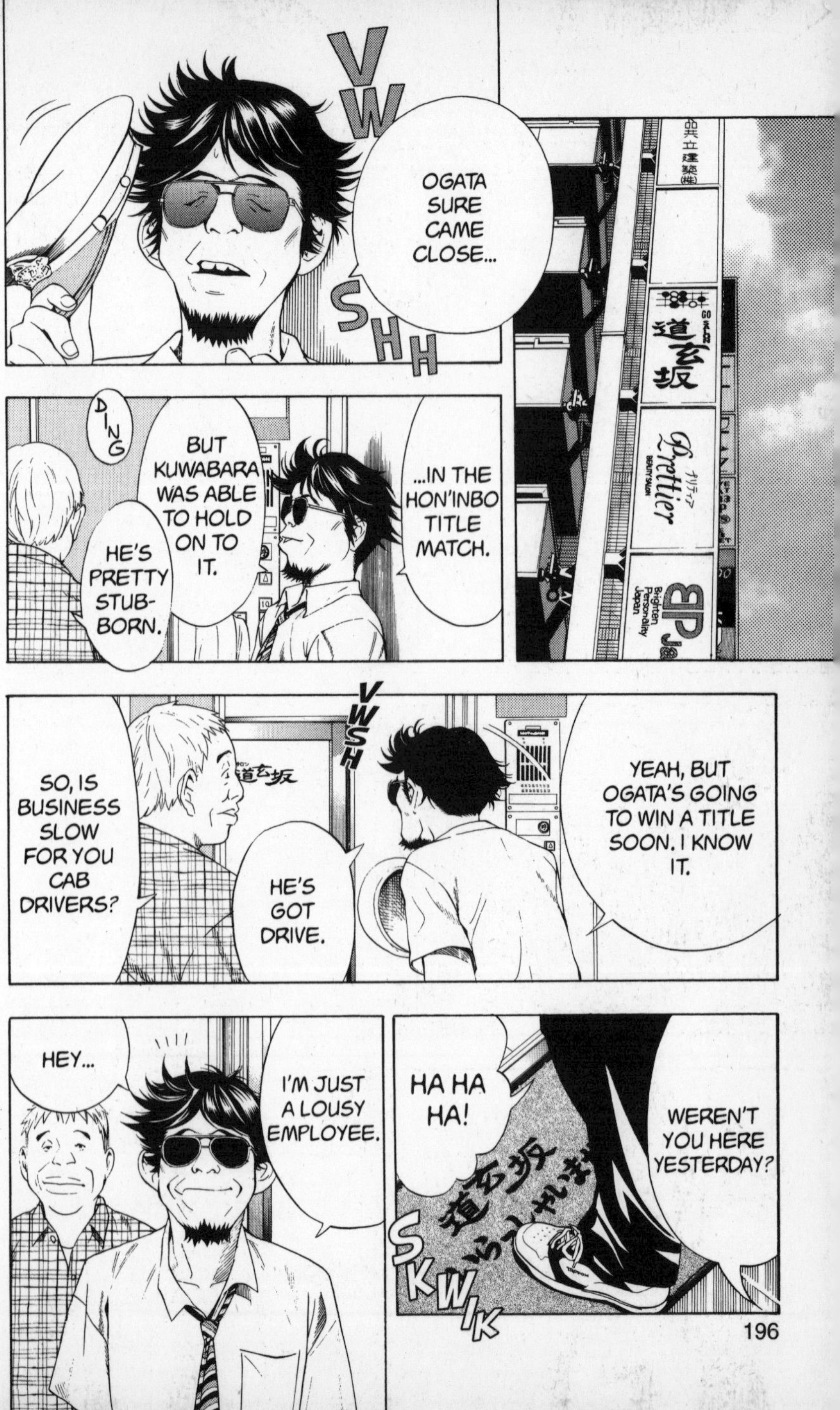

共立建築㈱
GO SALON
道玄坂
Prettier
BEAUTY SALON
プリティア
BP
Brighten Personality Japan
VWSHH
OGATA SURE CAME CLOSE...
...IN THE HON'INBO TITLE MATCH.
BUT KUWABARA WAS ABLE TO HOLD ON TO IT.
DING
HE'S PRETTY STUB-BORN.
YEAH, BUT OGATA'S GOING TO WIN A TITLE SOON. I KNOW IT.
VWSH
HE'S GOT DRIVE.
SO, IS BUSINESS SLOW FOR YOU CAB DRIVERS?
WEREN'T YOU HERE YESTERDAY?
HA HA HA!
道玄坂
SKWIK
I'M JUST A LOUSY EMPLOYEE.
HEY...

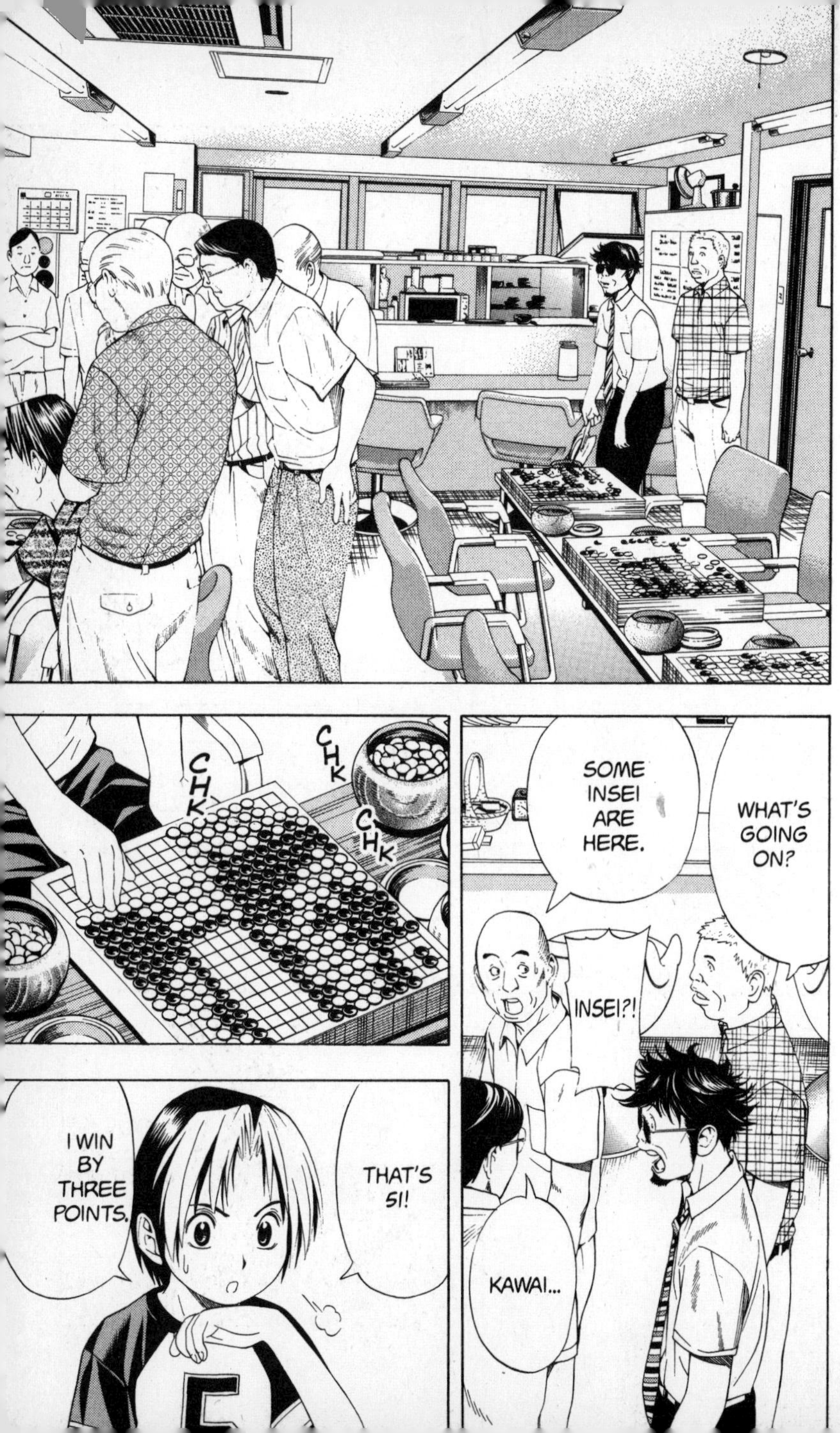
WHAT'S GOING ON?
SOME INSEI ARE HERE.
INSEI?!
KAWAI...
CHK
CHK
CHK
THAT'S 51!
I WIN BY THREE POINTS.

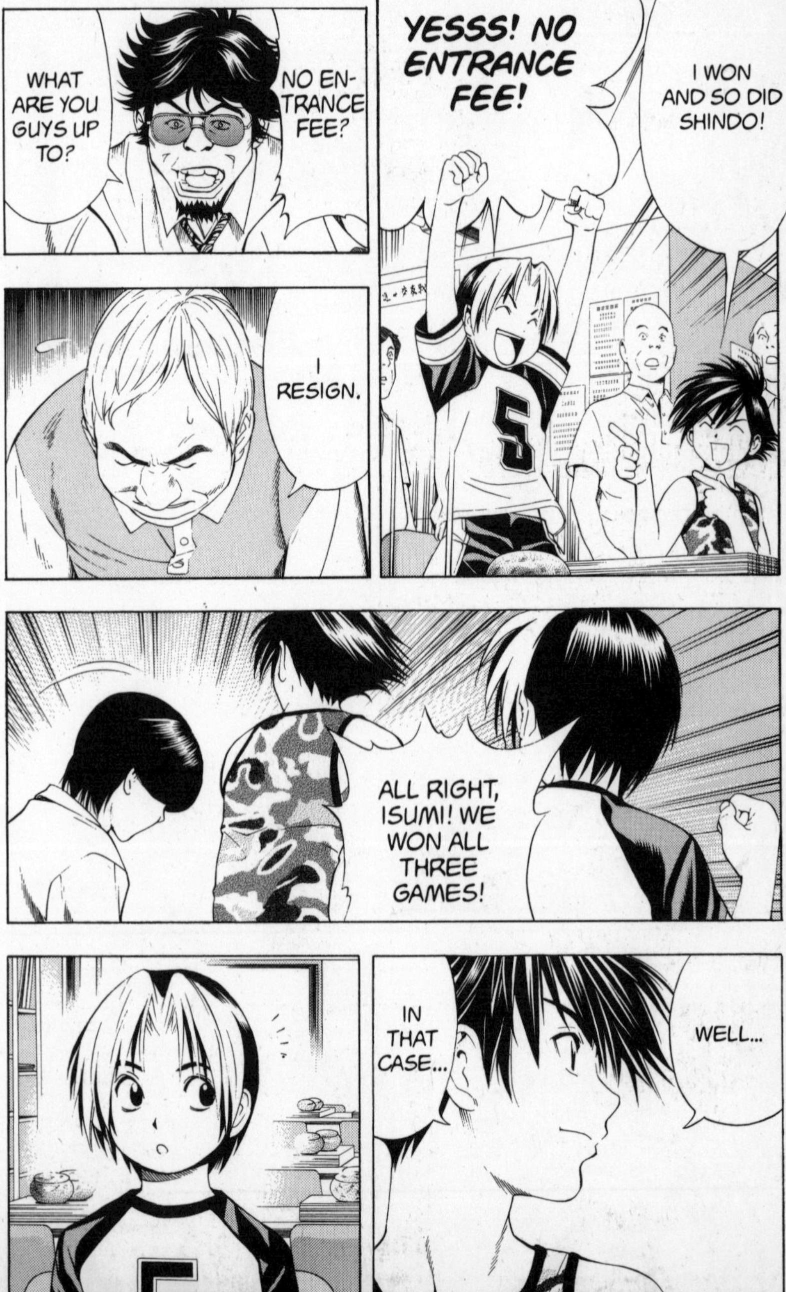
I WON AND SO DID SHINDO!
YESSS! NO ENTRANCE FEE!
NO EN-TRANCE FEE?
WHAT ARE YOU GUYS UP TO?
I RESIGN.
ALL RIGHT, ISUMI! WE WON ALL THREE GAMES!
WELL...
IN THAT CASE...

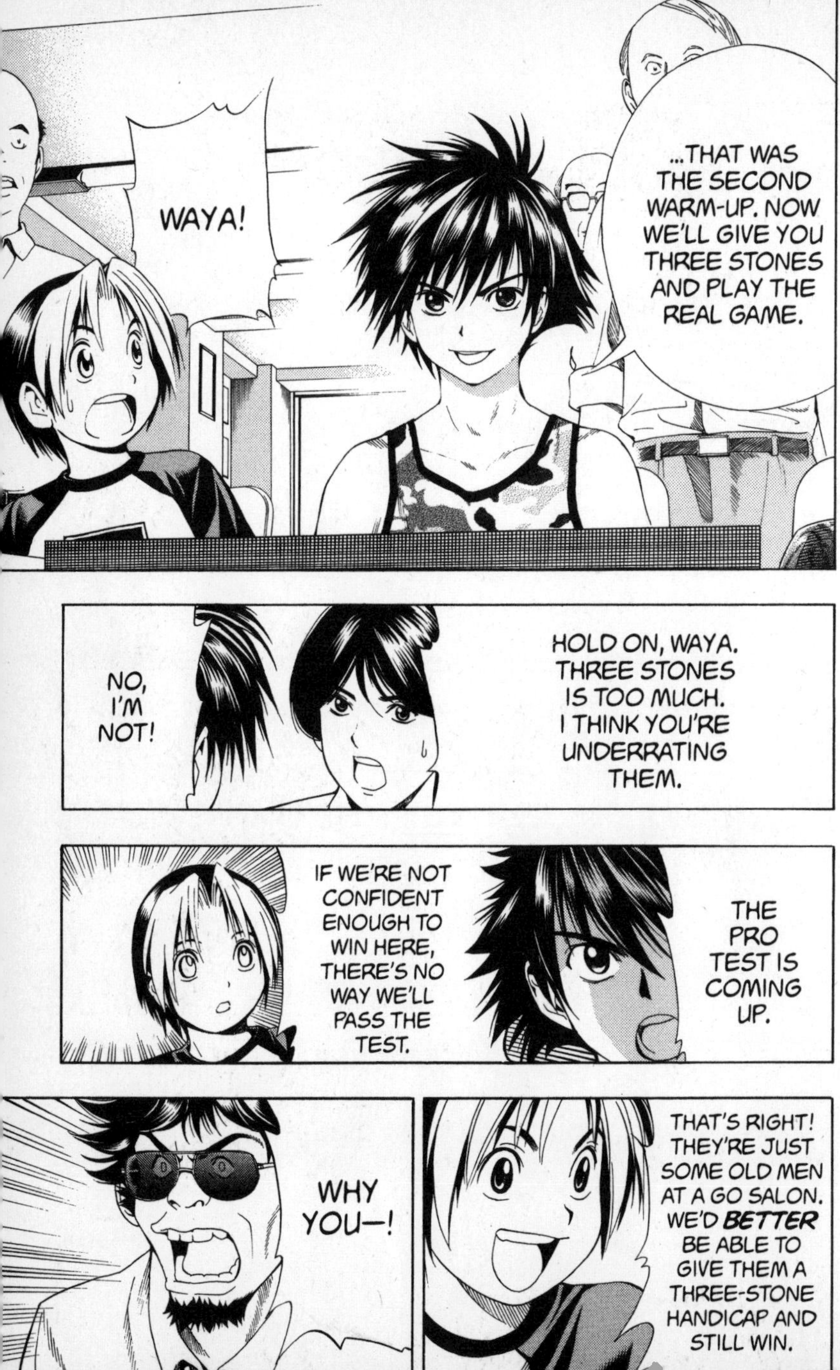
...THAT WAS THE SECOND WARM-UP. NOW WE'LL GIVE YOU THREE STONES AND PLAY THE REAL GAME.
WAYA!
HOLD ON, WAYA. THREE STONES IS TOO MUCH. I THINK YOU'RE UNDERRATING THEM.
NO, I'M NOT!
THE PRO TEST IS COMING UP.
IF WE'RE NOT CONFIDENT ENOUGH TO WIN HERE, THERE'S NO WAY WE'LL PASS THE TEST.
THAT'S RIGHT! THEY'RE JUST SOME OLD MEN AT A GO SALON. WE'D **BETTER** BE ABLE TO GIVE THEM A THREE-STONE HANDICAP AND STILL WIN.
WHY YOU—!

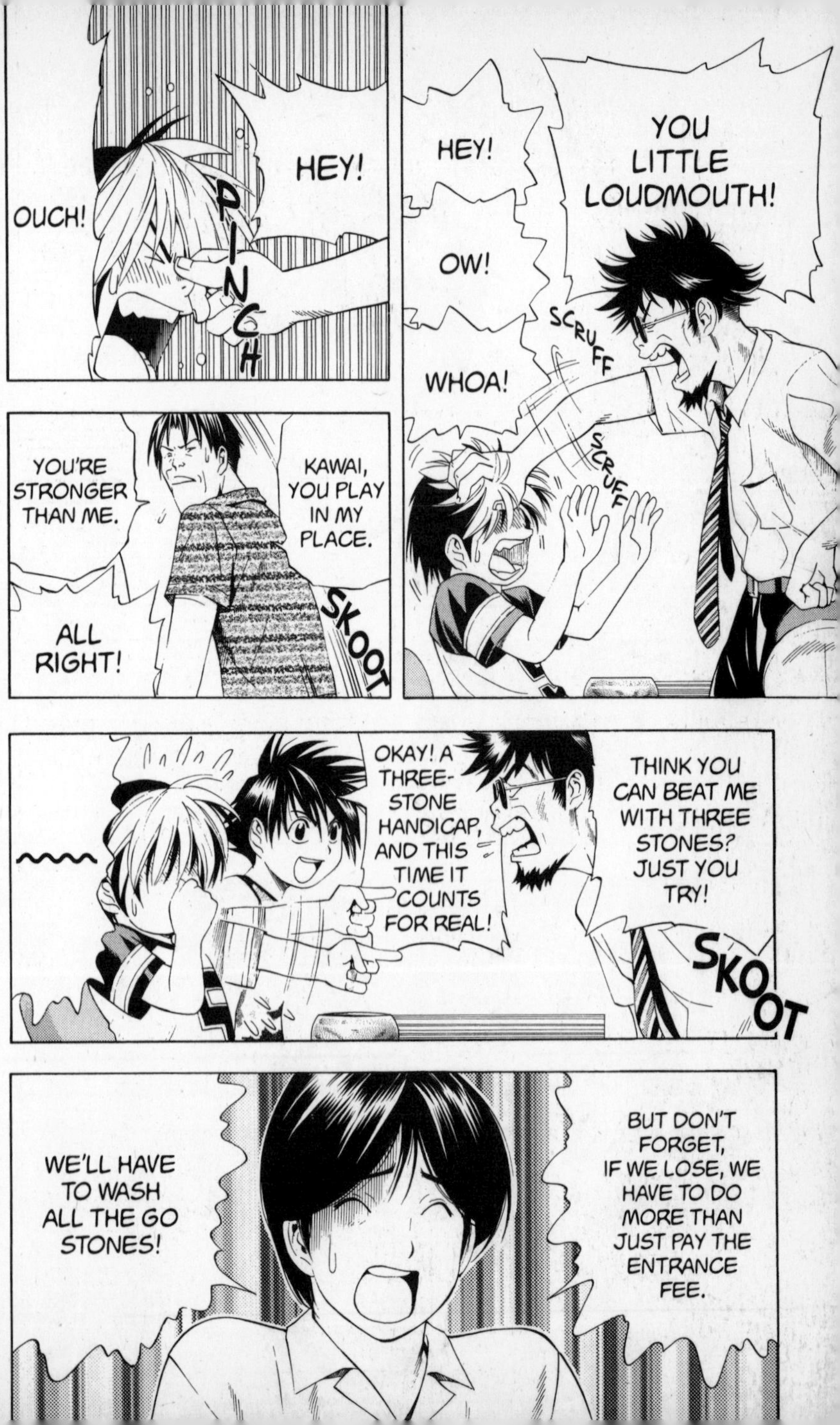
YOU LITTLE LOUDMOUTH!
HEY!
OW!
SCRUFF
SCRUFF
WHOA!
HEY!
PINCH
OUCH!
KAWAI, YOU PLAY IN MY PLACE.
YOU'RE STRONGER THAN ME.
SKOOT
ALL RIGHT!
THINK YOU CAN BEAT ME WITH THREE STONES? JUST YOU TRY!
SKOOT
OKAY! A THREE-STONE HANDICAP, AND THIS TIME IT COUNTS FOR REAL!
~~~
BUT DON'T FORGET, IF WE LOSE, WE HAVE TO DO MORE THAN JUST PAY THE ENTRANCE FEE.
WE'LL HAVE TO WASH ALL THE GO STONES!
~~~

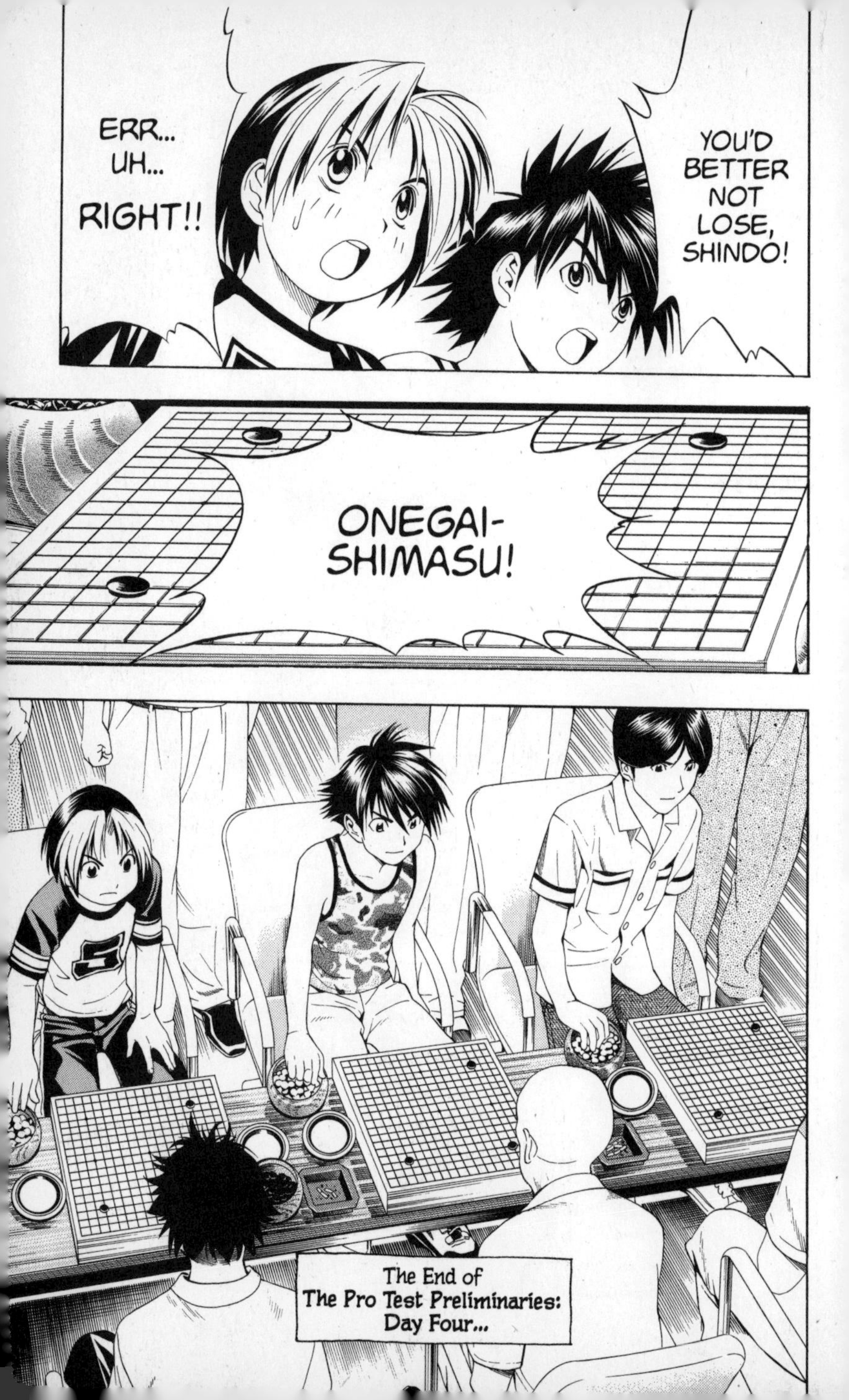
YOU'D BETTER NOT LOSE, SHINDO!
ERR... UH... RIGHT!!
ONEGAI-SHIMASU!
The End of The Pro Test Preliminaries: Day Four...

SPECIAL BONUS

THE HAZE MIDDLE SCHOOL ACTORS *present*

ASSASSINATION AT HONNOJI TEMPLE

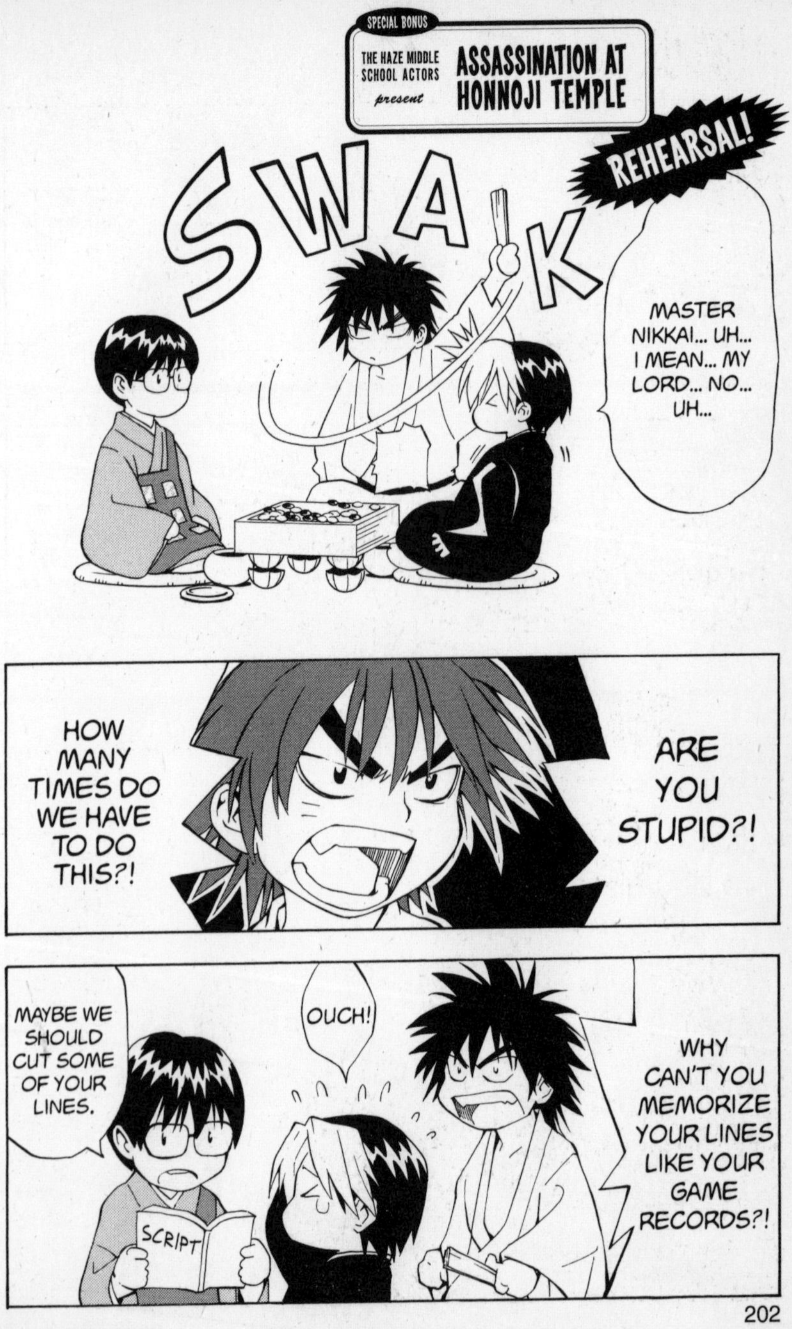
REHEARSAL!
SWAK
MASTER NIKKAI... UH... I MEAN... MY LORD... NO... UH...
ARE YOU STUPID?!
HOW MANY TIMES DO WE HAVE TO DO THIS?!
WHY CAN'T YOU MEMORIZE YOUR LINES LIKE YOUR GAME RECORDS?!
OUCH!
MAYBE WE SHOULD CUT SOME OF YOUR LINES.
SCRIPT

READ THIS WAY

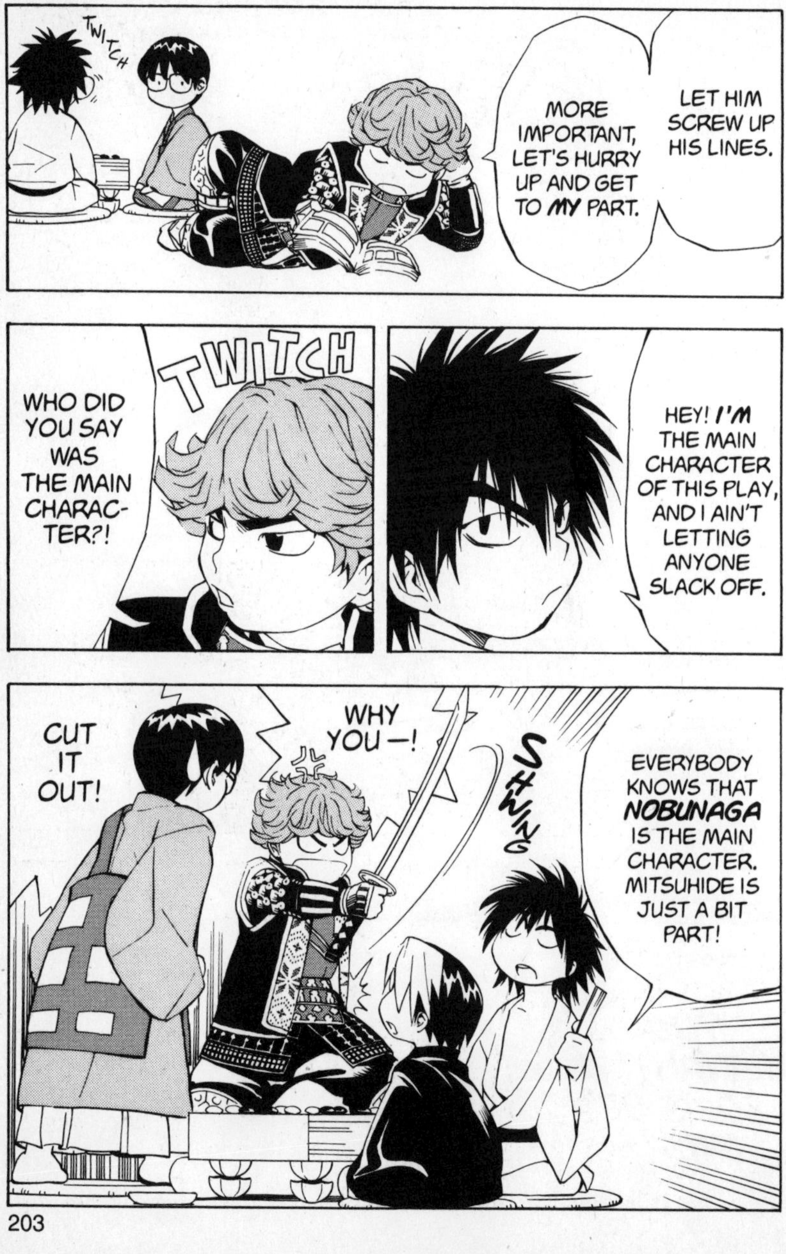
LET HIM SCREW UP HIS LINES.
MORE IMPORTANT, LET'S HURRY UP AND GET TO *MY* PART.
TWITCH
HEY! *I'M* THE MAIN CHARACTER OF THIS PLAY, AND I AIN'T LETTING ANYONE SLACK OFF.
TWITCH
WHO DID YOU SAY WAS THE MAIN CHARAC-TER?!
EVERYBODY KNOWS THAT ***NOBUNAGA*** IS THE MAIN CHARACTER. MITSUHIDE IS JUST A BIT PART!
SHWING
WHY YOU—!
CUT IT OUT!

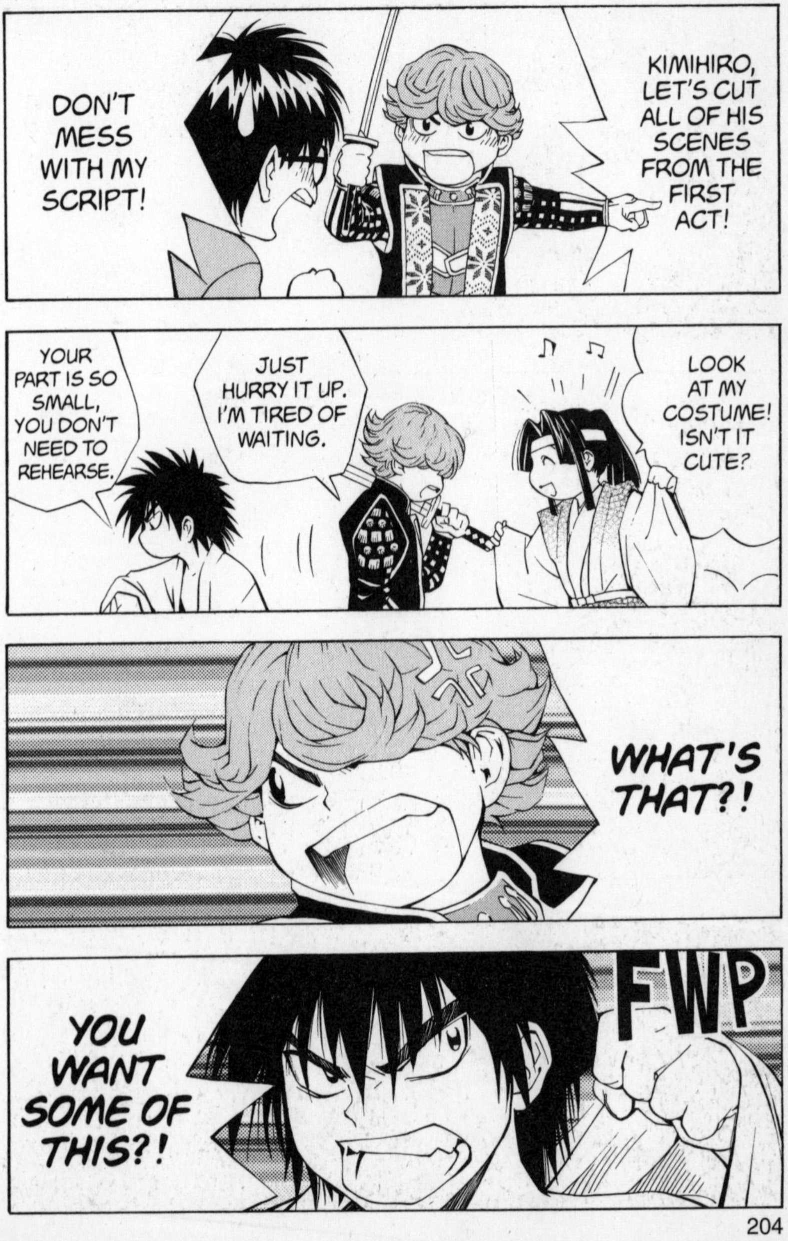
KIMIHIRO, LET'S CUT ALL OF HIS SCENES FROM THE FIRST ACT!
DON'T MESS WITH MY SCRIPT!
LOOK AT MY COSTUME! ISN'T IT CUTE?
JUST HURRY IT UP. I'M TIRED OF WAITING.
YOUR PART IS SO SMALL, YOU DON'T NEED TO REHEARSE.
WHAT'S THAT?!
FWP
YOU WANT SOME OF THIS?!

READ THIS WAY

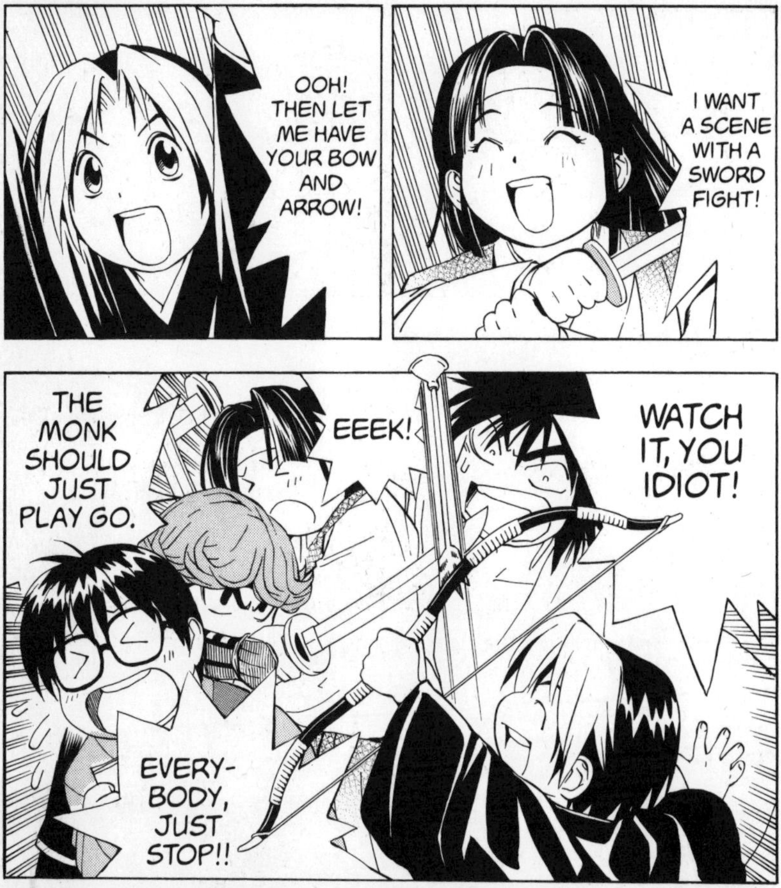
I WANT A SCENE WITH A SWORD FIGHT!
OOH! THEN LET ME HAVE YOUR BOW AND ARROW!
WATCH IT, YOU IDIOT!
EEEK!
THE MONK SHOULD JUST PLAY GO.
EVERY-BODY, JUST STOP!!

Starring: Tetsuo Kaga and Yuki Mitani Script by Kimihiro Tsutsui

ASSASSINATION AT HONNOJI TEMPLE

Playing now in volume 6!

Next Volume Preview

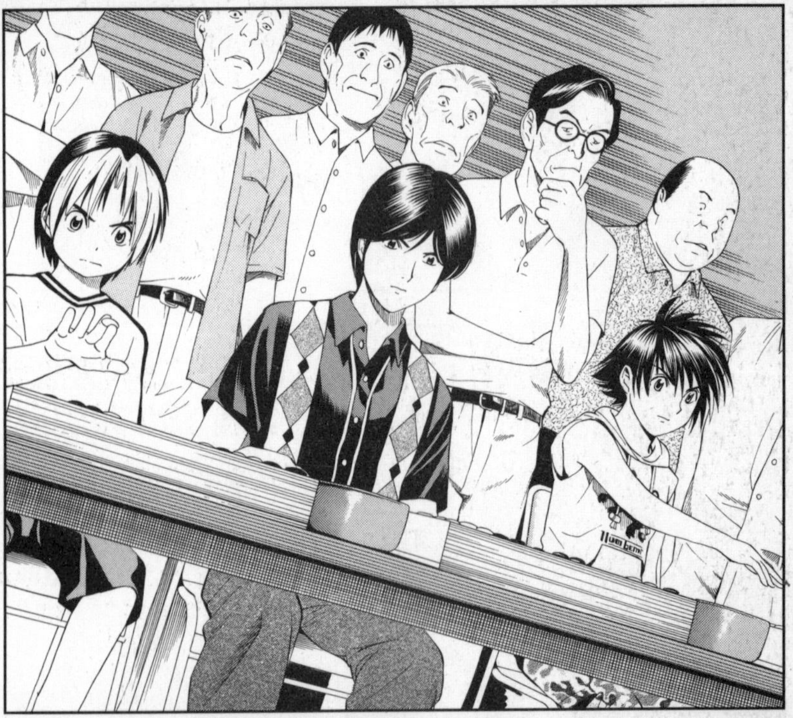

Hum ber

While Hikaru and his friends are practicing hard for the pro test, Akira is asked to play less than his best as a substitute Go instructor for an arrogant politician and his entourage. In fact, as a courtesy, Akira must lose his games on purpose. Will he swallow his pride and do as he's told?

AVAILABLE NOW

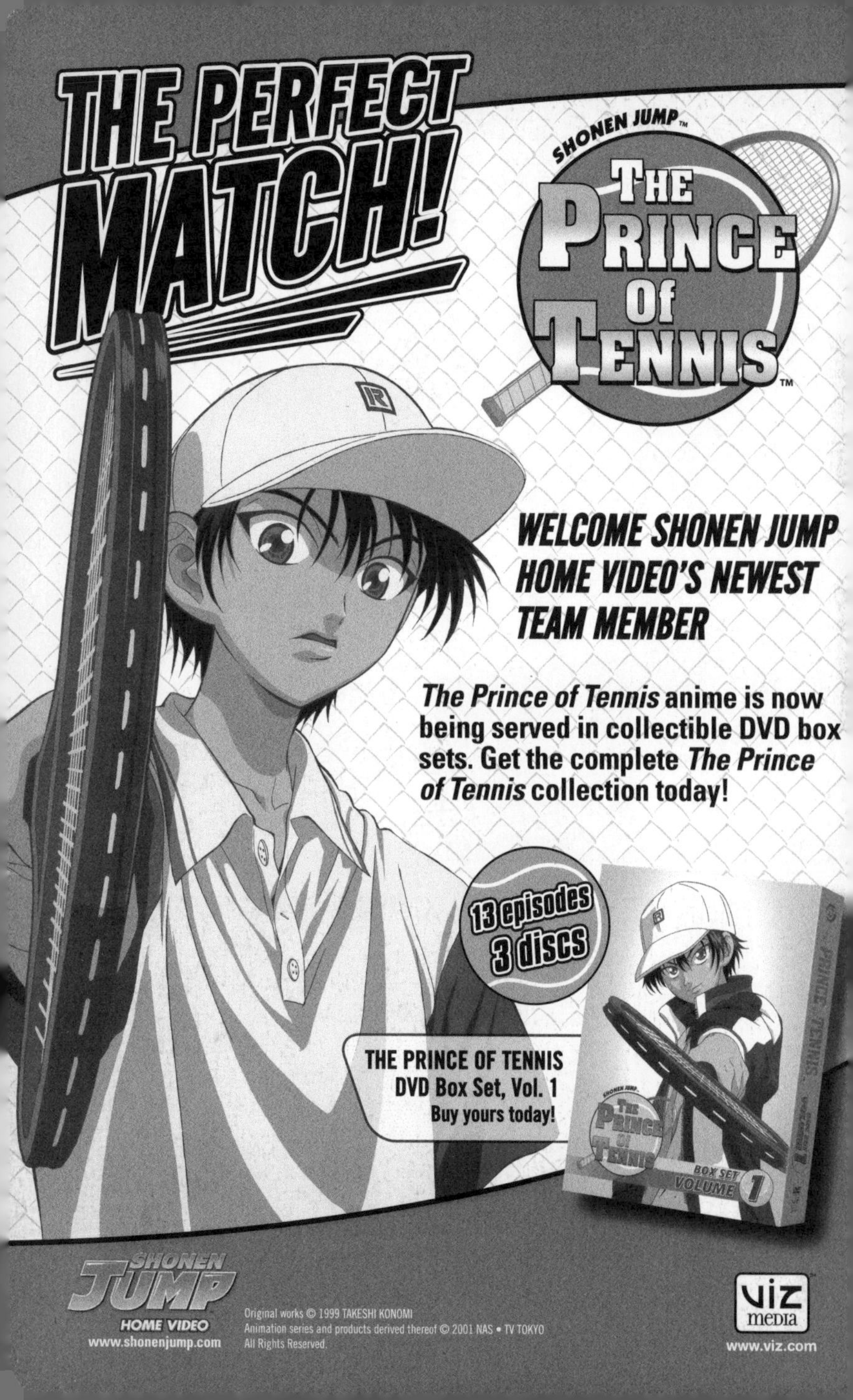
THE PERFECT MATCH!
SHONEN JUMP™
THE PRINCE OF TENNIS™
WELCOME SHONEN JUMP HOME VIDEO'S NEWEST TEAM MEMBER
The Prince of Tennis anime is now being served in collectible DVD box sets. Get the complete The Prince of Tennis collection today!
13 episodes 3 discs
THE PRINCE OF TENNIS DVD Box Set, Vol. 1
Buy yours today!
BOX SET VOLUME 1
SHONEN JUMP HOME VIDEO
www.shonenjump.com
Original works © 1999 TAKESHI KONOMI
Animation series and products derived thereof © 2001 NAS • TV TOKYO
All Rights Reserved.
viz media
www.viz.com

Change Your

From Akira Toriyama, the creator of *Dr. Slump*, *COWA!*, and *SandLand*

Relive Goku's quest with the new VIZBIG Editions of *Dragon Ball* and *Dragon Ball Z*! Each features:

- Three volumes in one
- Exclusive cover designs
- Color manga pages
- Larger trim size
- Color artwork
- Bonus content

And more!

* * * * * * * * * * * * * * * * * * *

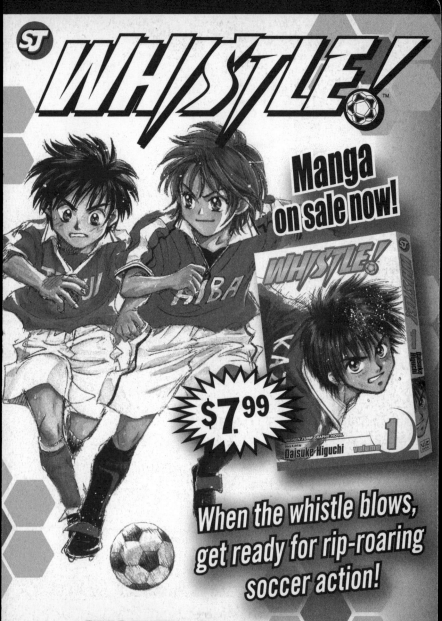

WHO'S GOT THE CURE FOR THE MONSTER FLU?

From AKIRA TORIYAMA, creator of *Dragon Ball*, *Dr. Slump*, and *Sand Land*

MANGA SERIES ON SALE NOW!

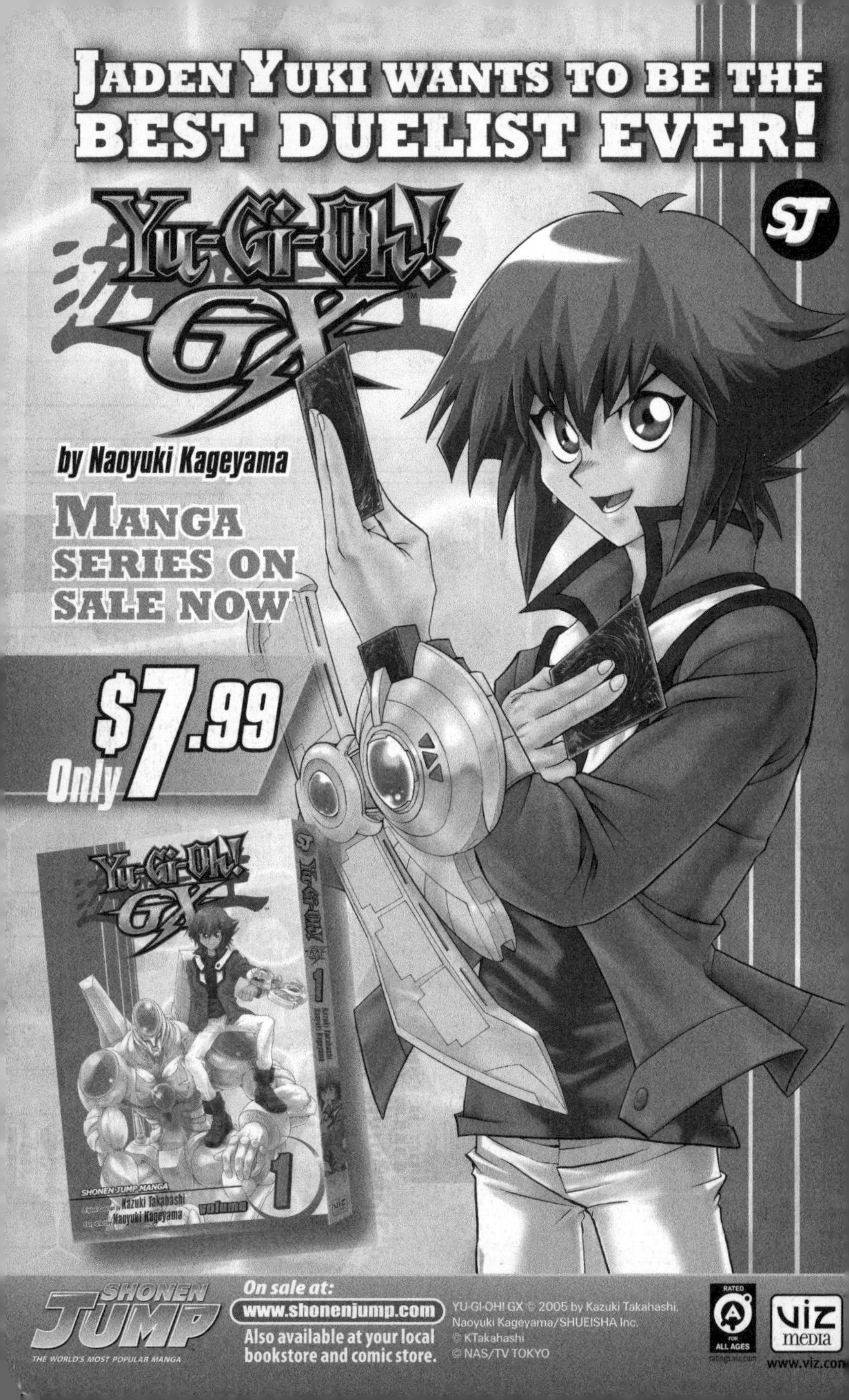
JADEN YUKI WANTS TO BE THE BEST DUELIST EVER!
SJ
YU-GI-OH! GX™
by Naoyuki Kageyama
MANGA SERIES ON SALE NOW
Only $7.99
YU-GI-OH! GX
1
SHONEN JUMP MANGA
Kazuki Takahashi
Naoyuki Kageyama
volume
1
SHONEN JUMP
THE WORLD'S MOST POPULAR MANGA
On sale at:
www.shonenjump.com
Also available at your local bookstore and comic store.
YU-GI-OH! GX © 2005 by Kazuki Takahashi, Naoyuki Kageyama/SHUEISHA Inc.
© KTakahashi
© NAS/TV TOKYO
RATED A FOR ALL AGES
ratings.viz.com
viz media
www.viz.com

Tell us what you think about SHONEN JUMP manga!

Our survey is now available online.
Go to: www.SHONENJUMP.com/mangasurvey

Help us make our product offering better!

THE REAL ACTION STARTS IN...
SHONEN JUMP
THE WORLD'S MOST POPULAR MANGA
www.shonenjump.com